AF473764

REMARKABLE GRAPHIC STYLES

FIERCE

SendPoints

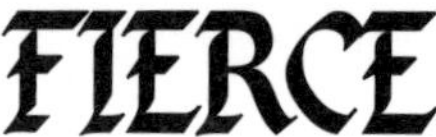

Second printing of the first edition, January 2020

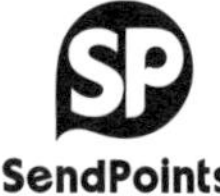

EDITED & PUBLISHED BY SendPoints Publishing Co., Ltd.

PUBLISHER: Lin Gengli

PUBLISHING DIRECTOR: Lin Shijian

ASSISTANT PUBLISHING-DIRECTOR: Chen Ting

CHIEF EDITOR: Lin Shijian

LEAD EDITOR: Li Weiji

EXECUTIVE EDITOR: Peggy Deng, Huang Qian

DESIGN DIRECTOR: Lin Shijian

EXECUTIVE ART EDITOR: Ding Jiaxin

PROOFREADING: James N. Powell, Li Weiji

REGISTERED ADDRESS: Room 15A Block 9 Tsui Chuk Garden, Wong Tai Sin, Kowloon, Hong Kong

TEL: +852-35832323 / **FAX**: +852-35832448

OFFICE ADDRESS: 7F, No.9-1 Anning Street, Jinshazhou Road, Baiyun District, Guangzhou, China

TEL: +86-20-89095121 / **FAX**: +86-20-89095206

BEIJING OFFICE: Flat 1701, Block C, BBMG International, Wangjing West Road no.48, Chaoyang District, Beijing, China

TEL: +86-10-84139071 / **FAX**: +86-10-84139071

SHANGHAI OFFICE: Room 302, Floor 3, Ningbo Road no.349, Huangpu District, Shanghai, China

TEL: +86-21-63523469 / **FAX**: +86-21-63523469

SALES TEAM

UK, Europe, Africa, Oceania: Sunnie sales02@sendpoints.cn

America, the Middle East: Mia sales03@sendpoints.cn

Asia: Hedy sales01@sendpoints.cn

TEL: +86-20-81007895

EMAIL: sales@sendpoints.cn

WEBSITE: www.sendpoints.cn / www.spbooks.cn

ISBN 978-988-78494-8-3

Printed and bound in China

CONTENTS

FIERCE HERITAGE

How does one express anger, fear, grief, or pain?

Many visual artists make powerful and striking visuals to release emotional powder kegs. The art of early predecessors seemed to be more reserved, but it was not uncommon that painting tapped into the sinister realms of macabre tales, narratives of redemption and punishment that appall or alarm, for example, Renaissance illustrations of Hell, and a modern artist's feelings about war.

In the contemporary graphic designs and illustrations in this book, the artists have produced penetrating, stupefying, even stinging images. They deform, decompose, or rearrange visual elements—often symbolic ones—just as in nature's ineluctable handling of birth and death. Today, when uncontrolled sensuous stimulation, amplified by techniques and discoveries in all possible fields, incessantly numbs our senses, the strike an image can launch has proved itself time and again. We believe that such visual fierceness offers unique aesthetic value and can inspire generations.

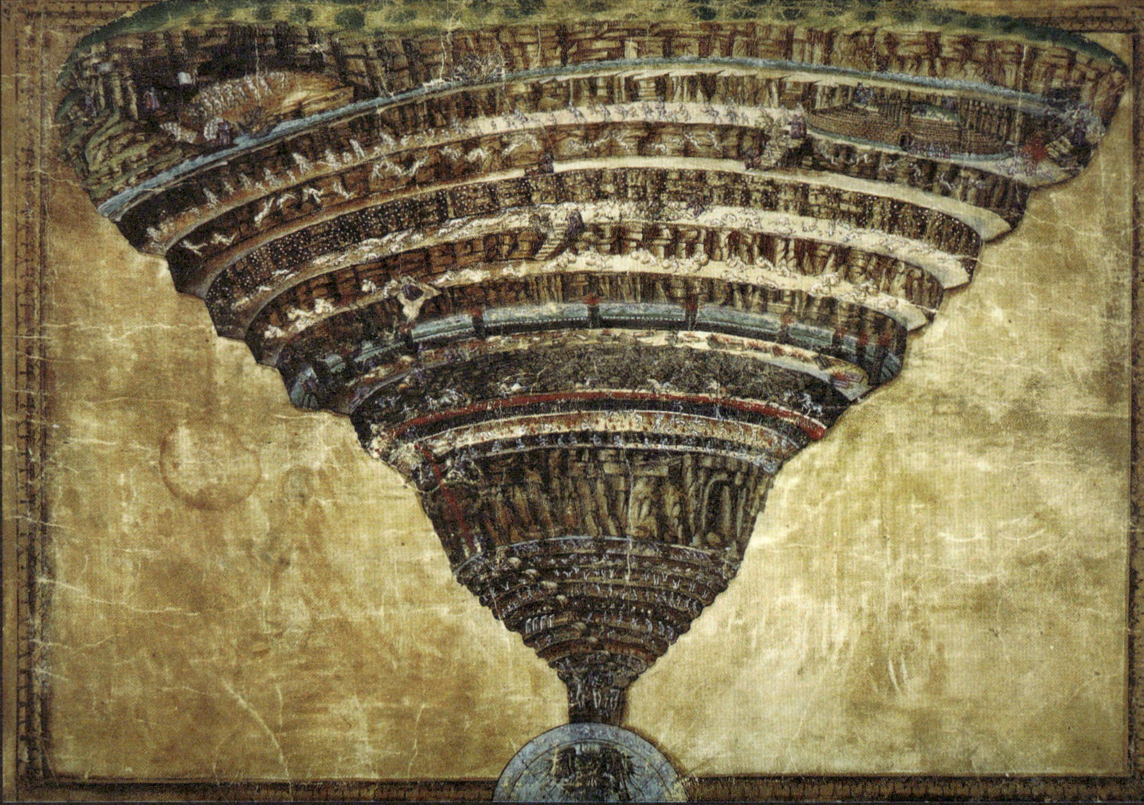

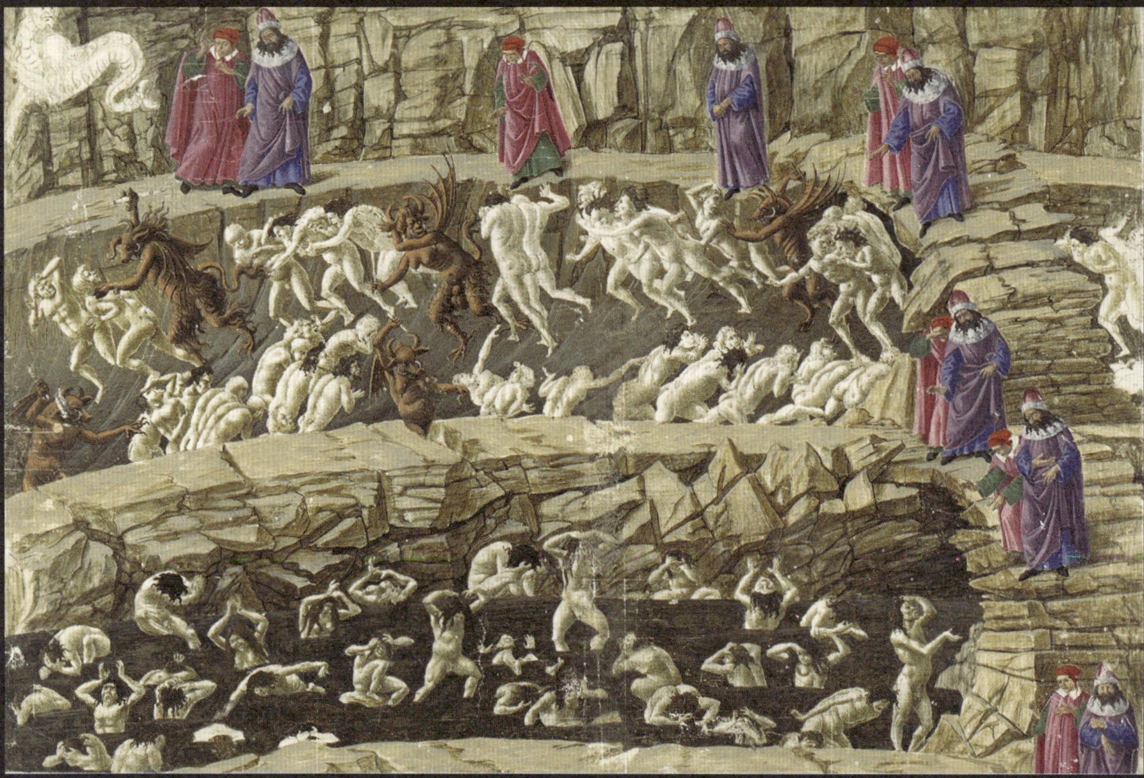

Illustrations of Hell for the Divine Comedy by Botticelli / Wikimedia Commons

BOTTICELLI'S ILLUSTRATION OF HELL

Almost 150 years after the appearance of the epochal narrative poem the *Divine Comedy* by the exiled Florentine poet Dante, Italian painter Sandro Botticelli (c. 1445–1510) unleashed the power of Dante's words into poignant graphical realism. Among the many illustrations, the one featuring the *Chart of Hell* stands out as the most impressive, with a gruesomely complete and organized hierarchy of the netherworld imprisoning all kinds of sinners, transforming Dante's unnerving imaginative depiction of the underworld into a reality for the eyes to take in .

Botticelli's rendering of the inferno unified multiple cantos on a single page, leading readers to proceed continuously downward through the nine circles of hell. Unfathomable chasms, scalding sepulchers, thorny forests, the condemned writhing in filthy swamps, debased sinners moaning dire laments in a river of boiling blood, the tormented steeping in burning pitch with backs occasionally arched to alleviate pain, weeping human piles with twisted heads facing backwards, flaming and quivering soles and joints of feet and legs protruding from holes that bury the damned upside-down, with no brand of torture or persecution left untouched. In sum, the painter conjured up appalling, daunting pictorial representations of the underworld.

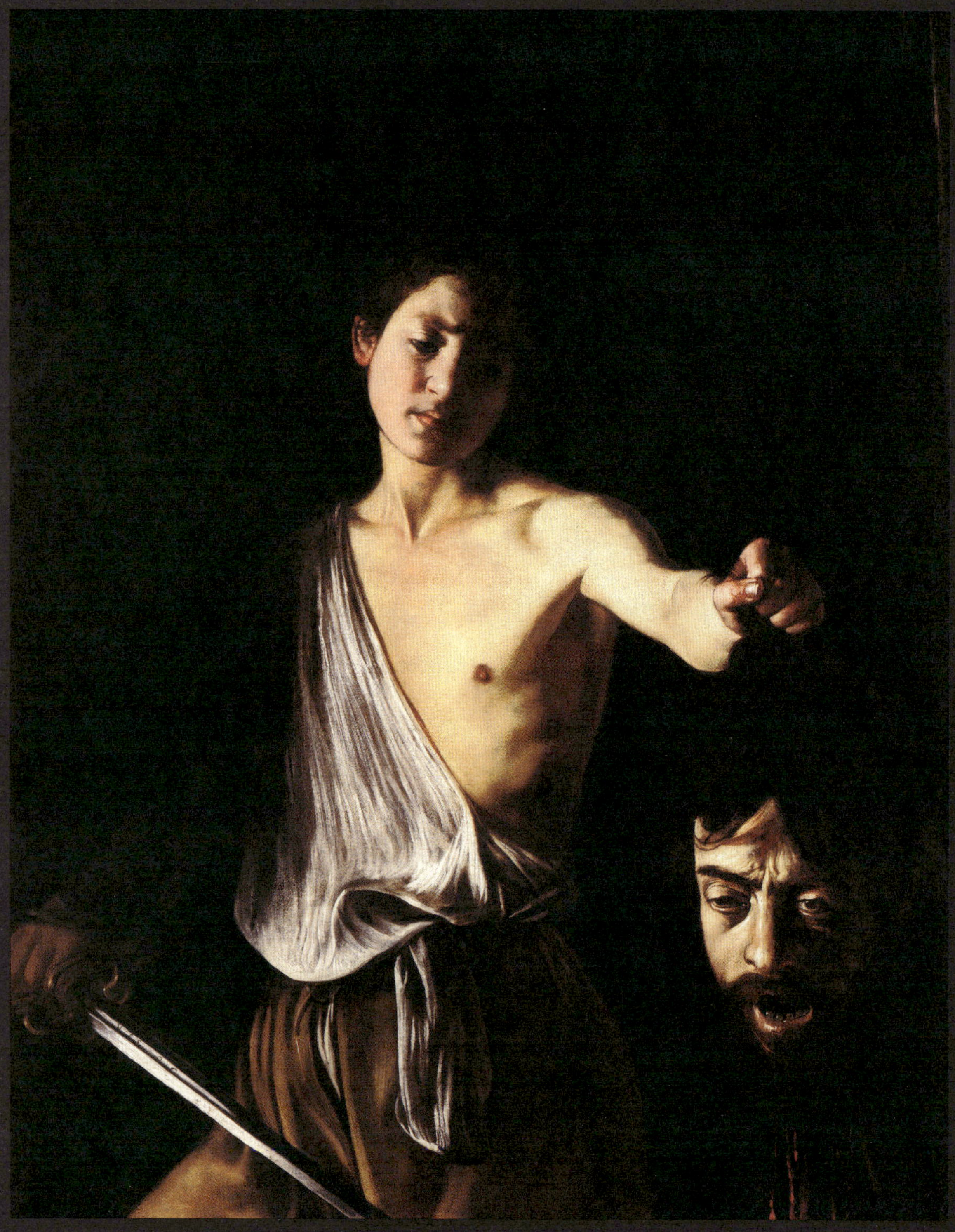

David with the Head of Goliath by Caravaggio / Wikimedia Commons

CARAVAGGIO AND TENEBRISM

The term "Tenebrism" (derived from Italian *tenebroso*, meaning "darkness") describes a painting technique characterized by the exaggerated contrast of light and dark. Tenebrist paintings often spotlight a small area via an unseen light source while the rest remains immersed in unfathomable darkness. The technique brought success to the talented yet controversial Italian painter Michelangelo Merisi da Caravaggio (1571–1610). He, amplified by his mastery of freezing critical moments before actions take place, created alarmingly faithful representations of profane subjects and bold explorations of visceral humanity: heart-rending pictures with intensive theatricality.

This dramatic employment of darkness—by directing attention to illuminated gestures and facial expressions—is an effective treatment to bring out the internalized strength of the figure. This technique therefore has won the favor of many later artists, who borrowed and adapted it: accentuating its internal conflicts and tensions. So far-reaching has been the influence of this style that it survives in the lighting and psychology of the dark camerawork of many classic examples of film noir and even contemporary horror films. Such overwhelming darkness stifles and entangles viewers, luring them into the obscurity of its thick, fear-infused shadows—where innermost fears invariably lurk and creep in consciously or subconsciously.

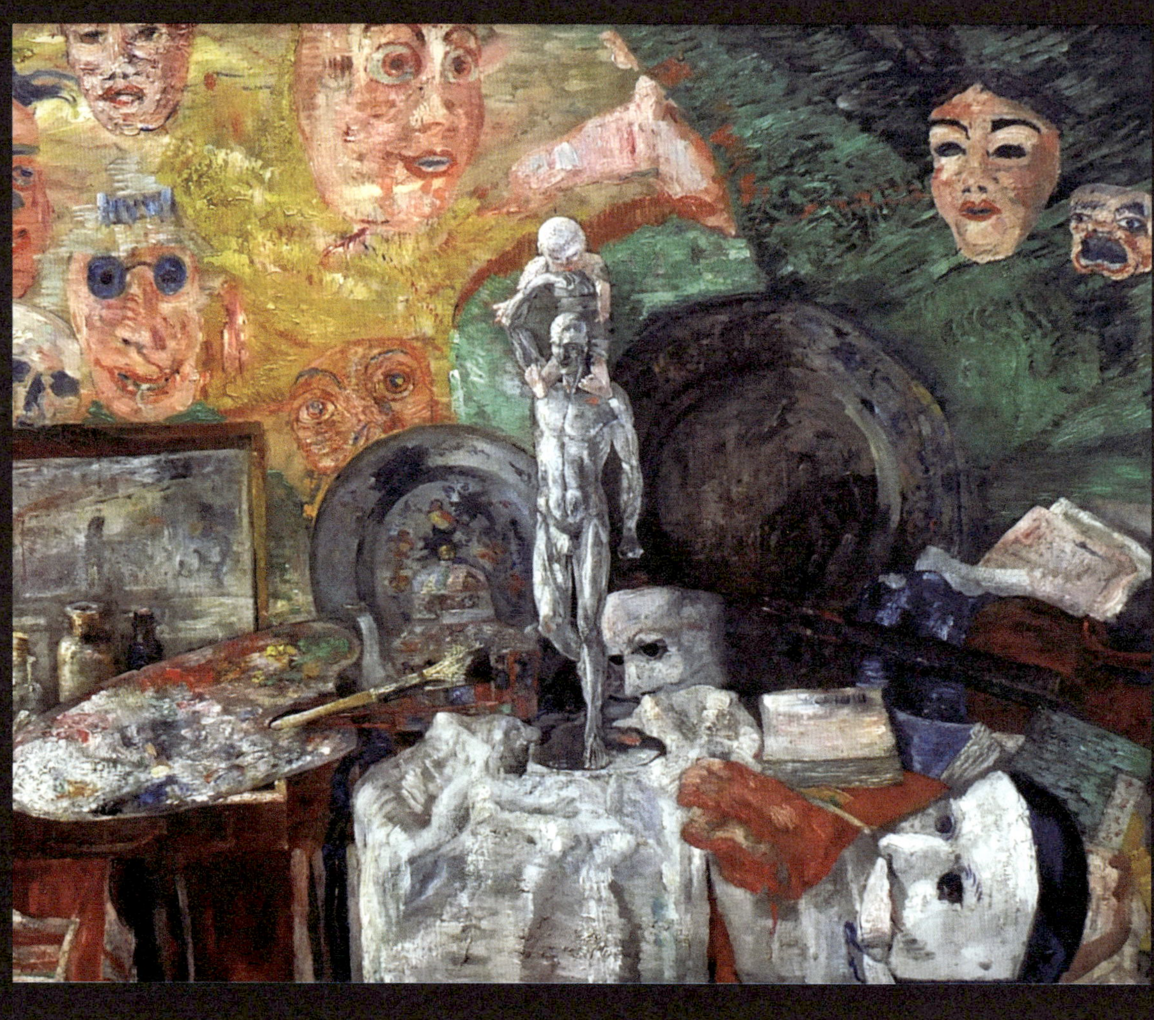

Still Life in the Studio by James Ensor

JAMES ENSOR

Revered as the "artist's artist," Belgian avant-garde painter James Ensor (1860–1949) does not belong to any specific artistic school, but his scathingly satirical and carnivalesque illusory imagery has influenced and nourished many later modernist movements such as expressionism and surrealism. His family operated a souvenir shop that catered to seasonal revelers and vacationers. Growing up in that environment, Ensor was well acquainted with grotesque carnival masks, iridescent seashells, puppets and dolls, and all kinds of exotic antiques. These later cluttered his "studio" and became his models, animating his fantastic paintings. He was as deeply obsessed with masks as he was with the allegorical employment of light: for both exhibit vast potentials for visual forcefulness and psychological impact. For Ensor, the bedazzling masks were ideal vehicles for subjective revelations displaying "freshness of color, sumptuous decoration, wild unexpected gestures, very shrill expressions, [and] exquisite turbulence" while light would "distort contour" with great intensity. Across his repertoire, the phantasmal masquerade speaks for the painter, in which the many clamorously clustered masks, skeletons, puppets, and dolls, in their grimacing, were seemingly pressing towards the viewer, their eyes vacuous, their faces wearing garish cosmetics, and their red mouths parted as if whispering and sneering.

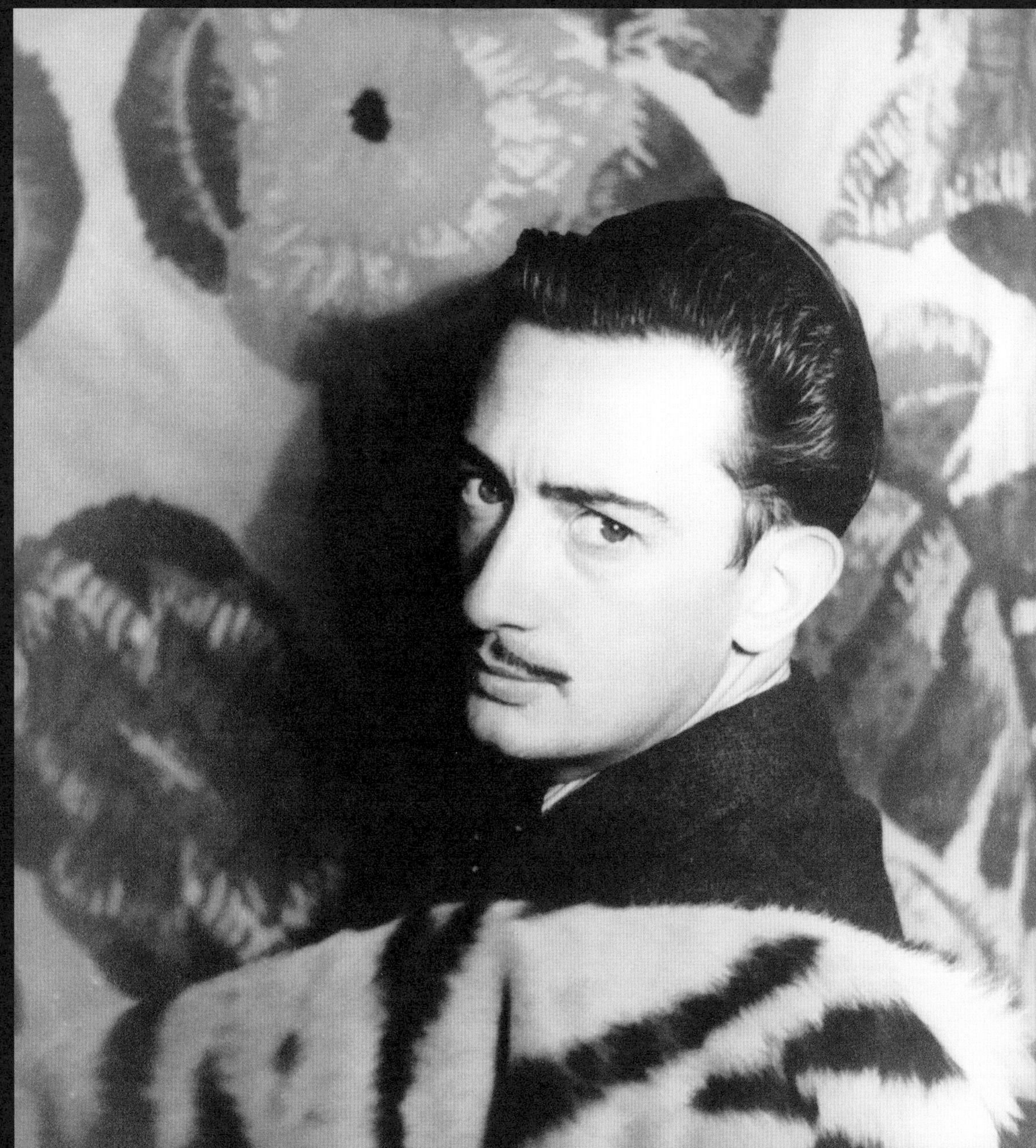

DAL AND HIS PREMONITION OF WAR

In 1936, with tension continuously accumulating in Spain, artist Salvador Dalí (1904–1989) executed the painting *Soft Construction with Boiled Beans*, later renamed *Premonition of Civil War*.

The painting is a thunderous pictorial accusation of war. In the painting, a gigantic monster with a human face is seen towering over a barren land devoid of life. Its face seems to be in an extreme paroxysm of either agony or ecstasy, as if combining both the countenances of the rapacious brutal aggressor and the wretched sufferers. Joining the shriveled neck are the flesh of legs and arms frenetically wrestling with each other in chaotic self-mutilation. The broken limbs, surrounding an area of void in the shape of the Spanish land, are dissected and distorted, emphatically stretching and struggling, as if signifying the breaking and devastation of the country, the disposition of its people, and the physical and psychological torment inflicted by war. A few "melancholy vegetables"—boiled beans—are "embellished," according to the painter, as if to append the absurdity for the cannibalism of the "unconscious meat" to procede. The sky behind the creature is progressively heavy with clouds, as if a deafening thunder is brewing to rip apart the sky at any moment, possibly implicating the looming of outbreak of conflicts.

An avid follower of Freud's theory of the psychoanalysis, the painter joined realistic details with an arbitrariness of exaggeration, decomposition, and deformation as well as allegorical elements. Together, these create a phantom, striking, and compellingly captivating world. The analogy of cannibalism to war also hints at something that deserves further contemplation—the underlying cruel nature of all mankind.

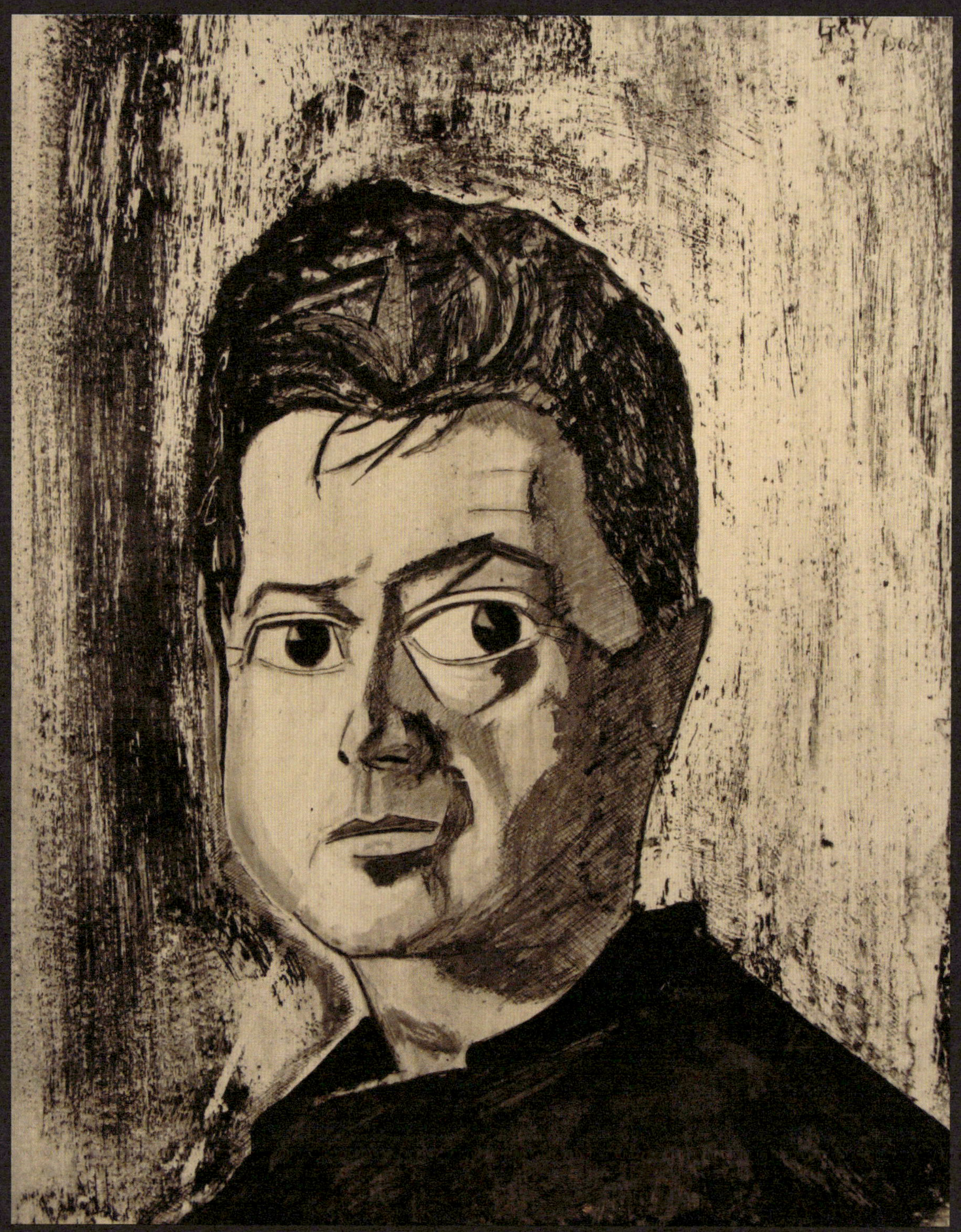

Portrait of Francis Bacon by Reginald Gray
Wikimedia Commons / CC BY-SA 3.0

FRANCIS BACON

Margaret Thatcher once referred to Irish painter Francis Bacon (1909–1992) as "that man who paints those dreadful pictures." Bacon, without question, is one exceptionally unusual figure of the 20th century. His paintings are ferociously stinging: the disturbing blood-red butchered carcasses; the chromatic confusion; as well as the many quasi-human magmas displaying sardonic grins, snarling mouths, lacerating screams, and snarling fangs dominating his canvases as if shouting fear, anguish, pain, and desperation. Through deformation of the subject into impenetrable, disfigured bodies, the painter deprived his paintings of any explicit and rational comprehension, leaving viewers with the only choice of being captive to the extreme expression.

Though his canvases explode with power and destructive fury, and he once described the execution of one painting as a "hand-to-hand combat," the painter denied his paintings were violent. "It's life that is violent," he contended. He always sought inspiration from photography: including images of slaughter houses, butchered meats, animals with throats being slit—all for a faithful and lucid revelation of our fragility. However, although Bacon's paintings are overwhelmingly poignant and oppressive, his simple attitude towards painting—"I painted to be loved"—might be even more disturbing because of its irony.

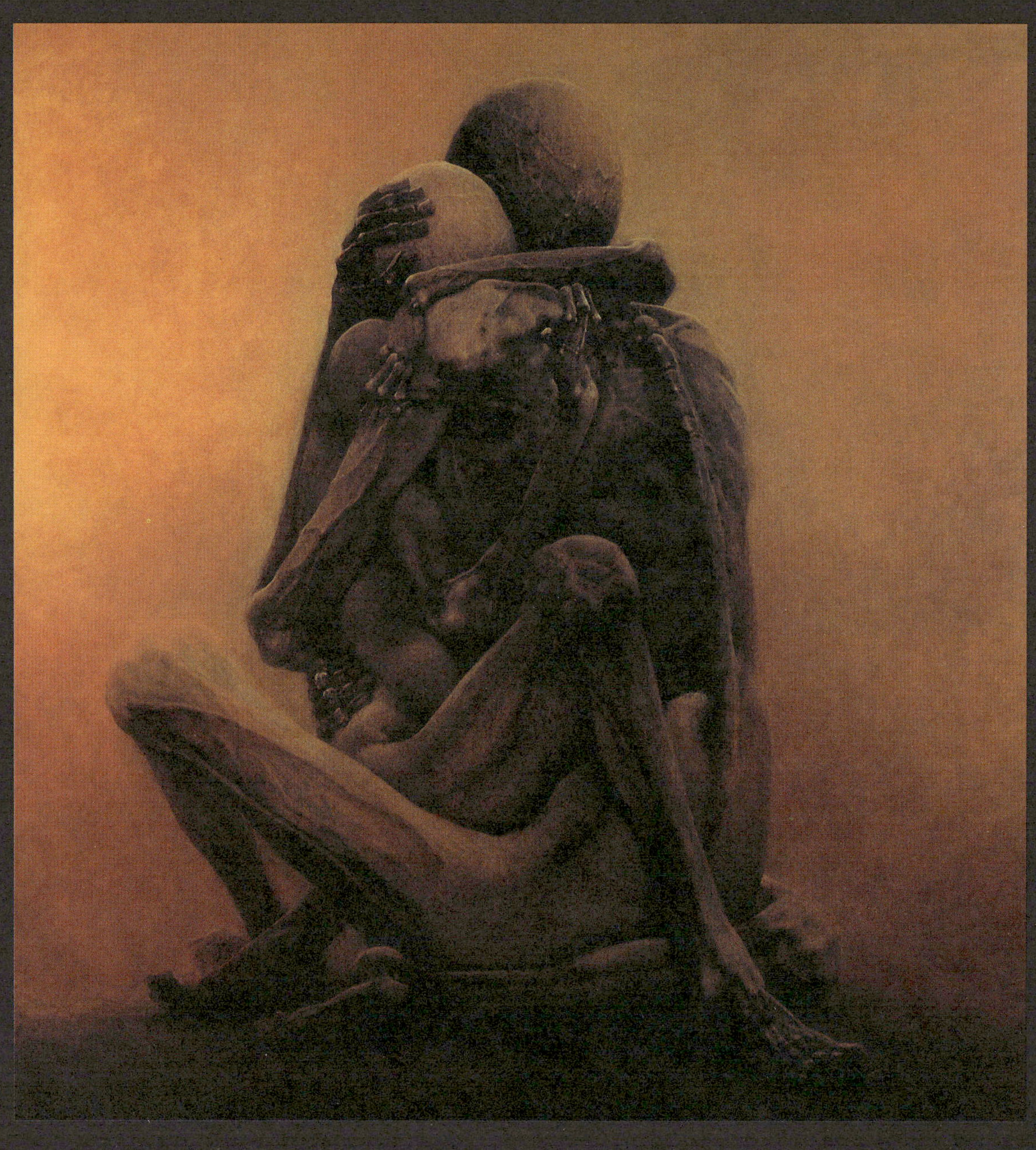

Untitled painting by Zdzislaw Beksinski

BEKSINSKI

Painter, photographer, and sculptor Zdzislaw Beksinski (1929–2005) is one of the most important figures in contemporary Polish art. His unique and eerie fantasies reveal a daunting, apocalyptic world where tombstones protrude gruesomely from bleak landscapes, with flames of fiery red leaping here and there; where desolate and decayed edifices stand erect against a sky veiled by dense fog that threatens to never evanesce; where skinned humanoid creatures baring their bones crouch on the dirt or crawl and roam about, many of the bodies wrapped or tied by spider webs or bandages; where some hug each other as if two would become one; where blood vessels with rampant tentacles of vermilion engulf cars or buildings. Such views are so striking and forceful that they instantly shock one's sensibilities, long before any logical decipherment can emerge.

Though Belsinkski's works are dominated by such mystic themes as the macabre, decomposition, and destruction, he objected to attributing any metaphorical interpretations to his works and even untitled them. As he gave expression and form to inner compulsions, he insisted his spectators do nothing more than see and feel, engaging in an unvoiced "soul-to-soul" conversation. Therefore, the best way to appreciate his paintings is perhaps to walk into the breathtaking, unsettling and hazy abyss of Belsinkski's artistic world with your mind, putting aside any reasoning, and let your heart feel thrilled, frightened, and spellbound.

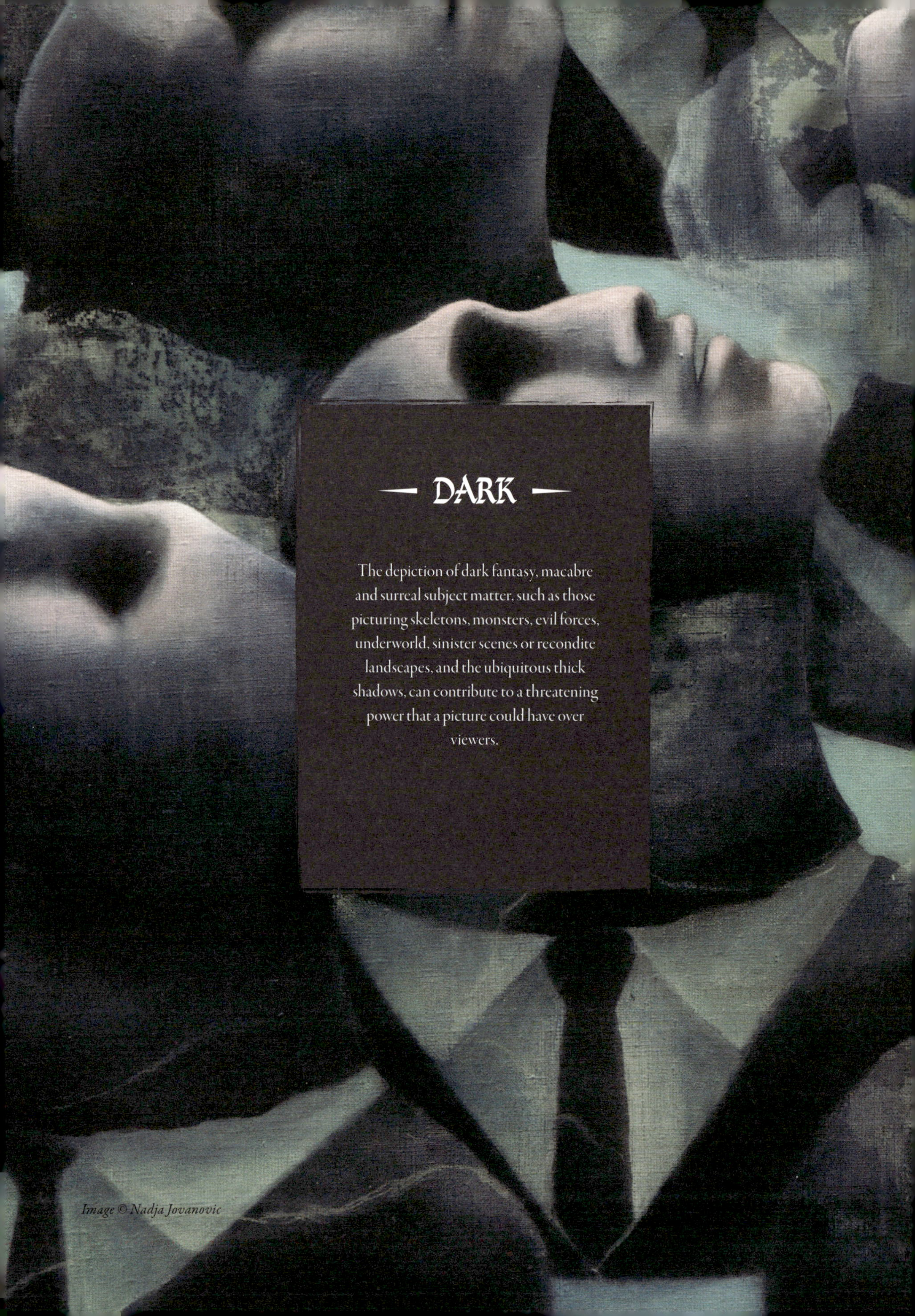

— DARK —

The depiction of dark fantasy, macabre and surreal subject matter, such as those picturing skeletons, monsters, evil forces, underworld, sinister scenes or recondite landscapes, and the ubiquitous thick shadows, can contribute to a threatening power that a picture could have over viewers.

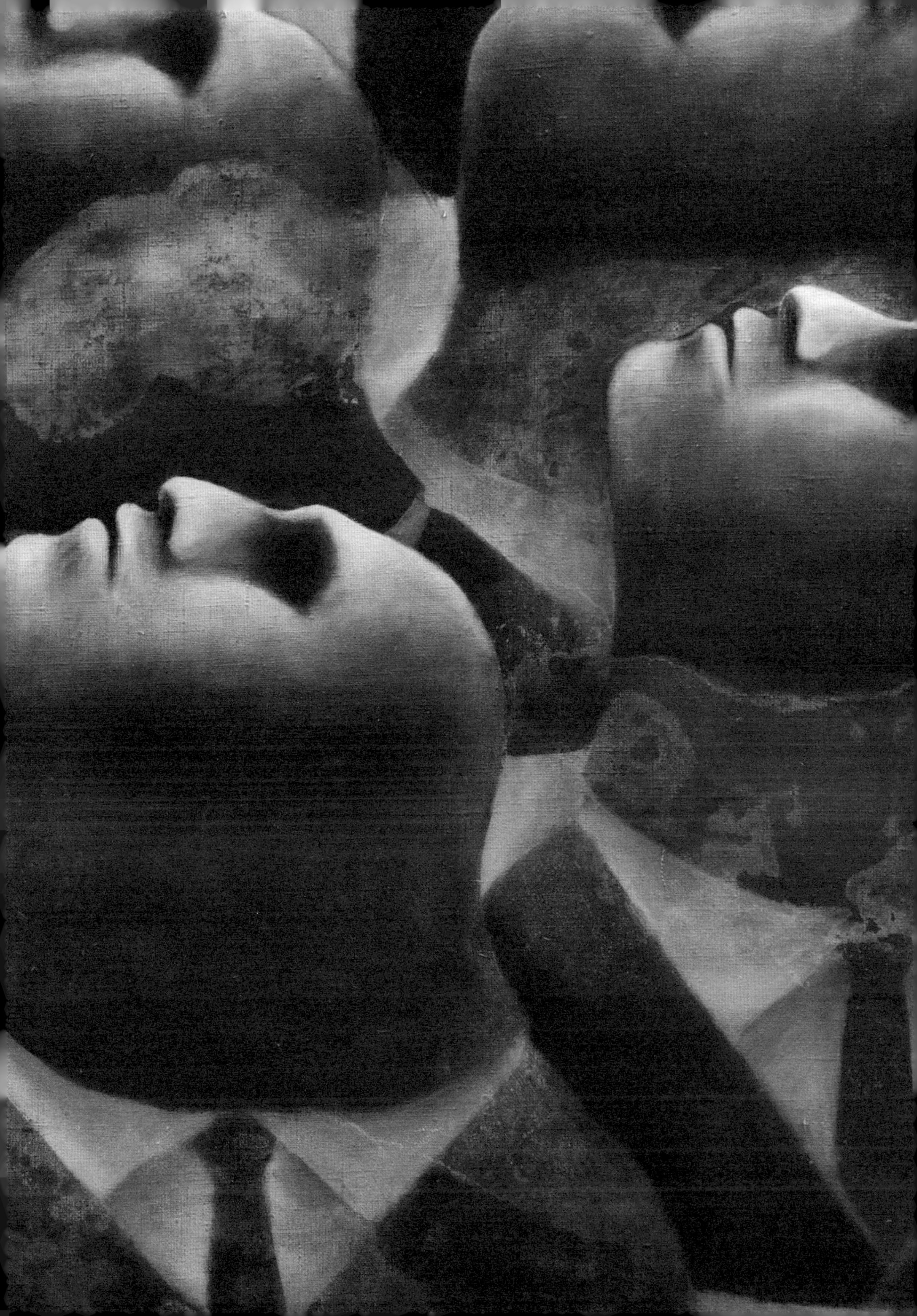

DYING GODS – ALL OUT WAR

Designer: Alexandre Goulet

This album cover was designed for the legendary band All Out War for their memorable album *Dying Gods*—the first album in 5 years with the same line-up of members as in 1998 when the team released their mythic album *For Those Who Crucified*.

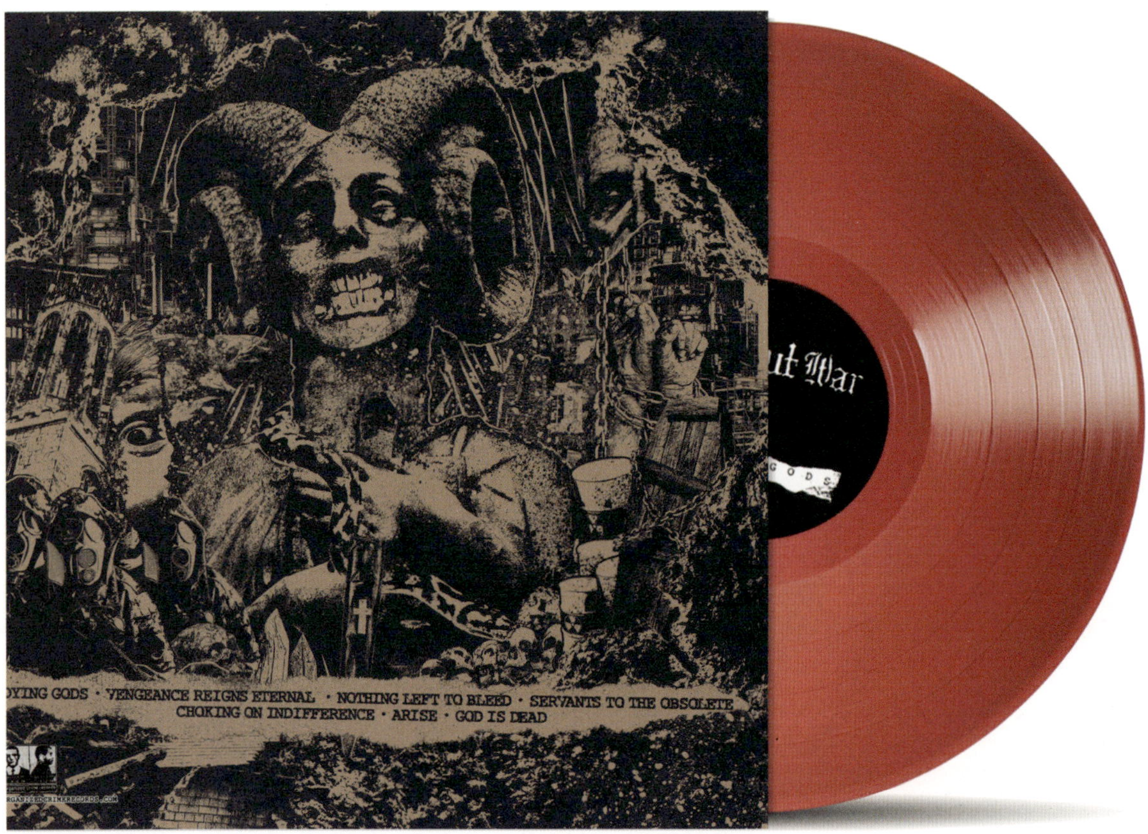

INTERVIEW

Why do you create such fierce visuals?

My main clients are from the metal music industry and they are all looking for the most vicious, aggressive thing they could get to fit their music. Sometimes I wish I could get more diverse clients but I truly love this style!

What are your common approaches to produce a fierce visual effect?

I usually sit at my desk and look at my computer for a good hour before figuring out what I want to do. Most of the time, I will build a "skeleton" of the project in less than an hour, then start the long process of adding all the tiny details that make the difference.

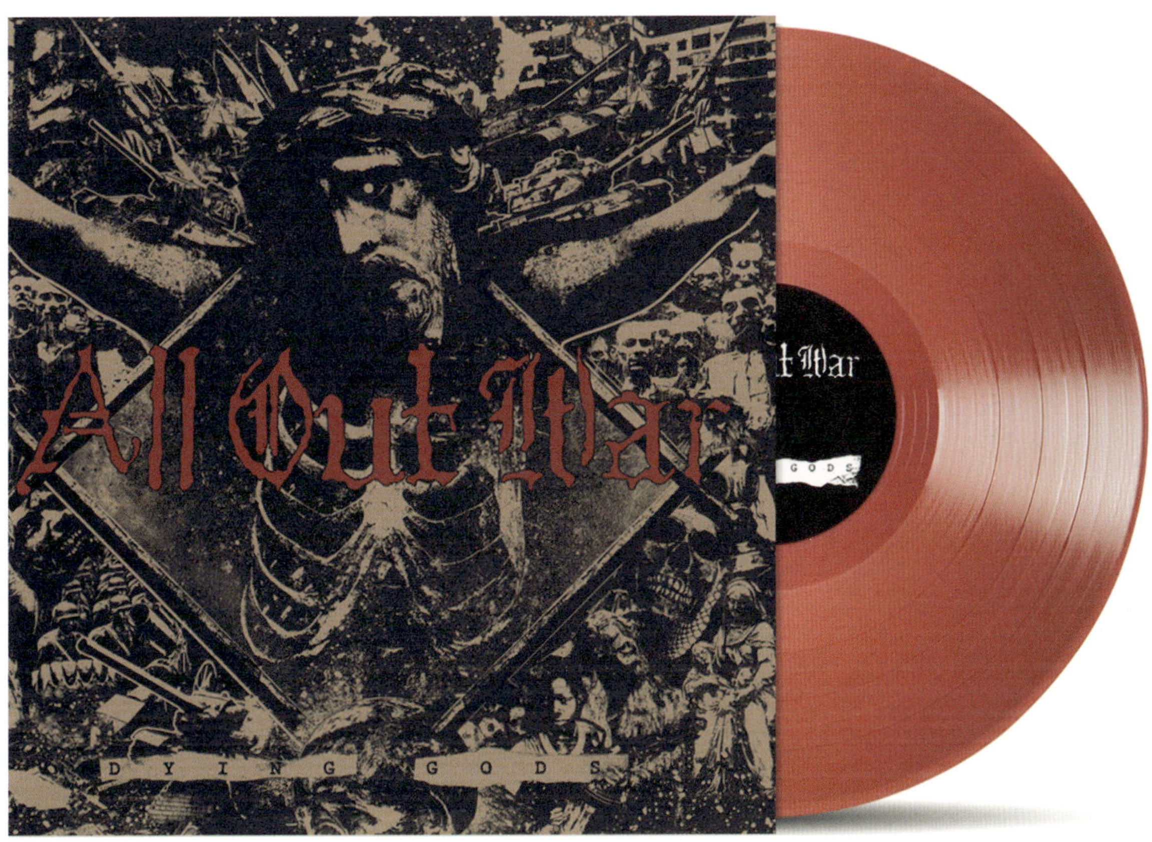

Where do your inspirations come from?

My style is highly influenced by the 70's horror and sci-fi posters and movie's artworks. Some of the favorites are (in no particular order): *Alien*, *2001 Space Odyssey*, *Blade Runner*, *Planet of the Apes*—I mostly love movies that have a strong political or social standpoint hidden in something that are visually stunning. And adding to this is a good dose of metal and hardcore and punk imagery.

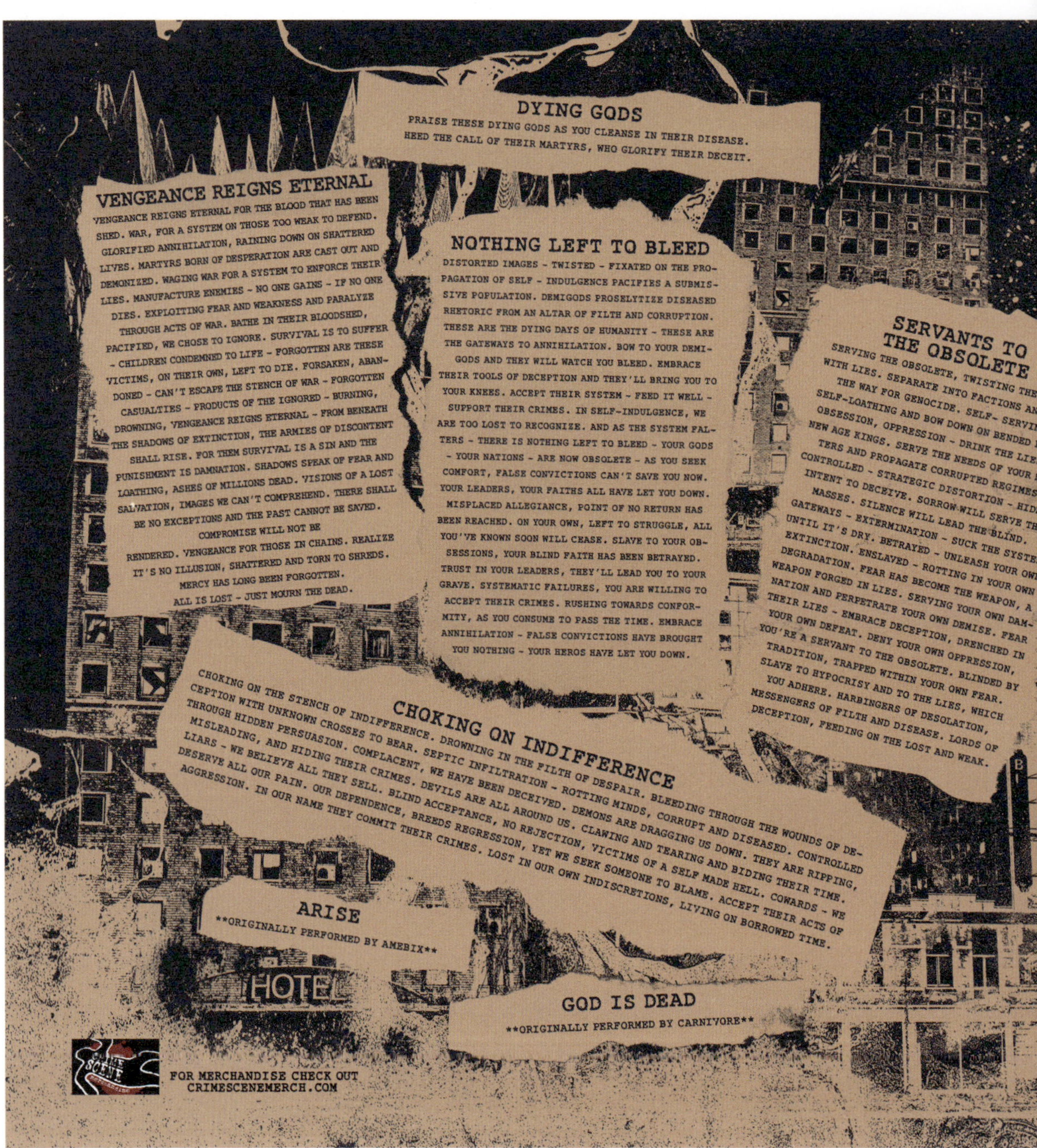
DYING GODS
PRAISE THESE DYING GODS AS YOU CLEANSE IN THEIR DISEASE.
HEED THE CALL OF THEIR MARTYRS, WHO GLORIFY THEIR DECEIT.
VENGEANCE REIGNS ETERNAL
VENGEANCE REIGNS ETERNAL FOR THE BLOOD THAT HAS BEEN SHED. WAR, FOR A SYSTEM ON THOSE TOO WEAK TO DEFEND. GLORIFIED ANNIHILATION, RAINING DOWN ON SHATTERED LIVES. MARTYRS BORN OF DESPERATION ARE CAST OUT AND DEMONIZED. WAGING WAR FOR A SYSTEM TO ENFORCE THEIR LIES. MANUFACTURE ENEMIES - NO ONE GAINS - IF NO ONE DIES. EXPLOITING FEAR AND WEAKNESS AND PARALYZE THROUGH ACTS OF WAR. BATHE IN THEIR BLOODSHED, PACIFIED, WE CHOSE TO IGNORE. SURVIVAL IS TO SUFFER - CHILDREN CONDEMNED TO LIFE - FORGOTTEN ARE THESE VICTIMS, ON THEIR OWN, LEFT TO DIE. FORSAKEN, ABANDONED - CAN'T ESCAPE THE STENCH OF WAR - FORGOTTEN CASUALTIES - PRODUCTS OF THE IGNORED - BURNING, DROWNING, VENGEANCE REIGNS ETERNAL - FROM BENEATH THE SHADOWS OF EXTINCTION, THE ARMIES OF DISCONTENT SHALL RISE. FOR THEM SURVIVAL IS A SIN AND THE PUNISHMENT IS DAMNATION. SHADOWS SPEAK OF FEAR AND LOATHING, ASHES OF MILLIONS DEAD. VISIONS OF A LOST SALVATION, IMAGES WE CAN'T COMPREHEND. THERE SHALL BE NO EXCEPTIONS AND THE PAST CANNOT BE SAVED.
COMPROMISE WILL NOT BE RENDERED. VENGEANCE FOR THOSE IN CHAINS. REALIZE IT'S NO ILLUSION, SHATTERED AND TORN TO SHREDS.
MERCY HAS LONG BEEN FORGOTTEN.
ALL IS LOST - JUST MOURN THE DEAD.
NOTHING LEFT TO BLEED
DISTORTED IMAGES - TWISTED - FIXATED ON THE PROPAGATION OF SELF - INDULGENCE PACIFIES A SUBMISSIVE POPULATION. DEMIGODS PROSELYTIZE DISEASED RHETORIC FROM AN ALTAR OF FILTH AND CORRUPTION. THESE ARE THE DYING DAYS OF HUMANITY - THESE ARE THE GATEWAYS TO ANNIHILATION. BOW TO YOUR DEMIGODS AND THEY WILL WATCH YOU BLEED. EMBRACE THEIR TOOLS OF DECEPTION AND THEY'LL BRING YOU TO YOUR KNEES. ACCEPT THEIR SYSTEM - FEED IT WELL - SUPPORT THEIR CRIMES. IN SELF-INDULGENCE, WE ARE TOO LOST TO RECOGNIZE. AND AS THE SYSTEM FALTERS - THERE IS NOTHING LEFT TO BLEED - YOUR GODS - YOUR NATIONS - ARE NOW OBSOLETE - AS YOU SEEK COMFORT, FALSE CONVICTIONS CAN'T SAVE YOU NOW. YOUR LEADERS, YOUR FAITHS ALL HAVE LET YOU DOWN. MISPLACED ALLEGIANCE, POINT OF NO RETURN HAS BEEN REACHED. ON YOUR OWN, LEFT TO STRUGGLE, ALL YOU'VE KNOWN SOON WILL CEASE. SLAVE TO YOUR OBSESSIONS, YOUR BLIND FAITH HAS BEEN BETRAYED. TRUST IN YOUR LEADERS, THEY'LL LEAD YOU TO YOUR GRAVE. SYSTEMATIC FAILURES, YOU ARE WILLING TO ACCEPT THEIR CRIMES. RUSHING TOWARDS CONFORMITY, AS YOU CONSUME TO PASS THE TIME. EMBRACE ANNIHILATION - FALSE CONVICTIONS HAVE BROUGHT YOU NOTHING - YOUR HEROS HAVE LET YOU DOWN.
SERVANTS TO THE OBSOLETE
SERVING THE OBSOLETE, TWISTING THE WITH LIES. SEPARATE INTO FACTIONS AN THE WAY FOR GENOCIDE. SELF- SERVIN SELF-LOATHING AND BOW DOWN ON BENDED K OBSESSION, OPPRESSION - DRINK THE LIES NEW AGE KINGS. SERVE THE NEEDS OF YOUR M TERS AND PROPAGATE CORRUPTED REGIMES CONTROLLED - STRATEGIC DISTORTION - HIDI INTENT TO DECEIVE. SORROW WILL SERVE TH MASSES. SILENCE WILL LEAD THE BLIND. GATEWAYS - EXTERMINATION - SUCK THE SYSTEM UNTIL IT'S DRY. BETRAYED - UNLEASH YOUR OWN EXTINCTION. ENSLAVED - ROTTING IN YOUR OWN DEGRADATION. FEAR HAS BECOME THE WEAPON, A WEAPON FORGED IN LIES. SERVING YOUR OWN DAMNATION AND PERPETRATE YOUR OWN DEMISE. FEAR THEIR LIES - EMBRACE DECEPTION, DRENCHED IN YOUR OWN DEFEAT. DENY YOUR OWN OPPRESSION, YOU'RE A SERVANT TO THE OBSOLETE. BLINDED BY TRADITION, TRAPPED WITHIN YOUR OWN FEAR. SLAVE TO HYPOCRISY AND TO THE LIES, WHICH YOU ADHERE. HARBINGERS OF DESOLATION, MESSENGERS OF FILTH AND DISEASE. LORDS OF DECEPTION, FEEDING ON THE LOST AND WEAK.
CHOKING ON INDIFFERENCE
CHOKING ON THE STENCH OF INDIFFERENCE. DROWNING IN THE FILTH OF DESPAIR. BLEEDING THROUGH THE WOUNDS OF DECEPTION WITH UNKNOWN CROSSES TO BEAR. SEPTIC INFILTRATION - ROTTING MINDS, CORRUPT AND DISEASED. CONTROLLED THROUGH HIDDEN PERSUASION. COMPLACENT, WE HAVE BEEN DECEIVED. DEMONS ARE DRAGGING US DOWN. THEY ARE RIPPING, MISLEADING, AND HIDING THEIR CRIMES. DEVILS ARE ALL AROUND US. CLAWING AND TEARING AND BIDING THEIR TIME. LIARS - WE BELIEVE ALL THEY SELL. BLIND ACCEPTANCE, NO REJECTION, VICTIMS OF A SELF MADE HELL. COWARDS - WE DESERVE ALL OUR PAIN. OUR DEPENDENCE, BREEDS REGRESSION, YET WE SEEK SOMEONE TO BLAME. ACCEPT THEIR ACTS OF AGGRESSION. IN OUR NAME THEY COMMIT THEIR CRIMES. LOST IN OUR OWN INDISCRETIONS, LIVING ON BORROWED TIME.
ARISE
ORIGINALLY PERFORMED BY AMEBIX
HOTEL
GOD IS DEAD
ORIGINALLY PERFORMED BY CARNIVORE
FOR MERCHANDISE CHECK OUT
CRIMESCENEMERCH.COM

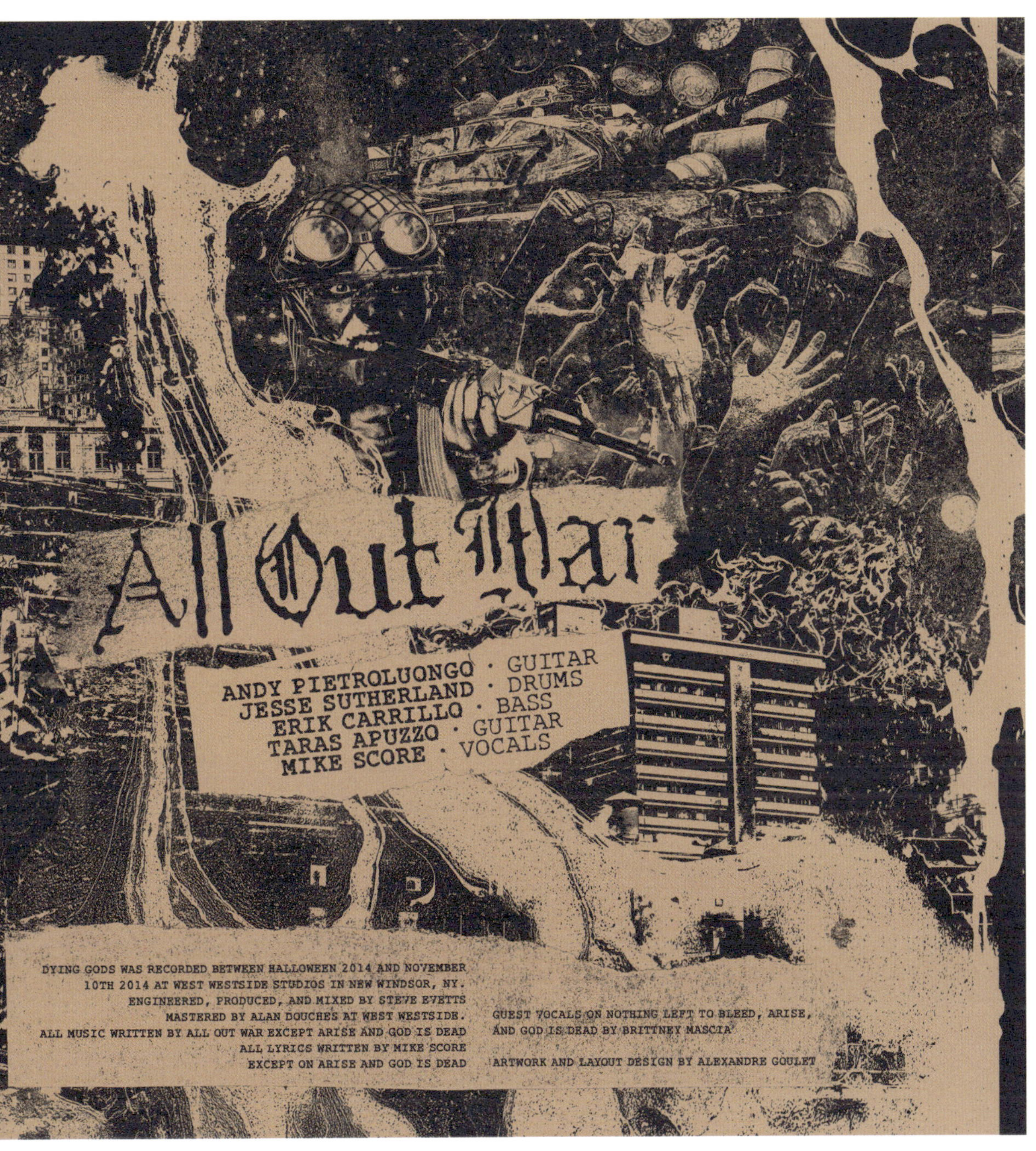
All Out War
ANDY PIETROLUONGO · GUITAR
JESSE SUTHERLAND · DRUMS
ERIK CARRILLO · BASS
TARAS APUZZO · GUITAR
MIKE SCORE · VOCALS
DYING GODS WAS RECORDED BETWEEN HALLOWEEN 2014 AND NOVEMBER
10TH 2014 AT WEST WESTSIDE STUDIOS IN NEW WINDSOR, NY.
ENGINEERED, PRODUCED, AND MIXED BY STEVE EVETTS
MASTERED BY ALAN DOUCHES AT WEST WESTSIDE.
ALL MUSIC WRITTEN BY ALL OUT WAR EXCEPT ARISE AND GOD IS DEAD
ALL LYRICS WRITTEN BY MIKE SCORE
EXCEPT ON ARISE AND GOD IS DEAD
GUEST VOCALS ON NOTHING LEFT TO BLEED, ARISE,
AND GOD IS DEAD BY BRITTNEY MASCIA
ARTWORK AND LAYOUT DESIGN BY ALEXANDRE GOULET

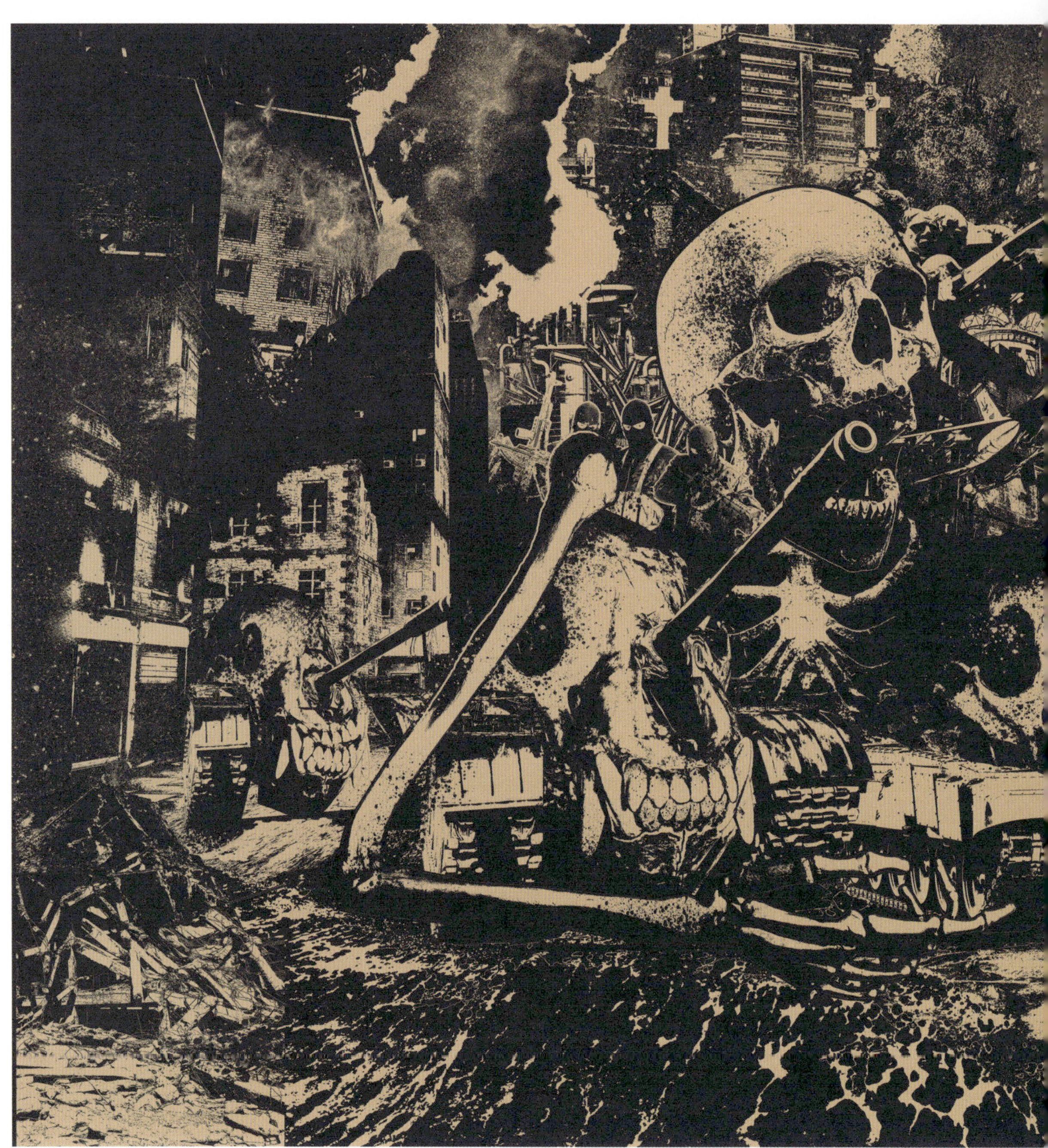

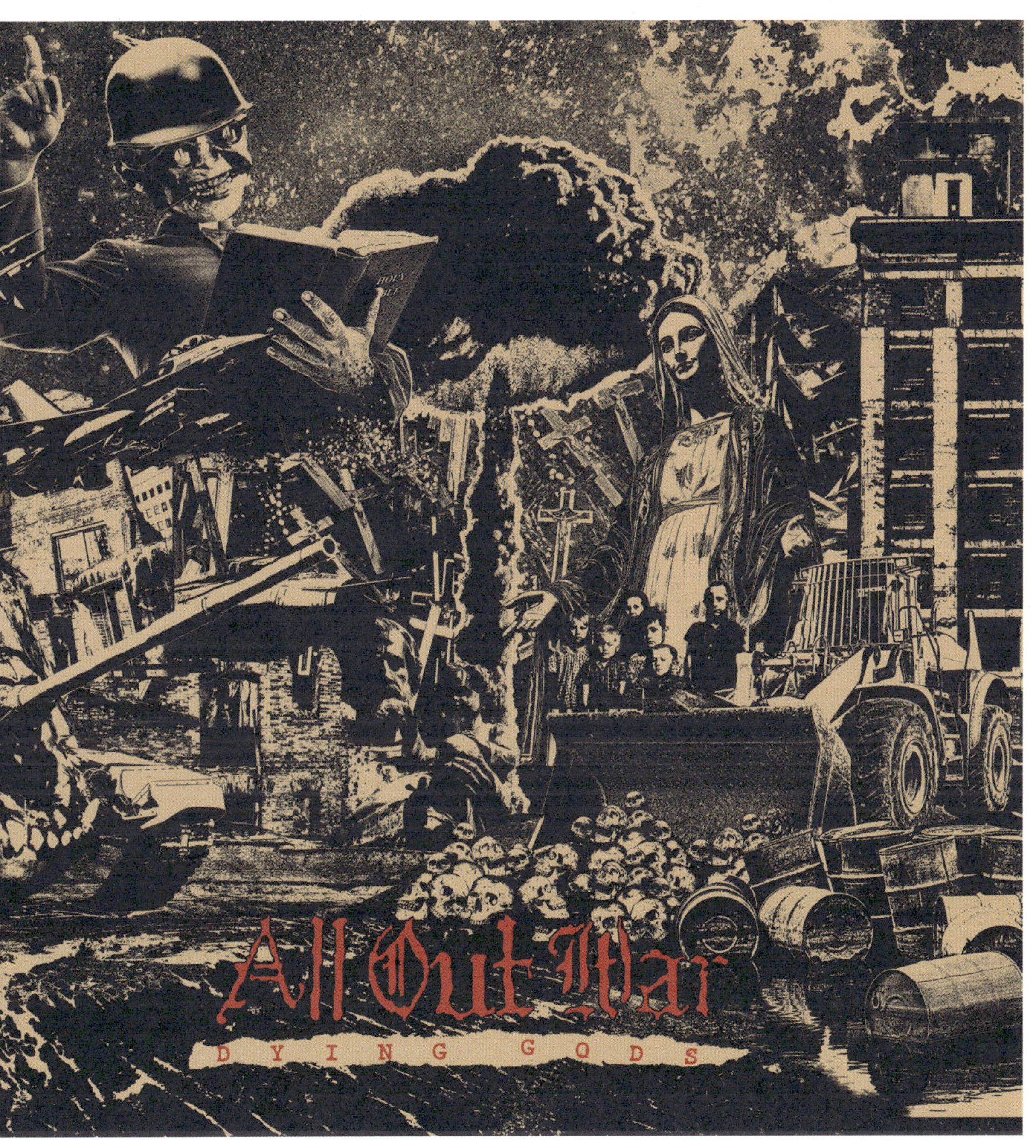
All Out War
DYING GODS

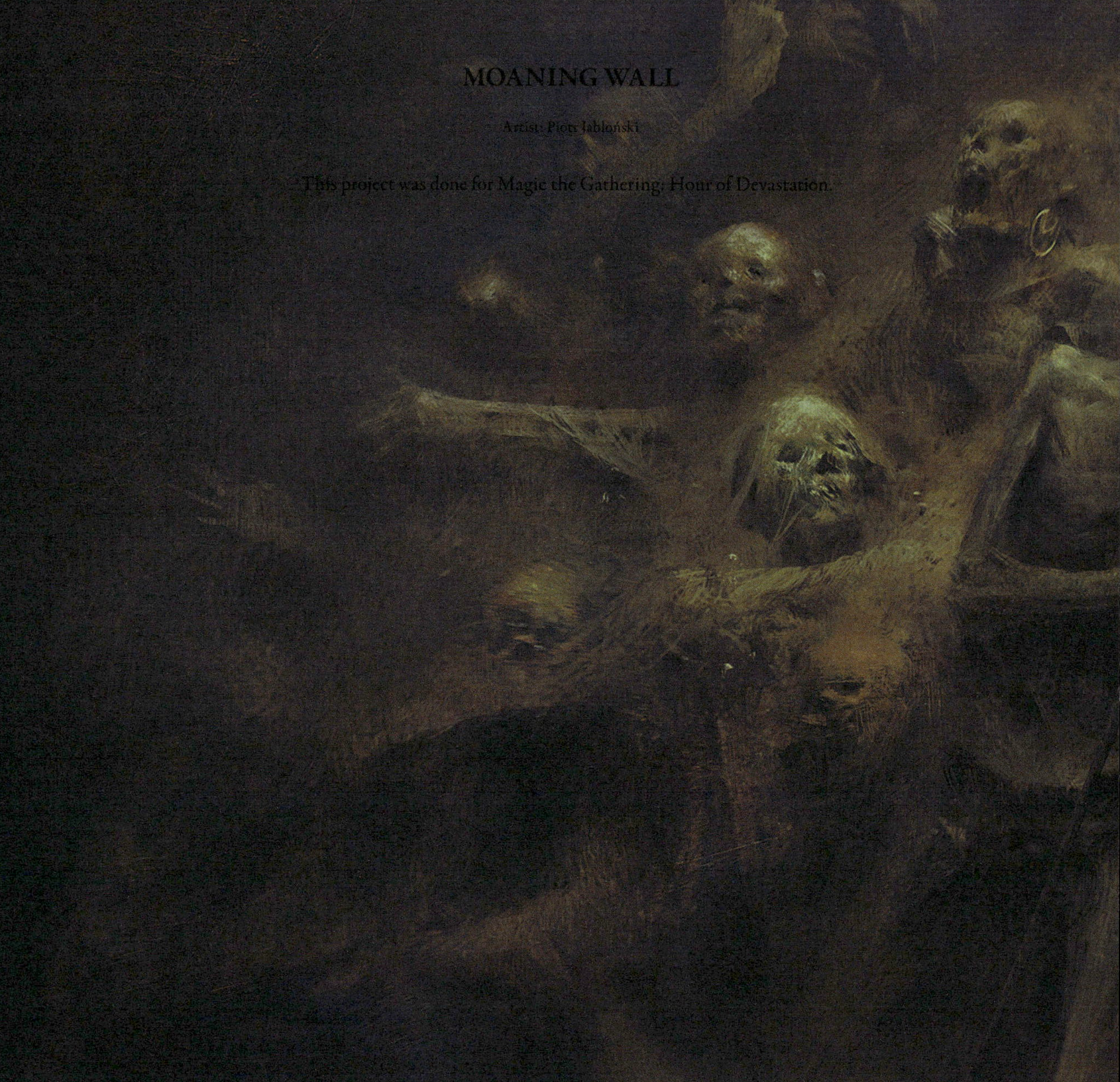

MOANING WALL

Artist: Piotr Jabłoński

This project was done for Magic the Gathering: Hour of Devastation.

INTERVIEW

Why do you create such fierce visuals?

It's a bit a tricky question, because it's not my intention to create only fierce arts. I just want to do my best with a theme I got from a client—that's all the secret. Fantasy art is not my top theme. When I was younger I used to paint graffiti, so some street arts themes are still close to my heart. I also like Swiss design and Polish poster, architecture, photography, movie, fashion, etc. It will be awesome to make more posters, covers, illustrations for music albums, maybe something for fashion company. Themes through which I can express my inspirations and interests will be great.

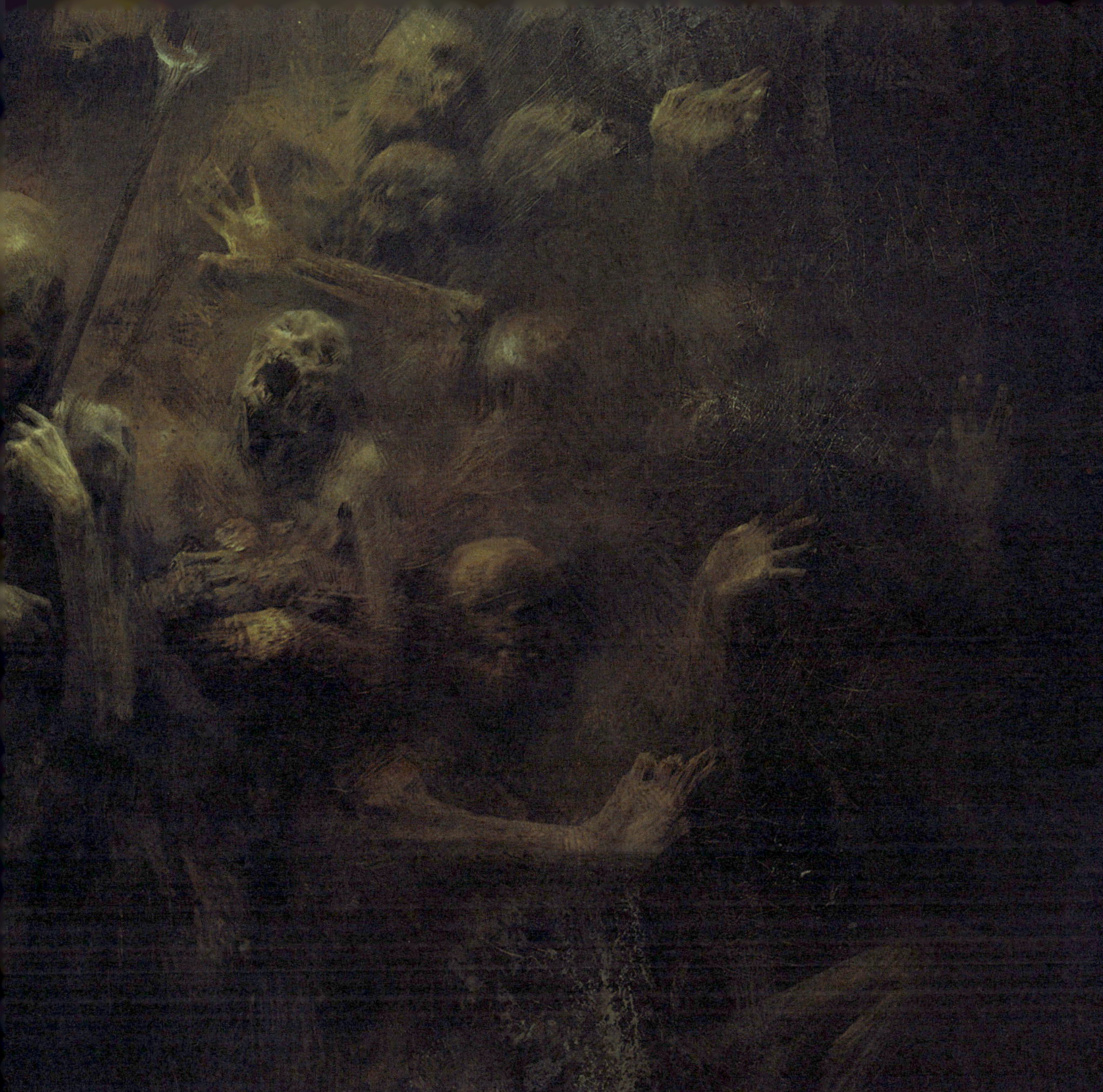

© Wizards of the Coast, LLC

What are your common approaches to produce a fierce visual effect?

There is no certain rules. Every theme needs totally different approach. Usually I will try to make a few fast and messy sketches on the paper to find a best composition of the mood and scene that I have in my mind. After that I will start sketching and painting on computer. And this latter stage takes the most of the time.

Where do your inspirations come from?

Paintings, movies, photography, fashion, architecture, design, music. Inspiration can be everywhere and everything can be an inspiration. Sometimes some random shapes or colors can bring a cool idea—cloud shape, element of small architecture, human pose, street scene or even color of sky can bring a good idea.

APOCALYPSE DEMON

Artist: Piotr Jabłoński

This project was done for Magic the Gathering: Hour of Devastation.

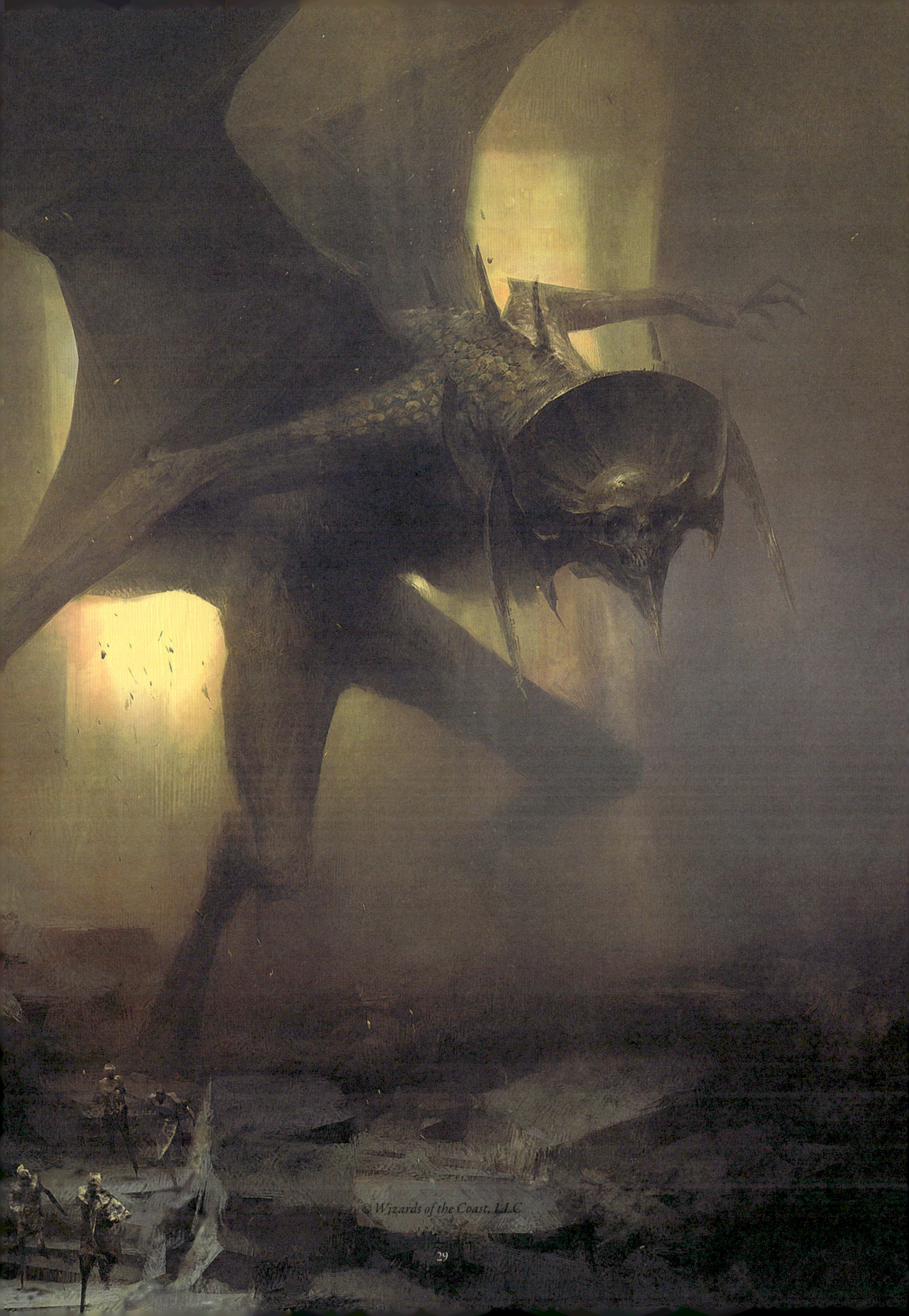

HELLS FOUNDRY – IRON GOLEM

Designer: Alexandre Goulet

For Canadian metal/hardcore band Iron Golem's first release, the designer aimed to create a desolate post-apocalyptic landscape which would reflect the band's really aggressive sound. A robotic man-eating-machine has been set as the focal point, while an inside panel shows the result of the digestion of human bodies—a grimy artwork for the *Hells Foundry*.

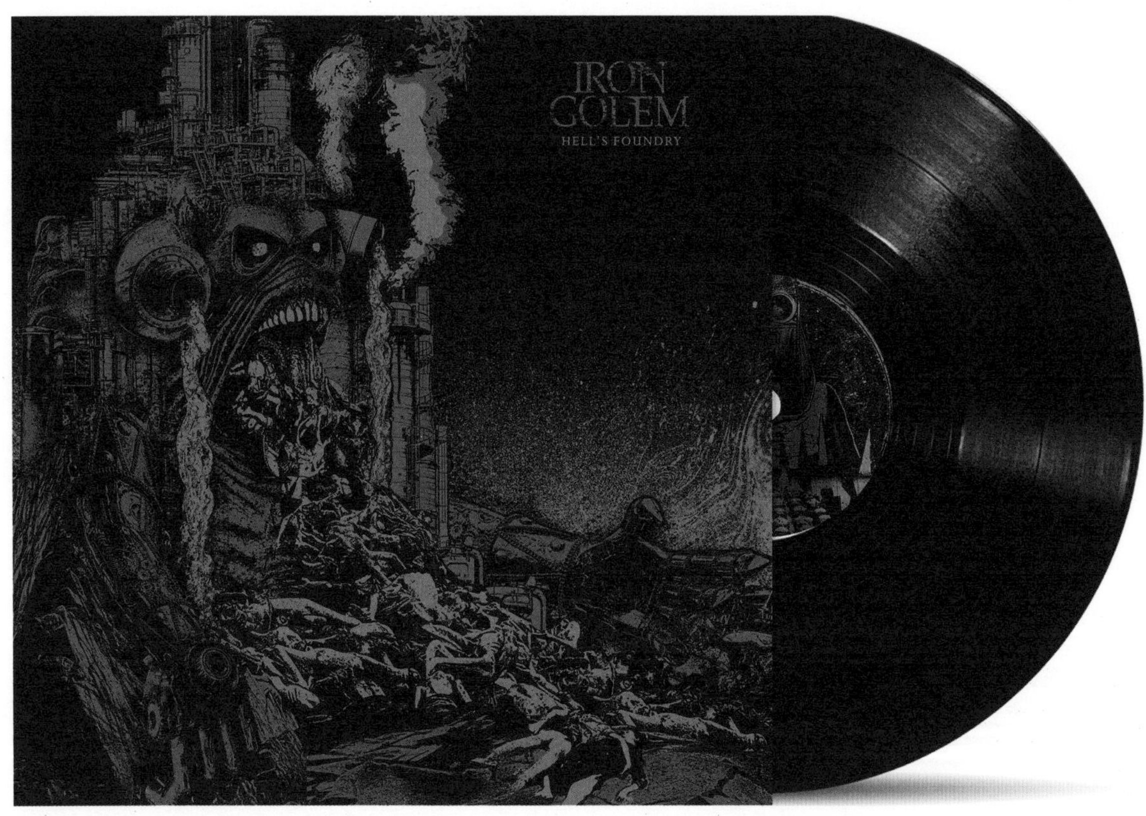

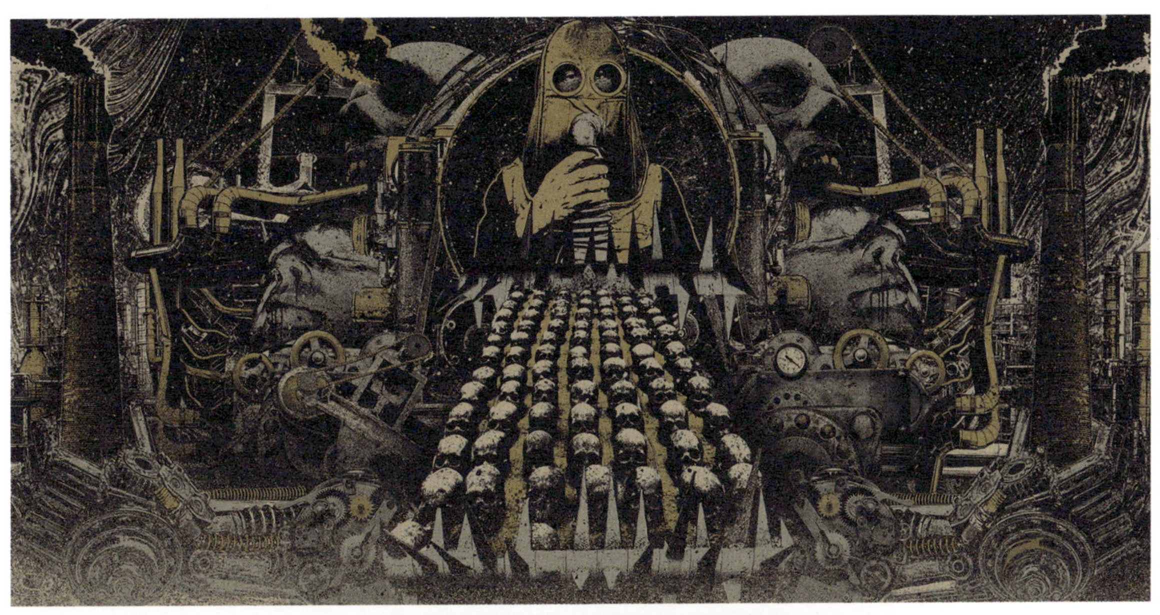

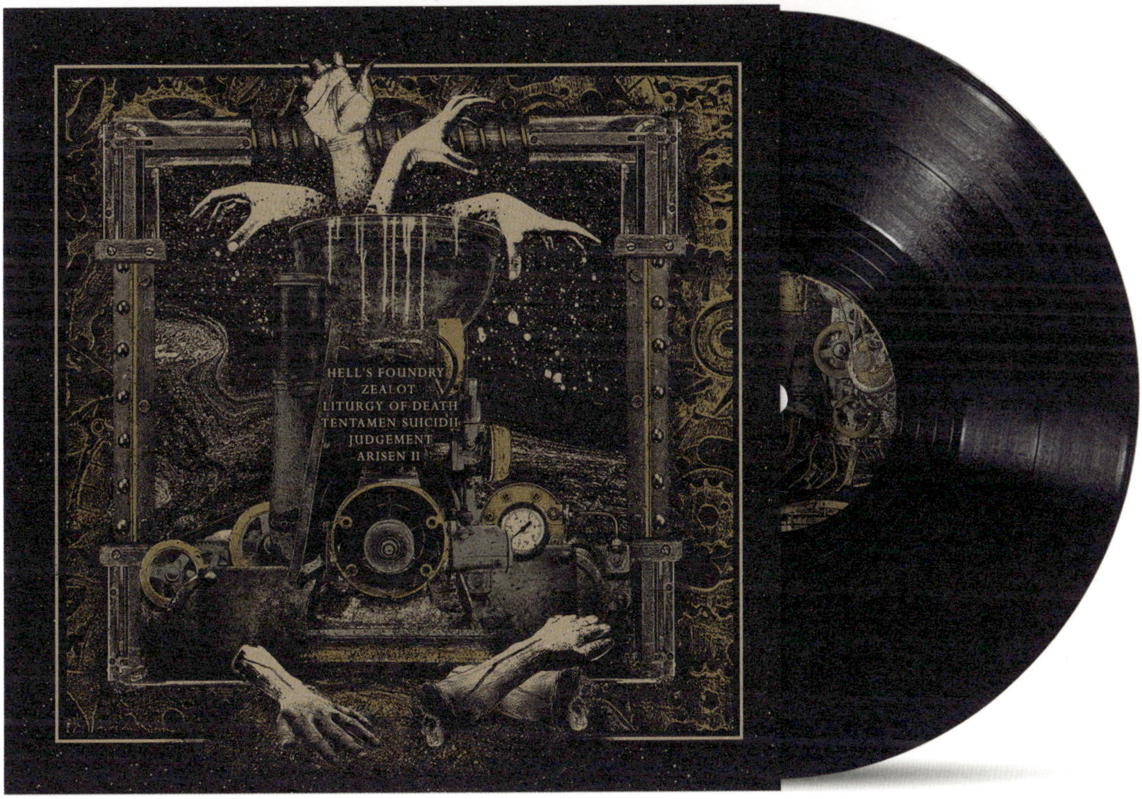

HELL'S FOUNDRY
ZEALOT
LITURGY OF DEATH
TENTAMEN SUICIDII
JUDGEMENT
ARISEN II

VVALBERG

Designer: Alexandre Goulet

For the first release of the hardcore band VVALBERG from Quebec, the aim was to produce a strong and dark imagery to show their style. The designer created this vibrantly aggressive and introspective artwork that relates to the lyrics of the music.

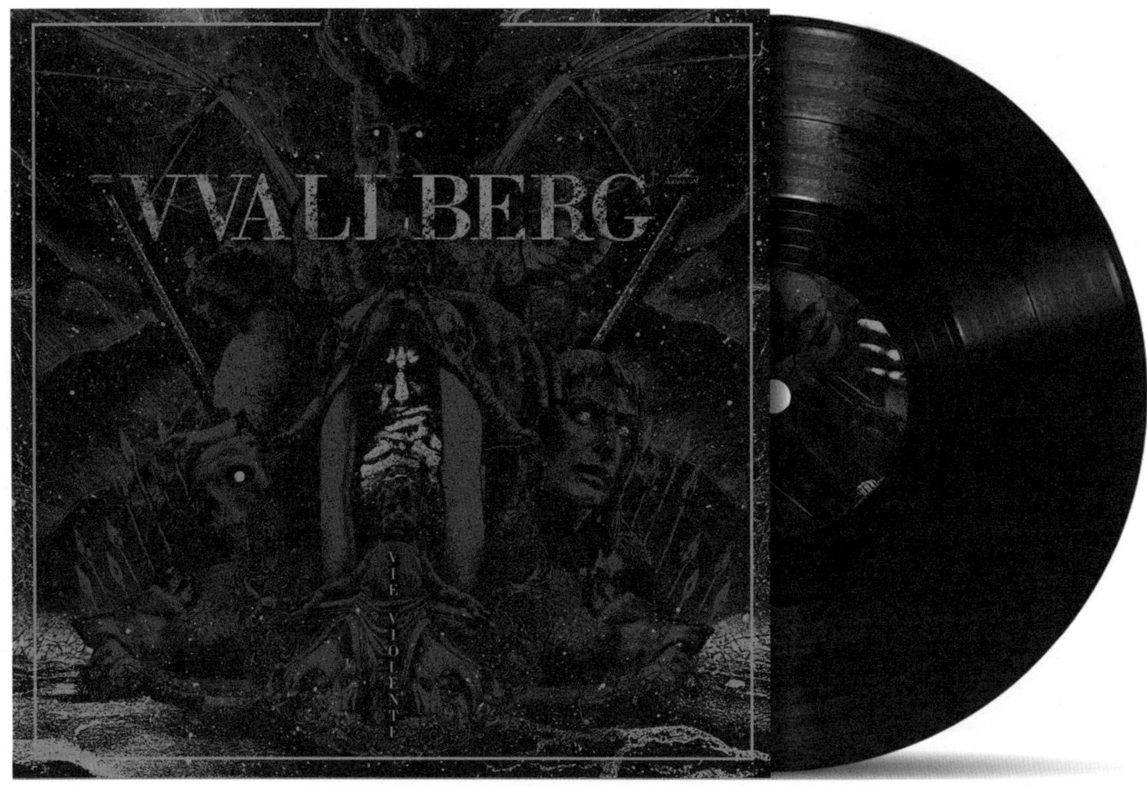

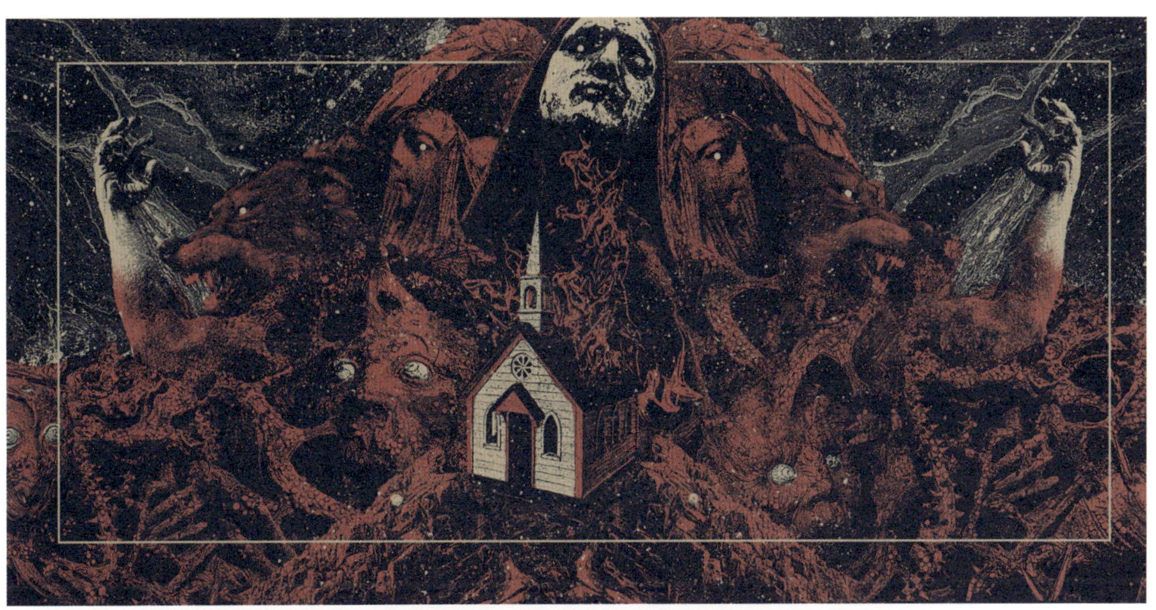

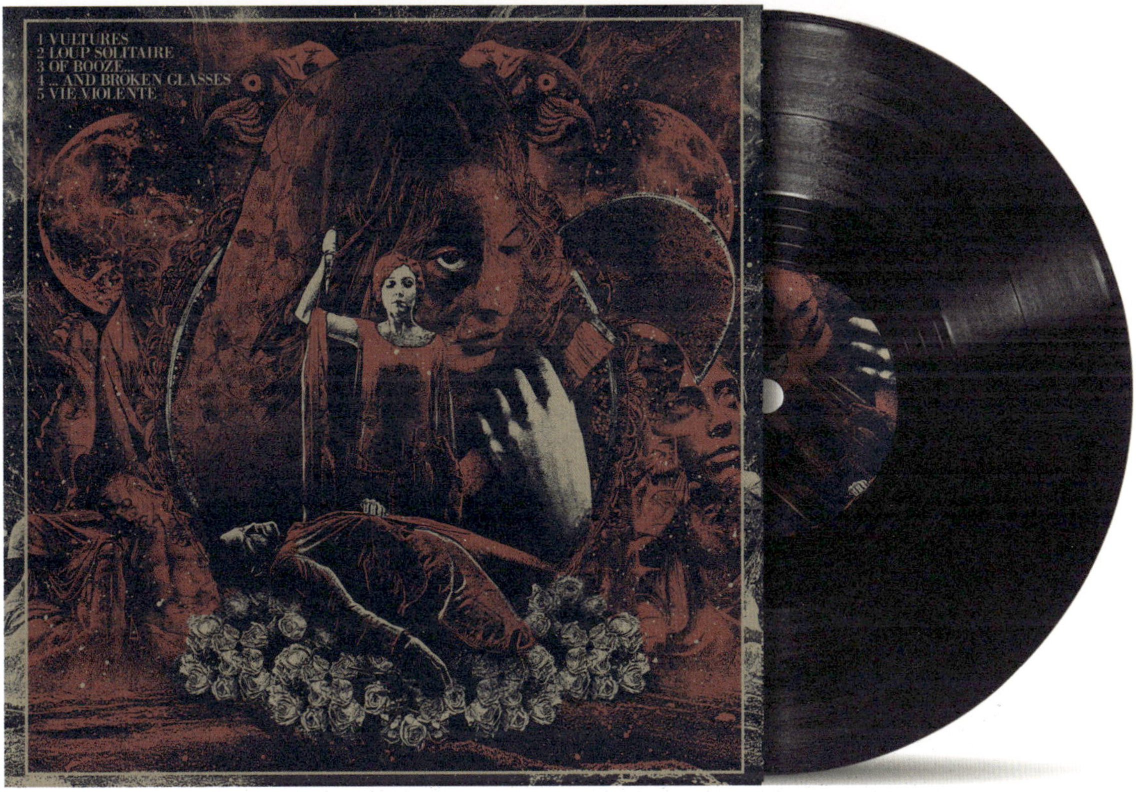

1 VULTURES
2 LOUP SOLITAIRE
3 OF BOOZE...
4 ... AND BROKEN GLASSES
5 VIE VIOLENTE

SOMNAMBULISM

Artist: Nadja Jovanovic

With an interest in transforming characters in mental images and creating illusions, the artist created these pictures as manifestations of illusions based on the various facets of existence. These allegorical representations of the state between sleep and wakefulness are the result of an examination of memory, past, present life and death with a focus on man in terms of the everlasting dualism, being either conscious or unconscious, and the imprisonment in his own illusion.

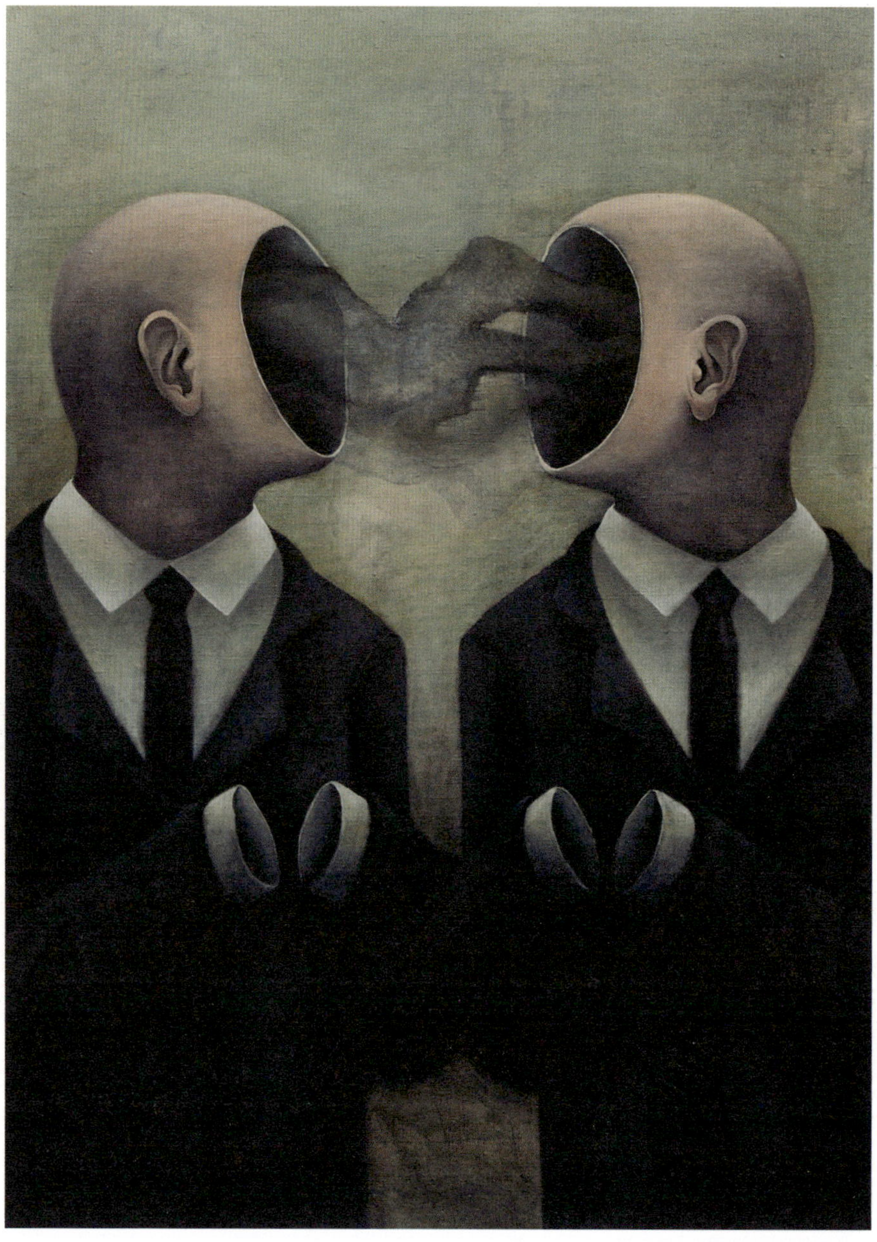

Empty Suit - Oil on Canvas

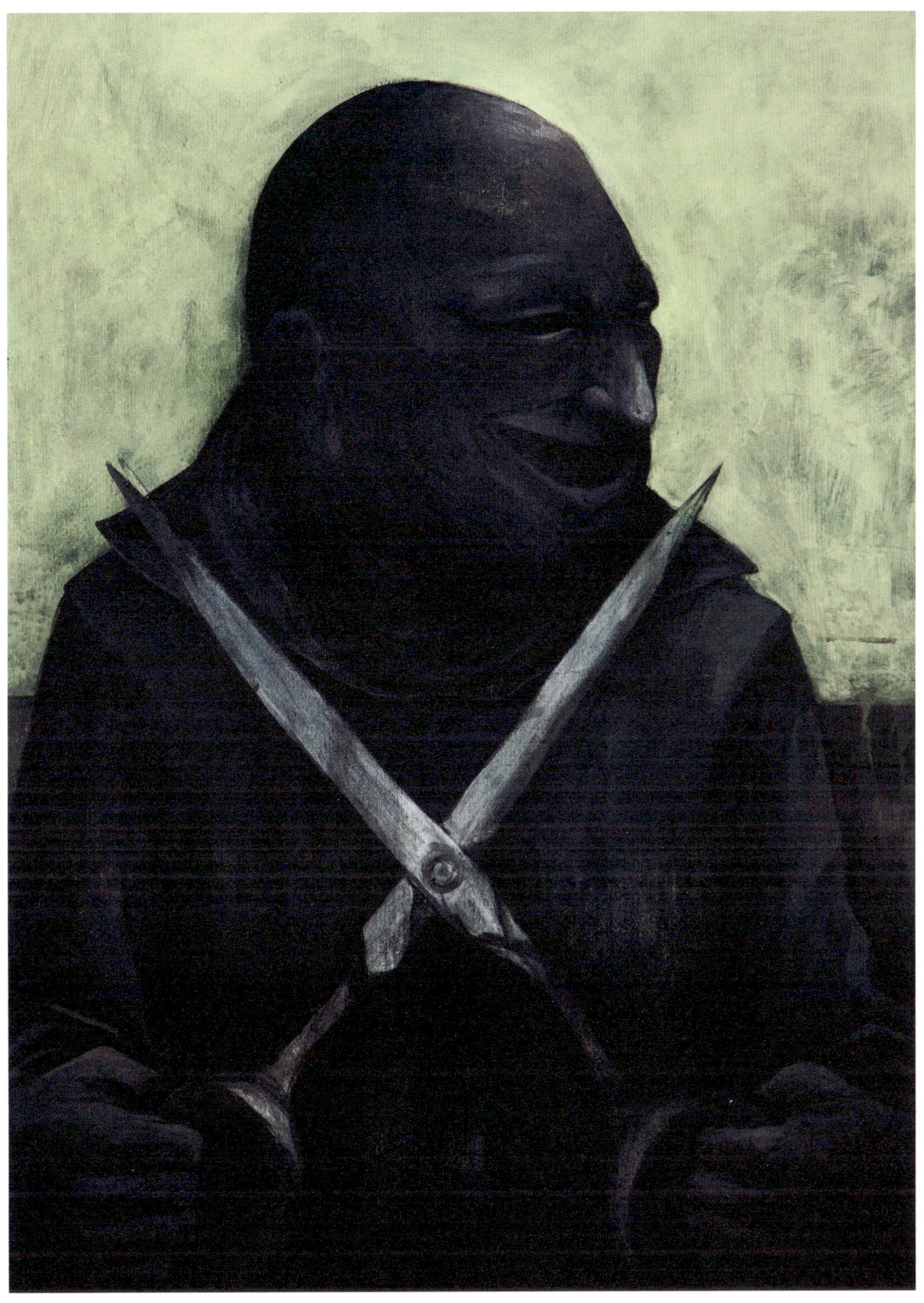

Nightmare - Acrylic on Paper

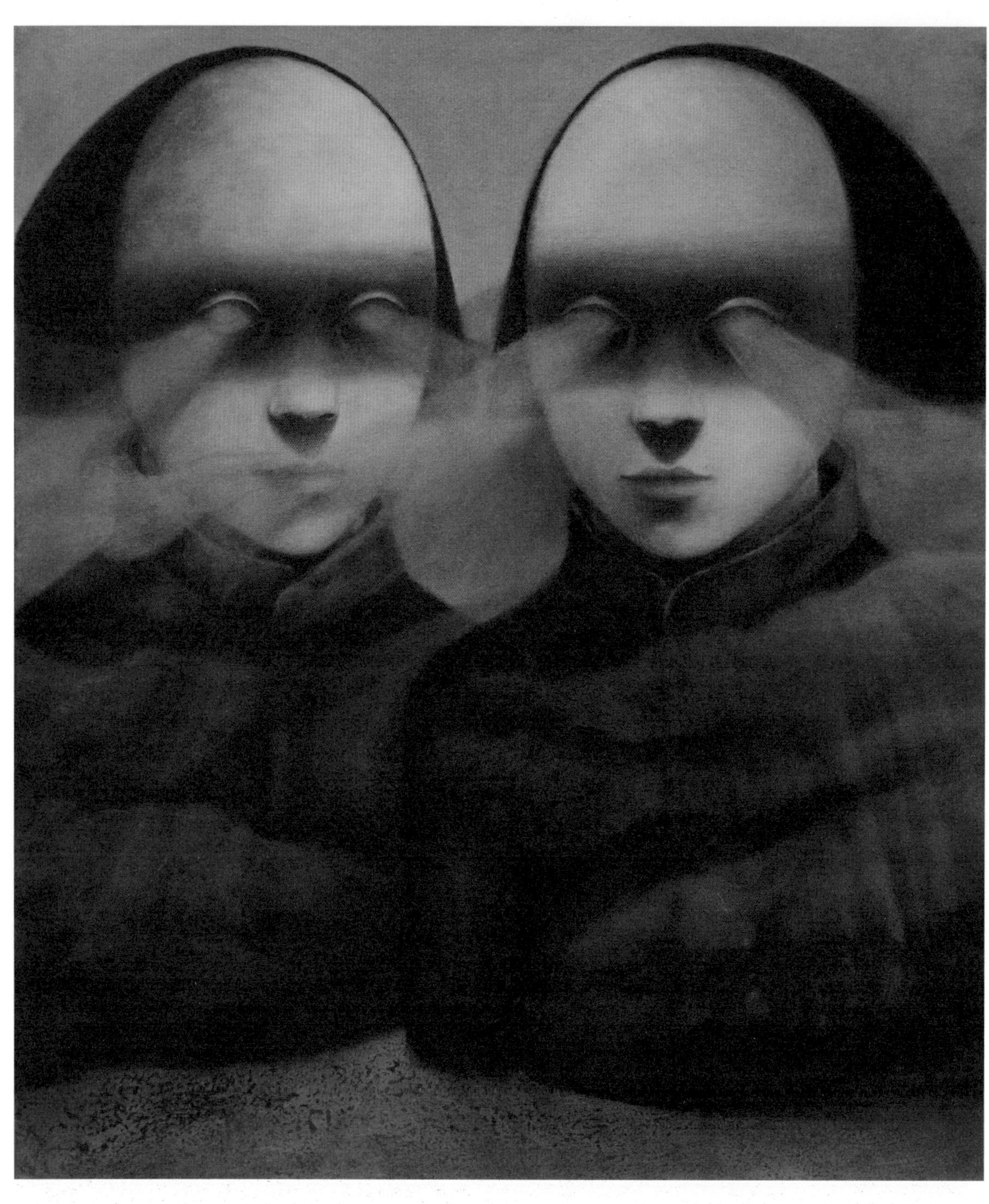

Dreamers - Oil on Canvas

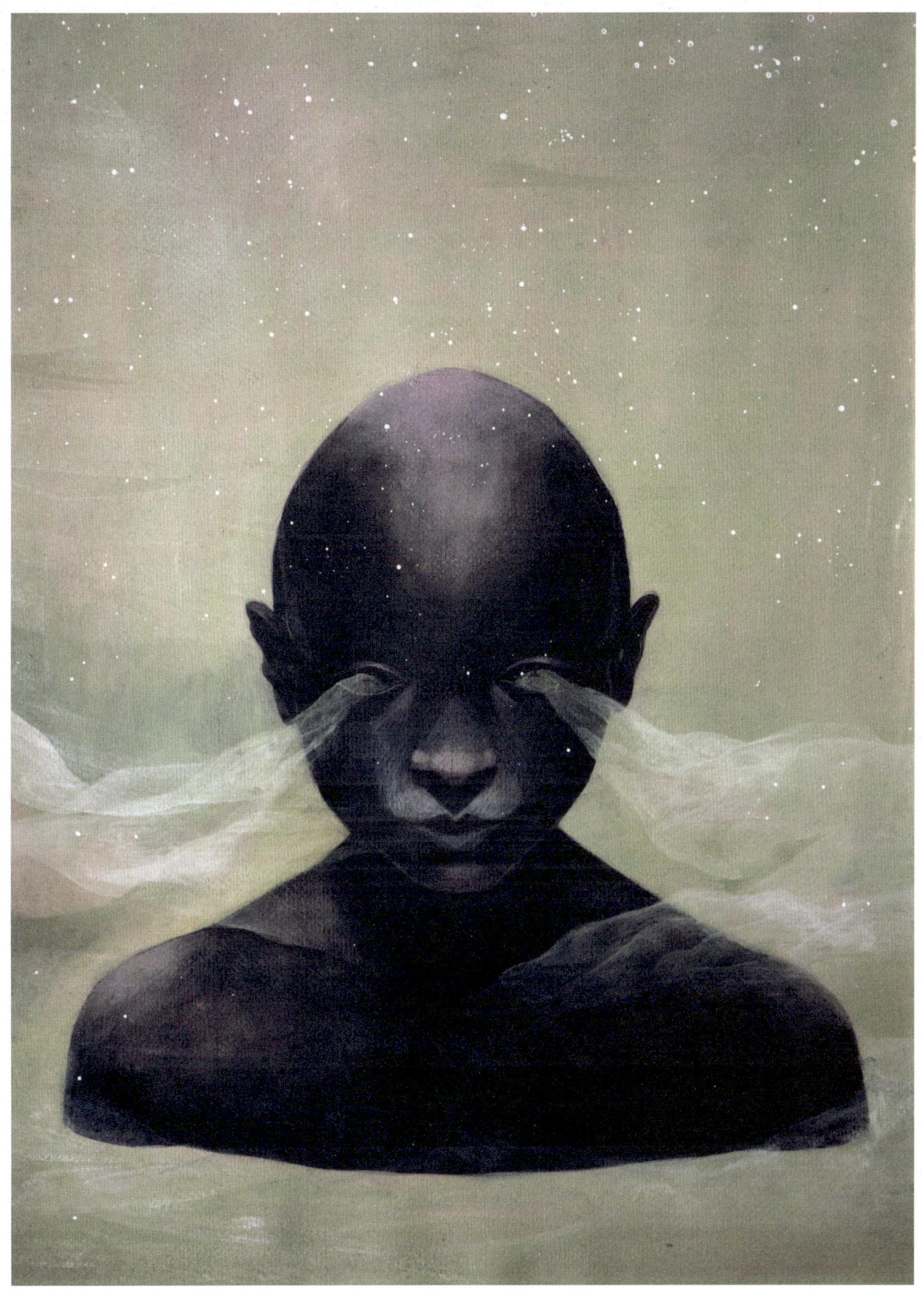

Sandmanss - Acrylic on Paper

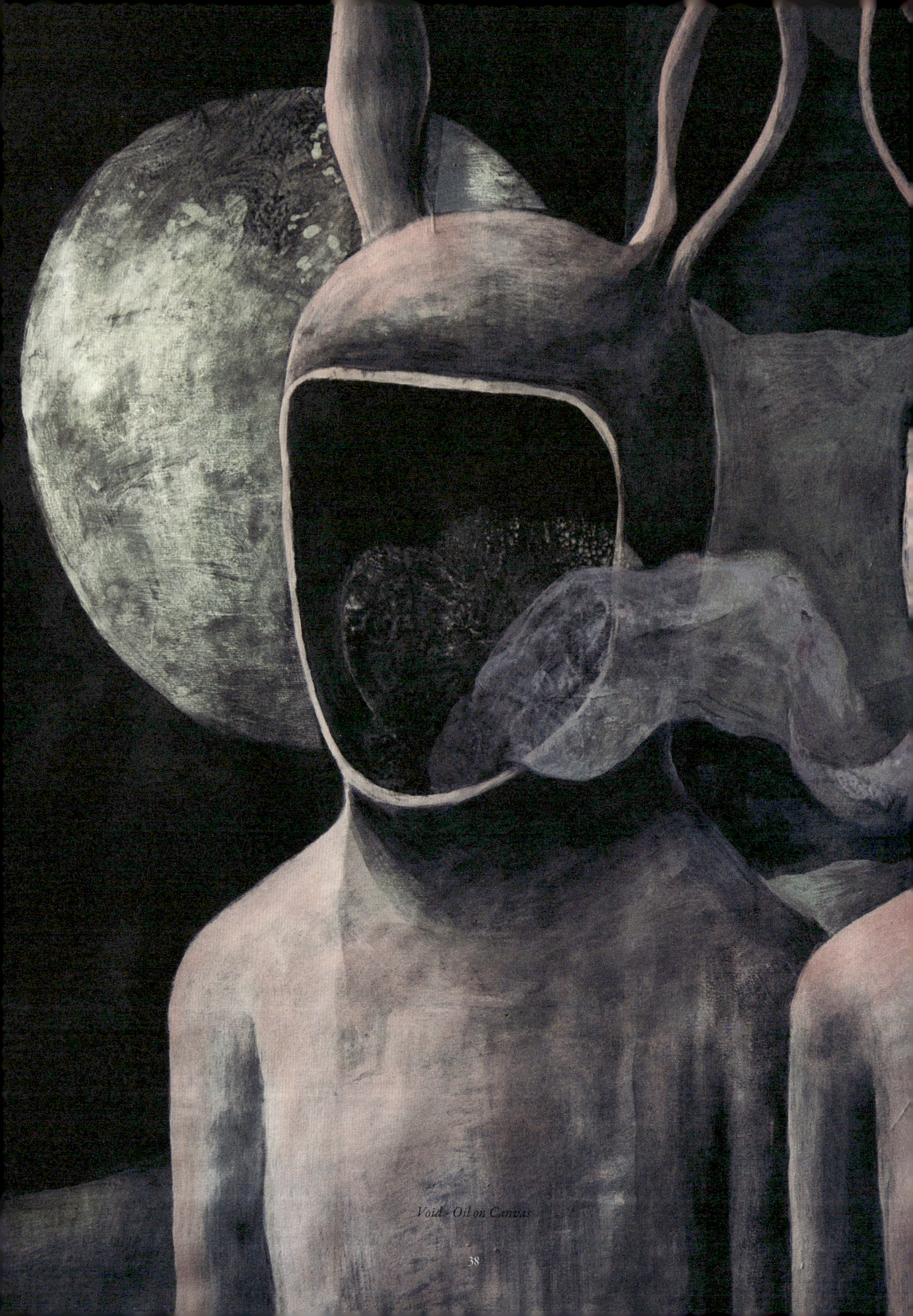

Void - Oil on Canvas

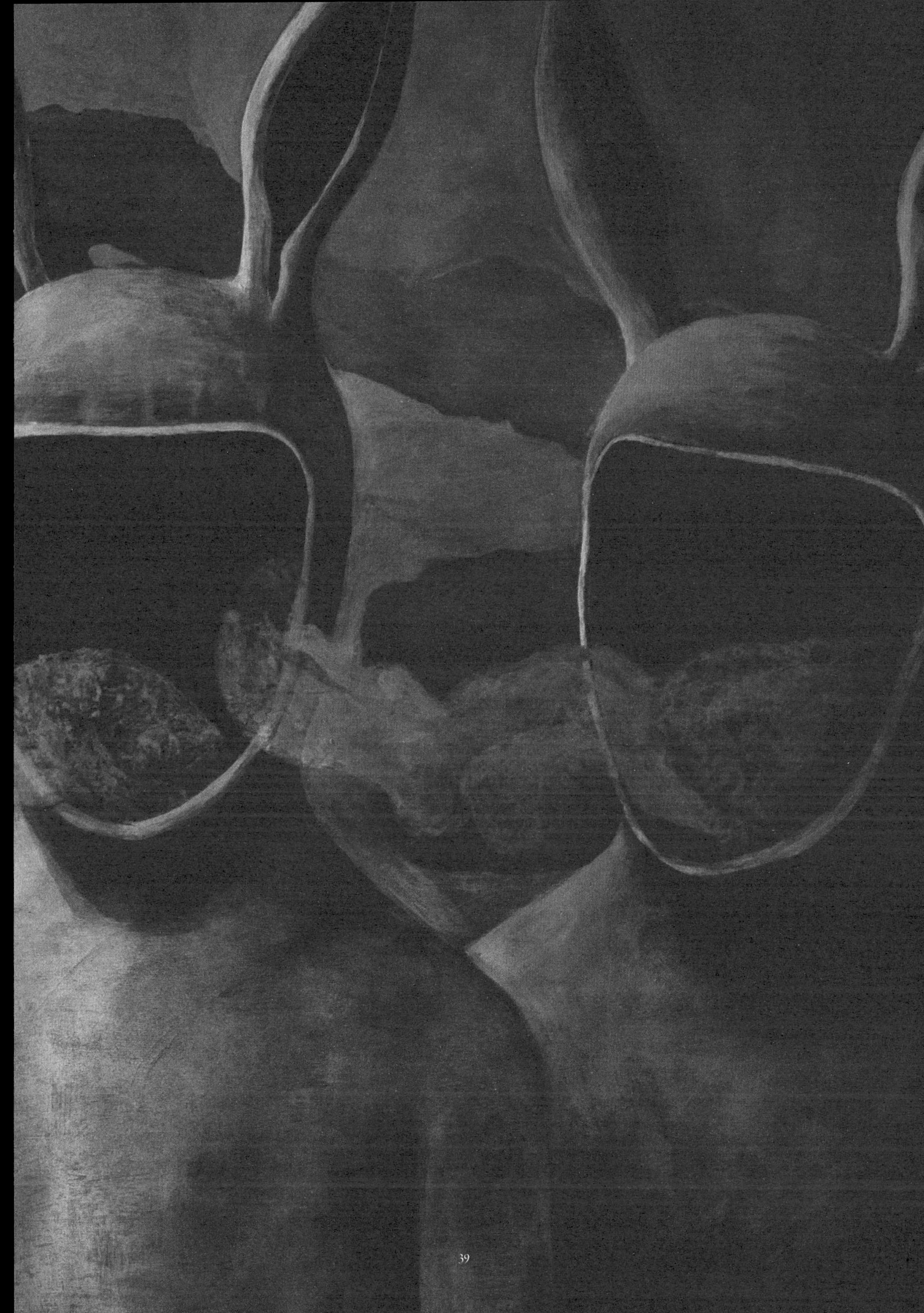

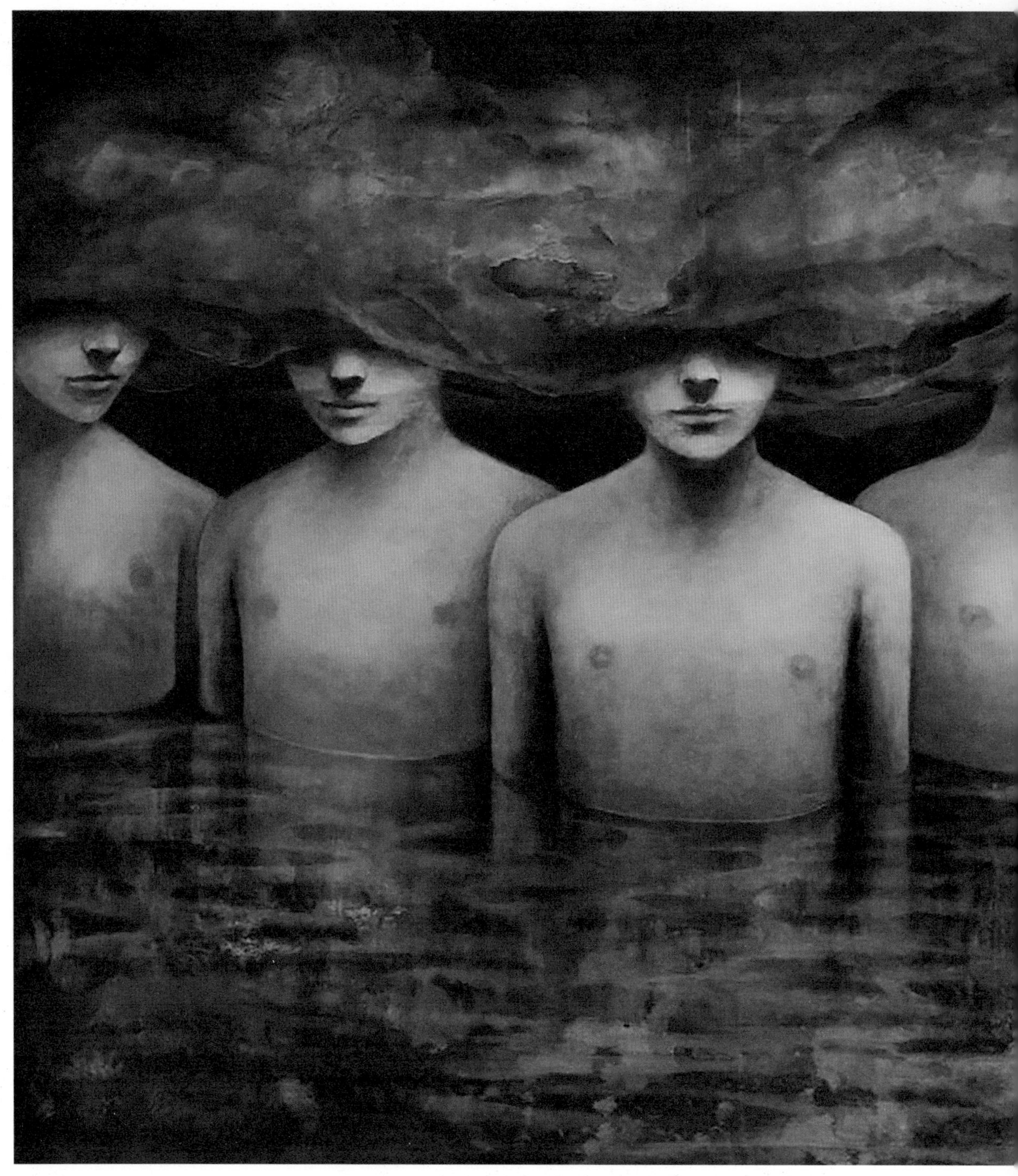

The Fog

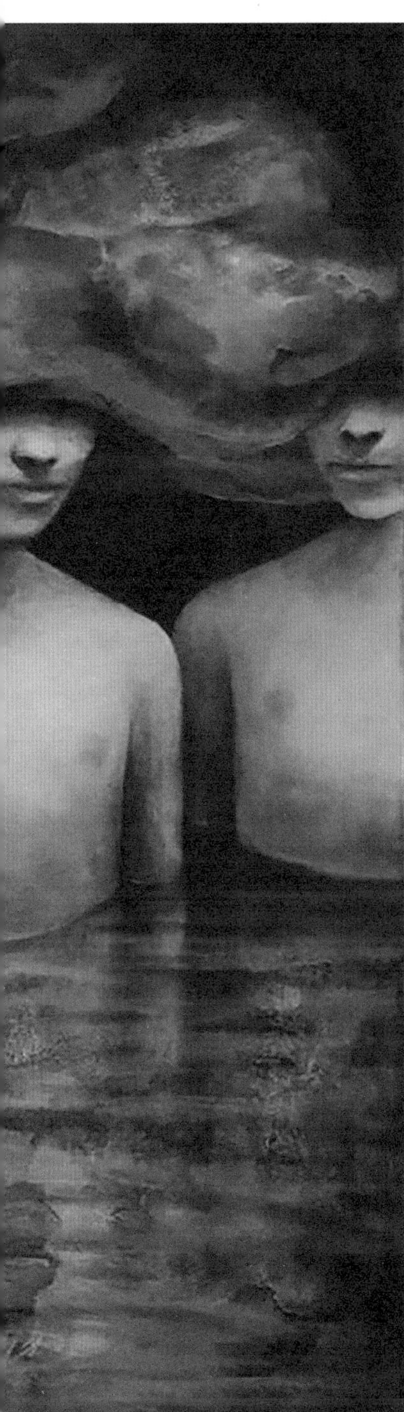

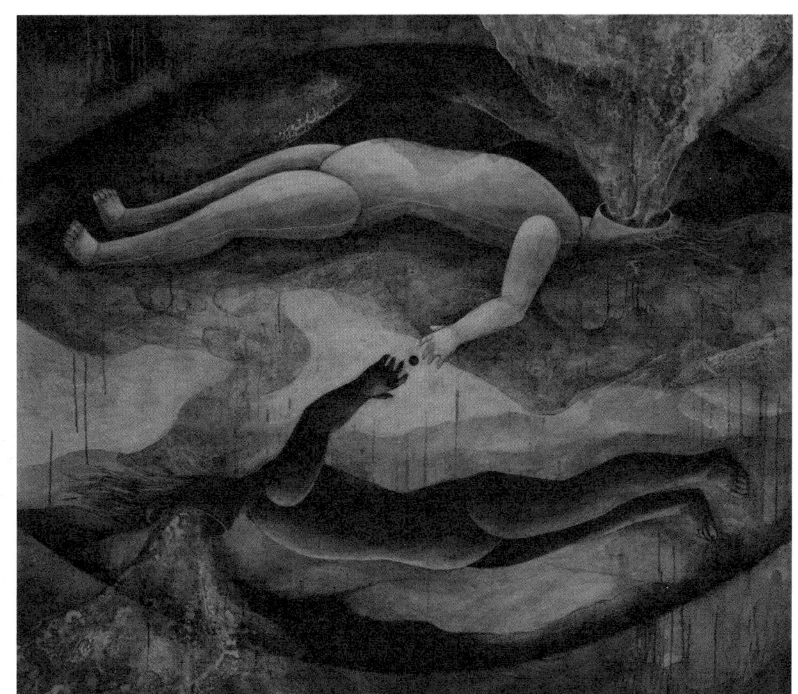

Shell - Oil on Canvas

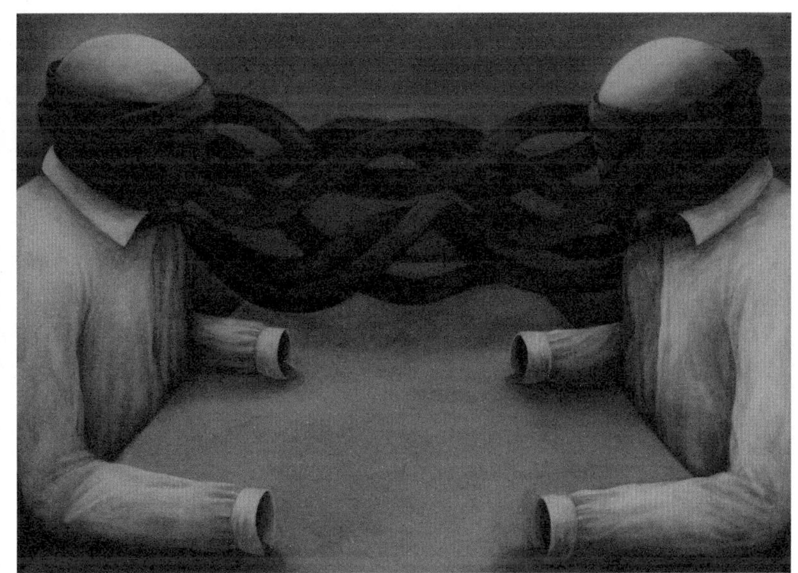

Overcome - Oil on Canvas

THE VISITOR

Artsist: Hu Rui, Xia Yun

These pictures are selected out of a short animation film "The Visitor", which is about a man's experience of fear, weird dream and surrealistic scenes.

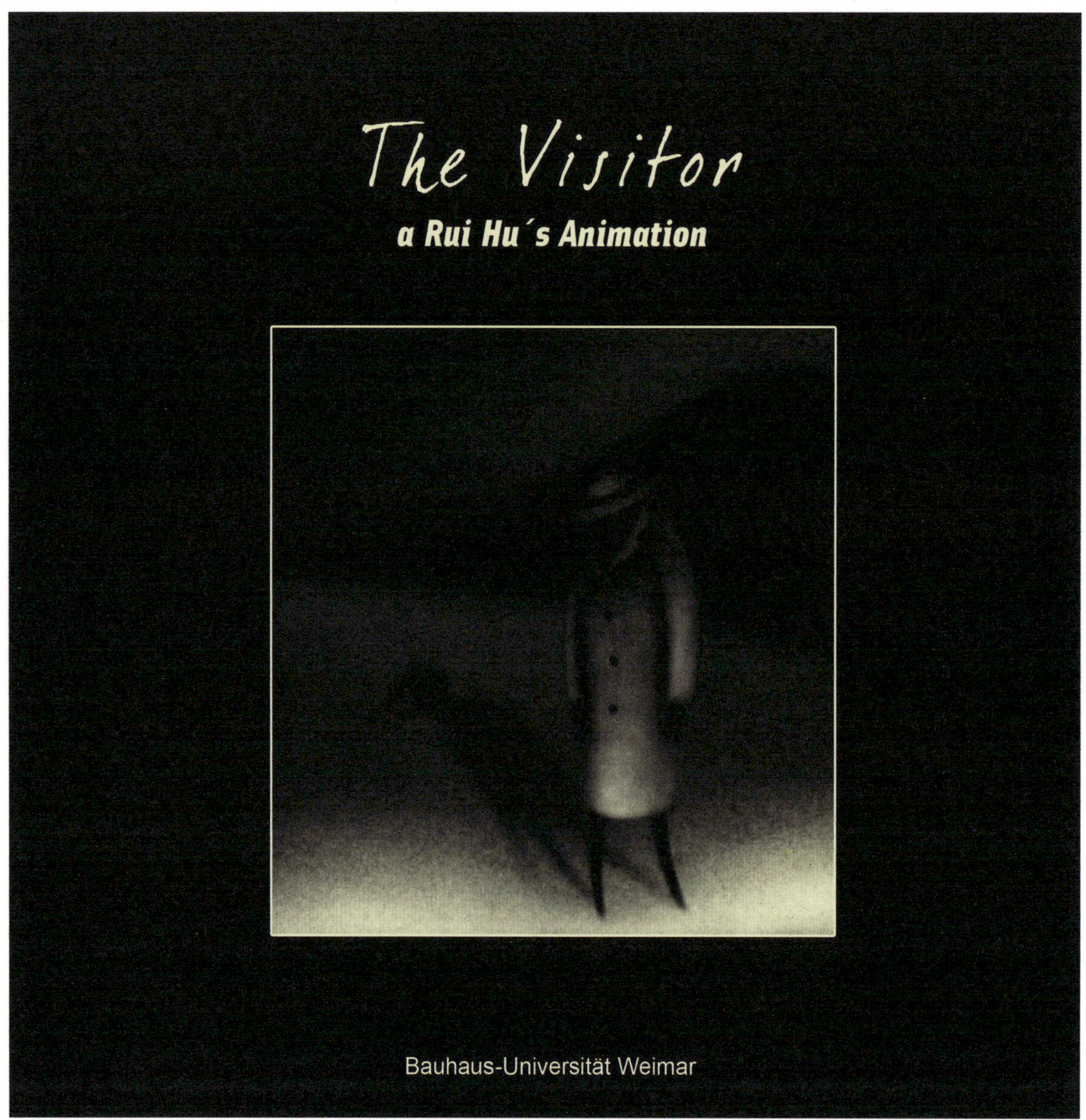

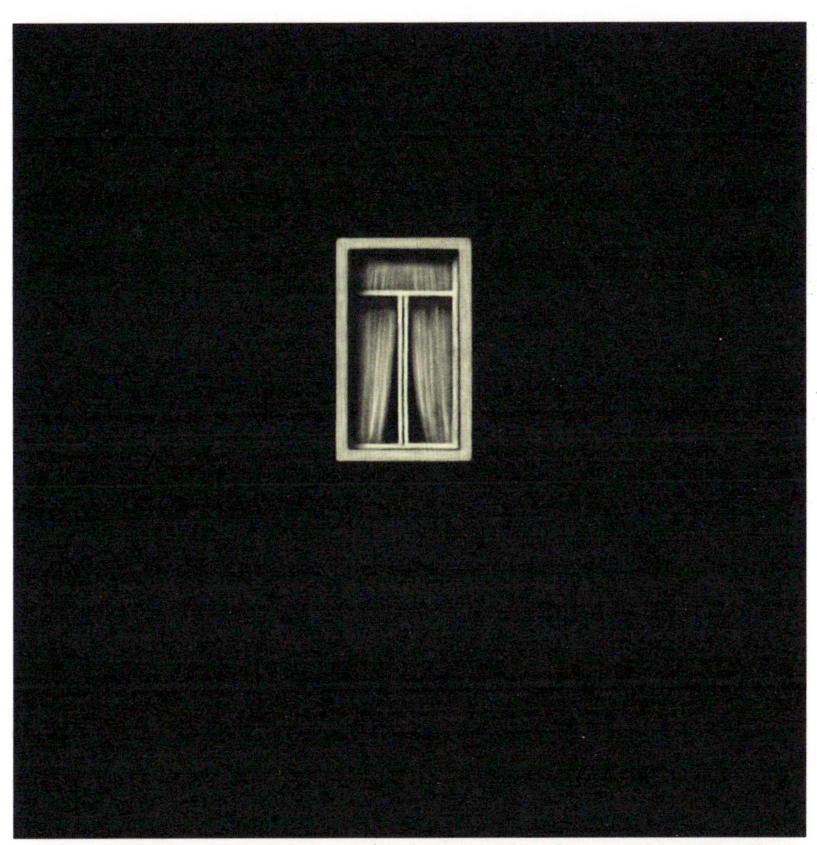

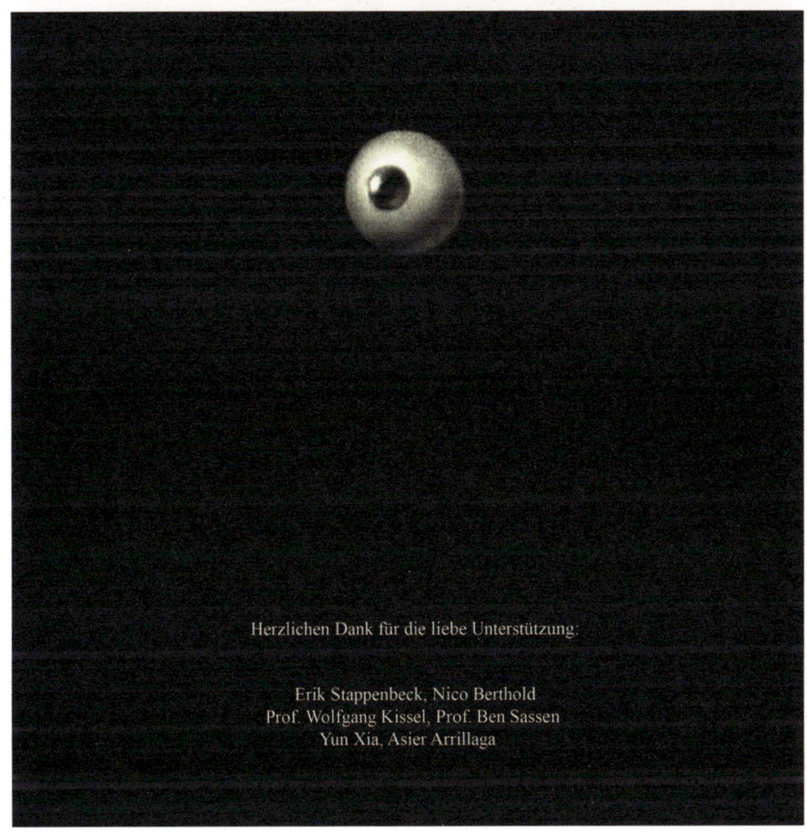
Herzlichen Dank für die liebe Unterstützung:
Erik Stappenbeck, Nico Berthold
Prof. Wolfgang Kissel, Prof. Ben Sassen
Yun Xia, Asier Arrillaga

1. Träume und Film

In der Geschichte geht es um einen Traum, der wahrscheinlich in der Realität wieder auftaucht und ein Alltagsbewusstein von Unheimlichkeit hervorbringt.
Wieso Träumen und Filme?

Film und Träume haben beide sehr viele mögliche materielle Ähnlichkeiten. In beiden Fällen wird eine primär visuelle Erfahrung, die Wahrnehmung von bewegten Bildern, der man in gewisser Weise passiv ausgeliefert war, in Sprache übersetzt und damit nachträglich strukturiert.

Ein Film ist offensichtlich eine gute Weise, Träume darzustellen oder wieder auszugeben.

Der Vergleich zwischen Träumen und Filmen beschränkt sich auf formale und strukturelle Aspekte und soll kein Versuch einer qualitativen Gleichstellung sein. Dieser scheitert schon daran, dass der Bewusstseinszustand des "Empfängers" in beiden Fällen grundverschieden ist. Der Filmzuschauer ist nicht der Träumende, sondern der wache Zeuge eines fremden (Traums) bzw. einer fremden Traums bzw. einer fremden "Aufzeichnung."

Das wichtigste Konzept des Film ist: die Imagination soll nicht so wild sein, es sollte classic sein, soll schon berechnend sein, dennoch extrem aber gleichzeitig cool bleiben.

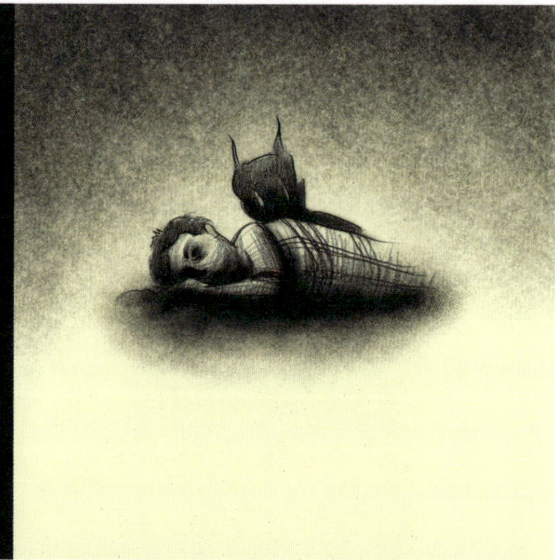

2. Über die Story

2.1 Alltagsbewusstsein aus den hinterlassenen Träume

Die Story entstand ursprünglich aus meinen eigenen Träumen und Erfahrungen. Es geht um die alltagsbewusste Unheimlichkeit, Verwandlung zwischen Traum und Realität, ein Status in der Dämmerungszone.

Es geht nicht darum, eine komplette Story mit durchgehenden Szenarios zu erzählen, sondern ein Gefühl oder einen Status zu interpretieren.

Mein Ziel ist nicht: Traum mit Sigmund Freud's Gustav Jung's Theorie oder Theorie, um die Träume zu analysieren. Obwohl die Gedanken von Gustav mehr überzeugend erscheinen als die von Freud.

Mich interessierte der Prozess, den Weg aus der Realität zu Träumen zu finden oder umgekehrt. Es erscheint für mich sehr entspannend, in die zwei Seiten - Träume und Realität - miteinander einzutauchen.

2.2 Ein Traum mit einem Vogel

Es war eine dunkle Nacht in meiner Heimatstadt. Ich und mein kleiner Cousin standen in der dunklen, engen Gasse. Unsere Schatten lagen ziemlich lang auf dem Boden durch die alte Laterne. Wir waren wahrscheinlich bei einem Spaziergang. Wenn ich meinen Schatten sah, habe ich einen großen Vogel auf der Gegenseite gesehen. Er lief langsam zu uns. Er war ganz schwarz, sah aus, als wäre er wie unterwegs, um jemanden zu besuchen; er war sehr elegant bekleidet, sein Kopf war etwas nach unten geduckt. Und wir versuchten Platz für ihn zu machen, damit er in der kleinen Gasse an uns vorbei gehen konnte. Wir sind einen Schritt nach rechts gegangen, allerdings hat er sich auch in die gleiche Richtung bewegt. Sind wir wieder nach links gegangen, so tat er es auch. Wir wagten uns in die Gasse und er lief ganz langsam zwischen uns vorbei. Seine Schritte waren sehr langsam und wohl bedacht.

Diese Begegnung mit dem Vogel hat mich sehr stark beeindruckt. Und dieser Moment, den wir mit ihm in der'Gasse standen, war für mich eine sehr geheimnisvolle Erfahrung, obwohl es ein Traum war.

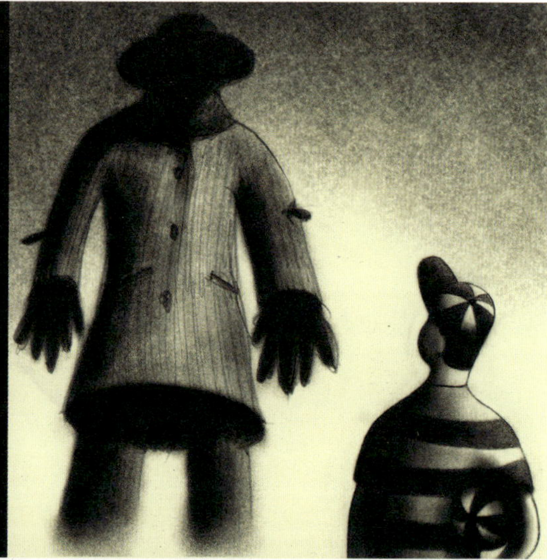

2.3 Die Begegnung mit einem Vogel

Vor einem Jahr habe ich bei einem Winterspaziergang an dem Ufer einen großen Vogel gesehen. Die Ausstrahlung dieses Vogels oder sozusagen die Identität oder Mentalität dieses Vogels war sehr ähnlich wie die des Herrn Vogel in meinem Traum. Was noch unheimlich war, dieser Vogel hielt ein Stückchen Flügel in seinem Schnabel. Der Flügel war von einem lebendigen Vogel oder einem toten, ich wusste es nicht, ob die Flügel zu ihm gehören.

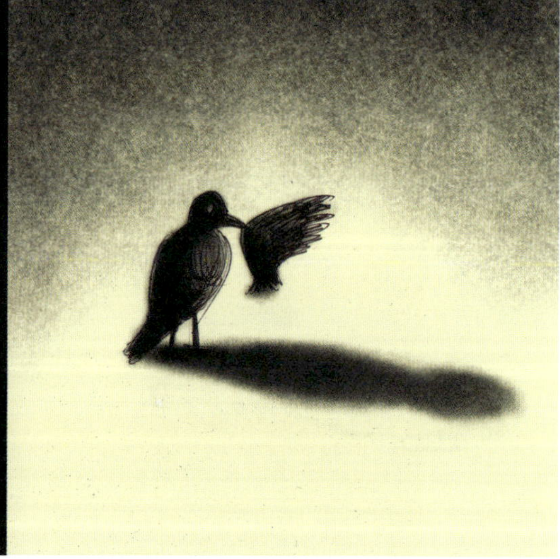

2.4 Eine andere Erzählung

Ich kann einige Situationen oder sozusagen Momente im Leben sehr gut erinnern. Bei einem Nachtessen hat mir ein Freund seine kurze Erfahrung aus der Kindheit erzählt.

Er wohnte in einem 8-geschossigen Hochhaus, die Wohnung seiner Eltern war ganz oben. Es war damals noch sehr dunkel in der kleinen Stadt. Es war spät in der Nacht, gegen 23 Uhr, kaum Menschen waren auf der Strasse zu sehen. Er legte sich auf das Bett und seine Mutter war in dem Badzimmer nebenan. Er versuchte die Augen zu schließen und einzuschlafen, aber es war doch ein aufregender Tag, er war noch nicht müde. Er hörte, dass das Wasser im Badezimmer lief, die Seife war nach unten gefallen und seine Mutter hob sie wieder auf. Er hielt die Augen noch immer geöffnet, da sah er etwas an dem Fenster, der Vorhang war noch nicht zugemacht. Da genau an diesem Fensterglas, da war etwas, sehr groß, es lehnte sich an das Fenster, es war ein Mann!! Er glaubte es nicht, da es das 8. Geschoss war, da laufen keine Menschen draußen vorbei. Aber es war wirklich ein Mann, wie auf das Fenster geklebt mit seinen Armen und Beinen. Sah er nur sein Gesicht nicht, der Mann war wie ein Schatten, ein schwarzes Papier auf das Glas geklebt, jedoch im Volumen.

Er hielt seinen Atmen an und wartete, bis der Mann etwas unternahm. Aber der Mann bewegte sich gar nicht. Er konnte gar nicht losschreien, obwohl er das wollte. Sein Hals war verstopft. Mein Freund wartete still auf den nächsten Schritt des Mannes.

Der Mann an dem Fenster hatte sich nach vorne bewegt, er versuchte wahrscheinlich durch das Fenster in das Zimmer zu gelangen. Mein Freund hatte seinen Mund sehr weit geöffnet, sein Speichel lief bereits heraus. Der Mann hatte langsam angehalten, sich zu bewegen und er drehte seinen Kopf zur Seite. Mein Freund dachte, dass er endlich seine Nase sehen könnte. Aber der Mann hatte keine Nase, er hatte nur einen riesig großen Mund, einen scharfen Mund wie ein Vogel. Sein Schatten strahlte auf den Vorhang.

Ein Vogels Mund, ein langer, riesiger Mund.

In dem Moment, als seine Mutter aus der Dusche kam, verschwand der Vogel-Mann von dem Fenster, sofort und ohne jede Spur.

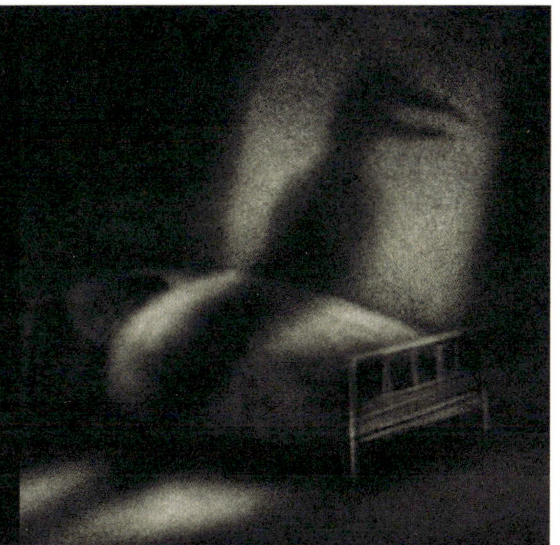

2.5 Einige Szene aus dem Leben

Manchmal machen wir viele unangenehme Erfahrungen und zwar sehr häufig.
Wie ein ständig tropfender Wasserhahn tröpfelt das Wasser besonders laut in der ruhigen Nacht. Und eine Stromunterbrochene Glühlampe, die immer wankt.

Solche Erfahrungen gehören zu dem Alltagsbewusstsein. Unheimlichkeit, wenn man es vergrößert. Es kann total anders aussehen oder unheimliche Bilder entstehen lassen.

Aus solchen Erfahrungen heraus hat mich das Image des Vogels sehr überzeugt, dass ich wahrscheinlich etwas daraus erkennen oder lernen kann. Und zwar mehr über das Mysterium Tier und Menschen, über ein surrealistisches Gefühl und Realität. Die Begrenzung zwischen Tier und Menschen, zwischen Traum und Realität, die Klarheit und das Überschreiten von Grenzen.

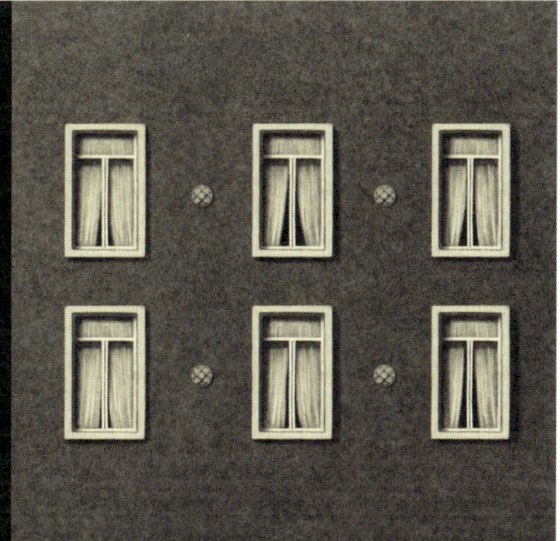

2.6 Über den Anfang - Eine Bild Reise

Eine Reise durch ein Bild habe ich in meiner Kindheit gelesen, die traditionelle chinesische Ghost Story. Eine Geschichte von einer Bildreise, ein Mann hat in 2 Minuten über 30 Jahre Zeit in seinem Kopf mit einer Nymphe im Bild verbracht. Als er aufwachte, fühlte er sich mit der Nymphe im Fresco sehr vertraut und die Figur der Nymphe im Fresco hat sich auch in der entsprechenden Weise geändert.

Für mich sind die vorherigen Werken, wie von David Lynch und Rene Magritte, sehr gute Beispiele für Alltagsbewusste Unheimlichkeiten.

Das Werk "Die Fixierte Idee" von Rene Magritte in der Neue Nationale Galerie hat mich an ein wunderschönes Erlebnis durch das Bild erinnert. Die vier Fenster mit unterschiedlich kleinen Gardinen. Ein wie ein Jäger bekleideter Mann mit einer Schrotflinte. Ein tiefer Wald und ein Stück blauer Himmel mit Wolke. Das Bild kann natürlich auch eine Geschichte aufbauen, je nach Gedanken und Erfahrung der verschiedenen Betrachter.

Aber das Bild hat mich irritiert, da es eine emotionale Intensität in mir bewirkte, die viel fantastischer als die Geschichte war und begründete somit ein Gefühl, eine Stimmung, eine Emotion für besonders Momente oder eine vergrößerte Reaktion von etwas.

Als Betrachter wirkt das Bild ein bisschen spannungsvoll, sogar unheimlich. Streng genommen ist aber zunächst nicht das Bild unheimlich, sondern- wenn überhaupt- die Szene, die es darstellt:
Unheimlich würde ich es empfinden, wenn es mir im Alltag widerfahren würde, was dem Mann in der dargestellten Szene widerfährt.Im Film symbolisierte das Fenster als ein Teil des Alltagslebens und ein Ausgangspunkt dass man die Unheimlichkeit erlebt.

Sowie meine Alltagserfahrungen und die Träume tauchen beide regelmäßig auf. Was spannungsvoll erscheint, sind diese auftauchenden Grenzen.

Diese Unterscheidung betont auch Sigmund Freud, wenn er in seinem Aufsatz über "das Unheimliche" zwar nicht für die bildende Kunst, aber doch auch auf sie anwendbar. Er schreibt "dass in der Dichtung vieles nicht unheimlich ist, was unheimlich wäre, wenn es sich im Leben ereignete." damit verweist er auf eine Distanzierung, die durch fiktionale Darstellungen möglich wird.

Was der Betrachter in seinem Alltag als unheimlich erleben würde, verliert für ihn als Betrachter eines Bildes, das eine unheimliche Szene

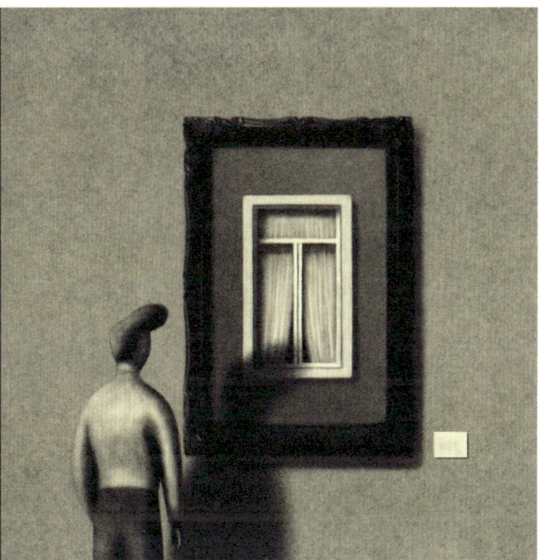

darstellt, an emotionaler Intensität. Vielleicht sogar soweit, dass gar keine unheimliche Wirkung mehr zustande kommt. Zu den Vorteilen einer solchen Distanzierung gehört, dass sich der Betrachter mit der dargestellten Szene probehandelnd auseinander setzen kann. Weiß er, dass er ein Bild sieht, dann behält er die Kontrolle über die Situation. Sie befähigt ihn erst zu überlegen, was er wohl erleben würde, wenn die im Bild dargestellte Szene kein Bild, sondern Alltagsrealität wäre.

Und mehr dazu habe ich ein anderes Motiv des Fensters als eine Übergangsbegrenzung der Realität und der Träume gewählt. Das Fenster wird als ein zu betrachtender Zugang zu diesen.

3. Die Darstellung meiner Animation

3.1 Das Bild und die Atmosphäre:

Aus den Zeichnungen habe ich mich bereits bemüht, bei dem Versuch meine eigenen identifizierten Zeichenstile auszugeben, was folgende Bilder gezeigt haben.

Die Neo-Impressismus Malerei sowie die Skizzen von Georges Seurat haben mich sehr stark beeinflusst. Die Stimmung des ganzen Films soll ähnlich wie der Film Noir, oder der von 1920- 1930 Expressionismus-Film Nosferatu * sein.

Aus beiden Werkstoffen: Das Licht spielt eine große Rolle in den Bildern.

Die übrigen Räume stehen in der Dunkelheit oder Halbdunkelheit, darin liegt die ursprüngliche Spannung.

Meine Träume haben meistens keine Farbe. Viele Dinge, die wir vergessen haben, stehen ewig in der Dunkelheit. Was wir schon gesehen haben oder gut erinnern können, ist nicht besonders, sondern bleibt im Dunkeln oder an der Begrenzung.

* Nosferatu: Nosferatu- Eine Symphonie des Grauens, ein deutscher Spielfilm aus dem Jahr 1922 von Friedrich Wilhelm Murnau.

3.2 Der Charakter

Es ist schwierig zu entscheiden, welche Rolle die Hauptrolle in diesem kurzen Film ist. Der Mann oder der Vogel oder beide oder sogar der Mann, der der Vogel ist.

3.2.1 Der Vogel:

Als kultureller Aspekt gelten Vögel seit alters her wegen ihres Fluges als dem Himmel verwandt, als Mittler zwischen Himmel und Erde. Als Verkörperung des Immateriellen, namentlich der Seele. Im Taoismus z.B. stellte man sich die Unsterblichkeit in Gestalt von Vögeln vor. Verarbeitet war die Auffassung, die Seele verlasse nach dem Tod den physischen Körper als Vogel. Sehr viele Religionen kennen himmlische Wesen mit Flügeln oder in Vogelgestalt, z.B. Engel oder Eroten.

Die psychoanalytische Traumdeutung sieht im Vogel oft ein Symbol für diePerson selbst des Träumenden. Obwohl nach Freuds Analyse ein Vogel eine unfertige Wunscherfüllung bedeutet.

Einer der fantastischen Vögel ist der Rabe. Über den Raben wird schon viel in der Literatur berichtet, so z.B. bei Edgar Allan Poe und den Brüdern Grimm. Da Rabenvögel Geräusche imitieren, können manche sogar menschliche Laute wiedergeben.
Die Figur des Vogels ist natürlich aus meinen eigenen Träumen und Erlebnissen gestaltet.

Außerdem ist meine Vorstellung die folgende: Der Vogel ist in Schwarz; er kann nicht fliegen; er hat einen Menschliche Natur; er ist elegant bekleidet; er sieht ein bisschen wie der Teufel aus; er bewegt sich wie ein Mensch und langsam; er spricht aber nicht und hat einen großen Mund. Er bleibt immer cool und still.

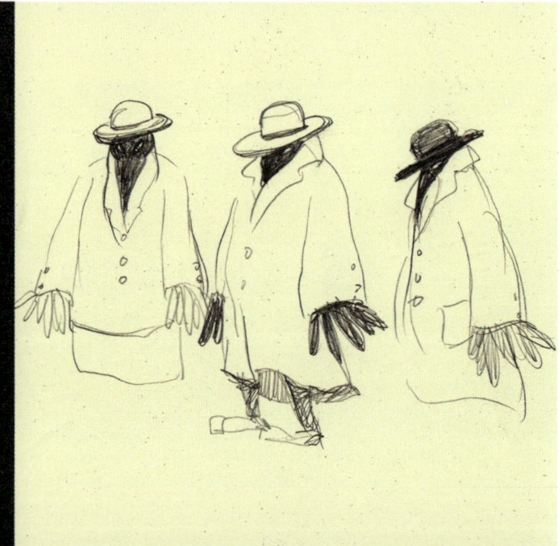

4. Extra Notizen

Als das Konzept ausgedacht wurde, bestand die Idee, dass der Film mit der Stimmung einer nicht wilden Imagination, einer klassischen Imagination, einer gerechten Imagination, einem zurückhaltenden Extrem entsprechen soll.

Deshalb sind die Schnitte und die Musik aus dem gleichen Ausgangspunkt gestaltet. Die Musik ist mit der Erlaubnis der deutschen Band 'Bohren & the Club of Gore' benutzt worden. Die Musik hat einen sehr ähnlichen musikalischen Raum wie der Film gebaut.

Dennoch habe ich ursprünglich daran gedacht, Orchestermusik als Filmmusik zu nutzen. Aber aufgrund des limitierten Budgets haben wir Probleme gehabt, Orchestermusik auszuwählen. Aber das Stück von 'Bohren & the Club of Gore's Musik hat wirklich meine Vorstellung der musikalischen Ebene weiter ausgebaut und mehr Fantasie erzeugt.

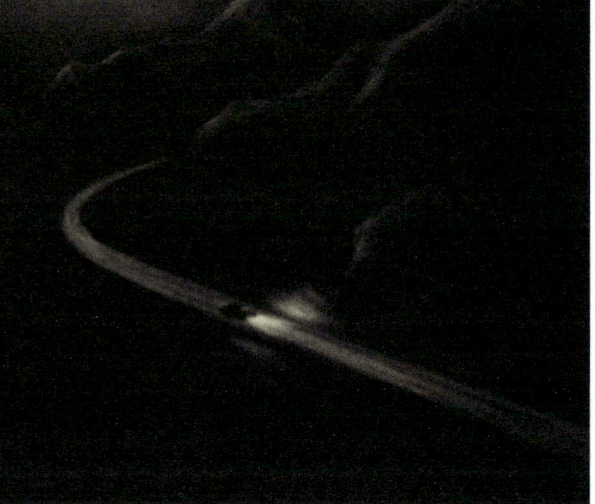

* Eraserhead : das Spielfim- Debüt des US- amerikanischen Regisseur David Lynch aus dem Jahr 1977

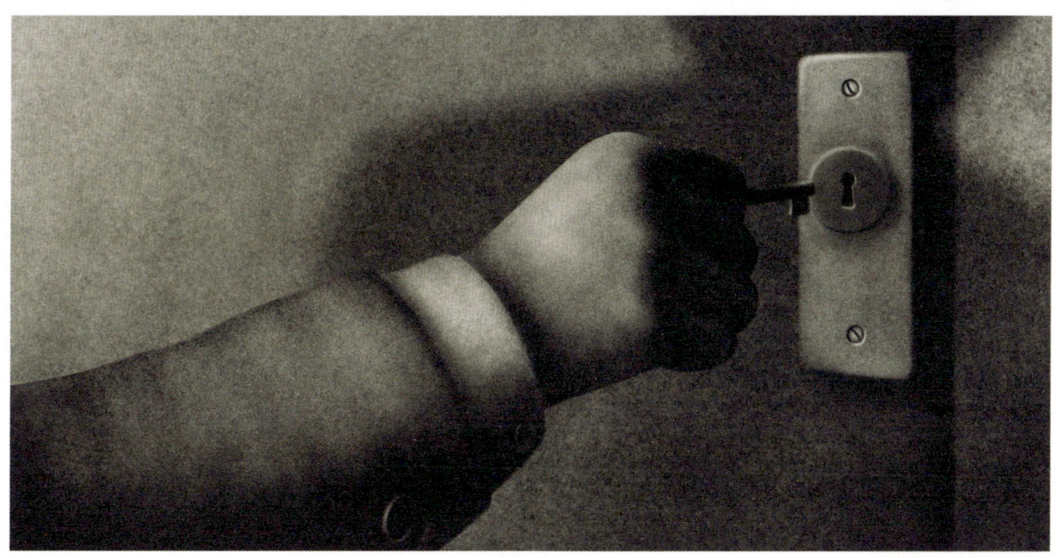

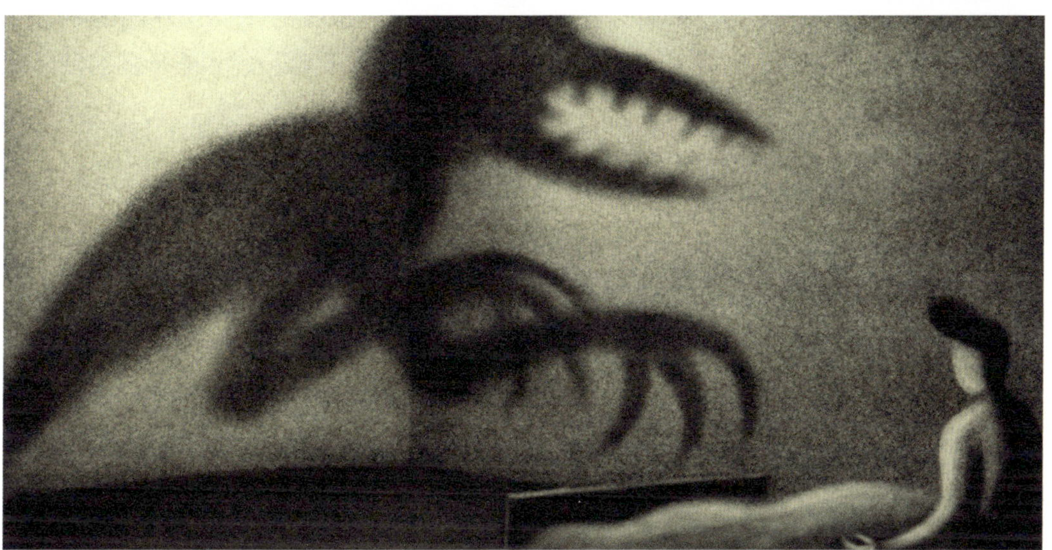

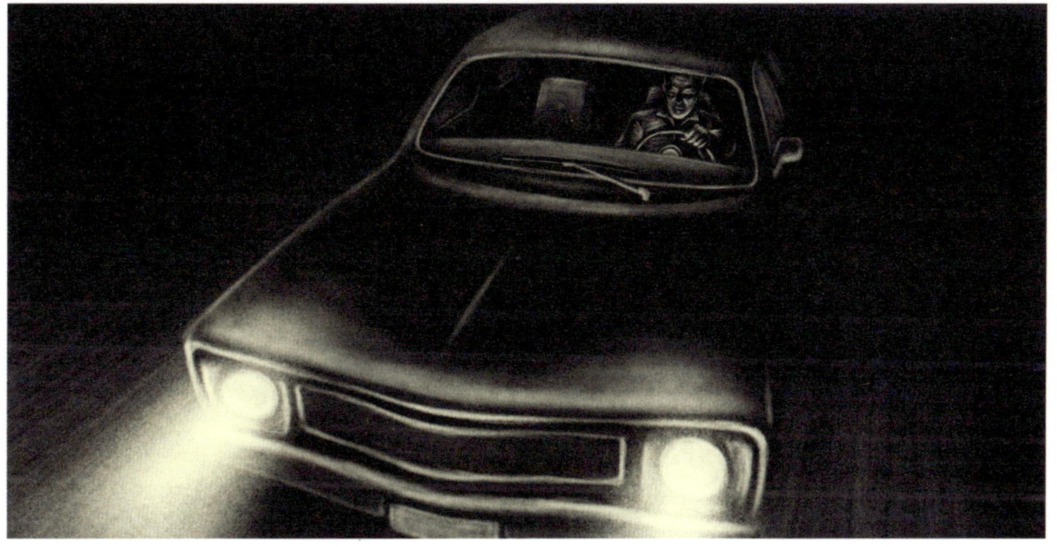

VOGUE ARTS FOR GUCCI CRUISE 2017

Artist: Virginia Mori   Creative director : Veronica Mazziotta

Inspired by Virginia Mori, this special project for Vogue Arts Gucci Cruise 2017 features real reproductions of some of Virginia Mori's surreal drawings.

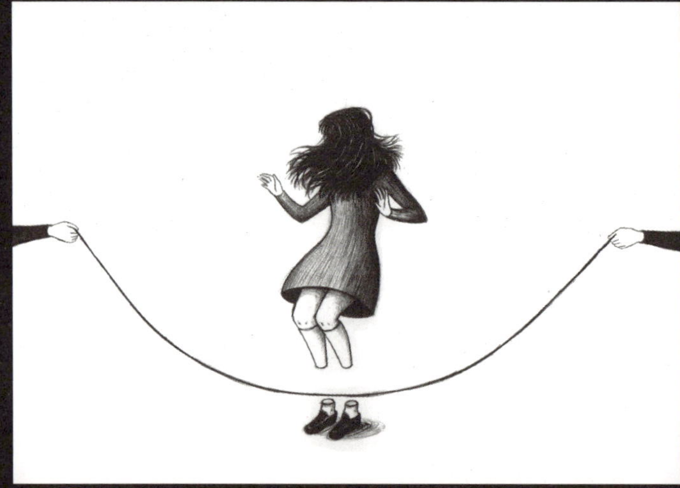

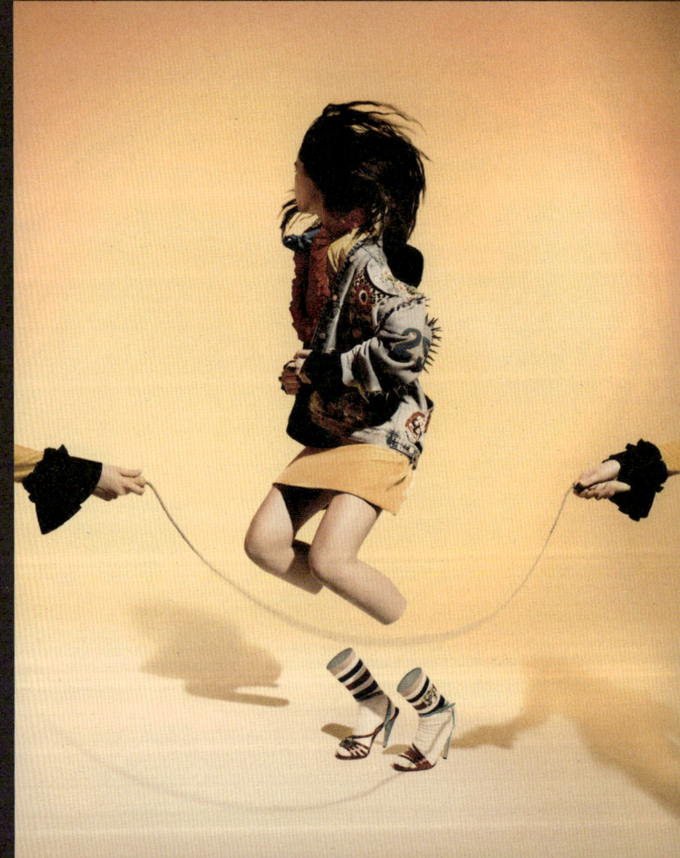

Photographer:
Filippo Fortis (@ MSK)

Model:
Yulduz (@ Monster)

3D Post production:
Darkslide

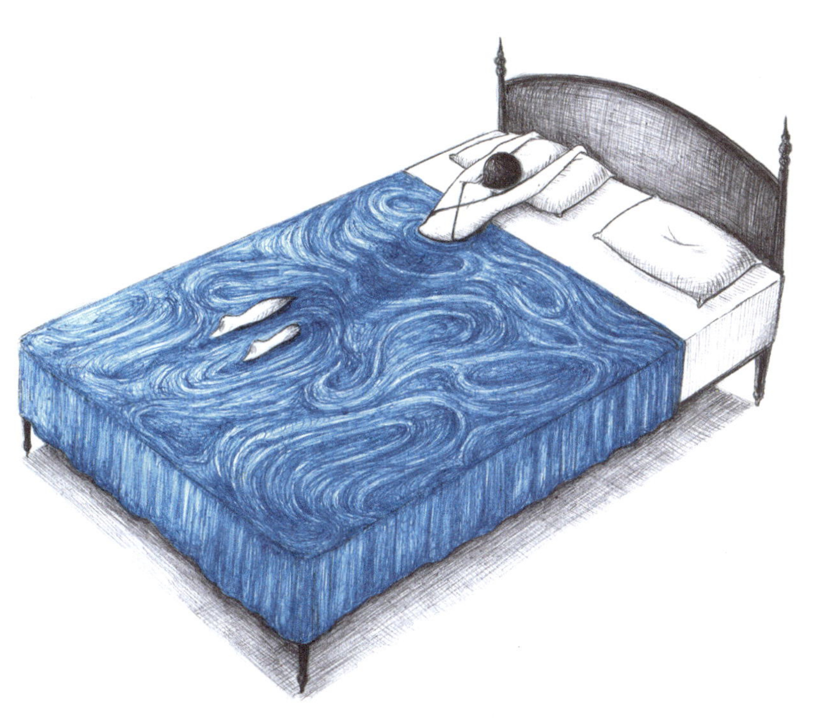

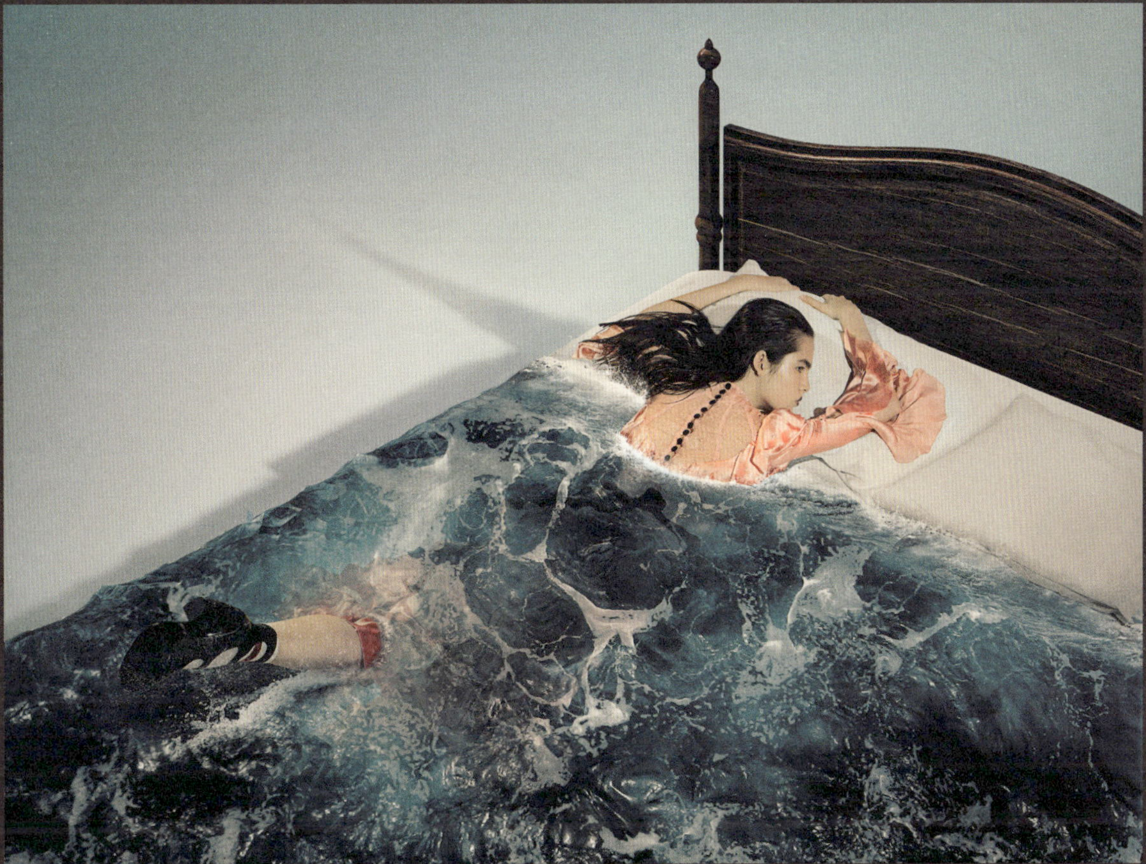

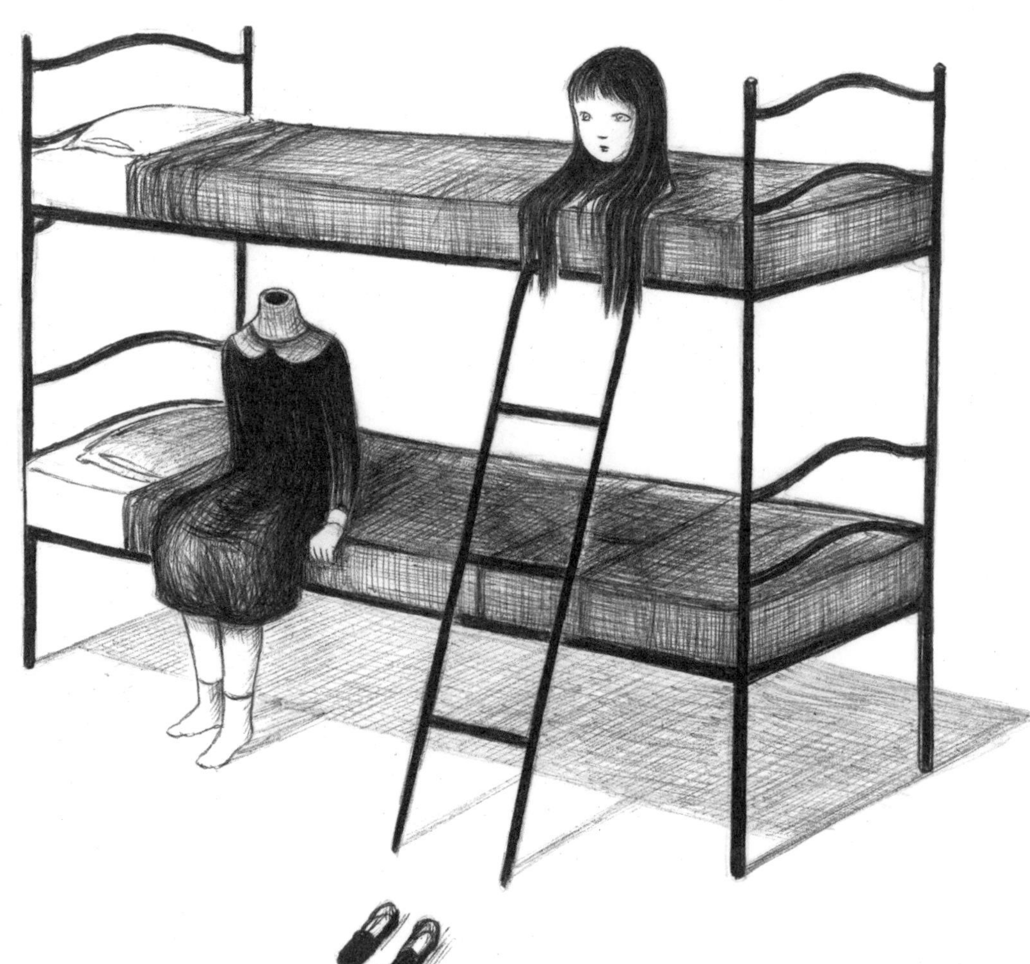

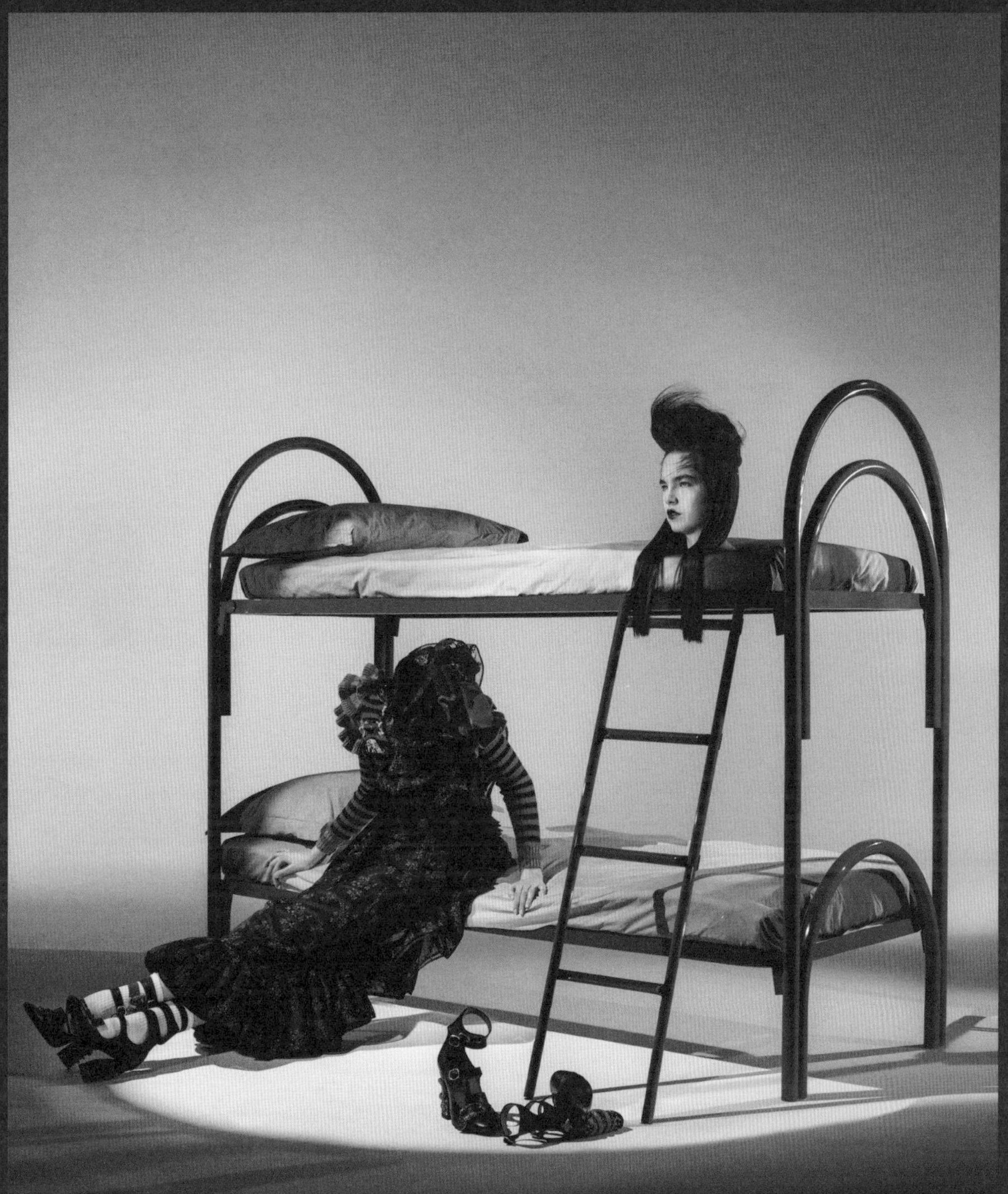

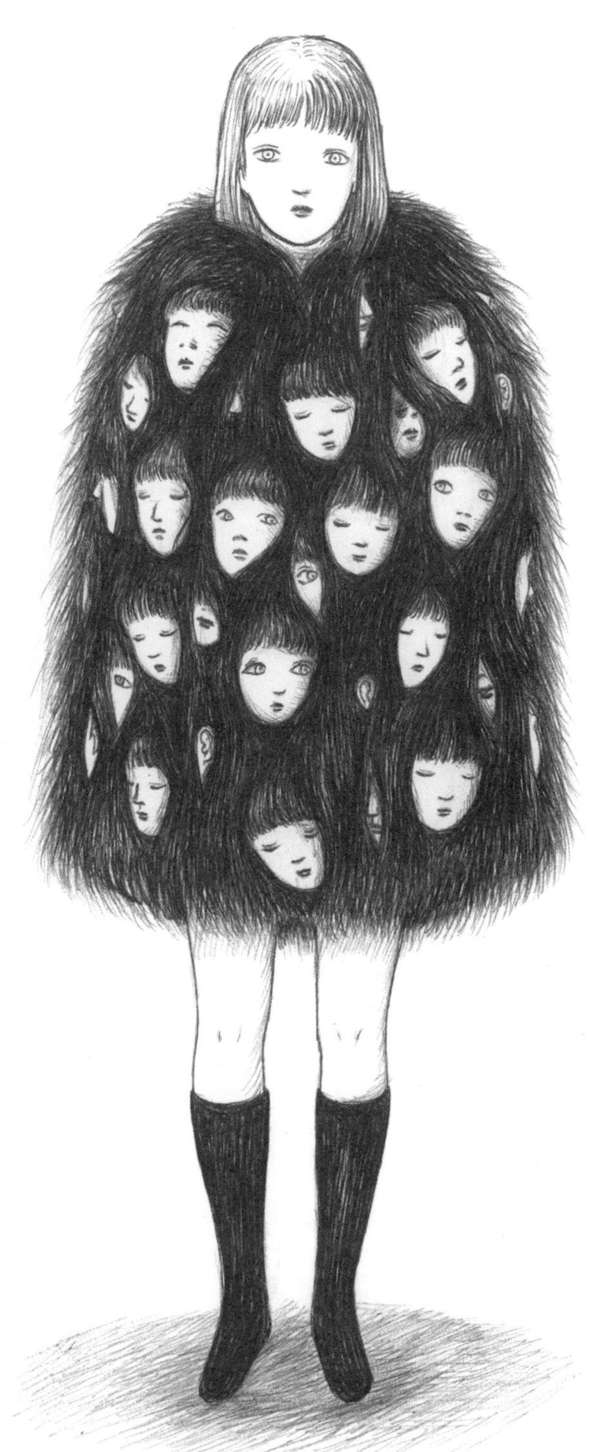

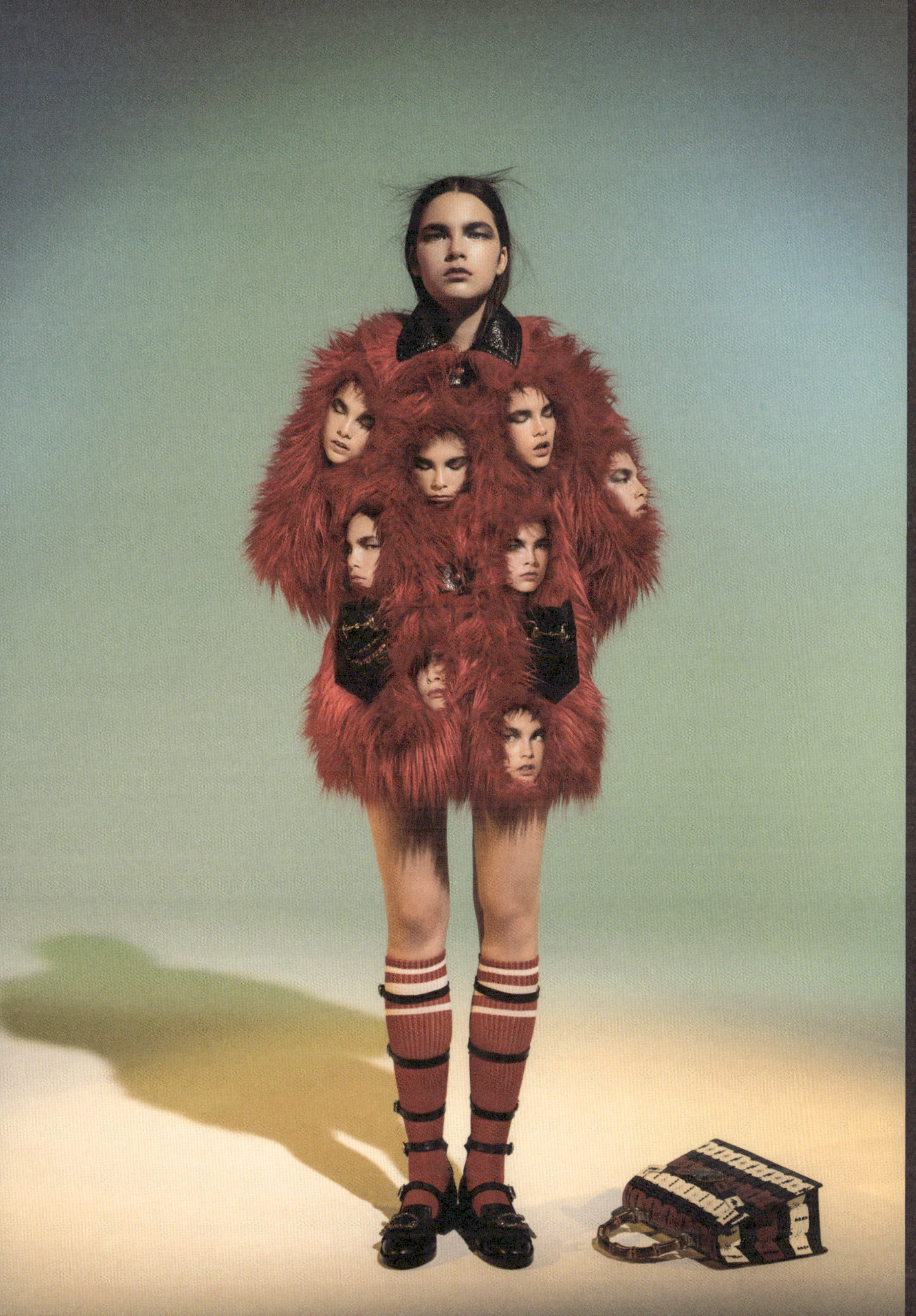

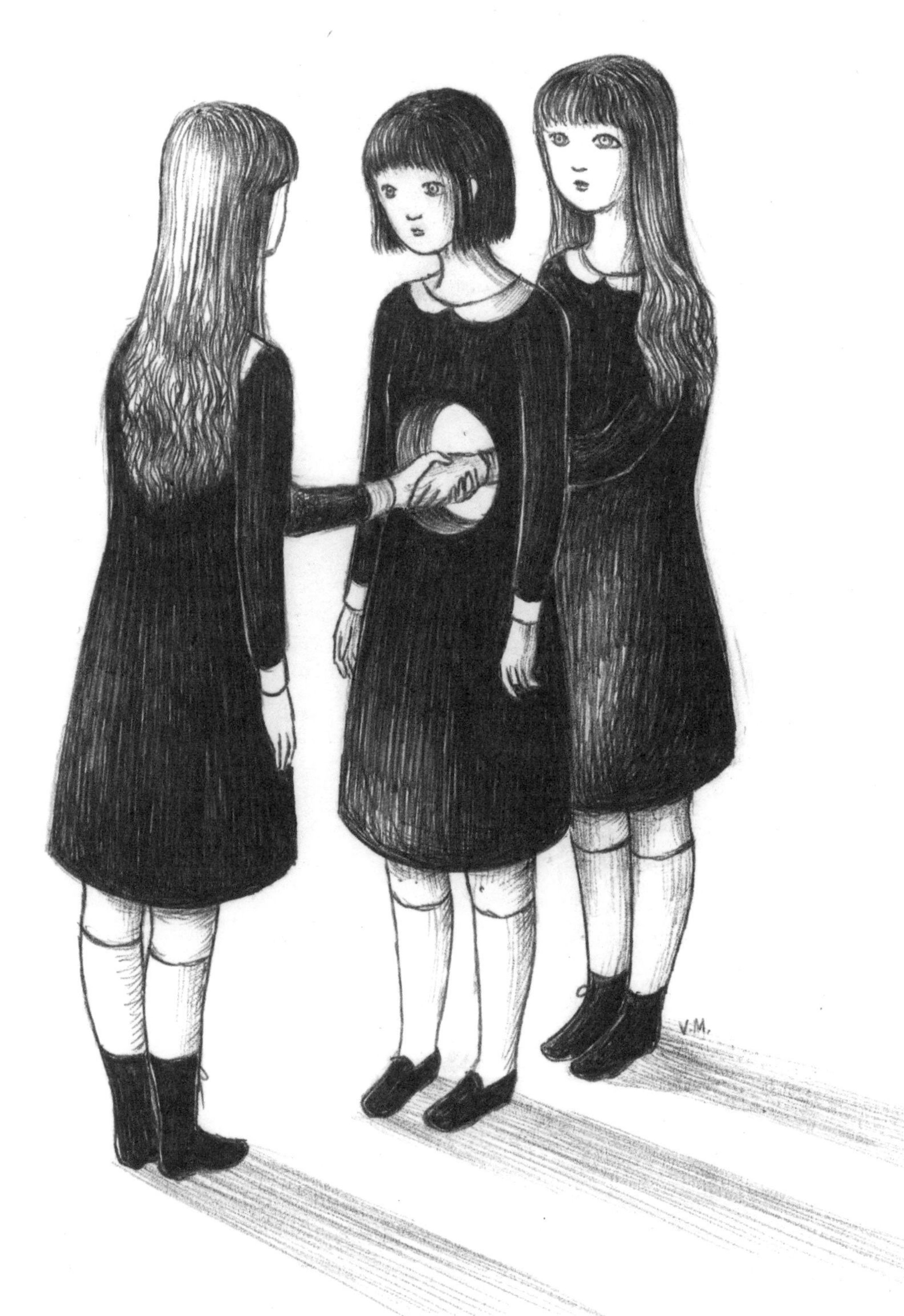
V.M.

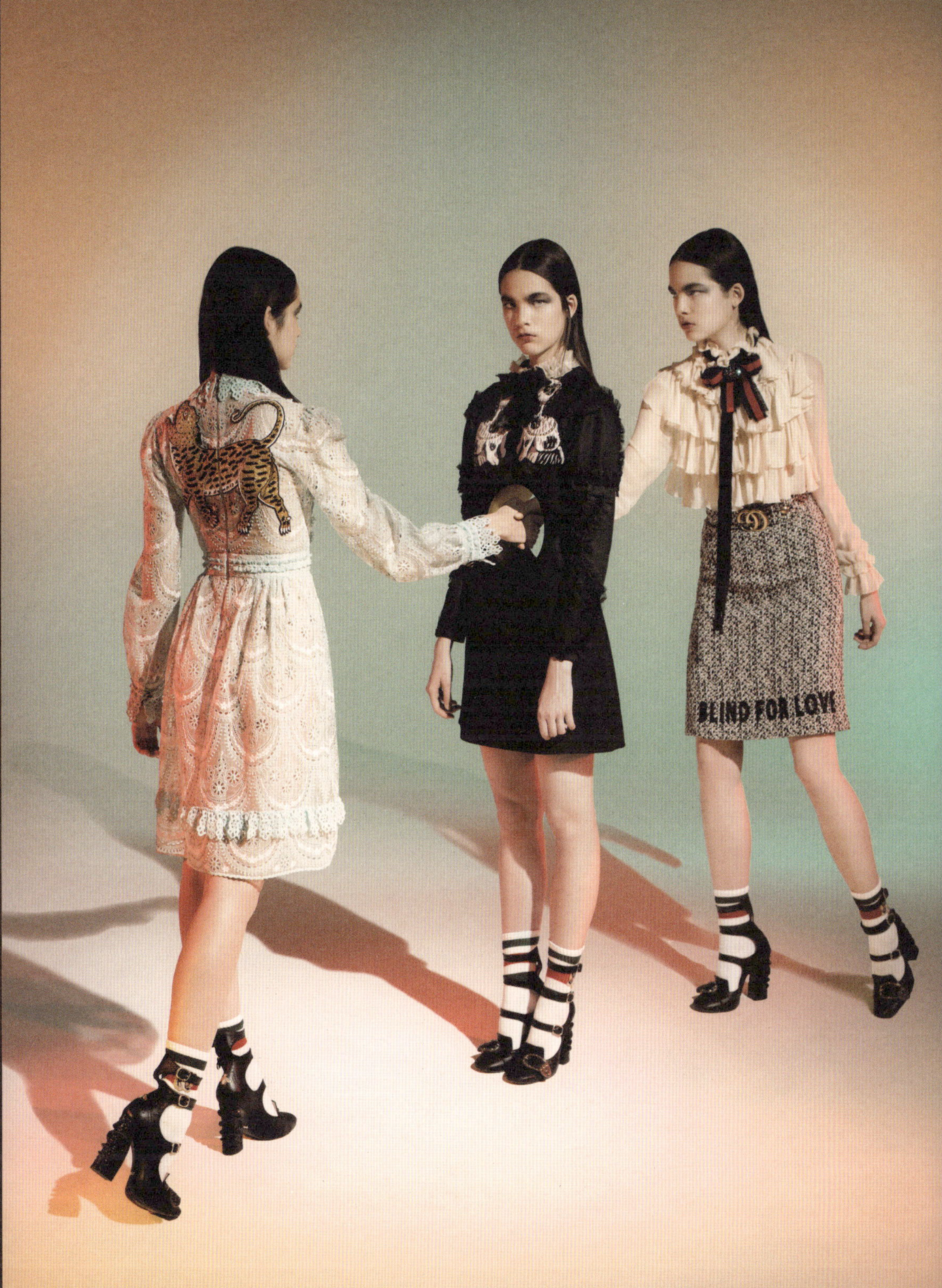
BLIND FOR LOVE

STICKMAN - THE VICISSITUDES OF CROHN'S

Artist: Spooky Pooka

The Stickman project was originally conceived as an attempt to reconcile the psychological and emotional, as well as physical impact of Crohn's disease. Based on personal experience, the artist considered these three to be linked by the common theme of metamorphosis or transformation—into the "other" that people become through disease. The dialectic between our well and unwell selves was mediated by pain, nausea and morbidity.

This personal journey through the inner landscape of Crohn's explored the multiple themes and emotional responses to the disease. From physical pain to the more abstract personification of disease, the Stickman project tried to encompass these myriad interrelated ideas in the form of a non-linear illustrated narrative.

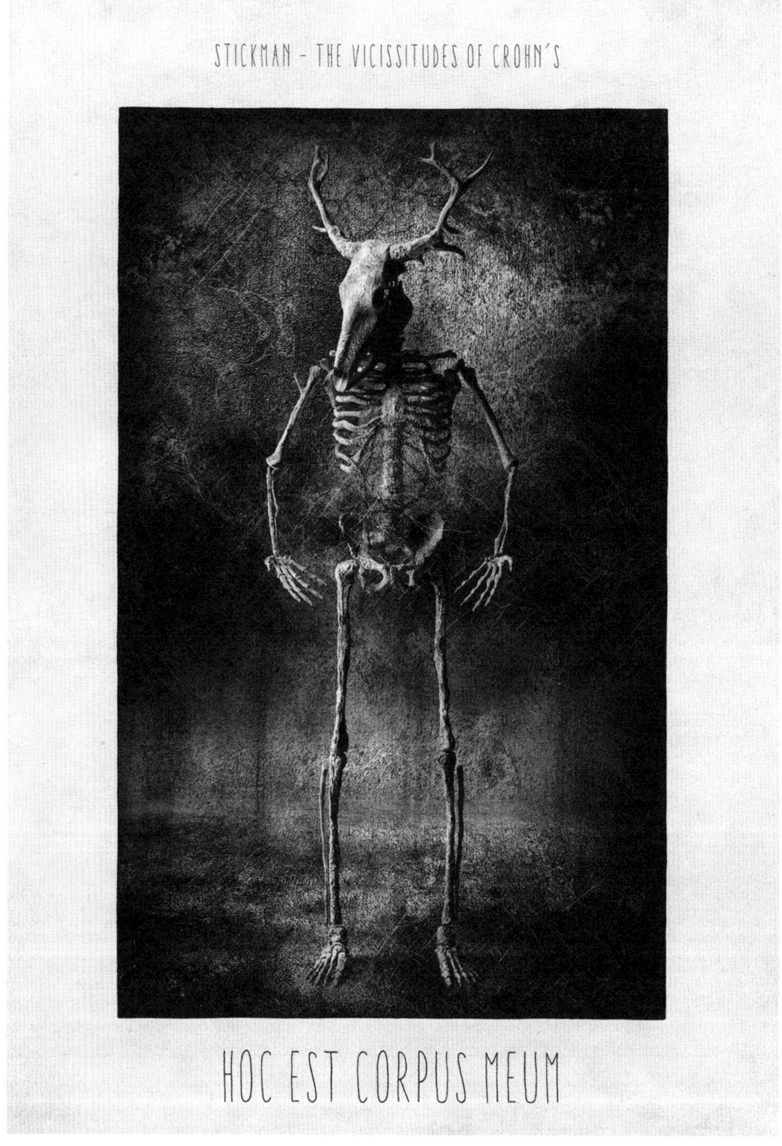

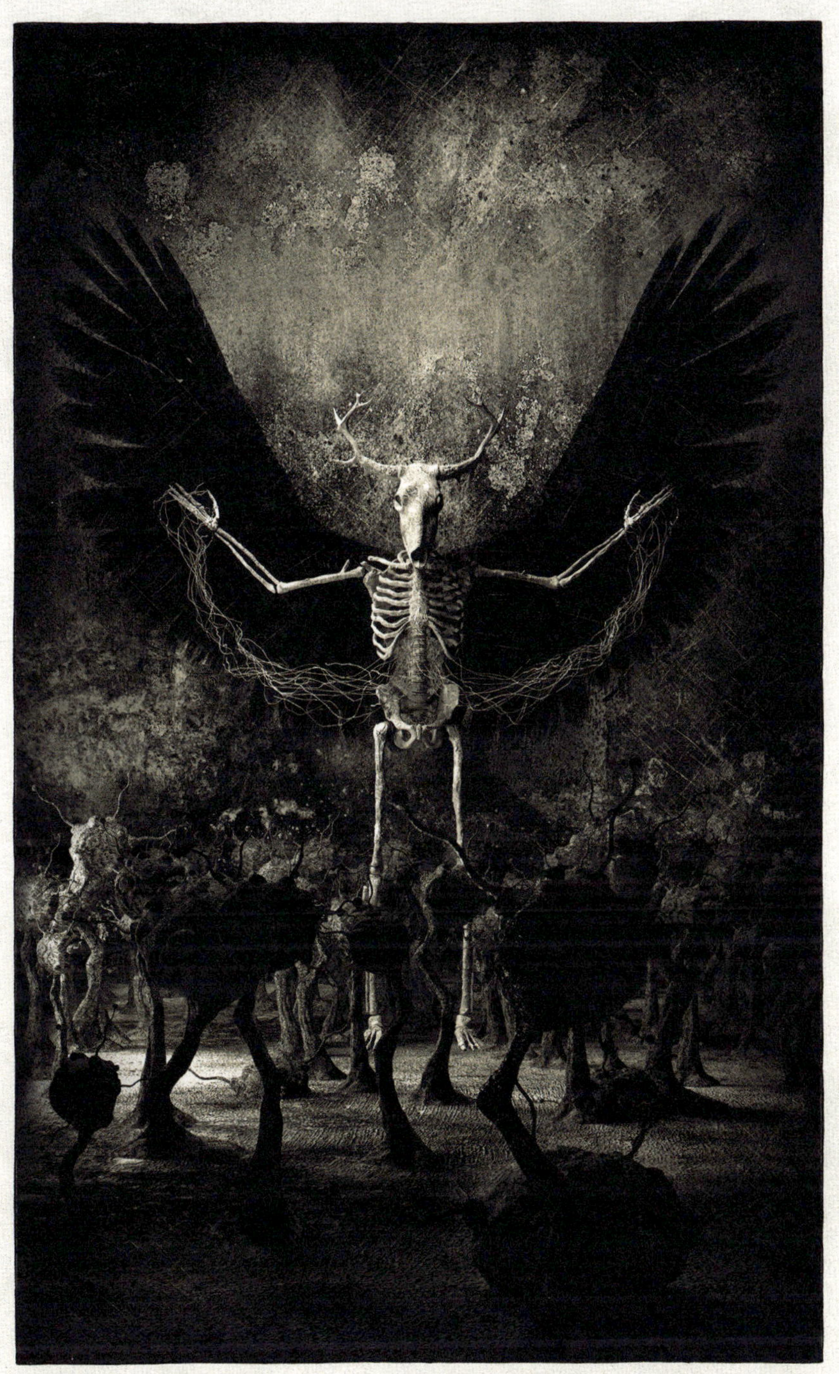

NULLAM DOLOREM SENTIRE

STICKMAN - THE VICISSITUDES OF CROHN'S

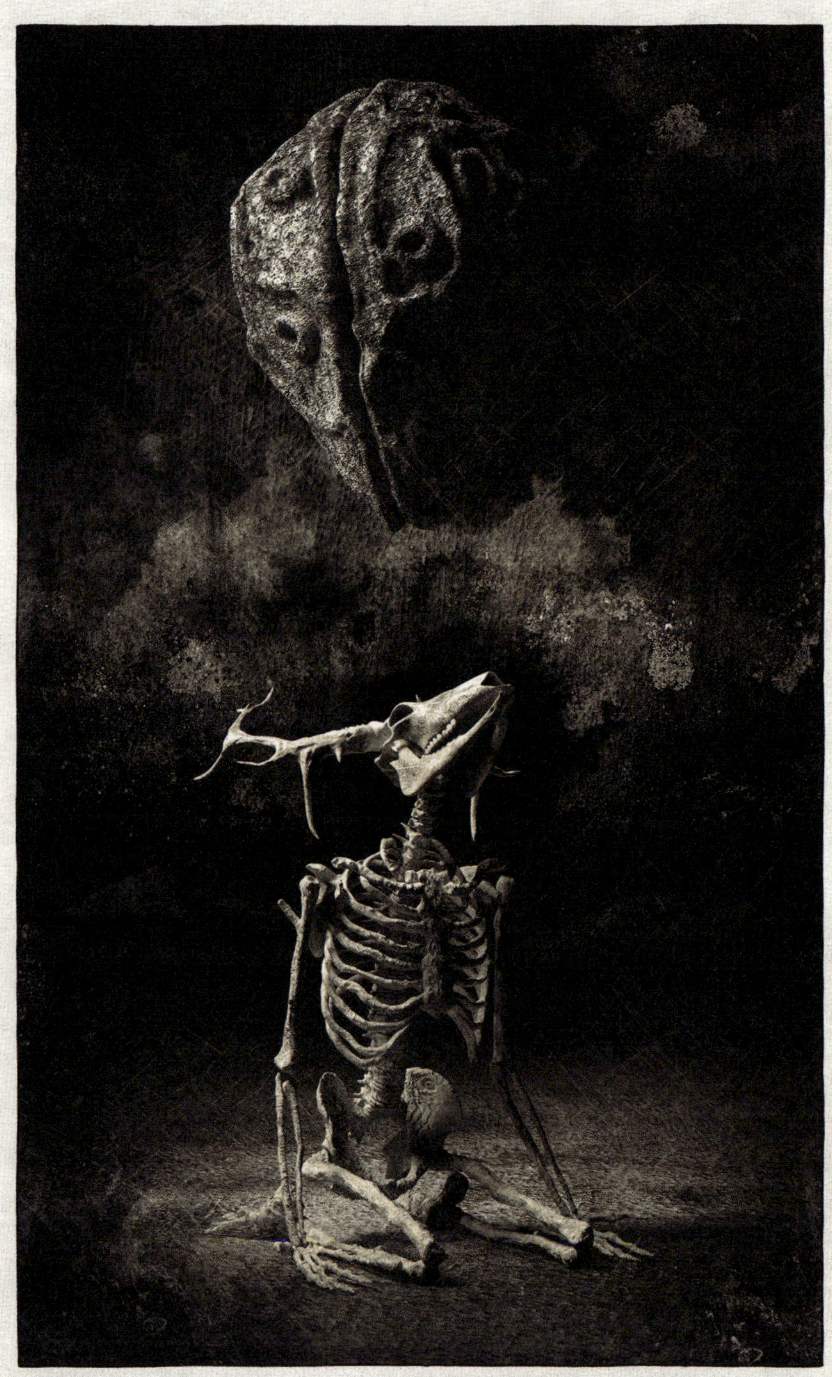

ET IN ARCADIA EGO

STICKMAN – THE VICISSITUDES OF CROHN'S

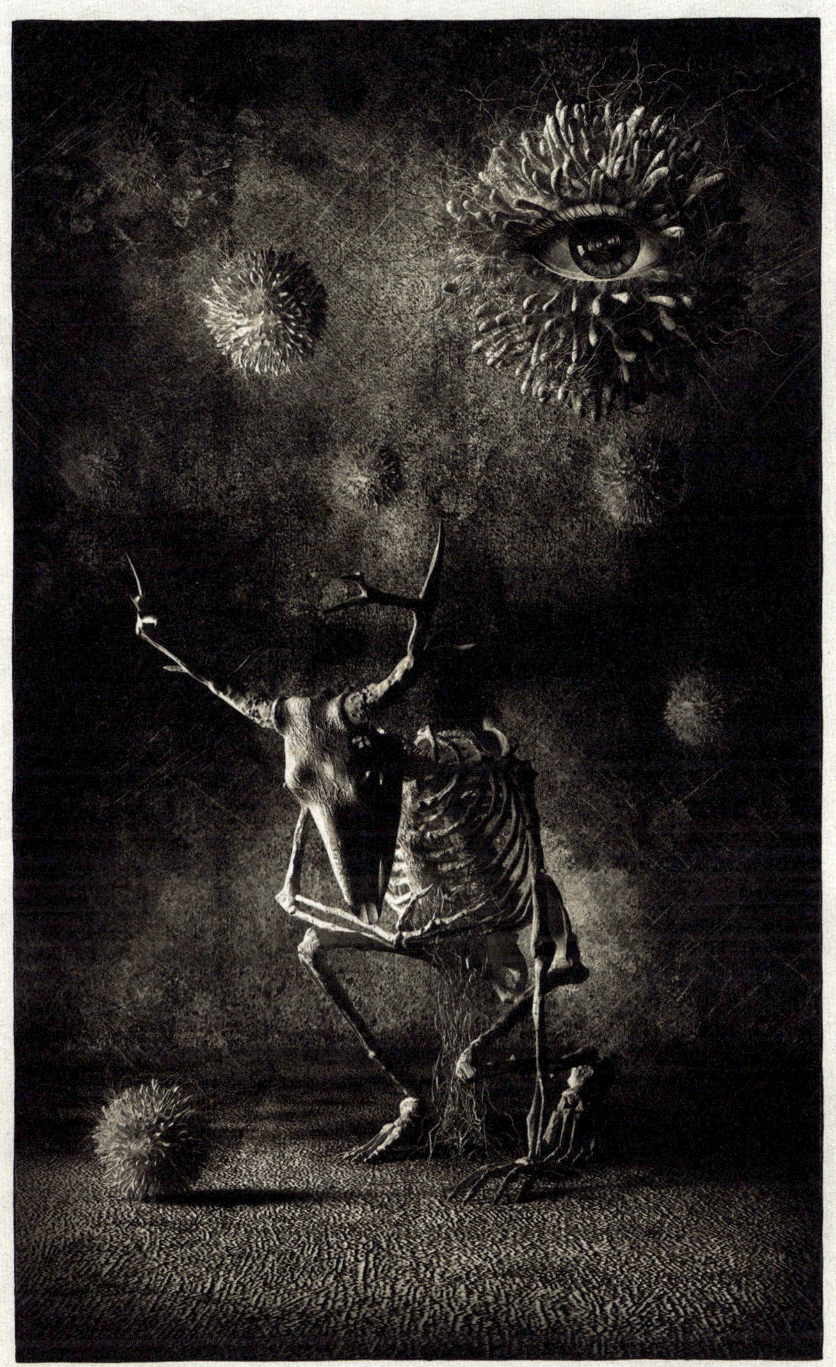

QUOD ME NUTRIT ME DESTRUIT

TAROT

Designer: Alex Panci, Davide Martini Studio: DOGMA

The Dogma's Major Arcana are the beginning of a set of 78 cards, every card of which features a unique and original hand-drawn illustration of DOGMA's macabre interpretation of the traditional Tarot. Inspired by the darkest and deepest fears, this deliciously dark and grimly enchanting tarot depicts a doomed realm of savage landscapes where dwell strange creatures and damned souls.

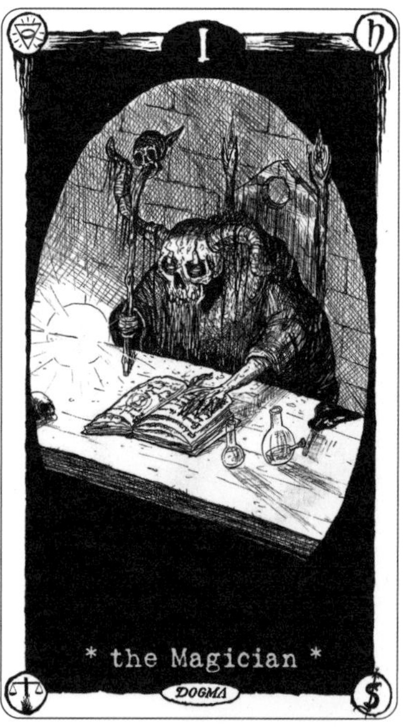

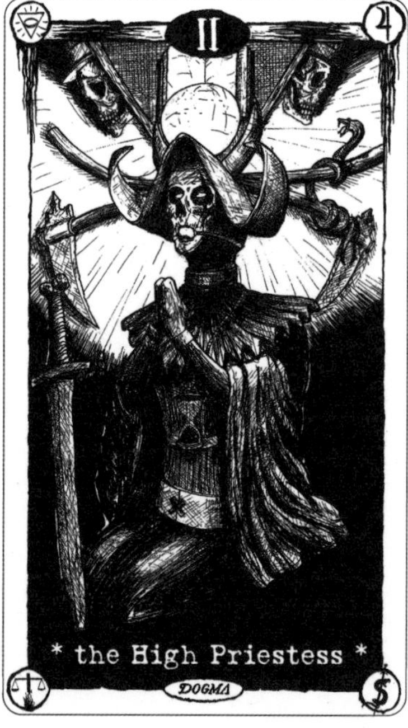

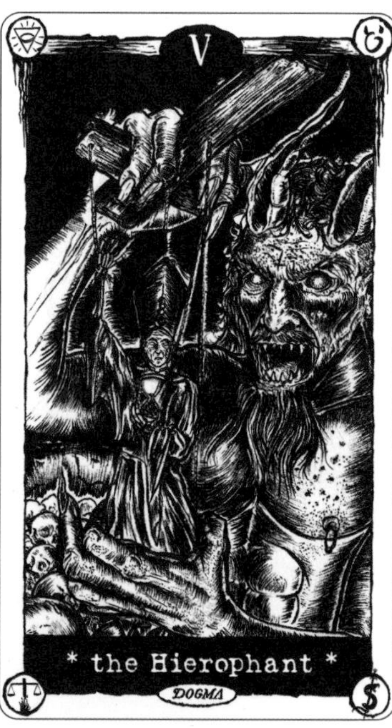

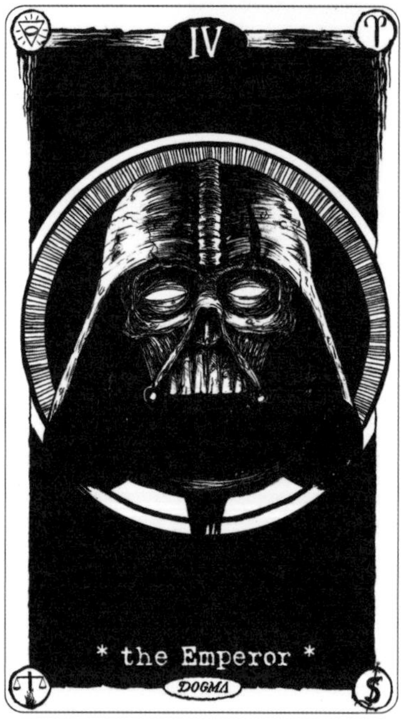

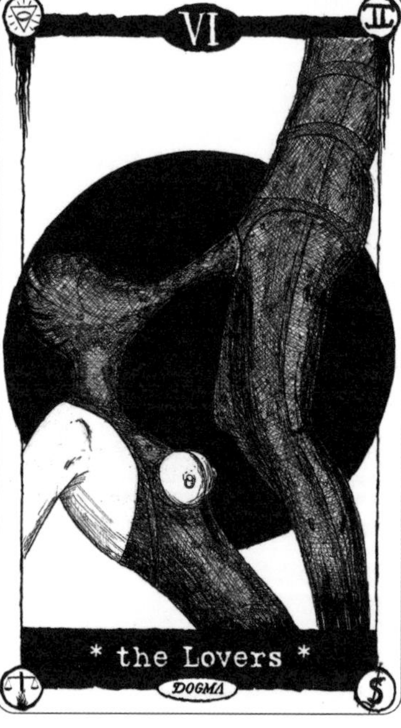

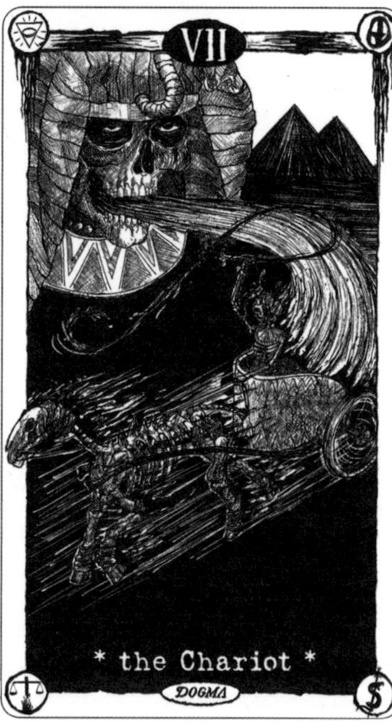

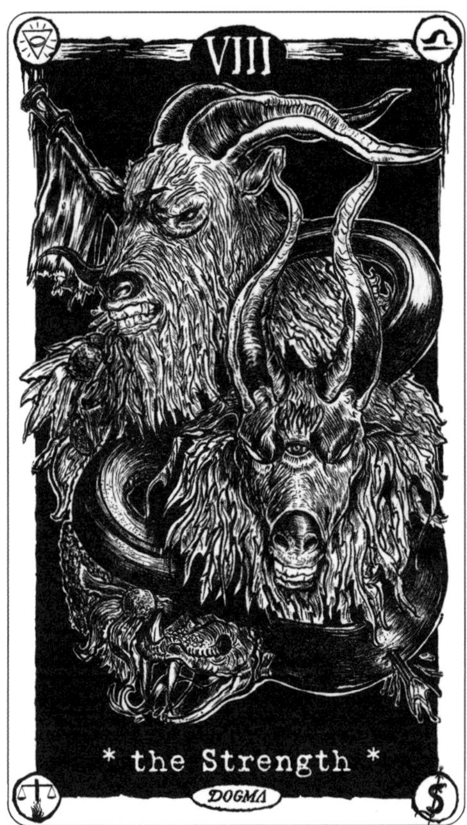
VIII
* the Strength *
DOGMA

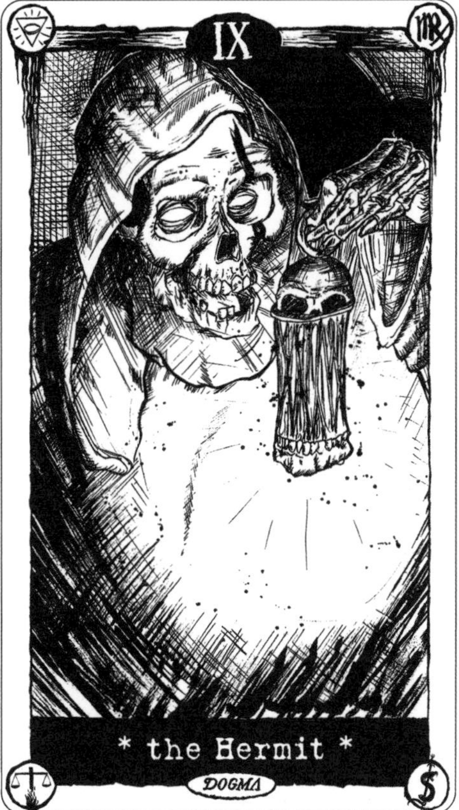
IX
* the Hermit *
DOGMA

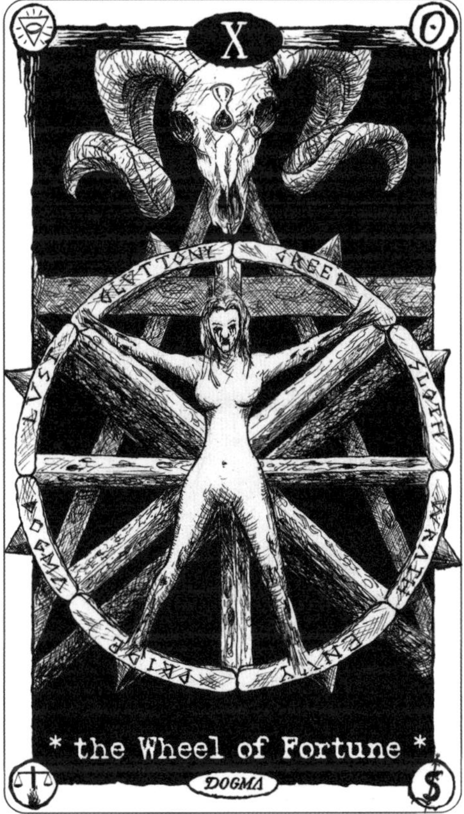
X
GREED
SLOTH
WRATH
ENVY
PRIDE
LUST
* the Wheel of Fortune *
DOGMA

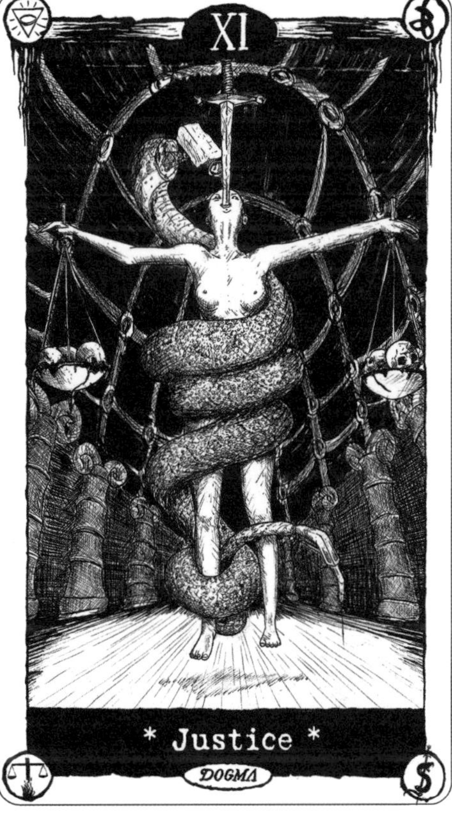
XI
* Justice *
DOGMA

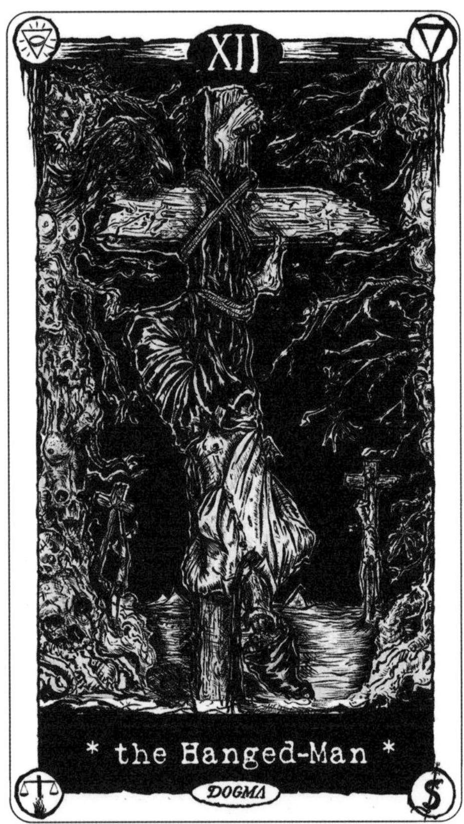
XII
* the Hanged-Man *
DOGMA

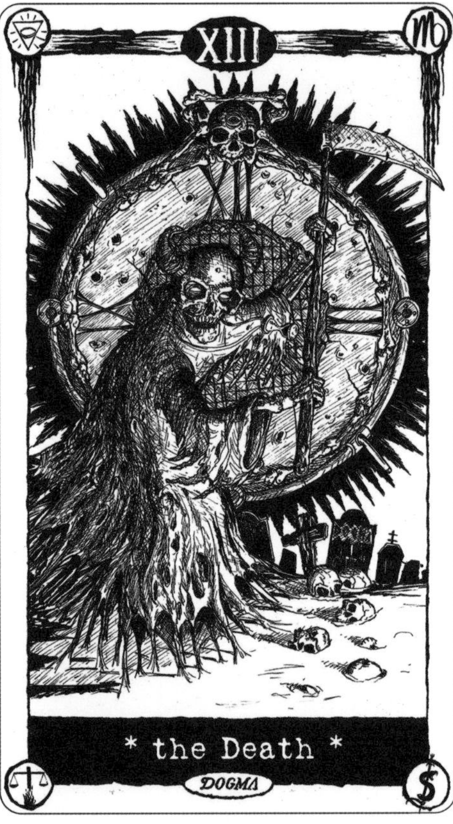
XIII
* the Death *
DOGMA

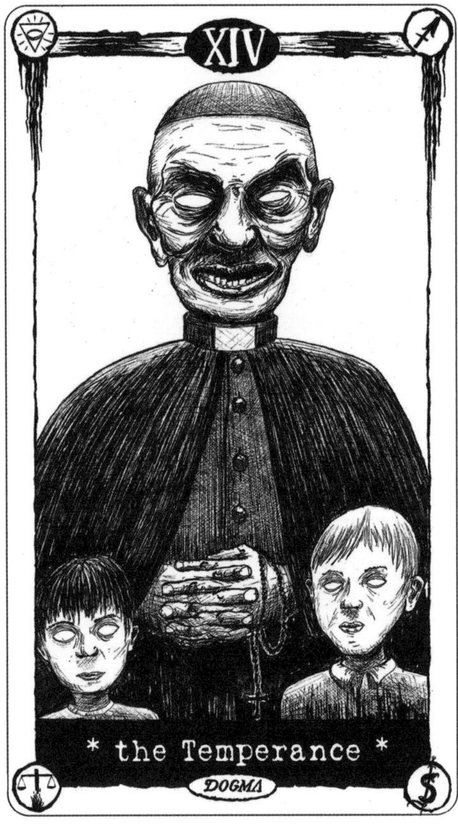
XIV
* the Temperance *
DOGMA

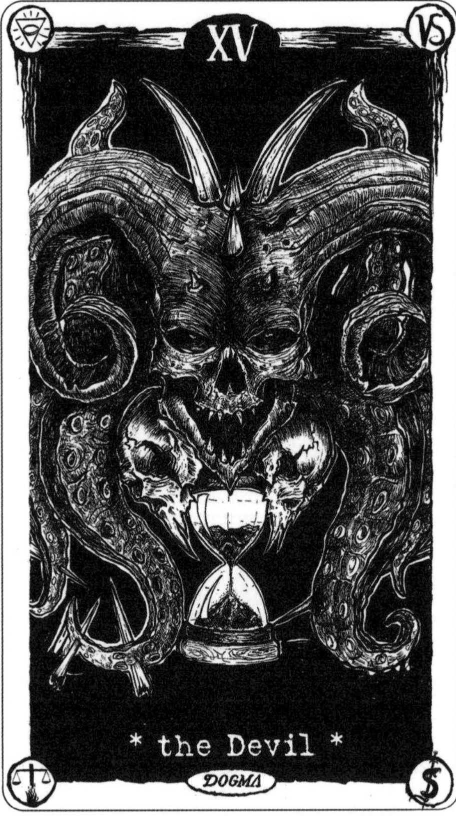
XV
* the Devil *
DOGMA

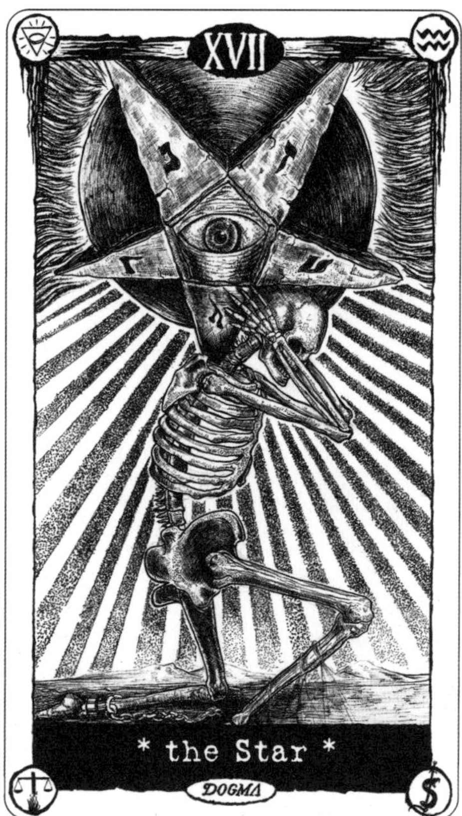
XVII
* the Star *
DOGMA

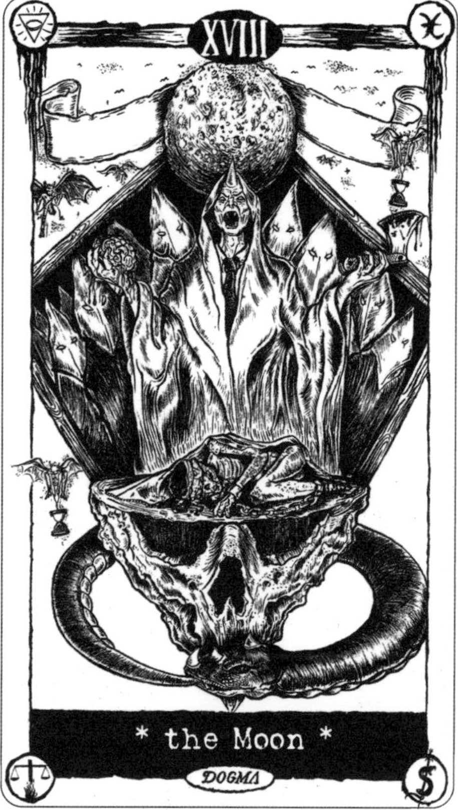
XVIII
* the Moon *
DOGMA

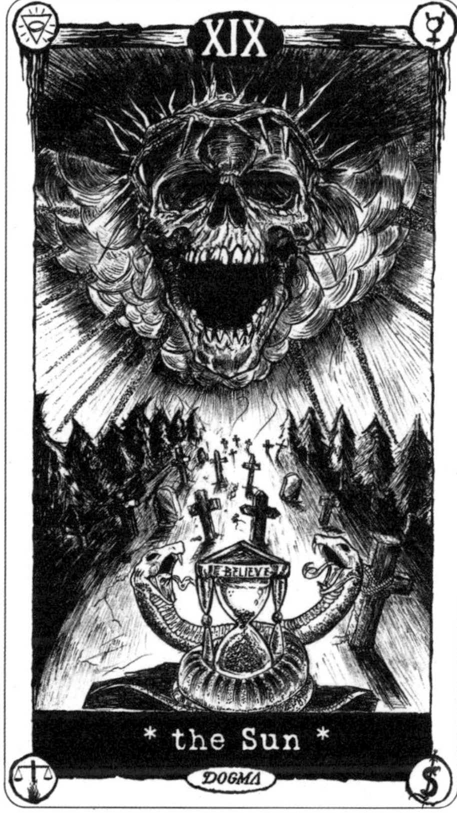
XIX
* the Sun *
DOGMA

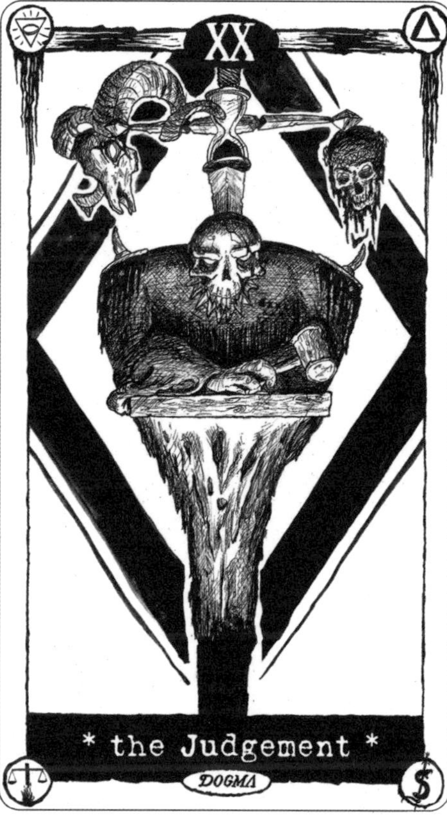
XX
* the Judgement *
DOGMA

SIAMESE WOMAN

Designer: Watcharaporn Thongaram Studio: Themushdrawing

The Illustration “The values of Thai woman” was created based on survey of the values of Thai woman, Thai astrology, and science of oracle card. With this project, the designer hopes to provide fortune tellers and general audiences with a new and unique set of tarot cards.

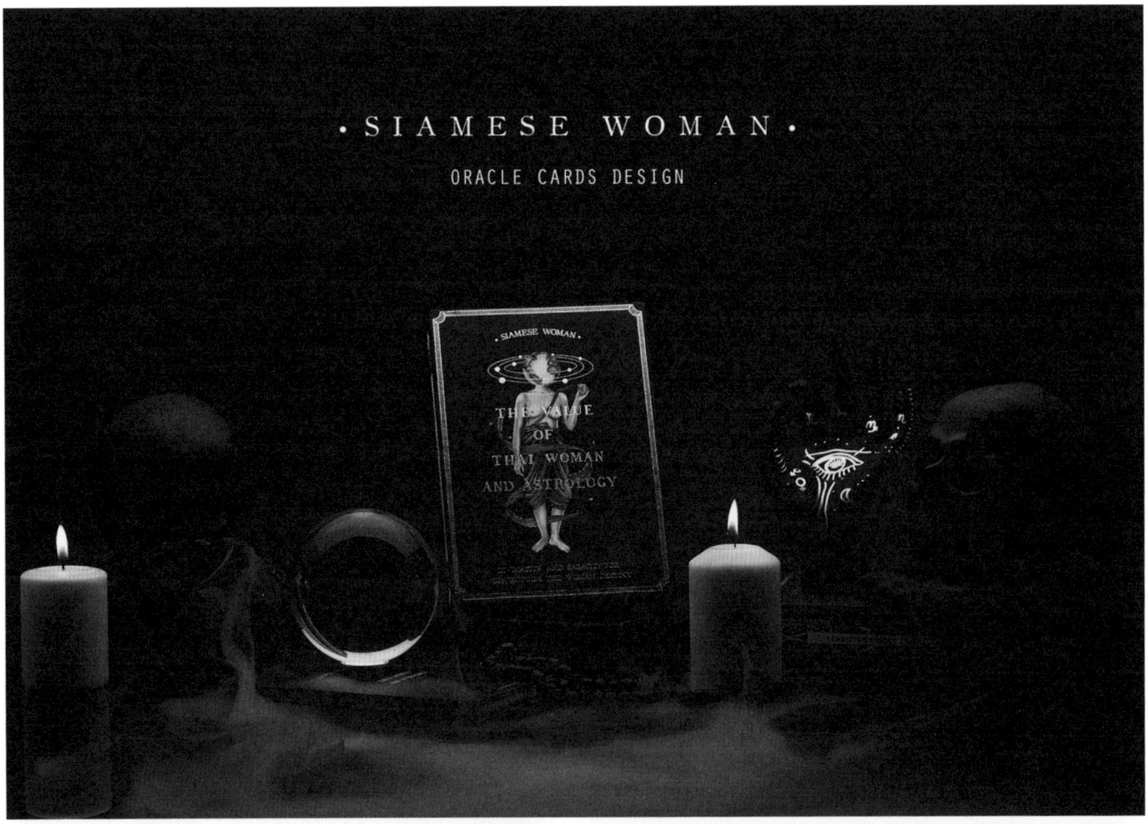

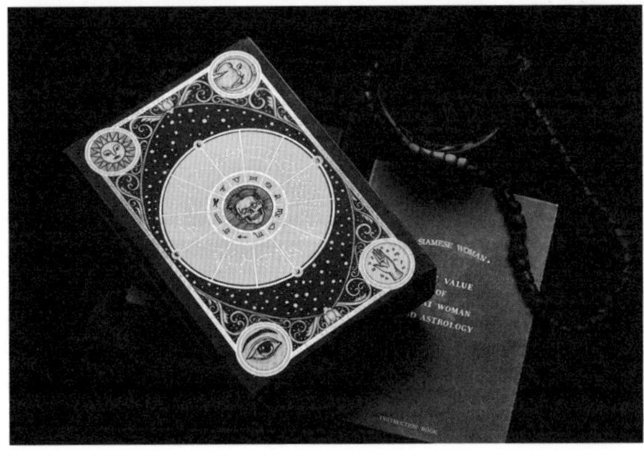

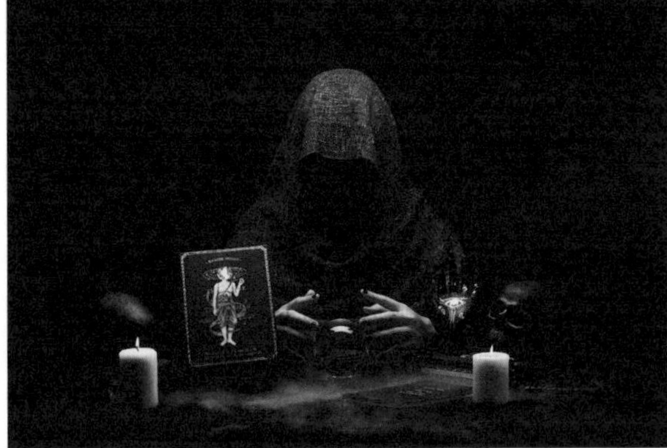

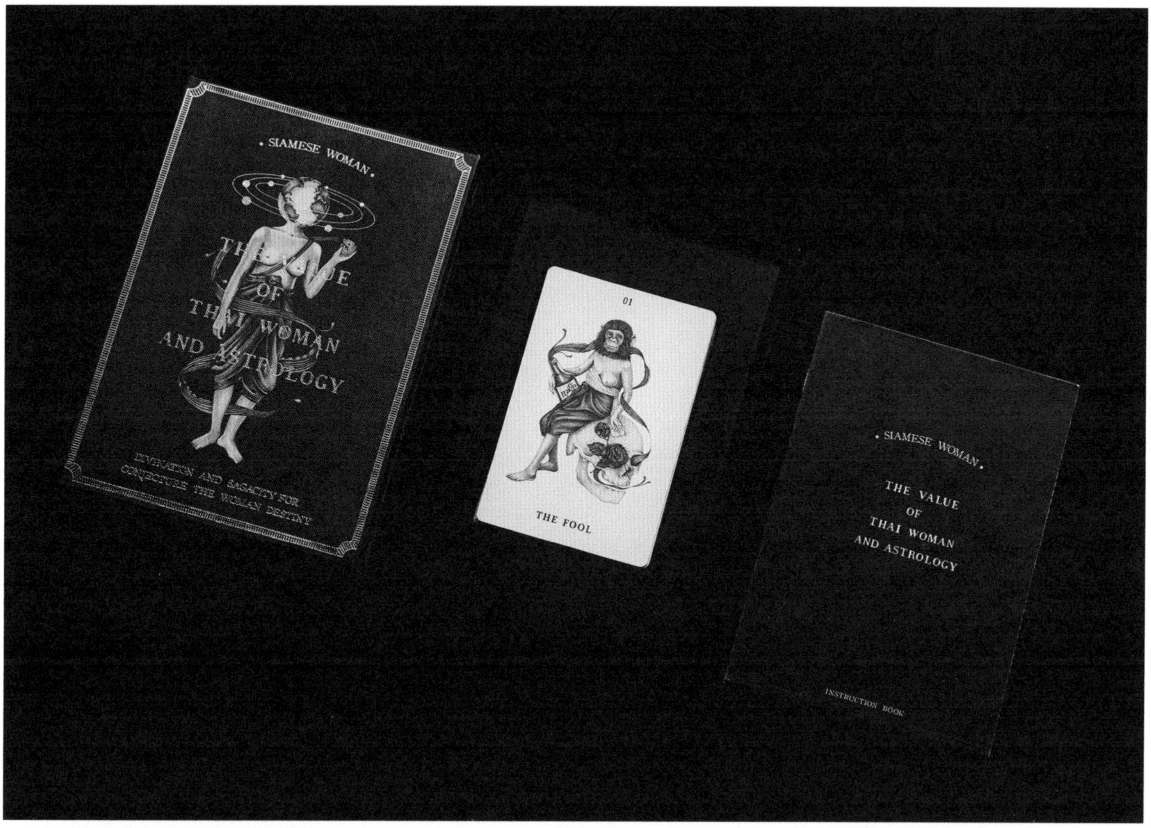

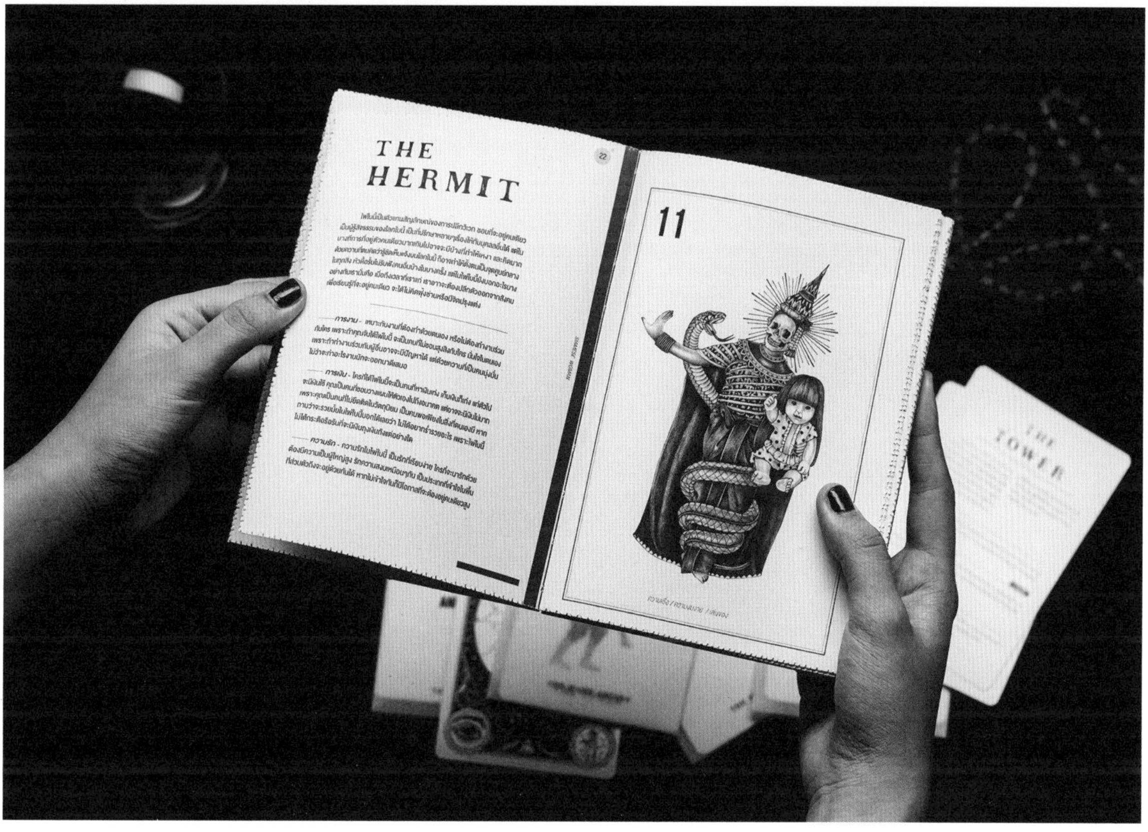

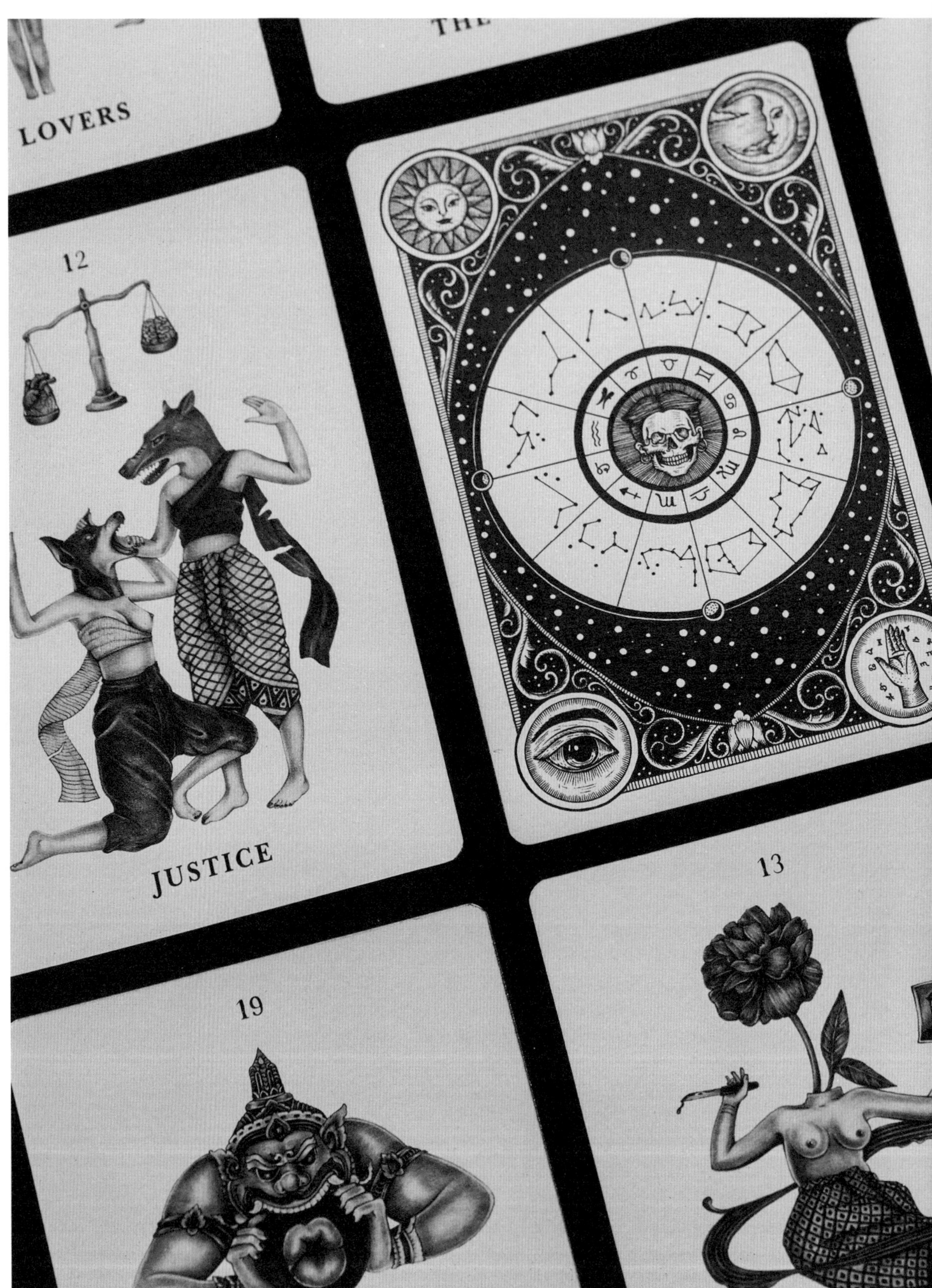
LOVERS
12
JUSTICE
13
19

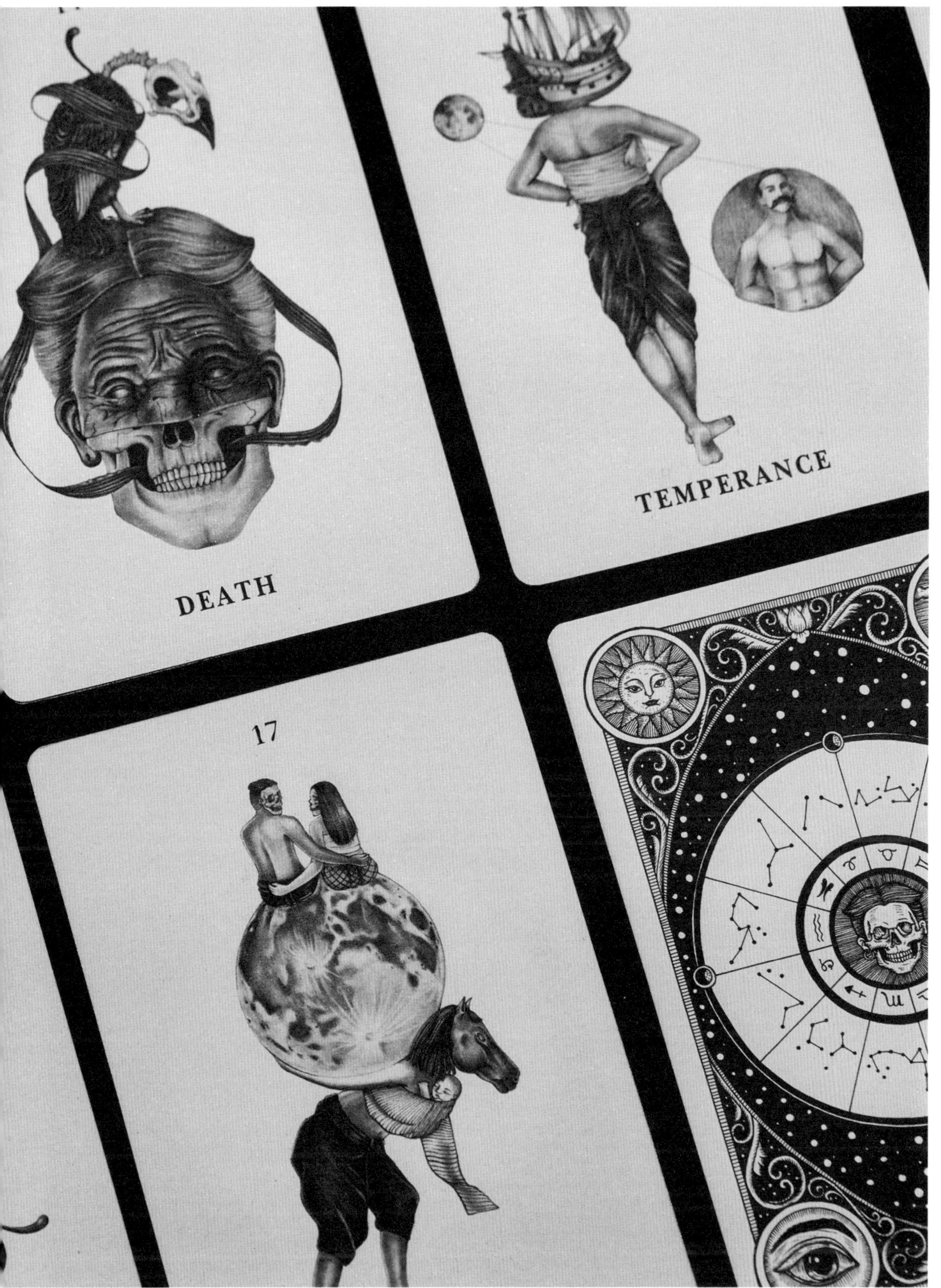
DEATH
TEMPERANCE
17

AEON-BURN AFTER ME

Designer/Artist: Davide Mancini   Studio: Dartworks

Aeon is a concept album of band Burn After Me, inspired by Dante's *Divine Comedy* with fantastic imagination. The album cover is composed of three circles, which represent respectively hell, purgatory and paradise, with a divine eye in the center. Every chapter in the booklet is distinguished by a specific color, and lyrics for each song are accompanied by unique illustrations. The creator started this creation using pencils before applying ink and digital colors.

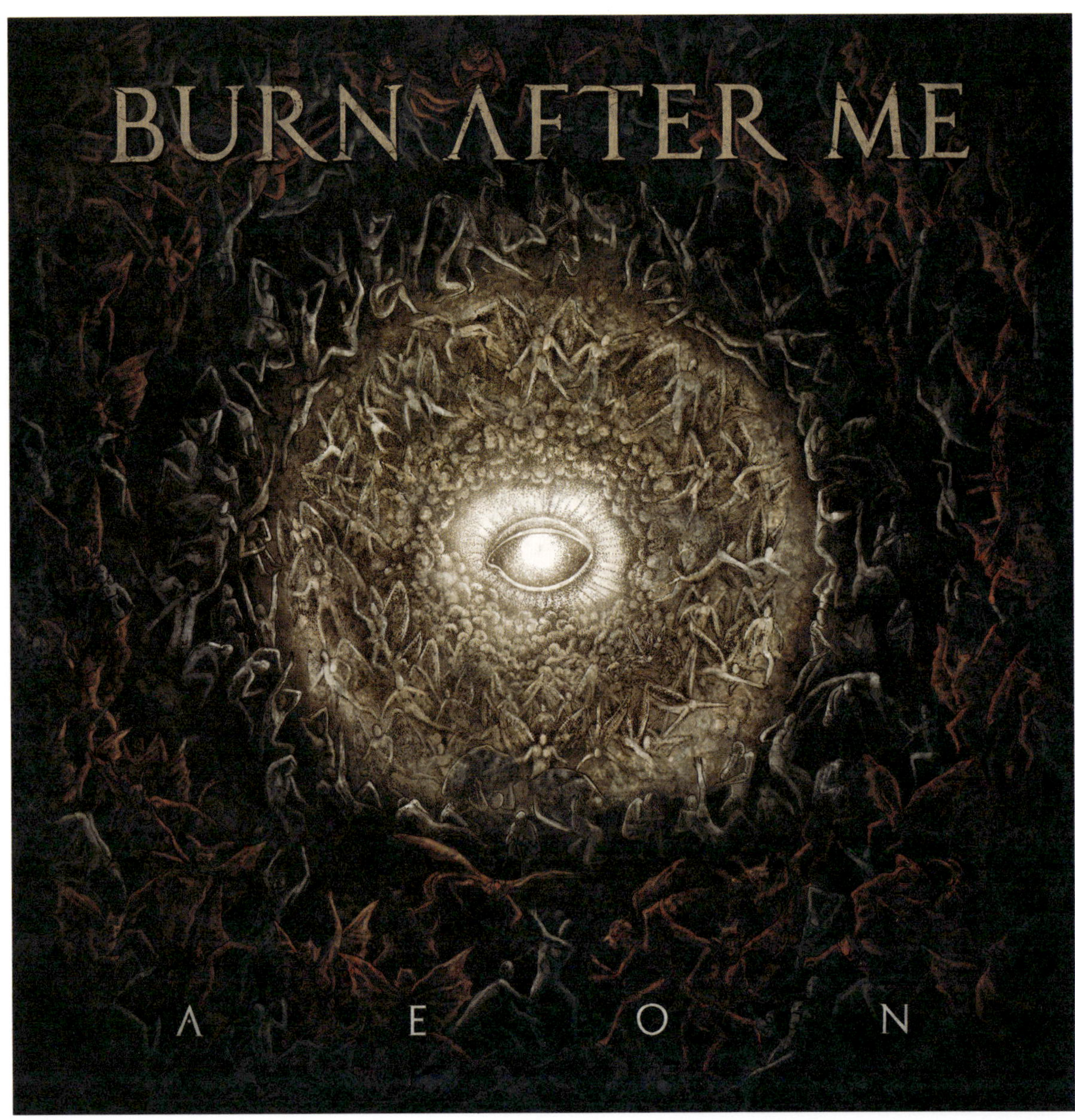

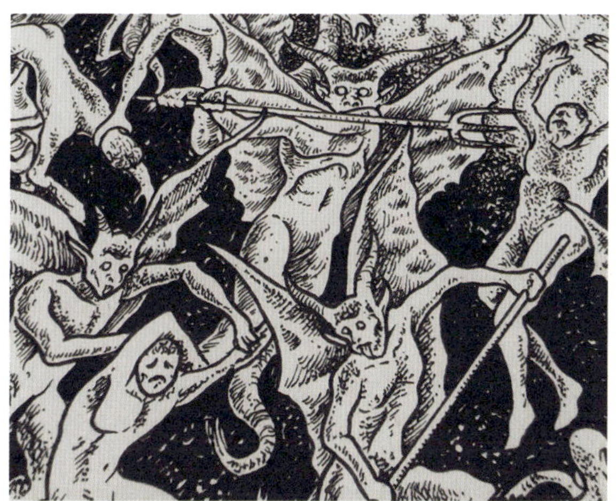

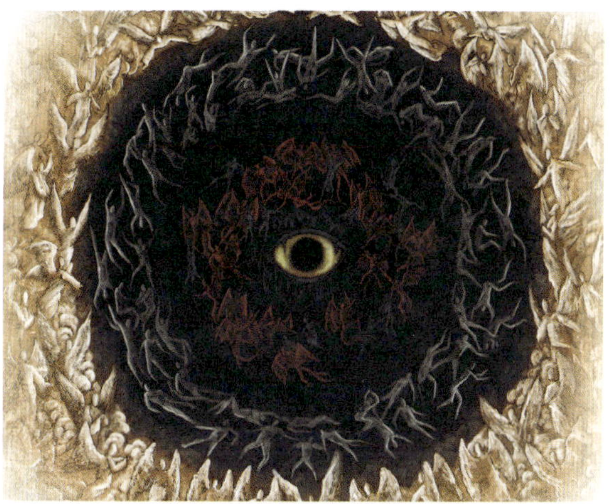

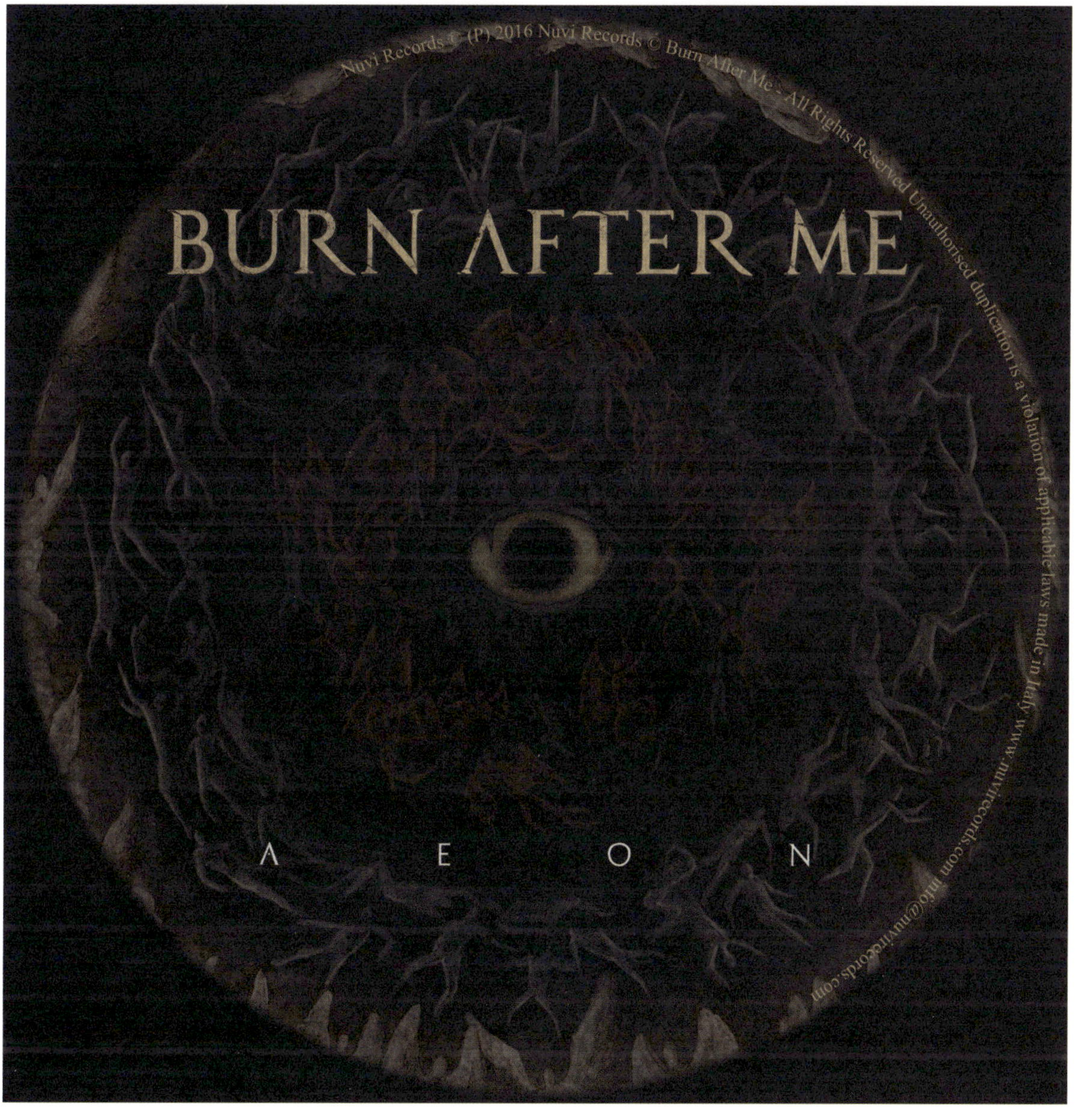

BURN AFTER ME

A E O N

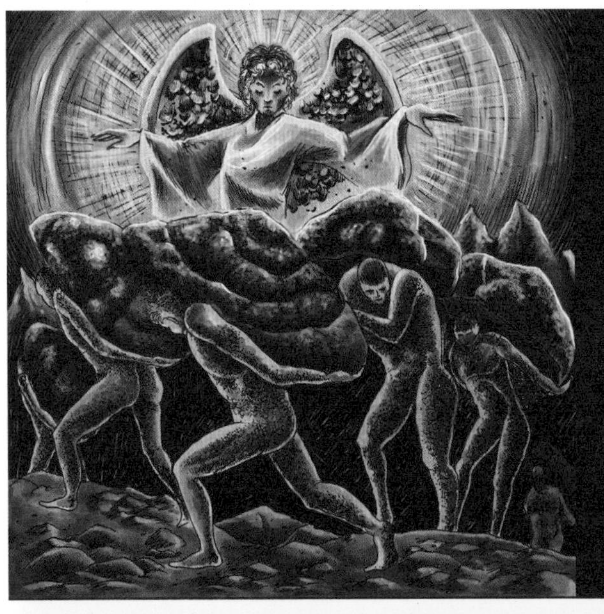

CHASTE KISS

Purifying fire
Of my impure side
Free me from the chains of carnality
Making my thoughts
Candid as innocence
A new awareness is born
Just brace yourselves out around her waist
A chaste kiss is gone again away
No time to taste it no time to feel it
Our soul still bare for another ride

Feed your hearts
Feed your souls
There's something more who can burn (x2)
Feed your hearts
Feed your souls
Just watch the smoke start to rise (x2)

Let's flow all wish
Hold tight your chest
A new light will take hold
River will let you forget
Once for all, all pain you've got (x2)

All memories

Is almost done
Still somewhat
Almost done (x3)

Feed your hearts
Feed your souls
There's something more who can burn (x2)
Feed your hearts
Feed your souls
Just watch the fire and let it burn (x2)

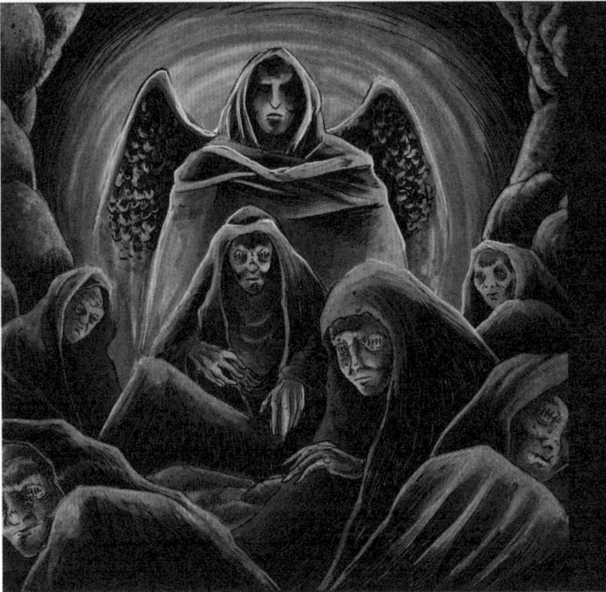

RIGHT FIT

Run! Run! (x2)
We are so close at the shore
Limpid water
Thirsty and hungry
Relentless desire infestor
Who mists moderation in minds
Right fit!
What we have to learn further to know
We have always known what was to be done
Greediness!
It has stayed with me for lifetime
Blinding my reason who now I have refund
I have refund
Emaciated and worn we run toward the trees
Branches retract stream up its banks subtracting us
One more time our sin
All I want
All I wanted is gone
It's now out of reach
Right!
Right fit! (x2)
We have always known
What was to be done
Right fit (x2)
Respawn
Can you feel in the air its scent?
I must go before the others come
Can you feel in the air its scent?
I must go (x2)
Is this burden to hard to carry?
Think your're next to your goal
Just keep your right fit
How much time you restart every time?
Think you're next to your goal
Just keep your right

Right!
Right fit! (x2)
Right fit (x2)

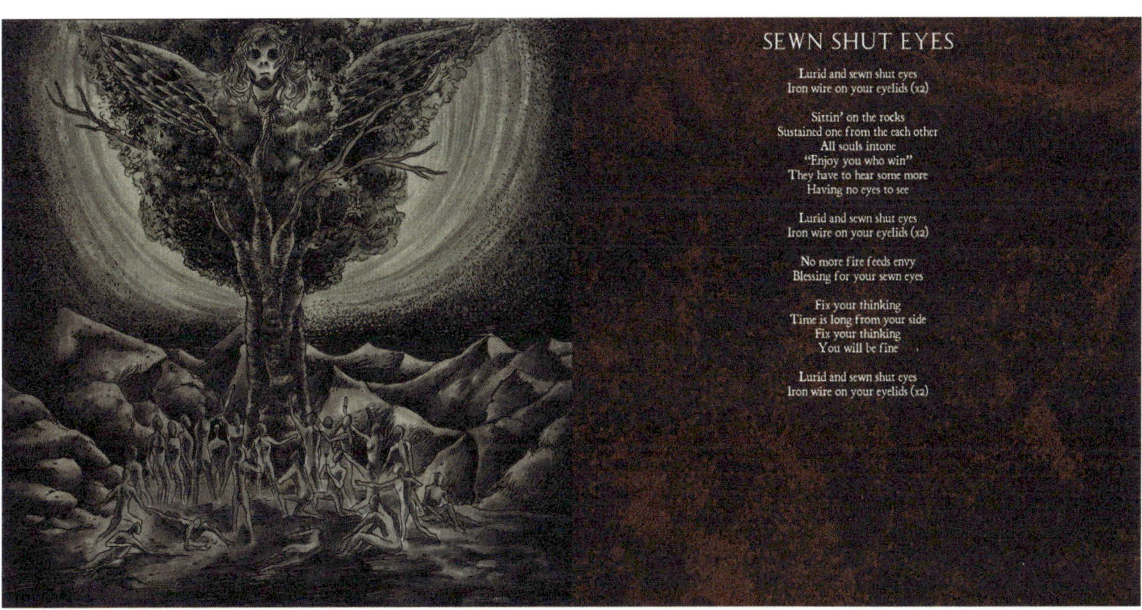

SEWN SHUT EYES

Lurid and sewn shut eyes
Iron wire on your eyelids (x2)

Sittin' on the rocks
Sustained one from the each other
All souls intone
"Enjoy you who win"
They have to hear some more
Having no eyes to see

Lurid and sewn shut eyes
Iron wire on your eyelids (x2)

No more fire feeds envy
Blessing for your sewn eyes

Fix your thinking
Time is long from your side
Fix your thinking
You will be fine

Lurid and sewn shut eyes
Iron wire on your eyelids (x2)

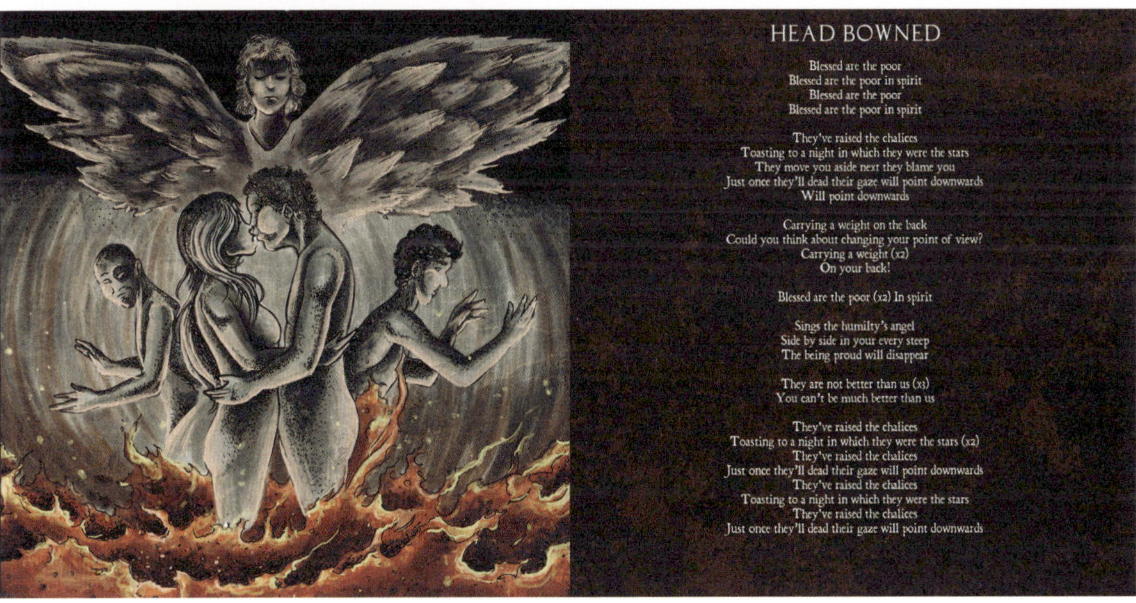

HEAD BOWNED

Blessed are the poor
Blessed are the poor in spirit
Blessed are the poor
Blessed are the poor in spirit

They've raised the chalices
Toasting to a night in which they were the stars
They move you aside next they blame you
Just once they'll dead their gaze will point downwards
Will point downwards

Carrying a weight on the back
Could you think about changing your point of view?
Carrying a weight (x2)
On your back!

Blessed are the poor (x2) In spirit

Sings the humilty's angel
Side by side in your every steep
The being proud will disappear

They are not better than us (x3)
You can't be much better than us

They've raised the chalices
Toasting to a night in which they were the stars (x2)
They've raised the chalices
Just once they'll dead their gaze will point downwards
They've raised the chalices
Toasting to a night in which they were the stars
They've raised the chalices
Just once they'll dead their gaze will point downwards

ÉRASE UNA VEZ

Designer: Emilio Rubione

Érase una vez (Once upon a time) is a retelling book written by five Argentinian booktubers. The designer was to create an image that could gather aspects of the different stories in the book. He decided to make a central image and from there divide the page so that the little specific things can be taken care of. The title and the names of the authors were also placed inside the frame.

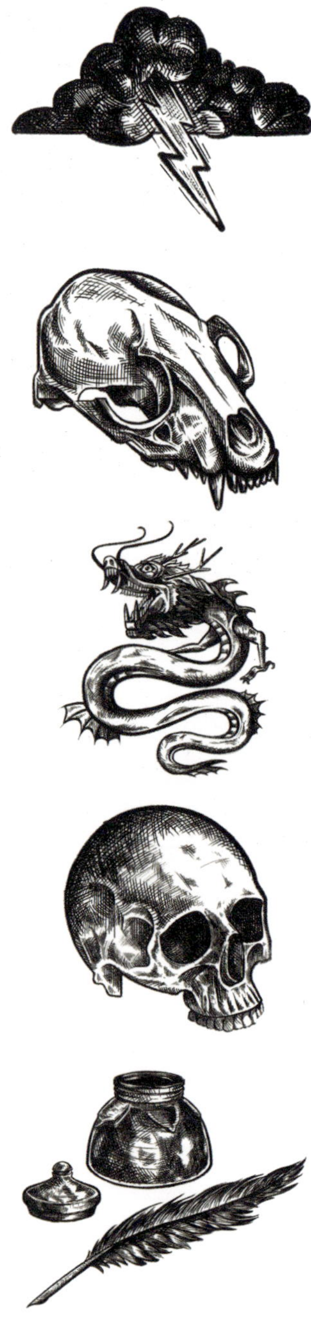

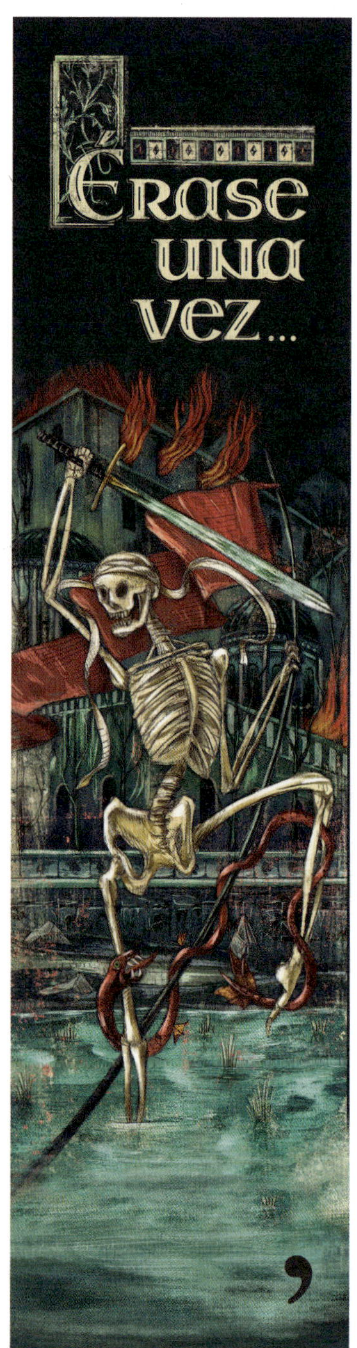

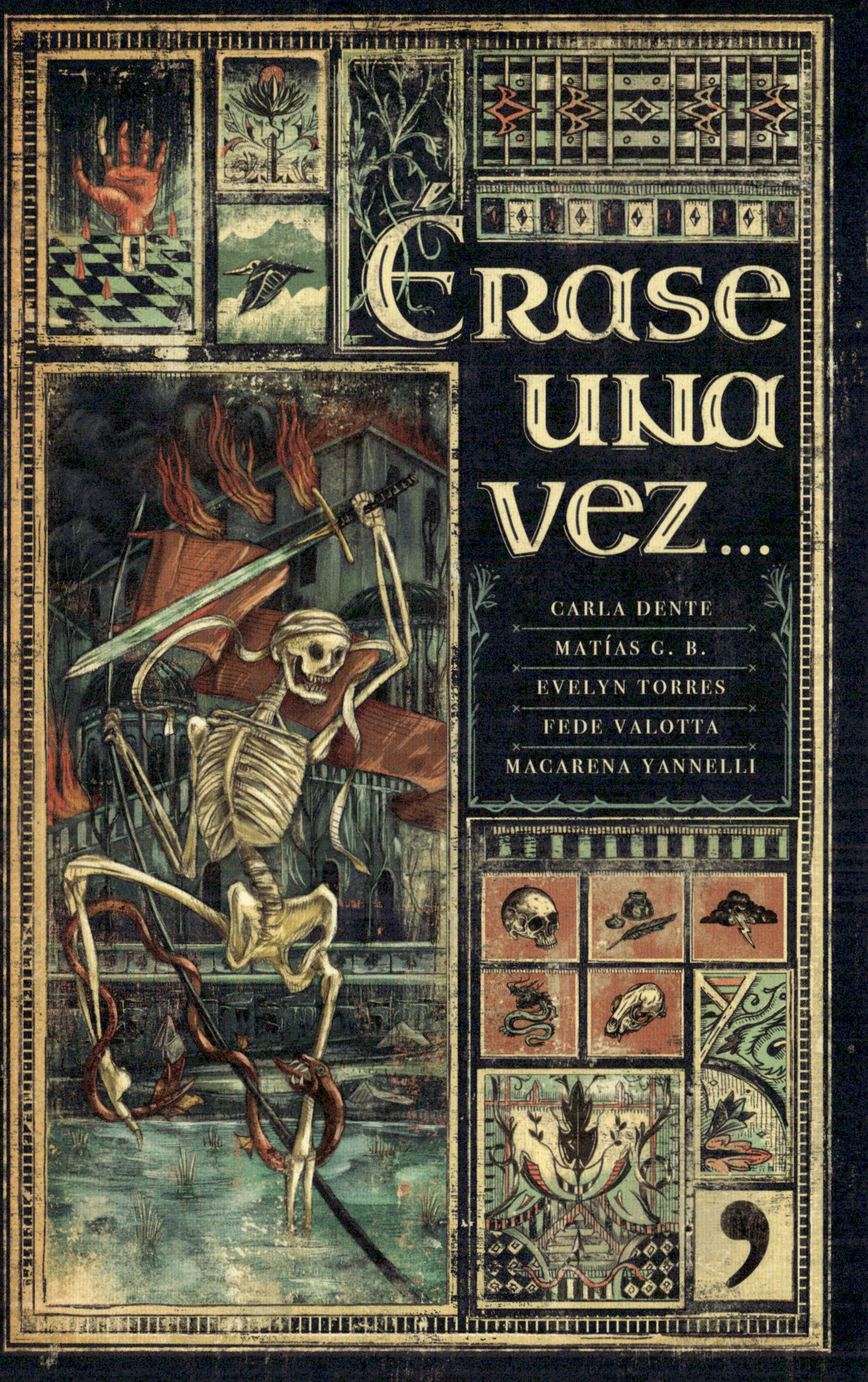
Érase
una
vez...
CARLA DENTE
MATÍAS G. B.
EVELYN TORRES
FEDE VALOTTA
MACARENA YANNELLI

STRANGE DAYS HAVE FOUND US

Artist: Danny van Ryswyk

For this work, 3D software and digital painting were mixed together to create an otherworldly sense of obscure absurdity. With all ideas being the influence of the artist's interest in and fascination for the supernatural, his work displays a fuse of dreamy imagery with a distinctly paranormal bent.

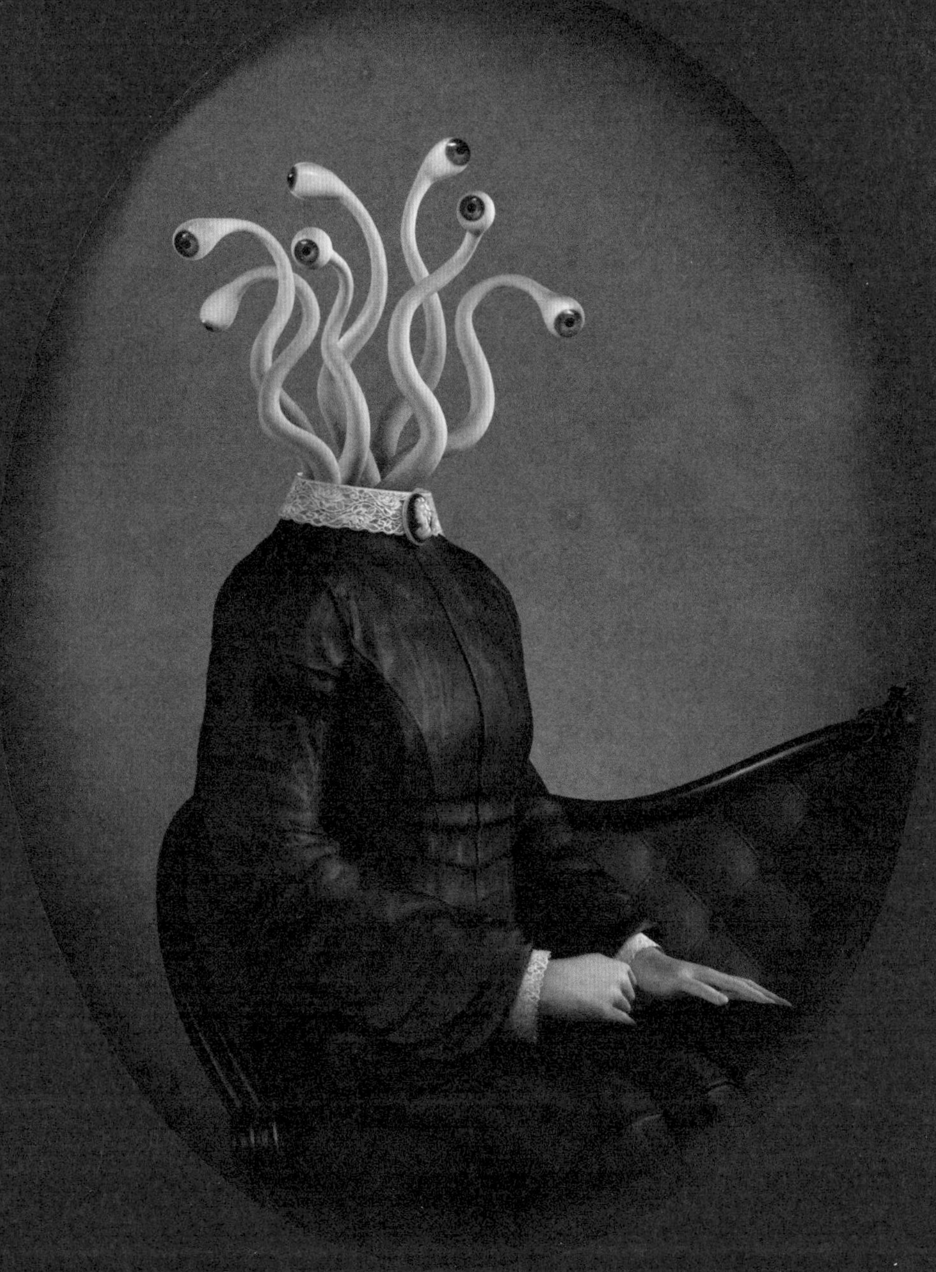

THE END AND THE BEGINNING

Artist: Diego Spezzoni

This is a personal project which illustrates the old and known walking uphill across a hazardous and horrid land, fighting against demons and ghosts, to bring to life the new-born and the unknown. Symbolic elements were incorporated to create this picture with a dark and mysterious atmosphere.

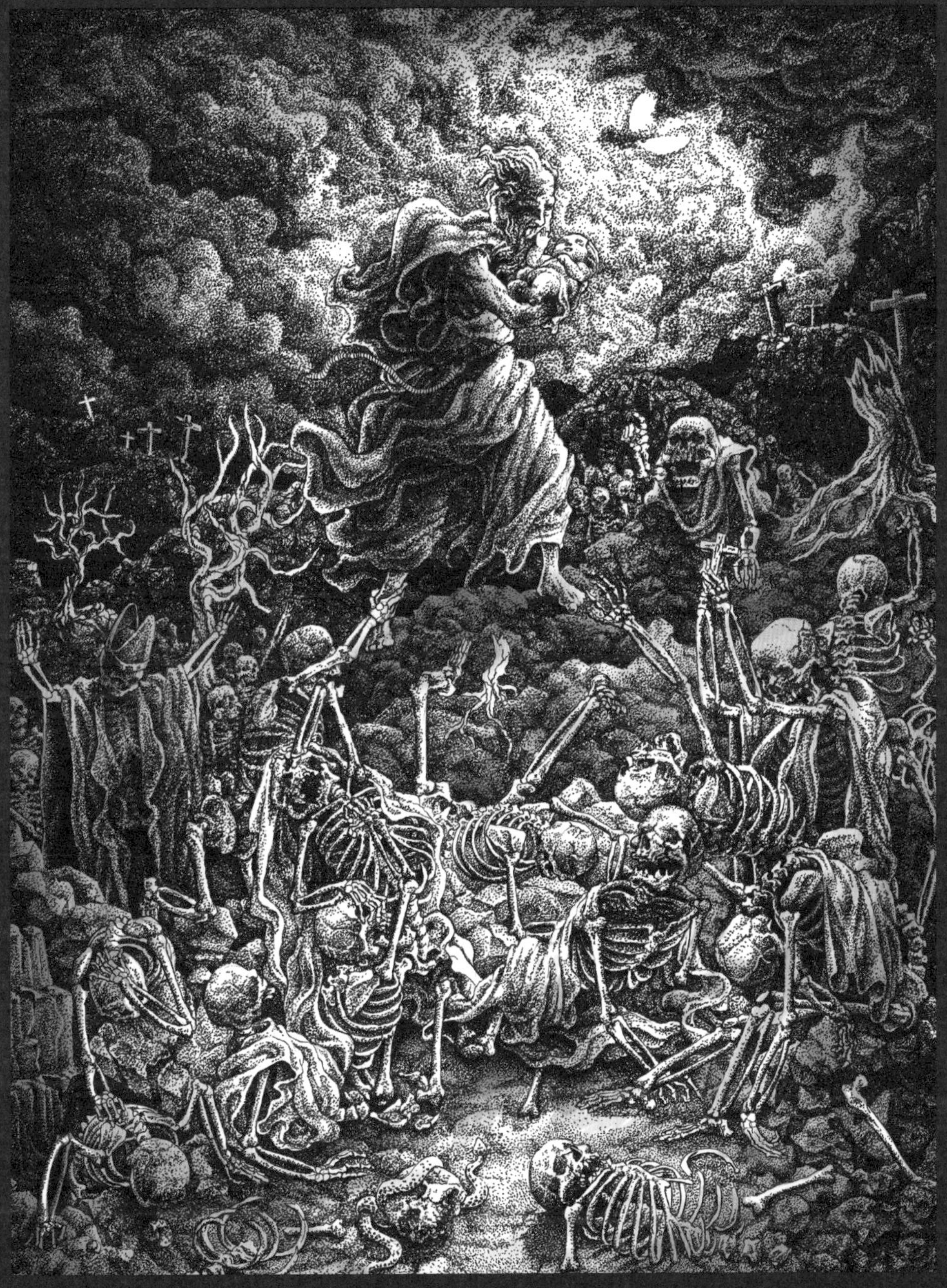

HUMAN SPRAWL

Designer: Ivan Meshkov

This image depicts the end of human existence and the earth when snakes will nest on human bones, symbolizing the insignificance of humans.

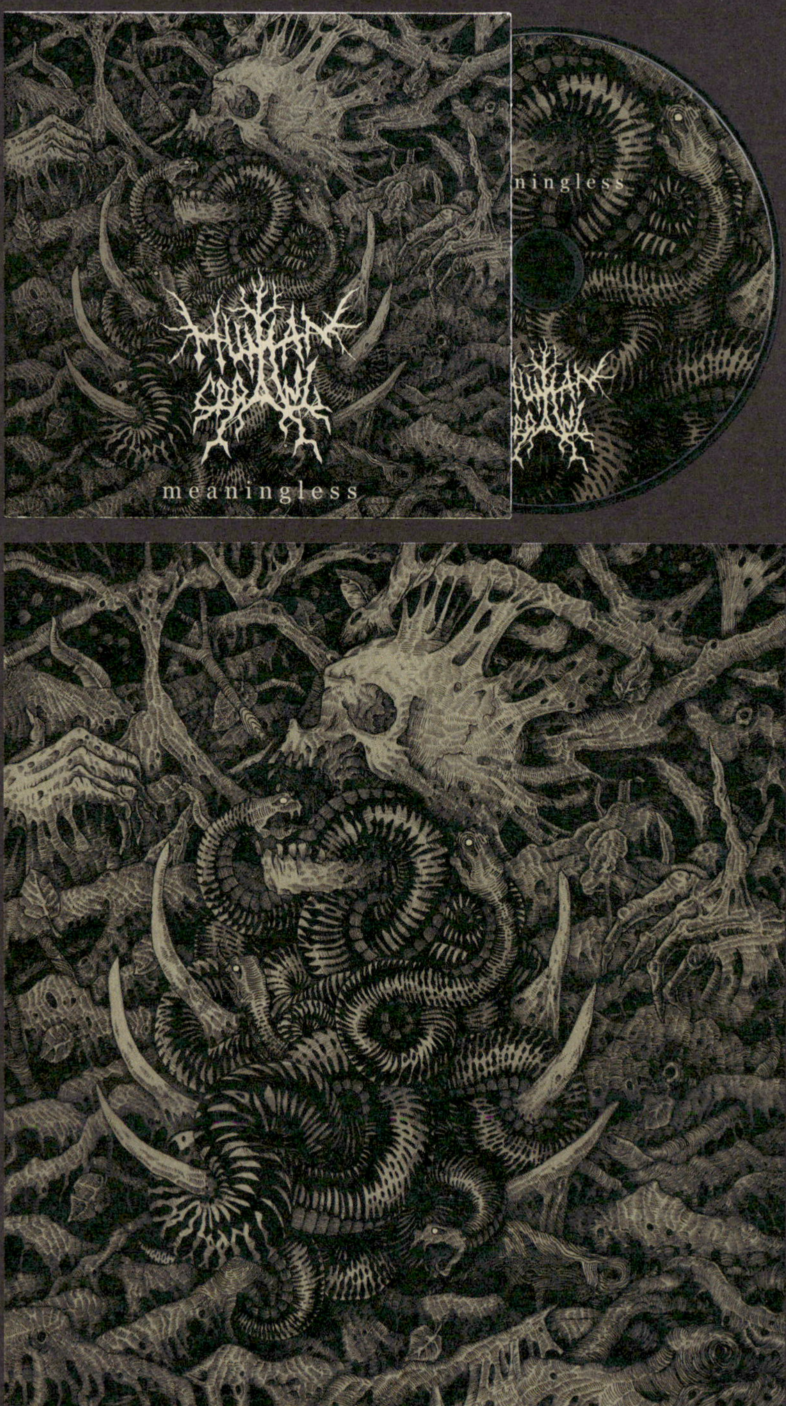

WORLD

Designer: Yang Shi Ching

This project aims to call for people to keep in mind the beginning of an idea or decision, to reflect from time to time so as to improve and evolve.

DEUEL

Designer: Aleksandar Živanov / Hardworkz

This poster artwork created for Croatian metal band Deuel.

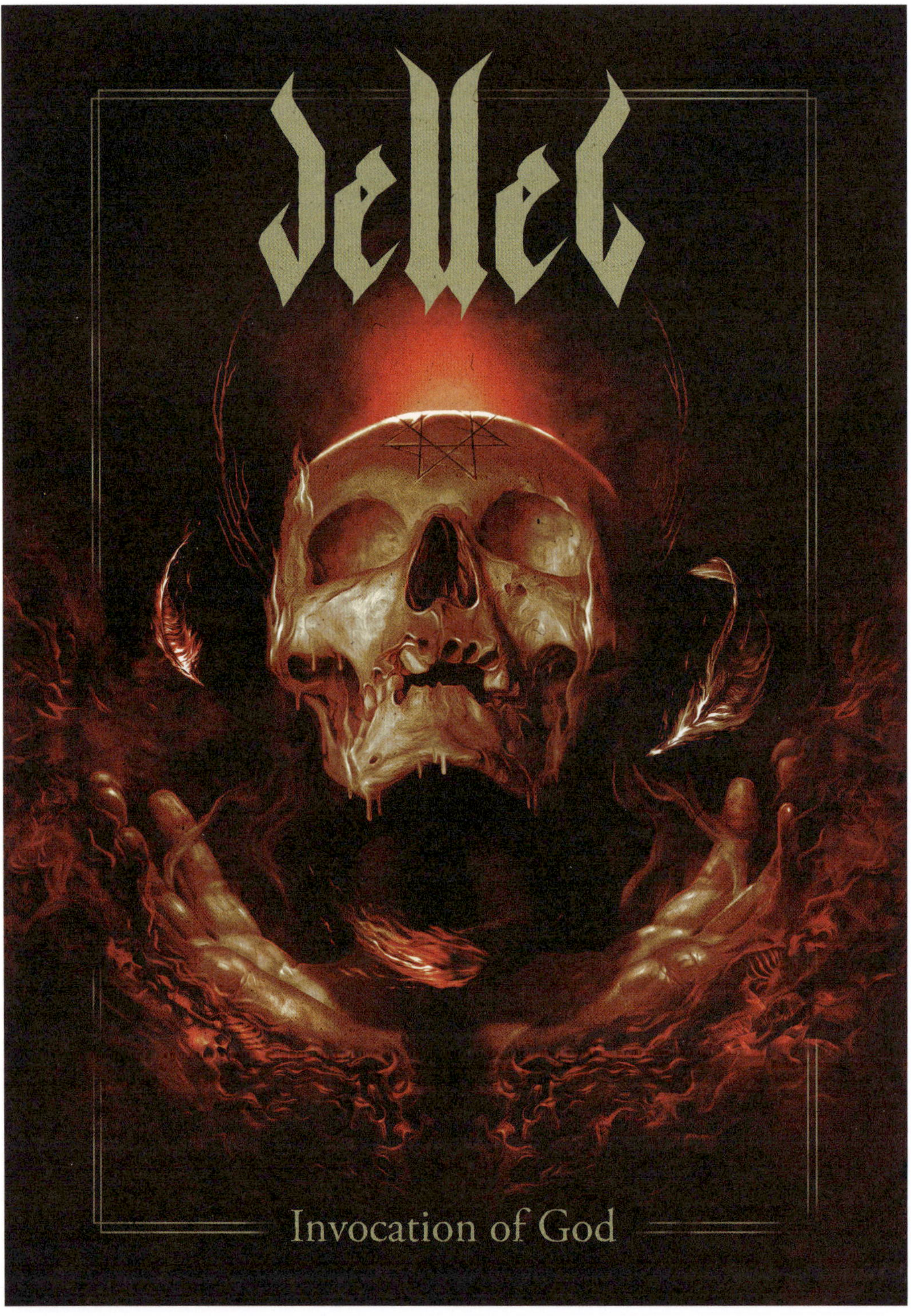

#OOTD

Artist: Esther Goh

With our generation being the first users of Instagram, an image-driven social media platform, the artist created this satiric piece. It shows how Instagram caused distortion in the perception of beauty by promoting the unhealthy act of idealization of our self-image. In a constant bid to one-up the others, some may even take on another persona. As the cycle of self-promotion continues with a need to validate our social status, some of us are drawn further from reality.

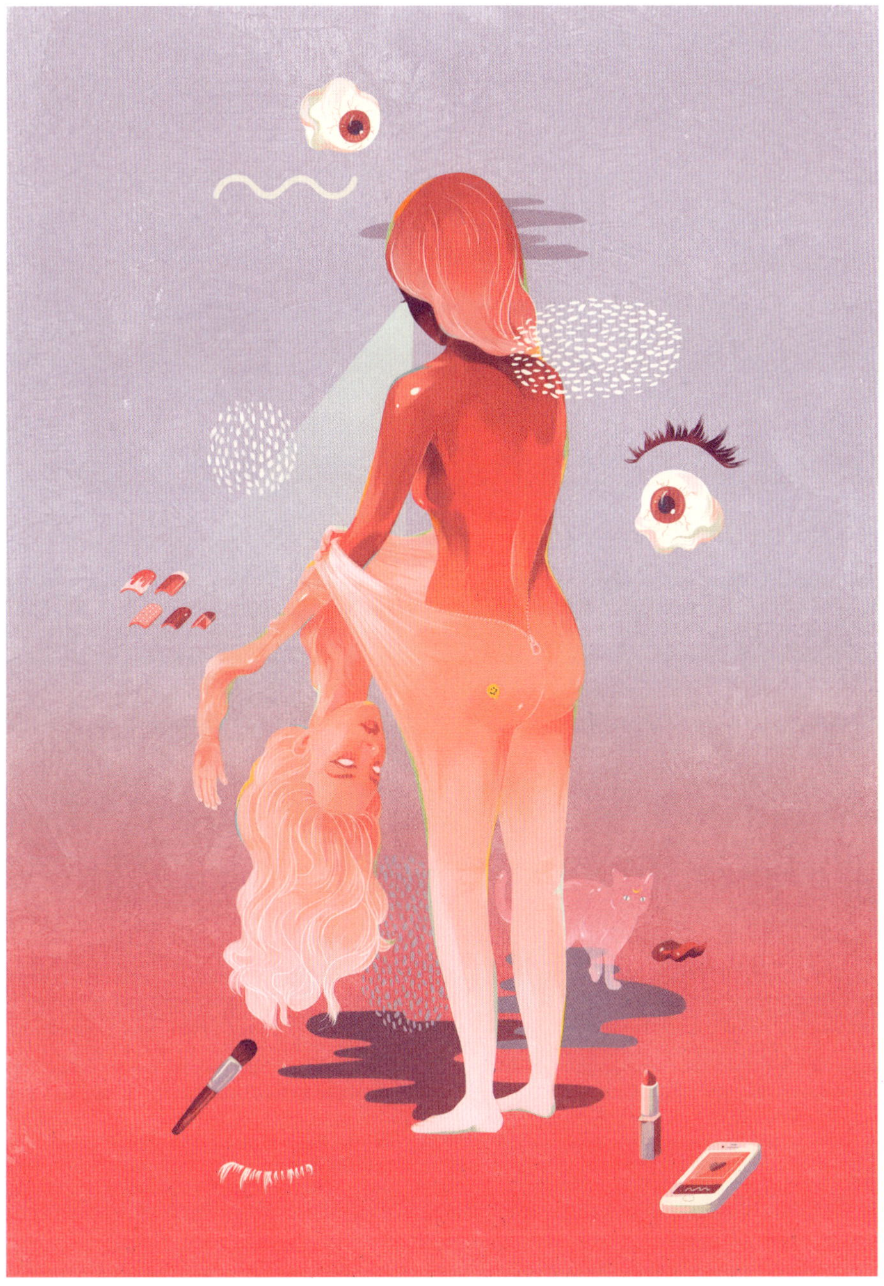

FUTAMONO

Artist: Randy Mora

This artwork was created as a promotional piece for the artist's first collage workshop in Bogotá, Colombia.

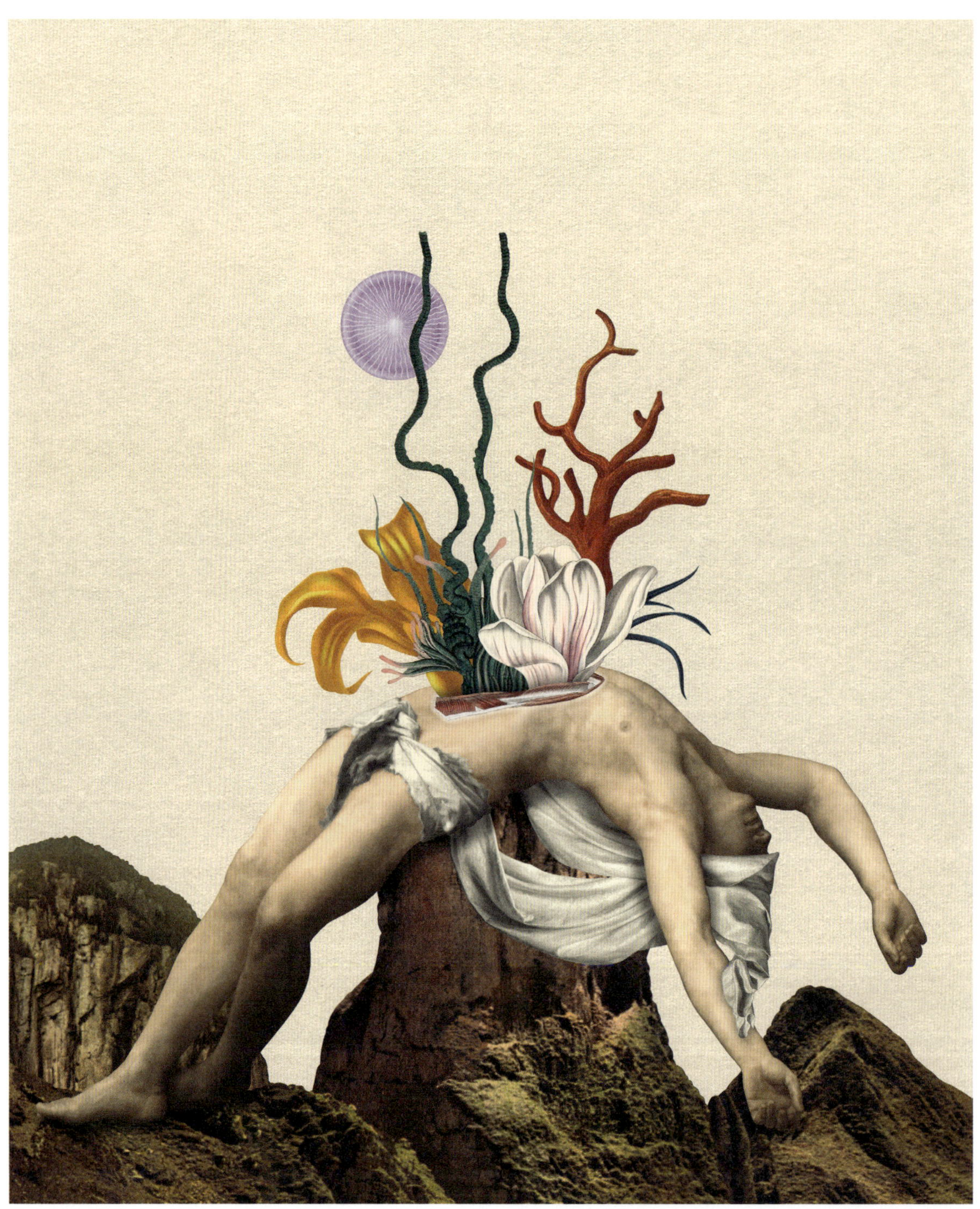

LOVE 2.0

Artist: Randy Mora

This work was created responding to The New York Times' question for five artists of what the past year meant to them and what their hopes, fancies and fears were for the coming year.

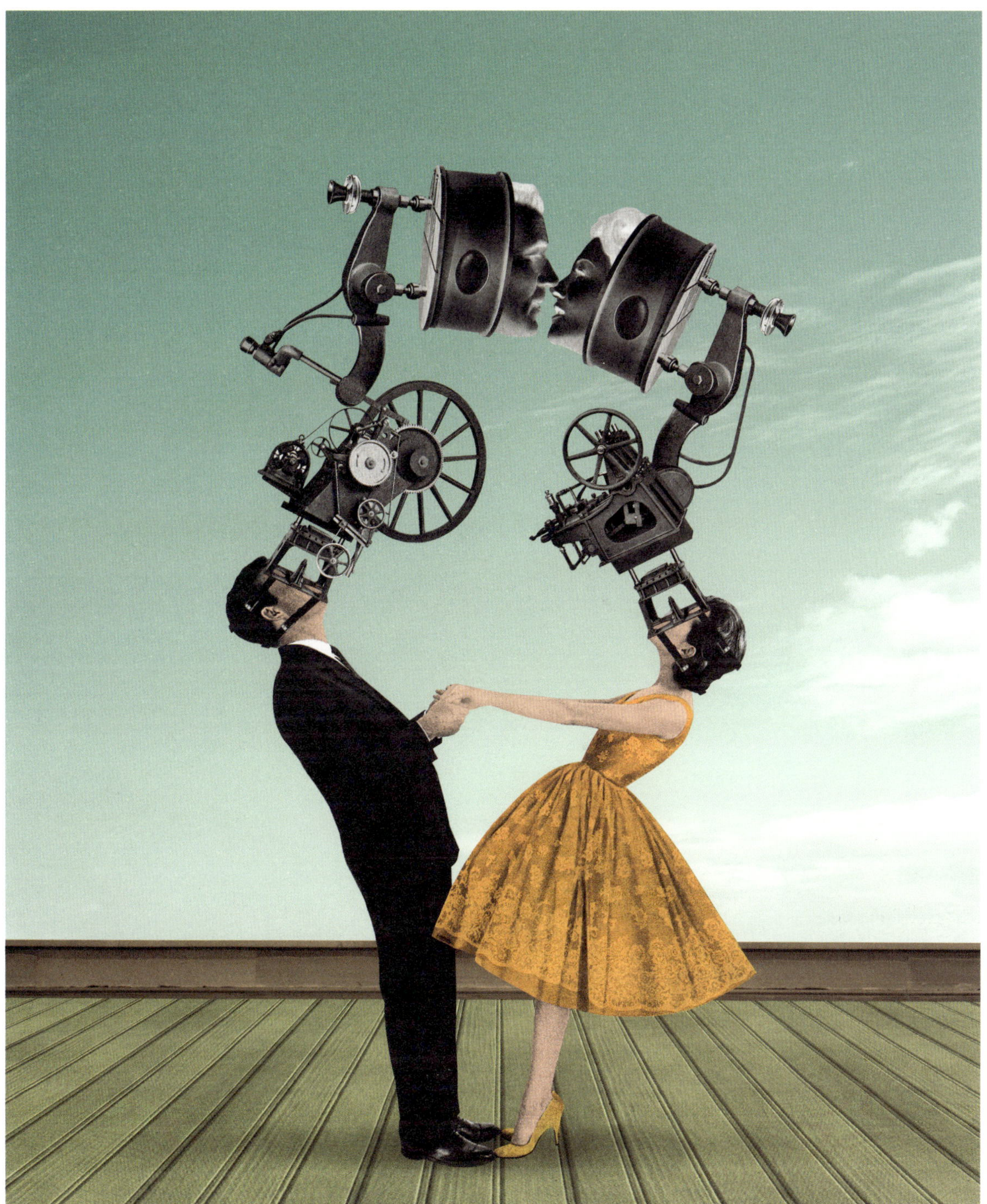

BE READY WHEN HE COMES

Artist: Randy Mora

This is a personal project inspired by the Skip James' song "Be Ready When He Comes".

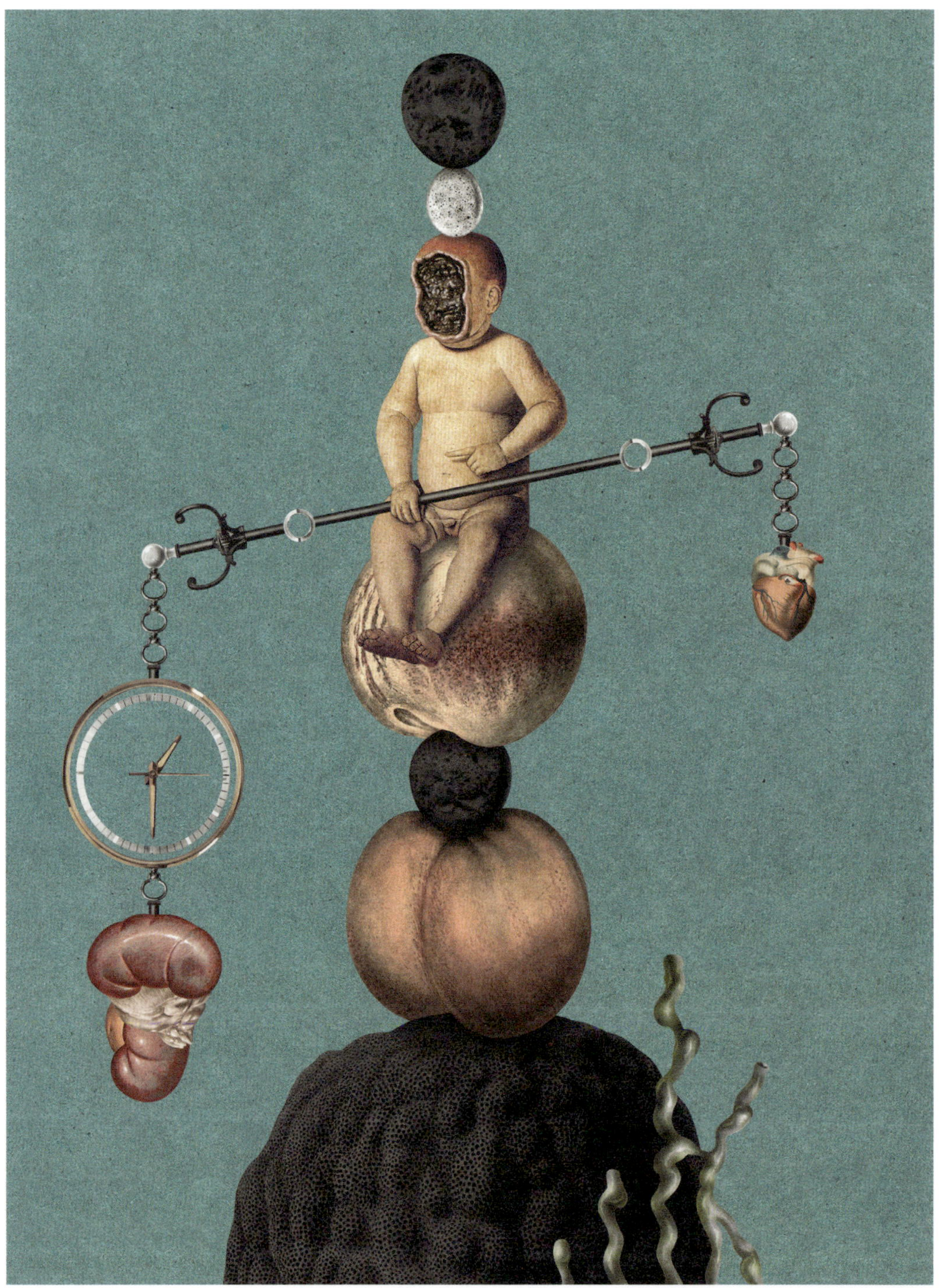

A DOG'S DINNER

Artist: Randy Mora

This artwork is for an exhibition named "A Baker's Dozen" organized by YCN and Ted Baker in its Meatpacking district store. Each participating illustrator was given a traditional British expression to be represented as an artwork. The expression for the artist was "A Dog's Dinner".

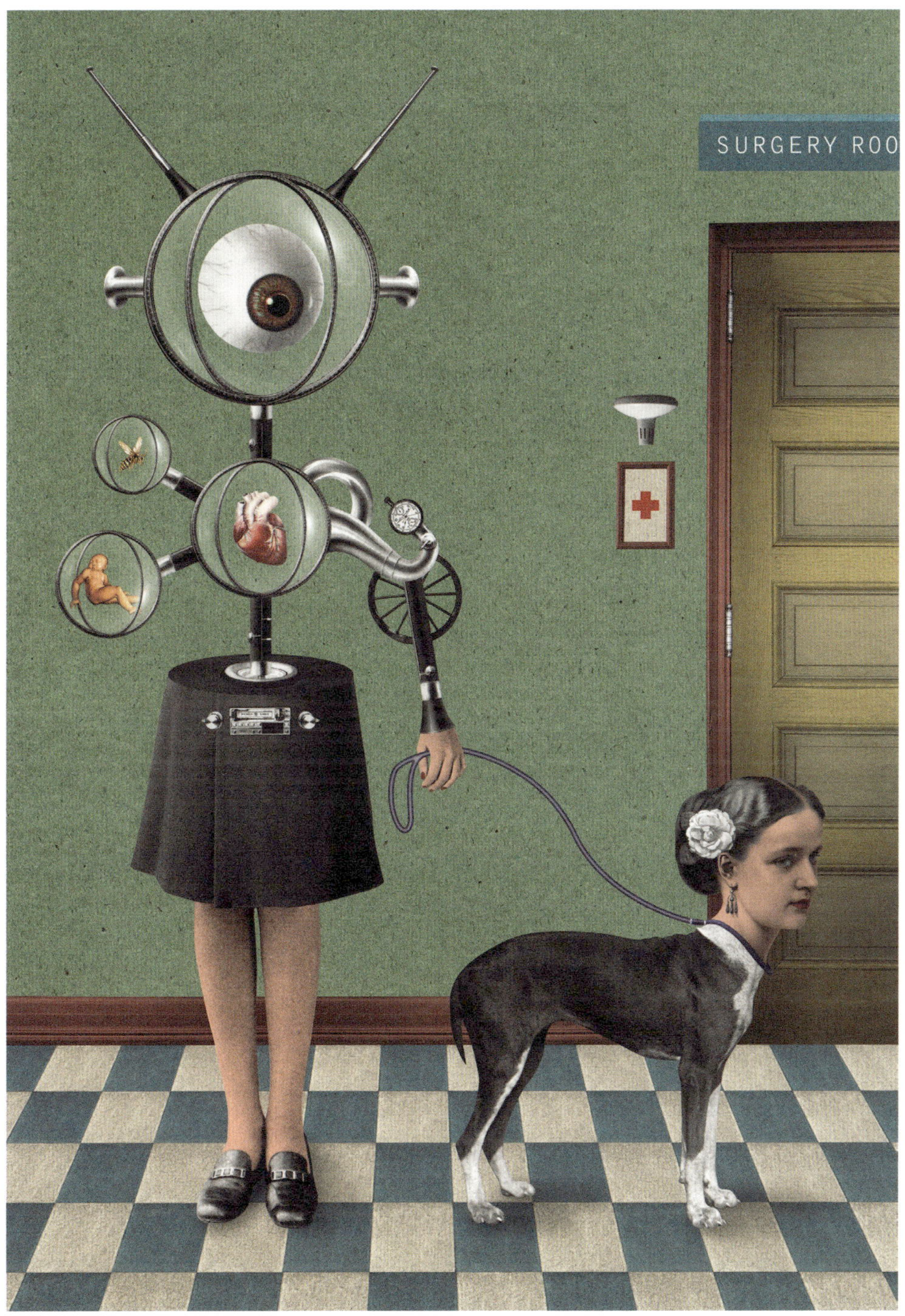

THE CURSED FOREST

Artist: Vlad Stankovic

The Cursed Forest is about a young entomologist who stumbles upon a great discovery in one of the magical woods where its many secrets are kept by various mysterious creatures. The illustrations were created with watercolor and colored pencils and were later scanned and processed in Photoshop.

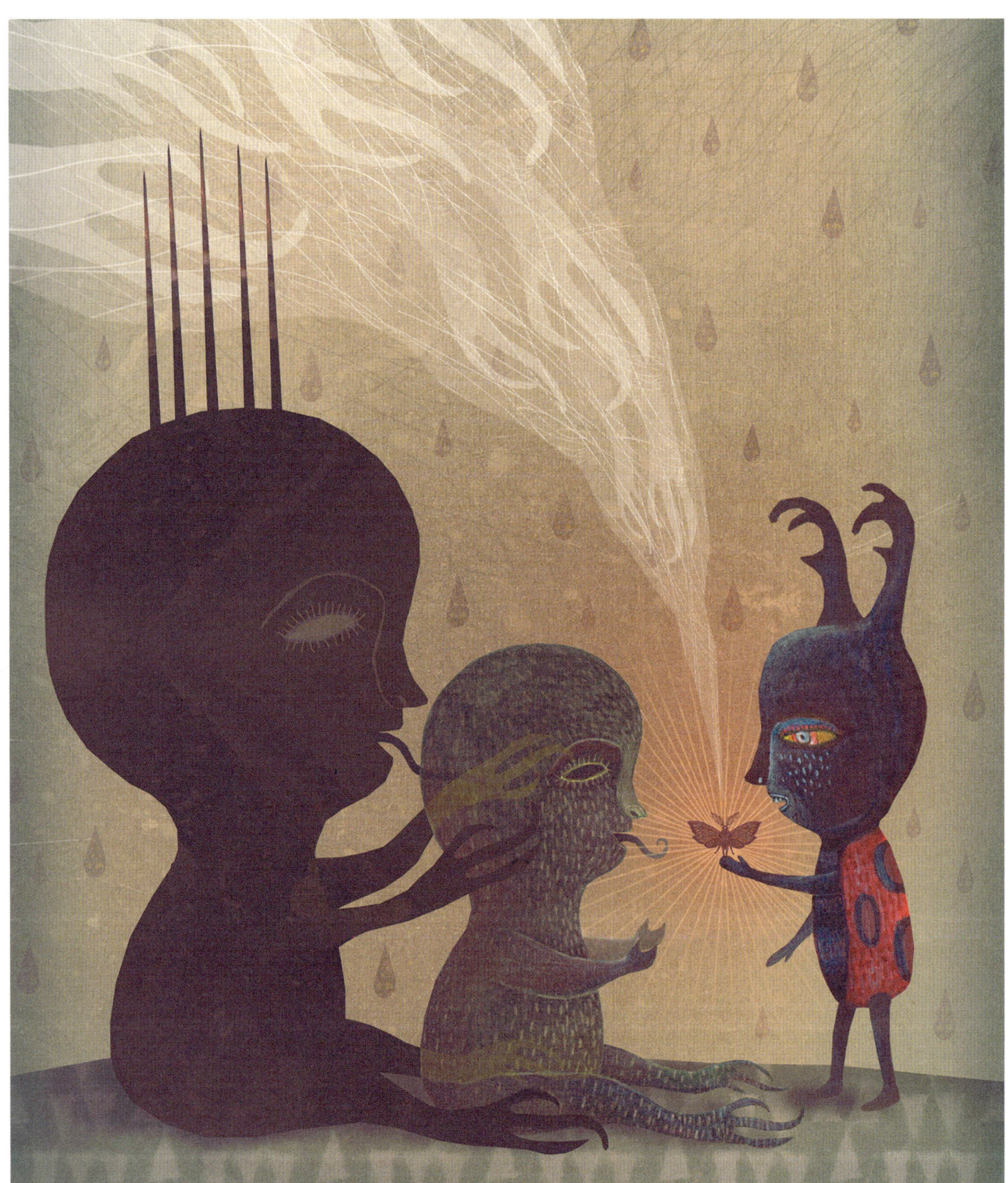

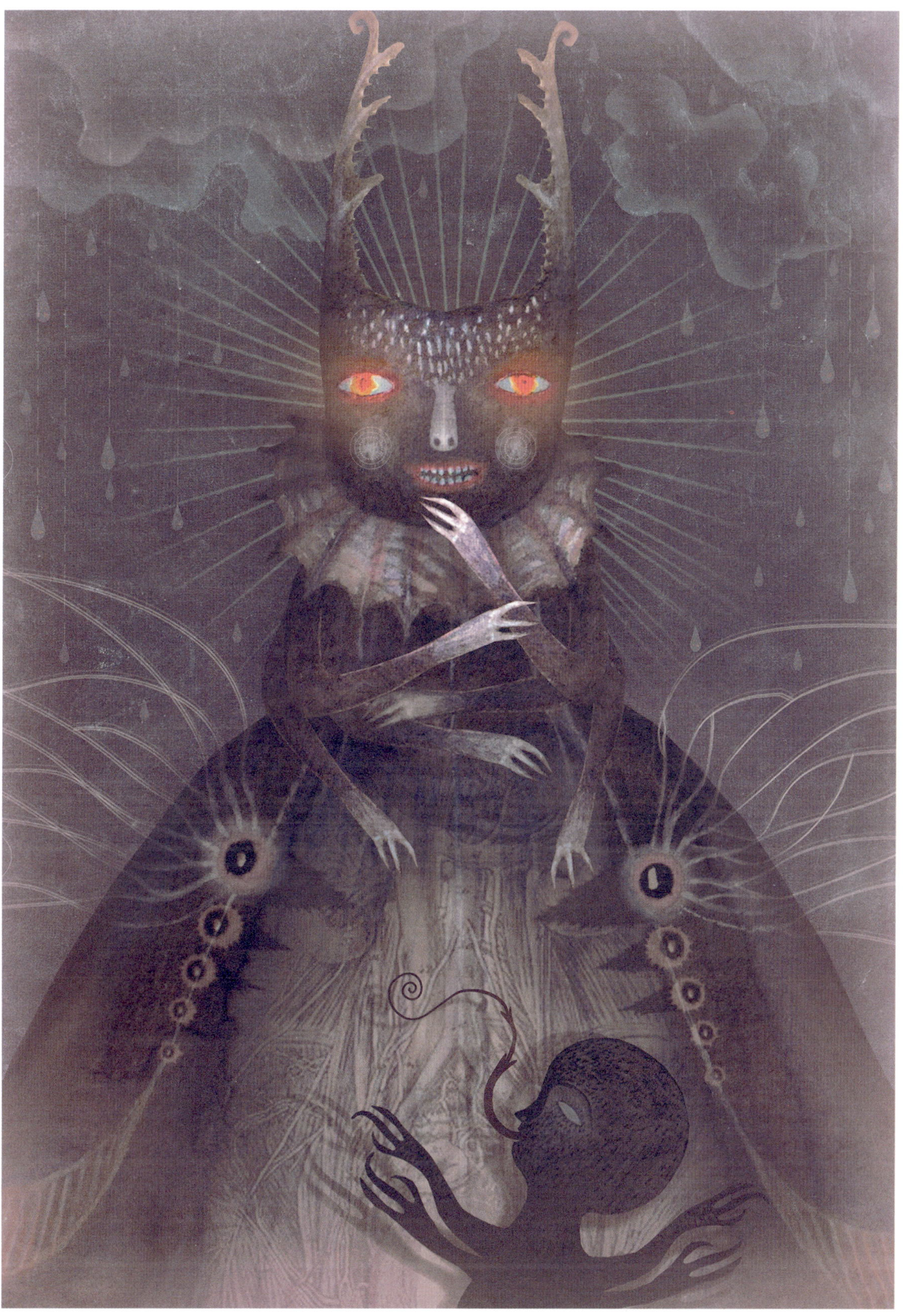

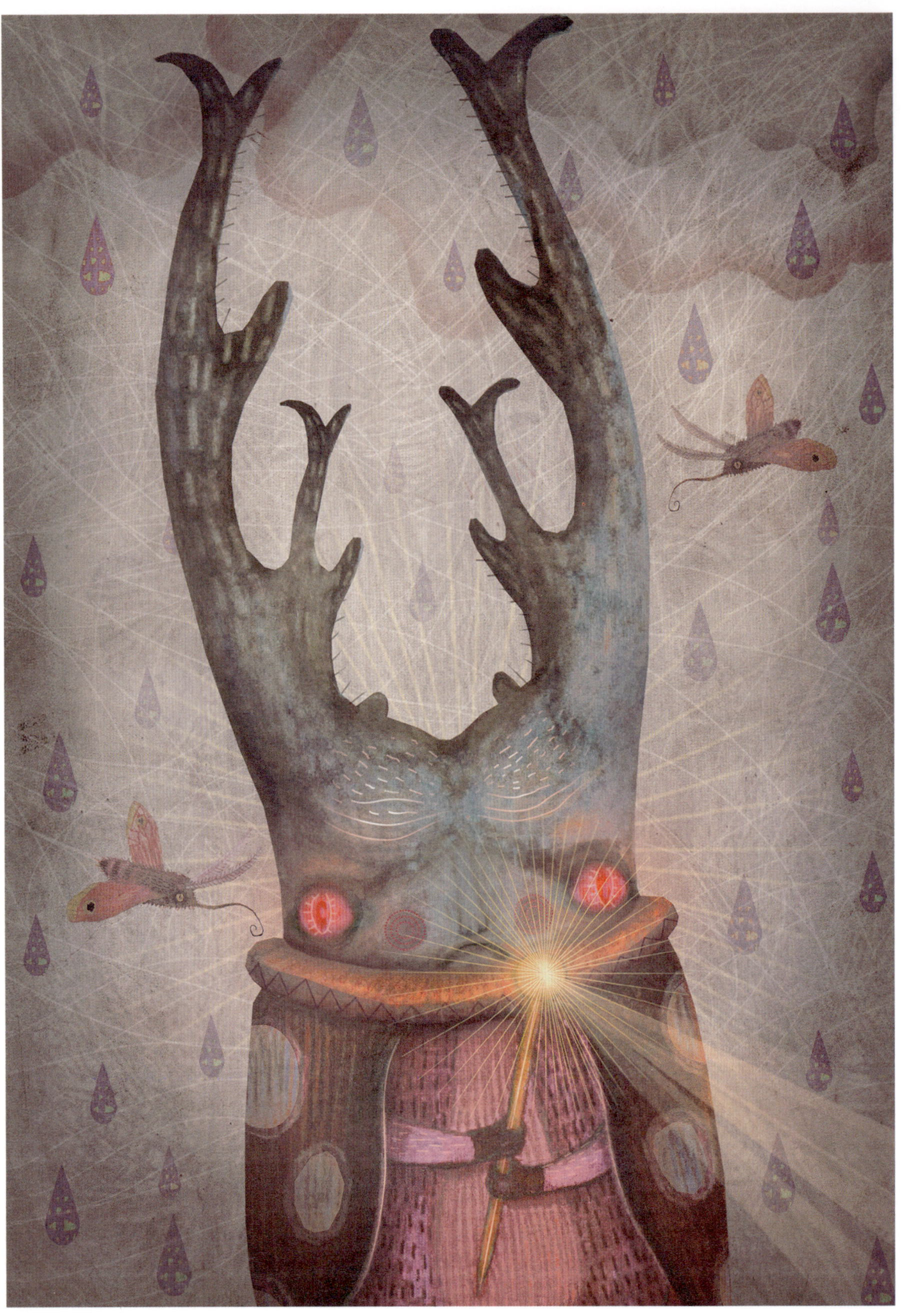

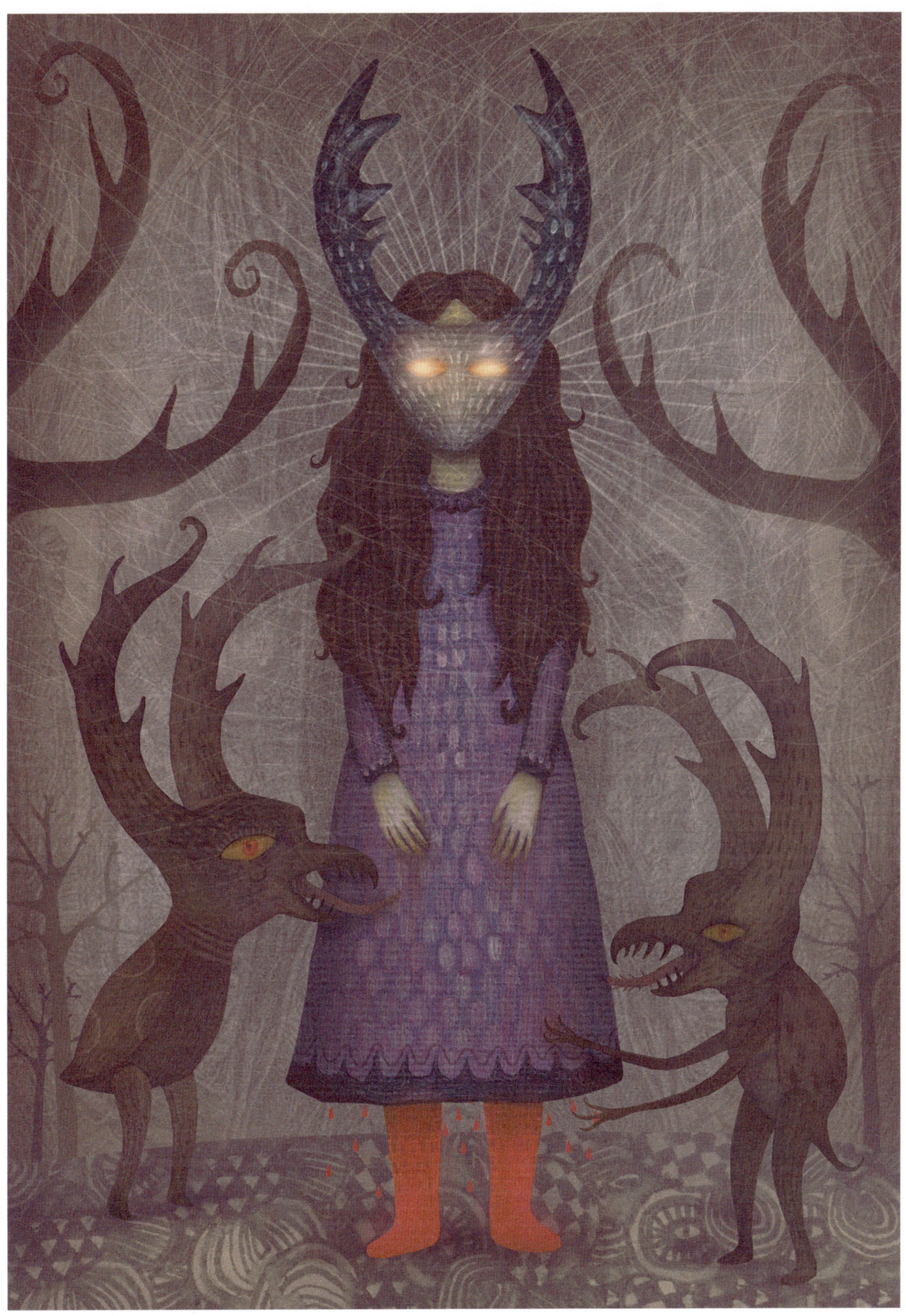

— DEPRESSING —

Depressing images are often seen portraying absurd and surreal scenes and disclosing the vulnerability and helplessness of human beings against negative forces. A gloomy, damp and unclear setting and a cold color palette can also contribute to the pressure such images have on viewers, provoking tension, anxiety and fear.

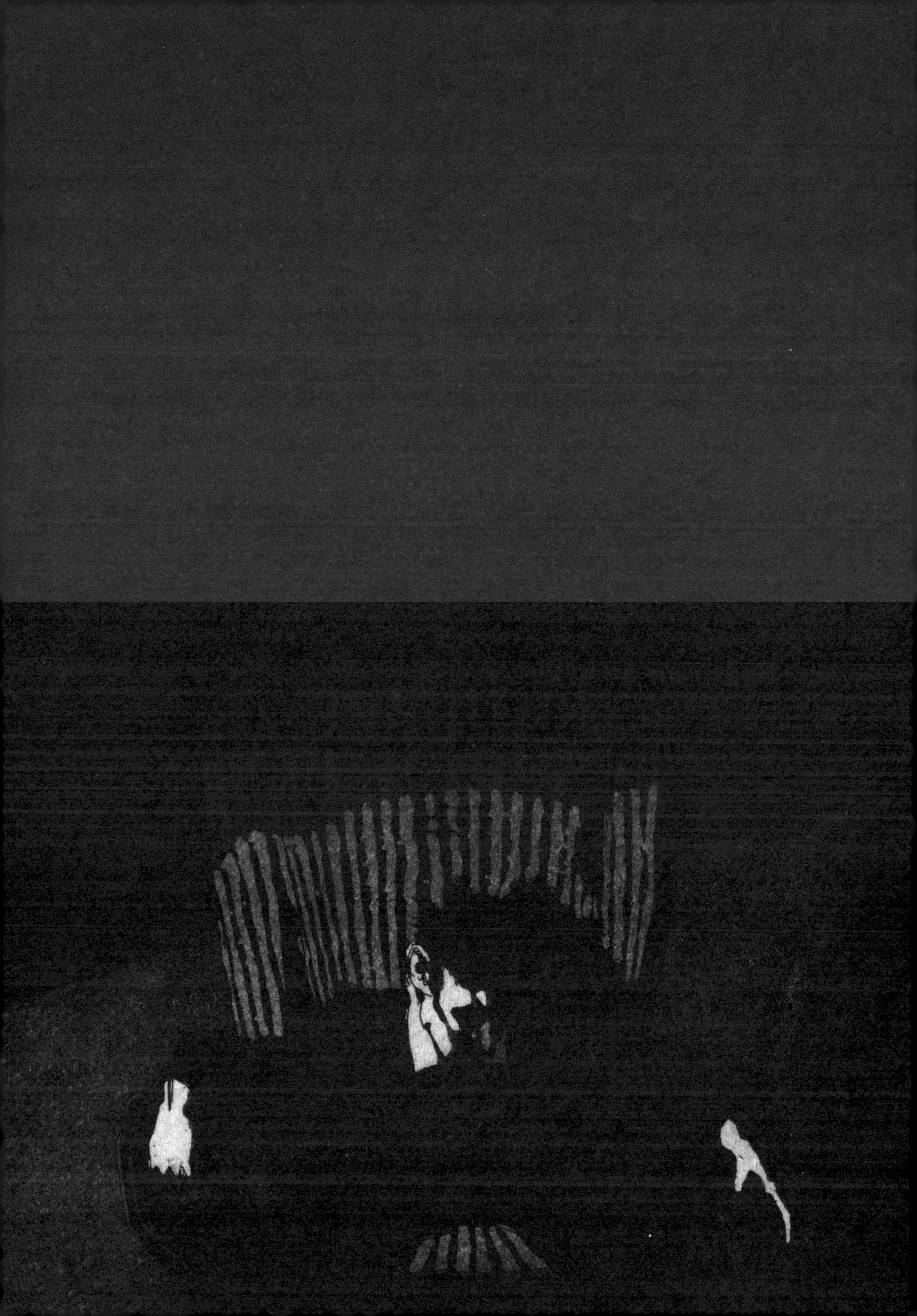

ALESSANDRO SICIOLDR'S PAINTINGS

Artist: Alessandro Sicioldr

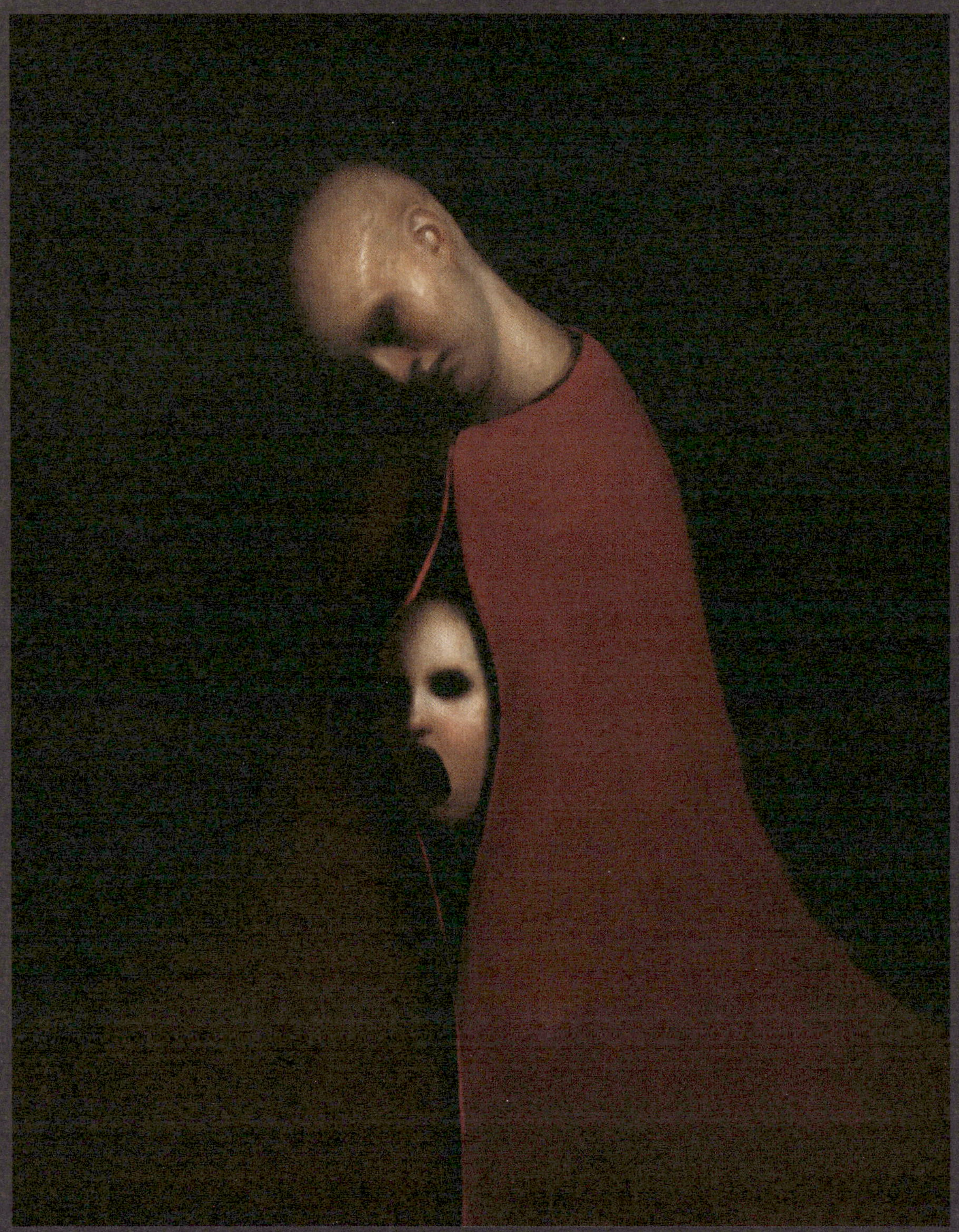

Ombra n.4 - oil on wood

INTERVIEW

Why do you create such fierce visuals?

My imagery is the result of a journey of introspection, a voyage that I make inside my imagination. I have not much power over my ideas. They just come and I manage to recognize them and try to give them a shape using the instruments of culture, taste, and science of classical painting. I only choose to represent some ideas, not others, because some images seem more striking to me. They have profound impact that touches me deep inside. You can say that they are fierce because I don't put any filters. I just follow my fascination without any limit, so the final result can be really uncanny and creepy. I think that they are related to dreams. Dreams are a mysterious product of free imagination. They always communicate inner realities with no filters nor boundaries so they are often a bit scary and weird. They show us fiercely forms of truth that we try to hide in order to be socially acceptable, which is fair, but if you don't accept the existence of the deep and wild part of your mind you are living a life that is not complete.

An artist contributes someway, often indirectly, to the awareness of people's unconscious mind. When something is considered scary or fierce it's because its' not accepted by the spirit of that particular time. But it's important to know and accept all parts of humanity, and art is a great way to exorcize the deepest fears-the unacceptable.

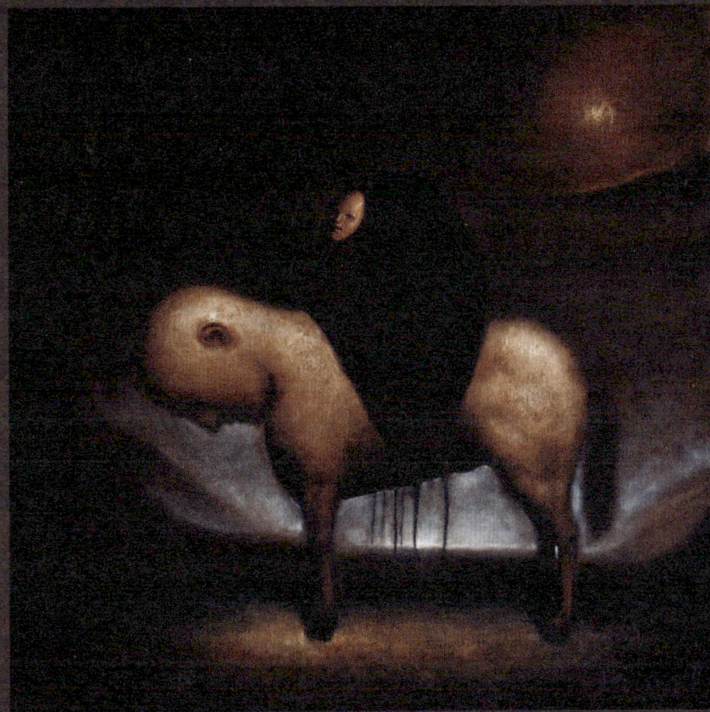

Ombra n.5 - oil on canvas

What are your common approaches to produce a fierce visual effect?

My paintings are often unsettling, odd and fierce. I work with techniques coming from the long tradition of oil painting. I keep a very limited palette that allows me to concentrate on the subject rather than the seduction of color, and among them I use a great amount of dark, earthy colors. But sometimes I love to put spots of intense glazed red, blue or green.

I work without a direct reference to models so the shapes on the canvas are coming directly from my inner world. Like vague shapes in the fog, they come to me, manifest themselves in the painted surface while I start adding details and layers until a tangible aspect has been reached. When I make drawings with charcoal I stop caring about techniques and just follow my instinct, my 6th sense, and I go freely on a large piece of paper. The result is a direct photography of my unconsciousness.

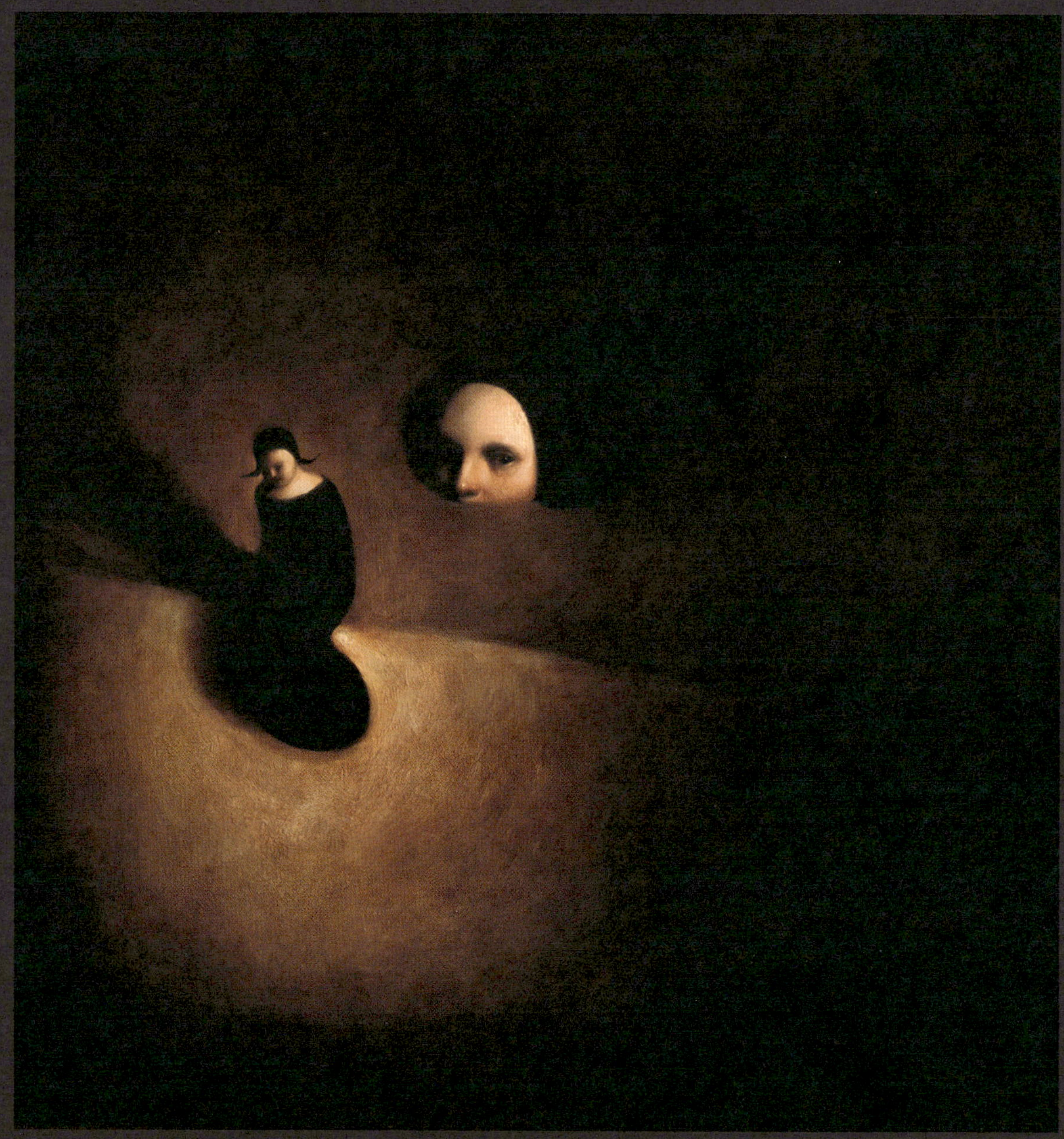

Ombra n.6 - oil on canvas

Where do your inspirations come from?

I don't believe in inspiration, I believe in ideas. They are blessings for human beings: mysterious connections that emerge inside our brains. I have a very deep fascination for them. In ancient times people believed that ideas were coming from Muses, and in my opinion it is a beautiful point of view. We don't own our ideas, they are given to us. We can't choose to have ideas. Our only responsibility is not to throw them away and not to waste these important gifts. Ideas are like seeds and artists are farmers who should take care of them, seeding them every day and respecting their rhythms with humility and patience. I have a lot of sketchbooks where I keep the "seeds" , waiting to transform them into painting. Culture, technical skills and craftsmanship are instruments to give ideas definitive and meaningful shapes. And this, in my opinion, is the duty of an artist.

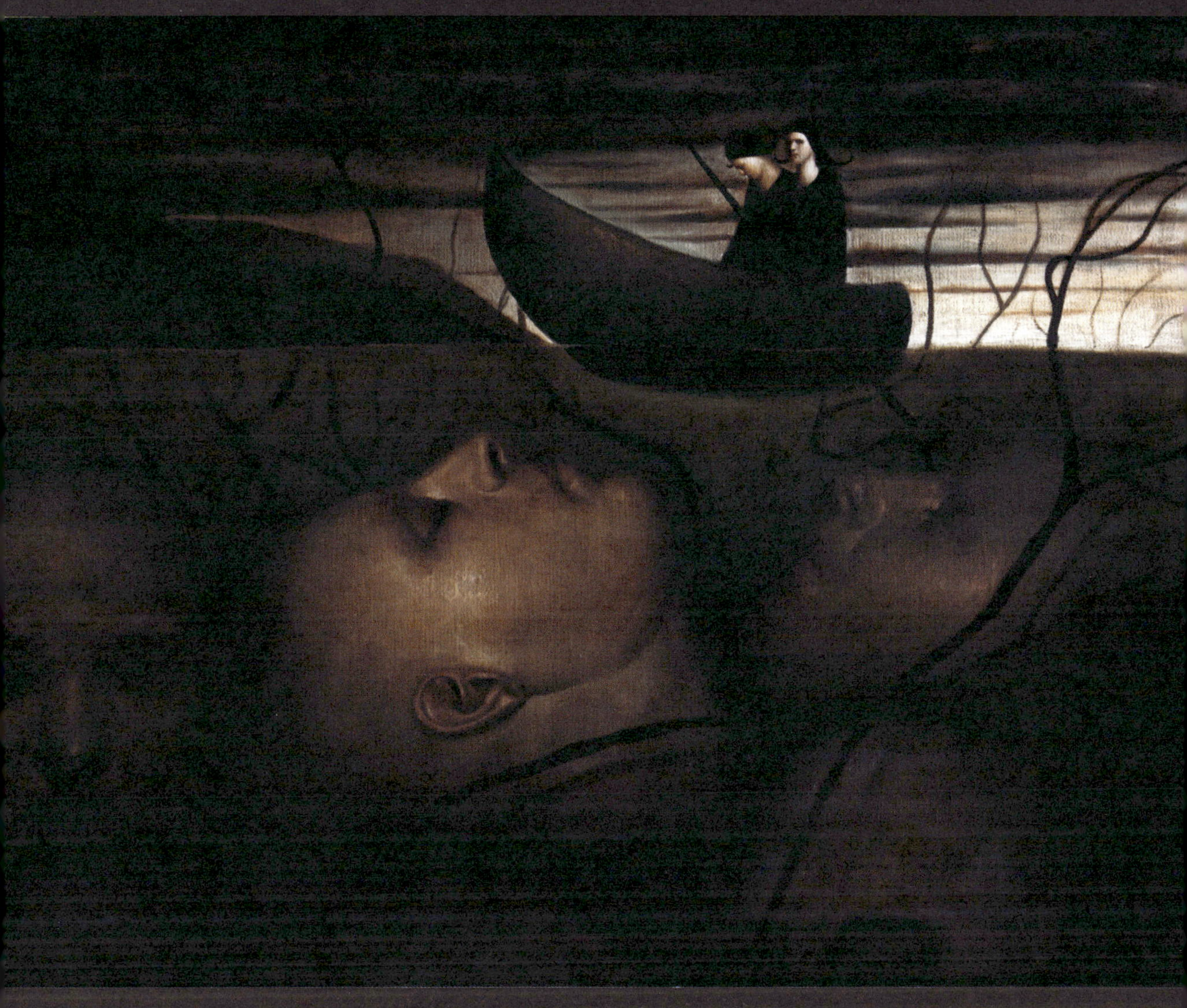

Ombra n.7 - oil on canvas

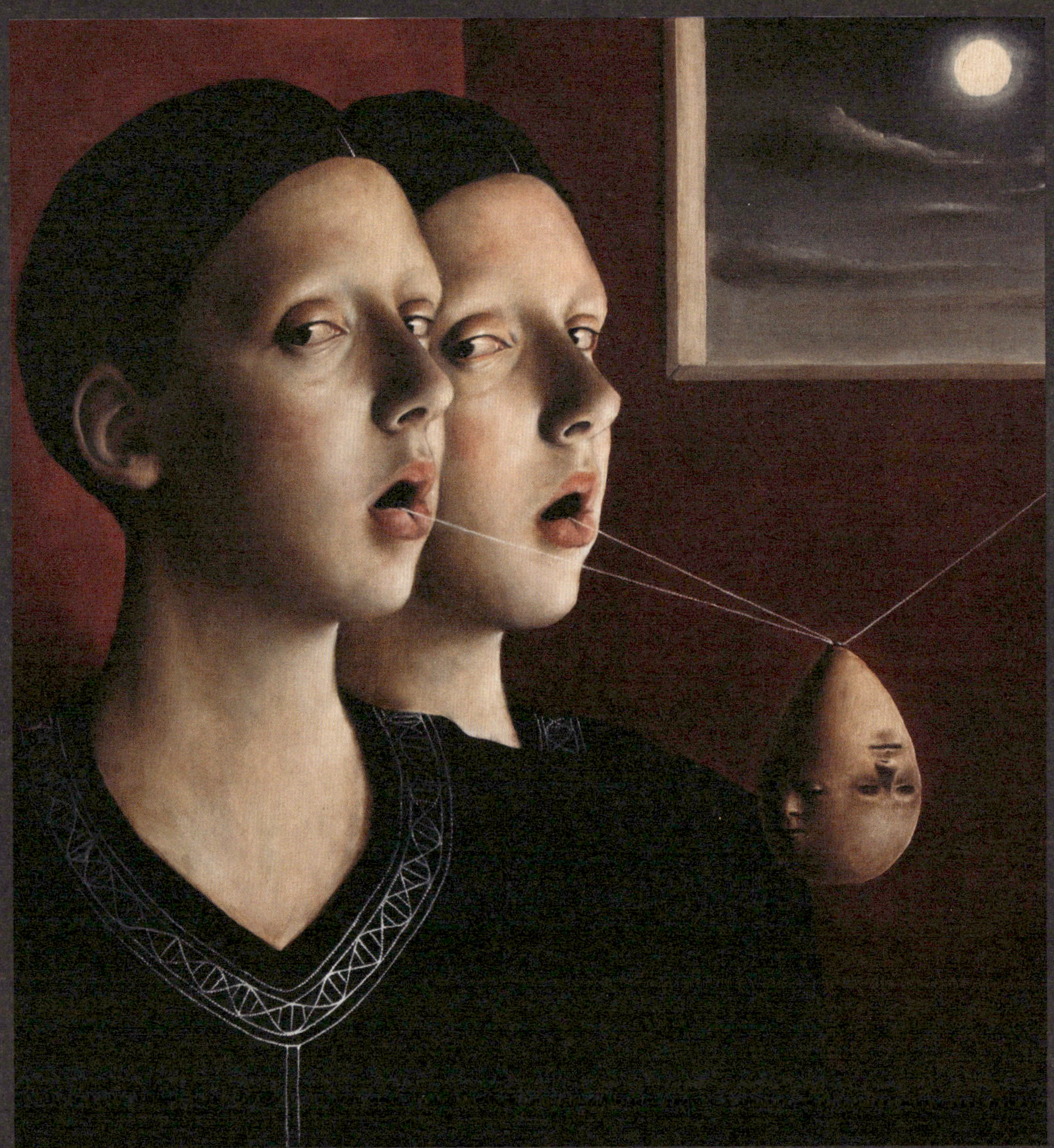

Mystic Egg - oil on wood

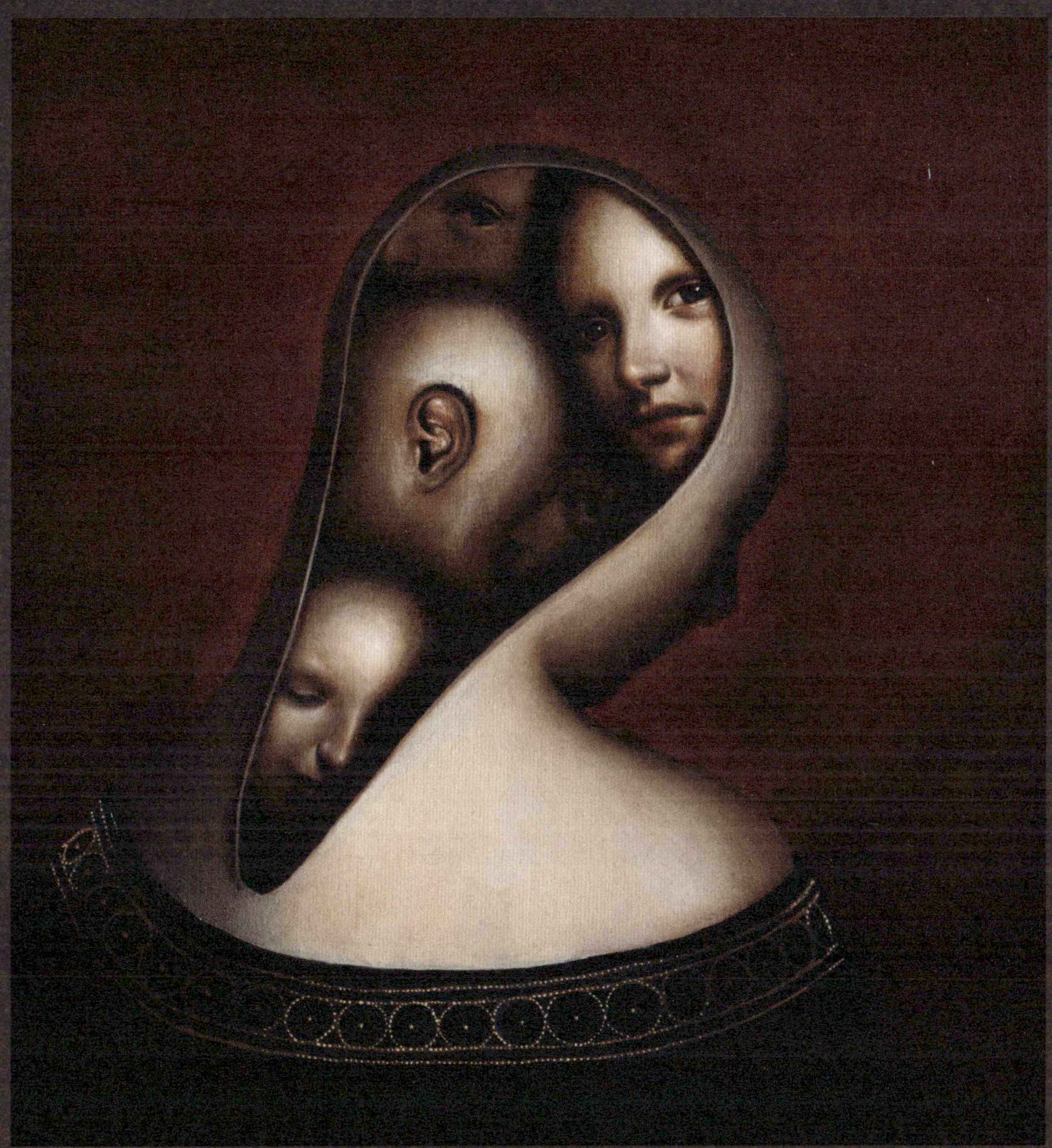

The Other Side - oil on wood

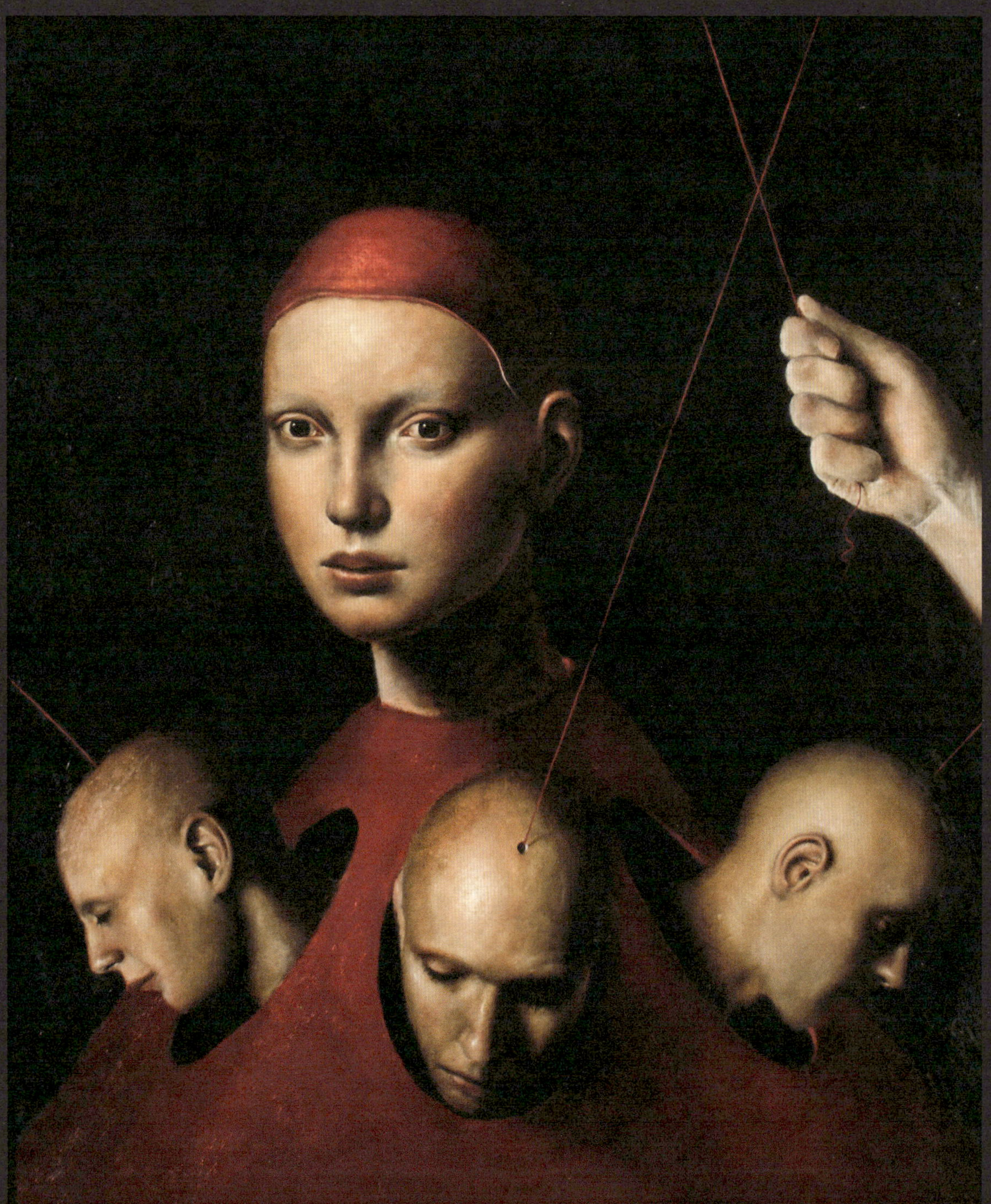

Enlightenment - oil on wood

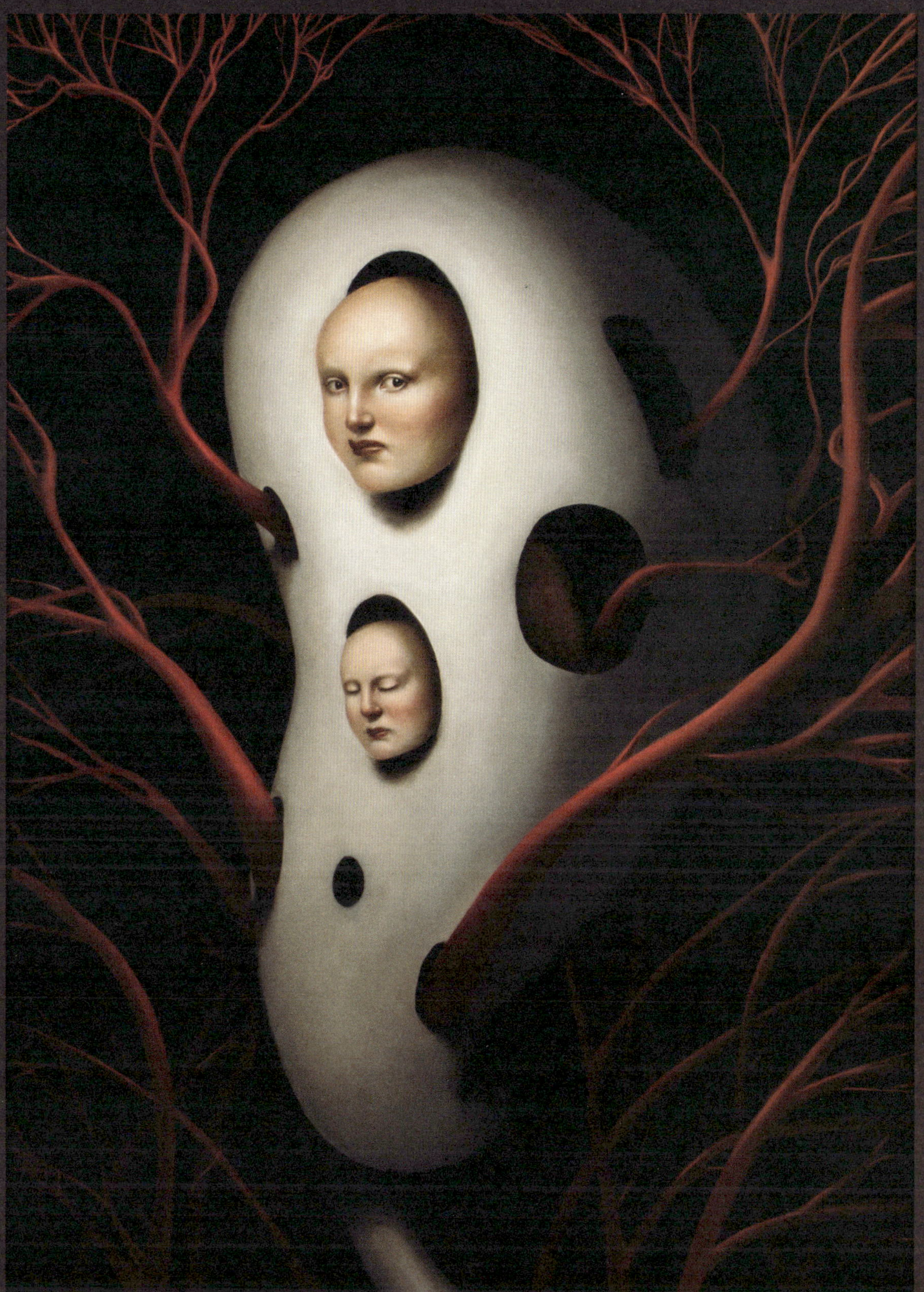

In Utero (The Forest) - oil on wood

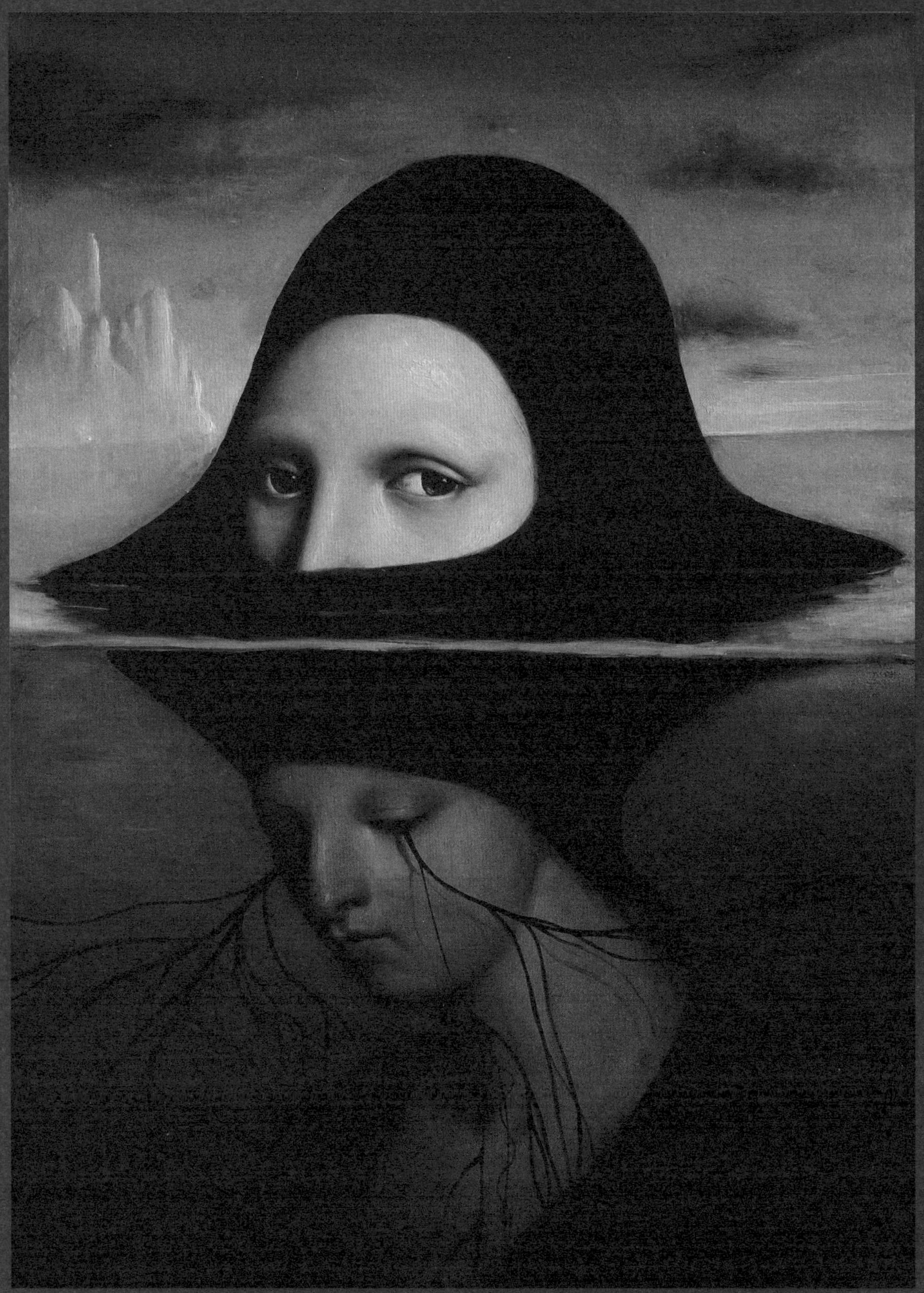

La Sibilla - oil on wood

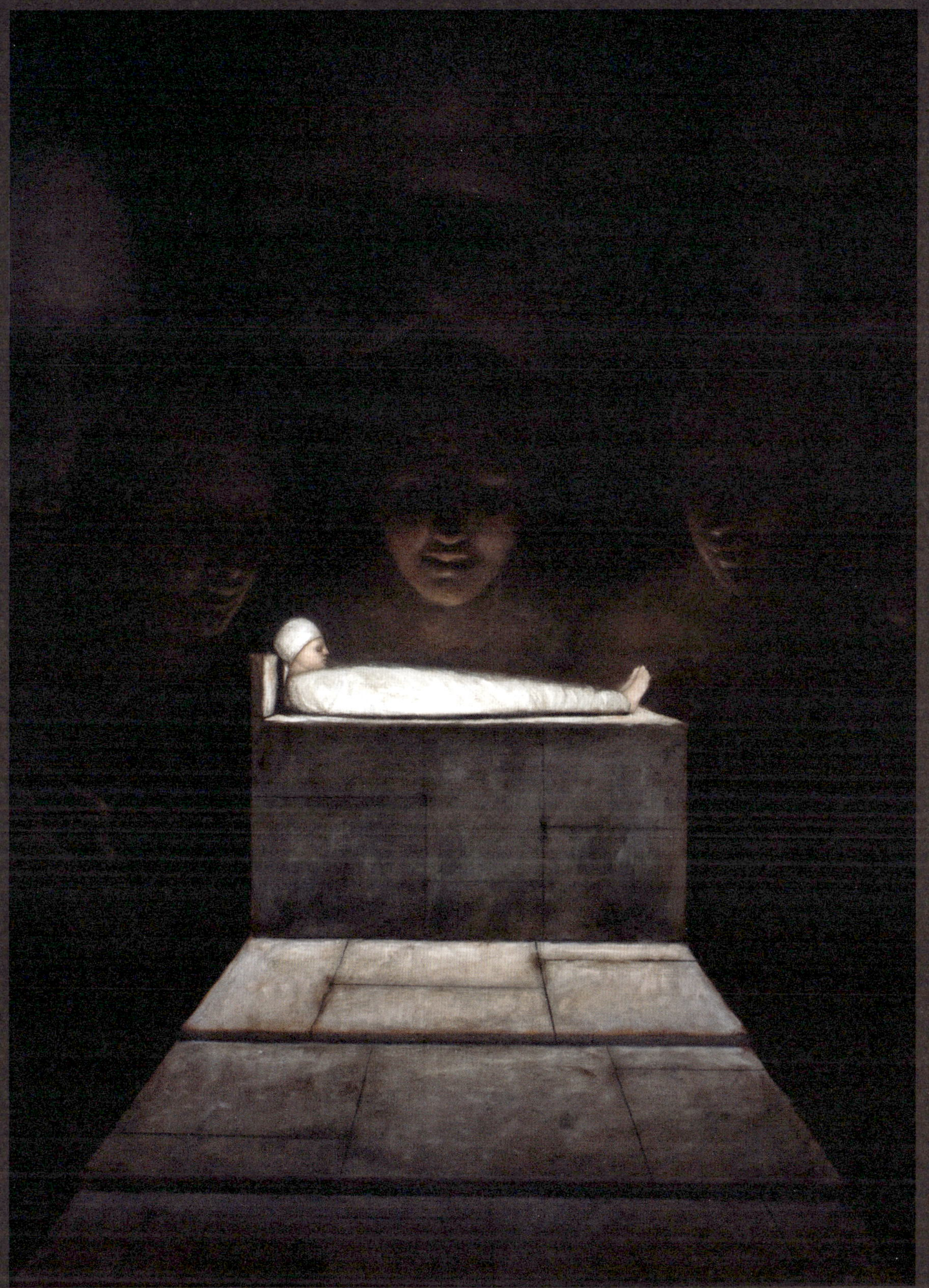

Enigma Del Sogno - oil on canvas

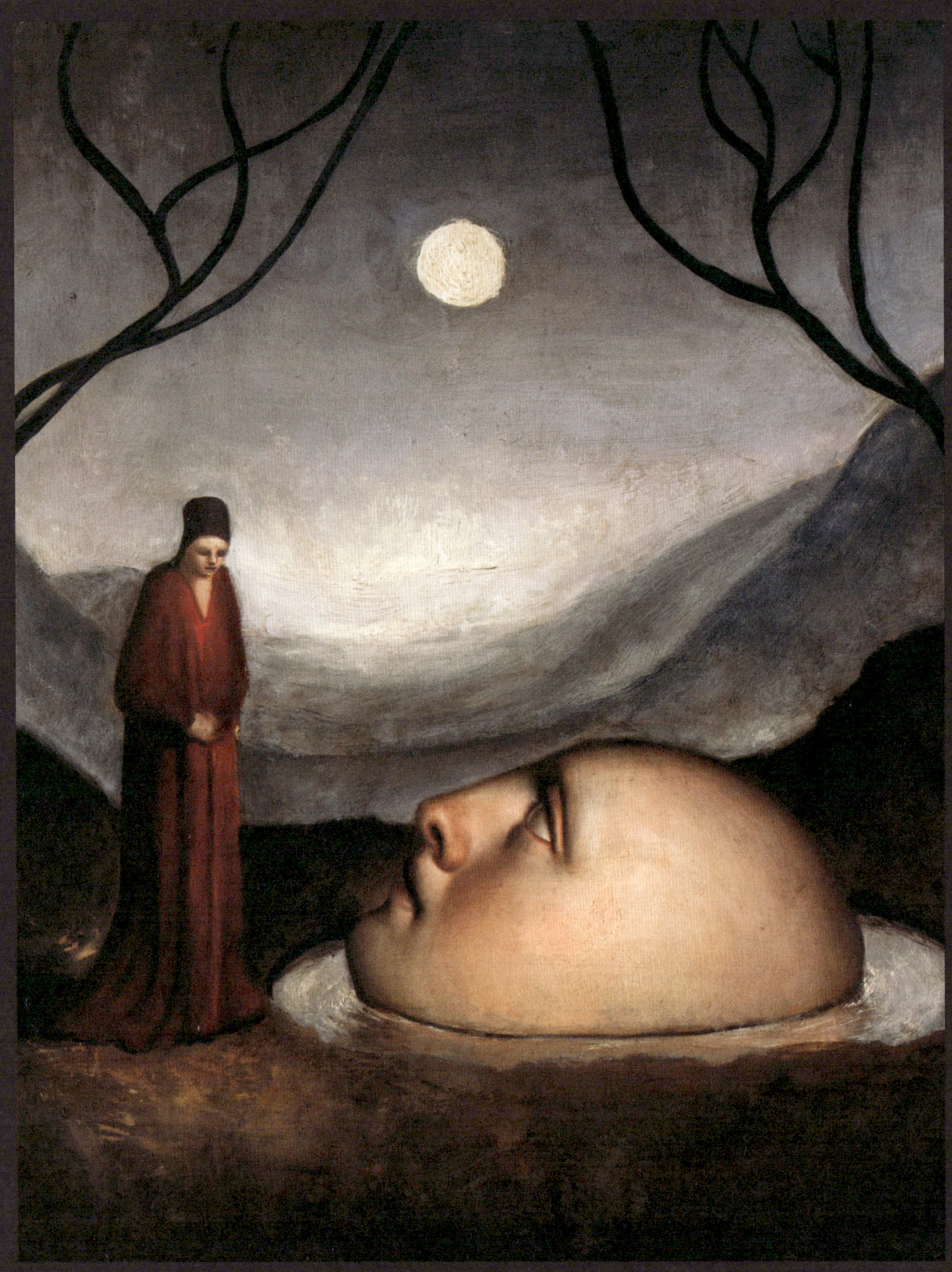

ORacolo - oil on wood

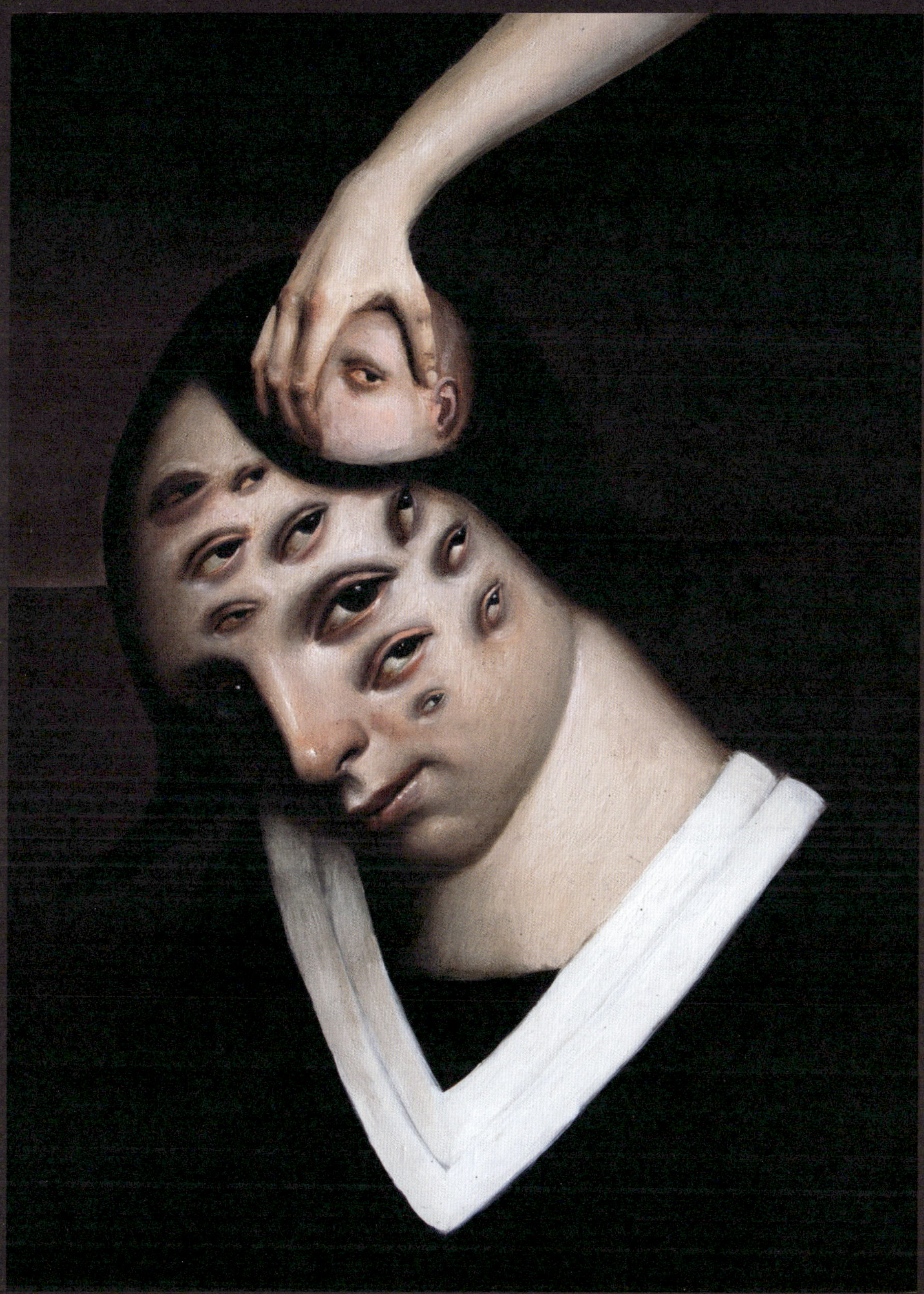

Estrazione - oil on wood

DAYMARE BOOGIE

Designer / Artist: Max Loeffler

Daymare Boogie is an attempt to understand and grasp this raging current called modern life. The black and white illustrations address our imperfections as well as the anxieties faced by all and look at the issues surrounding individuals in society. It's part of "100 for 10", an art book project iniated by Melville Brand Design, in which each issue contains 100 black and white pages.

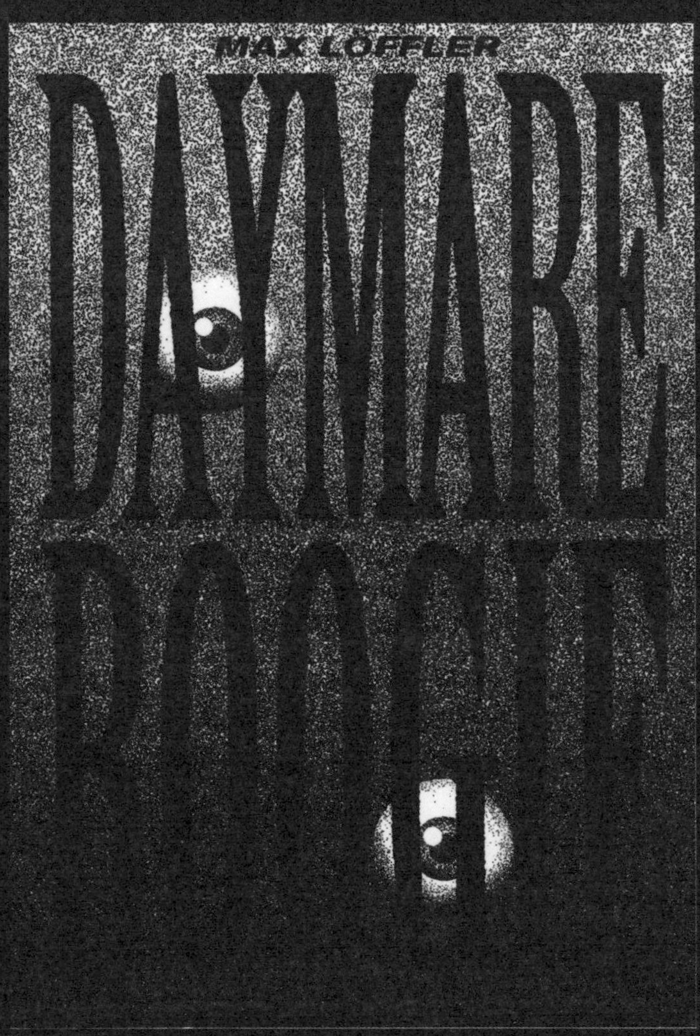

INTERVIEW

Why do you create such fierce visuals?

I think this fierceness derives immediately from my inner self as an individual. On one hand I enjoy wrapping myself with the old, rough blanket called melancholy. On the other, there's a lot of things happening in this world right now which make me discontent or mad. For example I'm feeling overwhelmed by an increasingly fast-paced stream of information and media. For me, the digital era is an age of distraction or dissociation, with social media establishing a "having a good time" digital society in which people chase and display only positiveness. Maybe we need to be more honest with ourselves: accept the full spectrum of emotions instead of hiding the negative parts behind habitual pretending and small-talk attitudes.

So I guess my fierce visuals act in some way as a valve for myself, through which I try to dissociate from the mad things in order to avoid drowning in it. What's even more important is that I hope to call people's attention to these issues and get them to rethink the status quo. It's also a call for reflection.

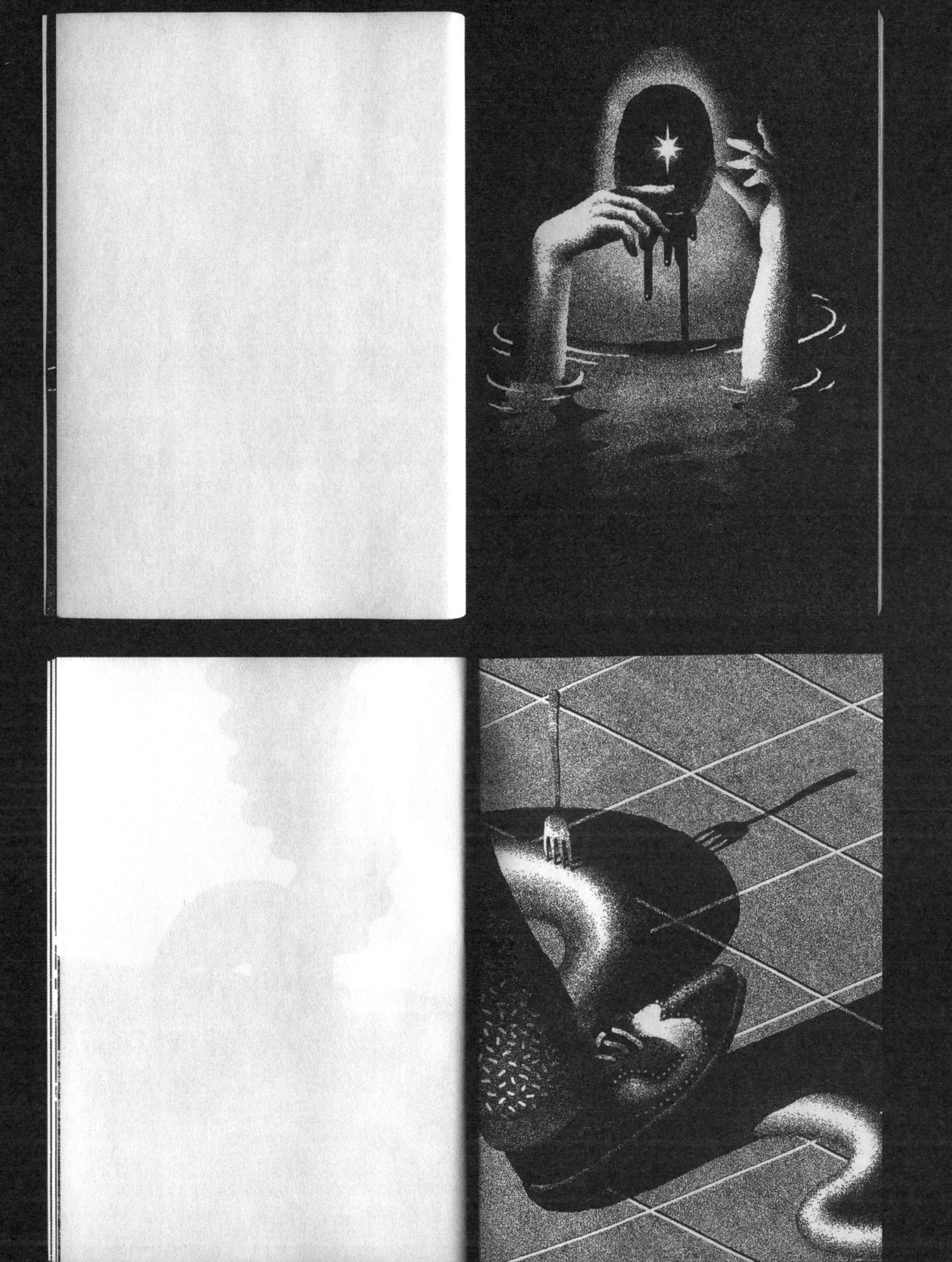

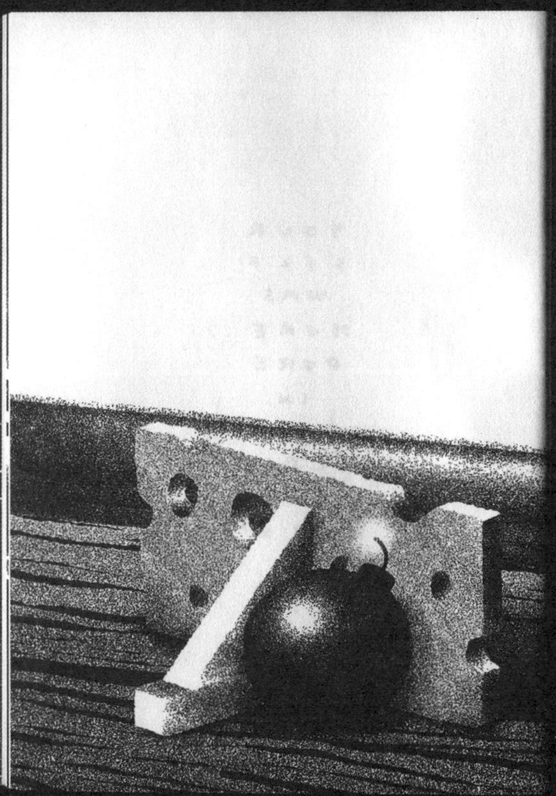
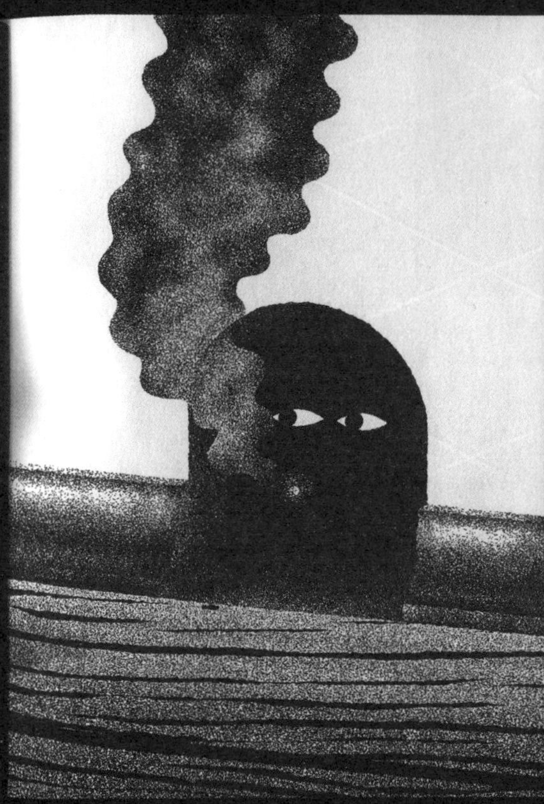

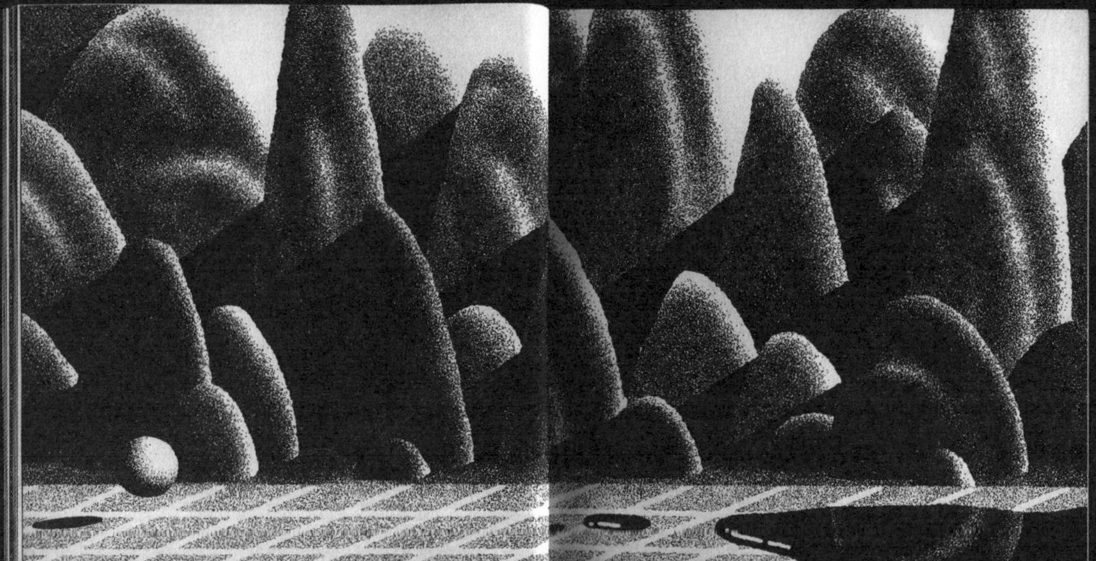

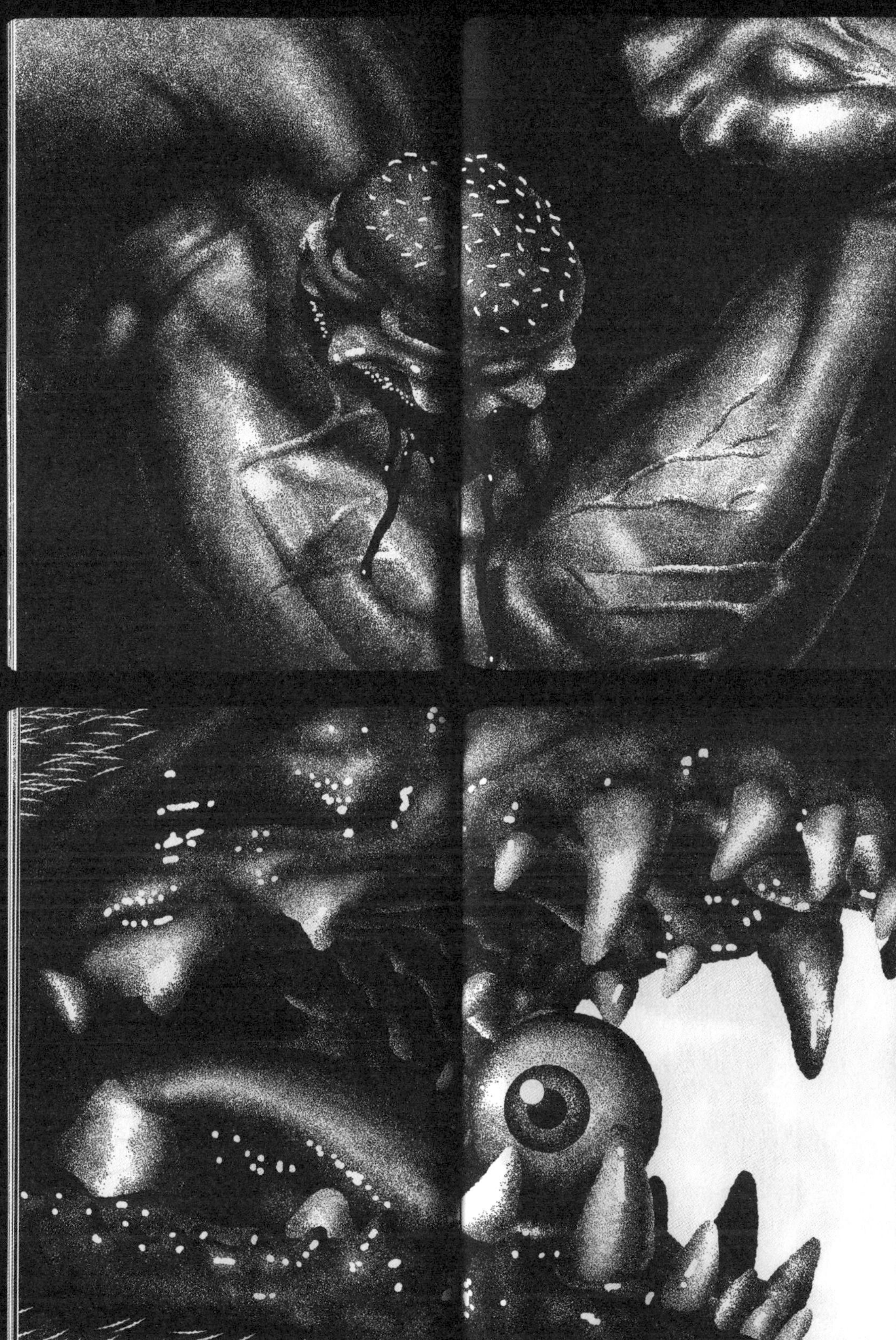

I USE MY HANDS TO PULL MY EYELIDS DOWN AND WATCH THE INSIDE OF MY FACE

Designer / Artist: Max Loeffler

As an extension of Braille Face's 12 album project in 2015, this risograph zine contained lyrics from one song from each of the 12 albums. The designer was commissioned to interpret each of the song's lyrics with a custom illustration. The result was a dark, vulnerable and beguiling take on the 12 albums.

I
USE
MY
HANDS
TO
PULL
MY
EYELIDS
DOWN
...

A zine by Braille Face & Max Löffler

What are your common approaches to produce a fierce visual effect?

I like to create a dark and heavy atmosphere with a lot of shadows and a lot of blacks as well as an attacking language of form. This means I like to depict spiky elements like teeth, knifes, spikes, nails and other nasty stuff, and place them beneath vulnerable objects, e.g. eyeballs. With the color black and the raw grain I'd like to amplify the rough and confronting effect on the viewer.

Anyway, it's more often the case that—as my brain sometimes feels like an old rusty sieve, letting me forget things and lose memories—my approach is a rather visceral one. But this also means that I realize only afterwards—if at all—what the meaning of a piece could be. In any case, it's always far more exciting to learn what a viewer sees in a piece than talking about what that work means to me.

Where do your inspirations come from?

A big (if not the most) influential discovery may have been Moebius(Jean Henri Gaston Giraud). I deeply adore his otherworldly imagination and sense for amorphic shapes. Speaking of Moebius, I recently discovered his mate Philippe Druillet, who is such a master at creating fantastic worlds as well. Talking about the French, it's the Belgian Painter René Magritte whom I owe a lot to when it comes to disassembling things and rearranging/thinking them through in a new context. A list like this wouldn't be complete without the magical landscapes of Eyvind Earle, who inspires me when I look for a language of form with this certain fantastic retro vibe. Another source of inspiration that can't be missed is films by Hayao Myazaki! Hard to find words to describe his sublime pieces of animation magic! Explicit recommendation to watch them all!

DISTANCE FROM DEPARTURE

II.

Distance from departure
Temporarily faster
If it takes you to leave
Just to see all the doors you closed up

Finally we are much quieter
The sound of this ageing disaster
Silence speaks through the walls for fifty kilometres

Please take what you need

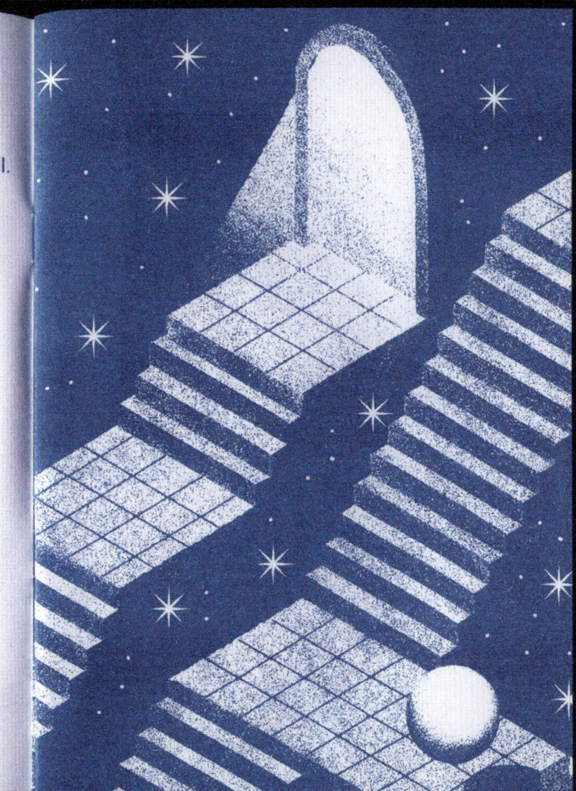

RAIN FALLS WITHIN ME

III.

I wasn't afraid
Deep in those entrapment parades
You couldn't, you wouldn't complain
Why we're drowning in all of this shade

Silence come around me
The rain falls within me

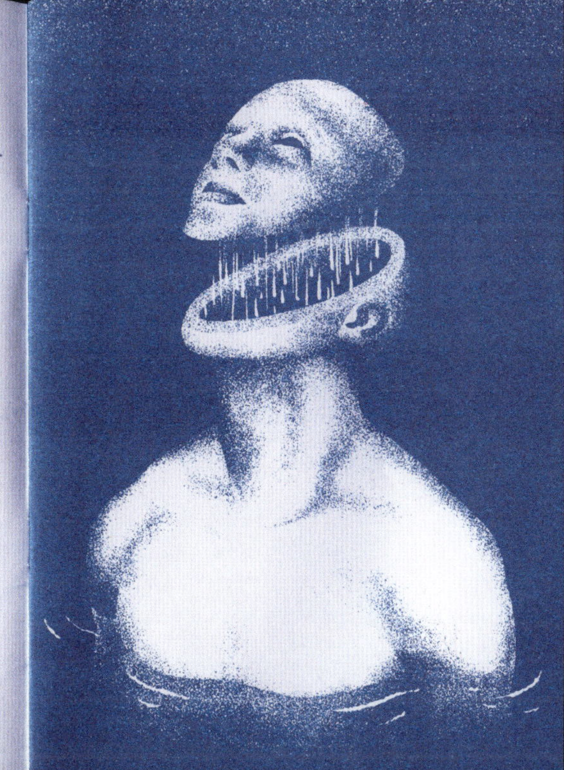

COLOURED PEN

V.

With your father's injury we all thougt he'd be okay
All the fairness of the world would let him down,
Before your face would break my heart

Drawing pictures of the world
Through waving lines and coloured pen
There's a fear I have inside,
never clear if it's mine or theirs
At least I'm here with you again

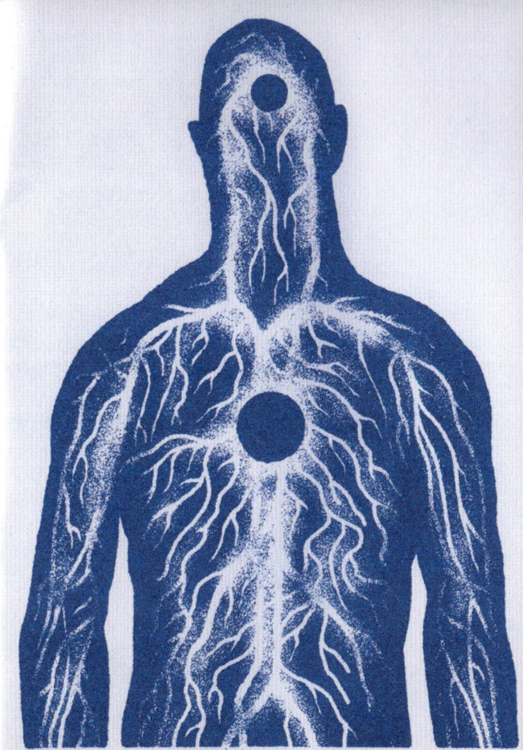

YES/NO

VIII.

I cannot let
I cannot beg
When you barter, child
With your waking life
When the sleeping giant
Takes me home to bed

We don't want your war
We don't want your war

Take the petals off,
Off one by one
Yes no yes no yes no yes no

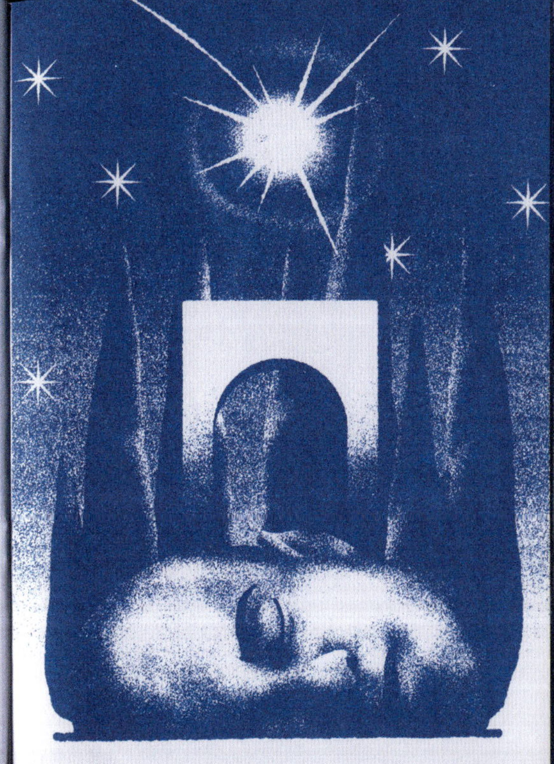

KINDNESS

XI.

Backslash, the forward takes the best of me sometimes
It helps me move back to the centre
This rant could break the night in spite of what you heard
You don't need to tell me that it's over

When does what you missed in front of you
Have anything to do with me?
When does what you need wake you from your sleep?
To shake you? It shamed you?

Broken lines carved in my hands, estragon's fortune
Have I told you I can't wait forever
Can you pull the rabbit from the box you left it in
Is this a trapdoor or a mirror?

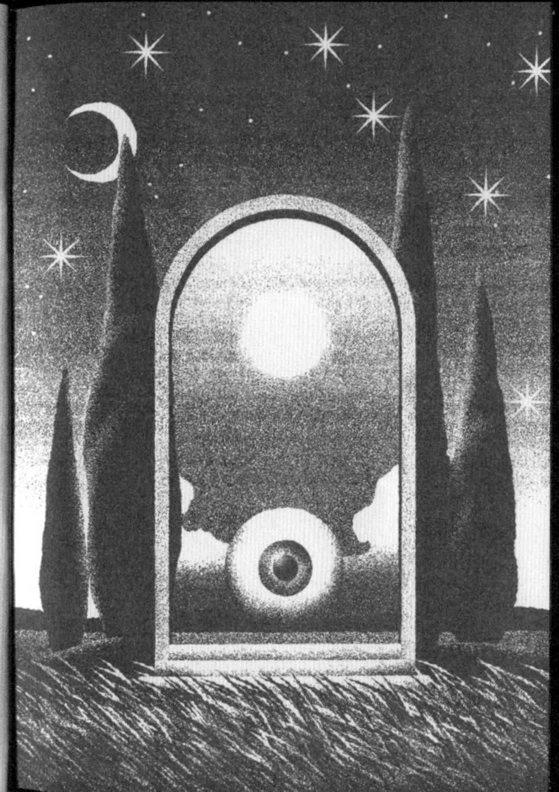

LEVER

XII.

New face to the same talk
Next mouth on a string
Old limbs remain fickle
Pull this lever to sing

I'm surprised by the folly
That's blown about like a leaf
Old nerves will be tested
Pull the lever

I can't believe what you see

New stride of the same walk
Same slip of the peel
Got parched in the ocean
Caught lapped at the heels
I'm a pawn you can place me, wherever you feel
I'm your guts on the sidewalk
Pull the lever

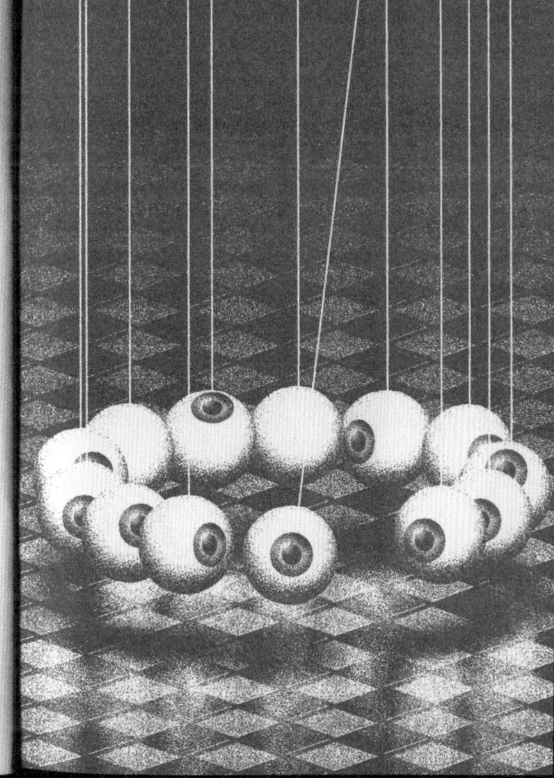

EL SORPRENDENTE MÉTODO ADIVINATORIO DE MADAME MALHEUREUX

Designer: Daniel Santiago Dubin

This scheduler was designed for people to organize any kind of project where random conditions are involved. The project, segmented in different goals, will be laid on a board where specifically design tarot cards would then be used to determine every goal's destiny. Since its use introduces random factors, mishaps and accidents that may occur in the process, the divining character of this scheduler was designed for a fully understanding of the final duration of the project. The scheduler consisted of tarot cards, eight cards of accidents, a book of interpretations for the arcane, magnets, and a metal folding board.

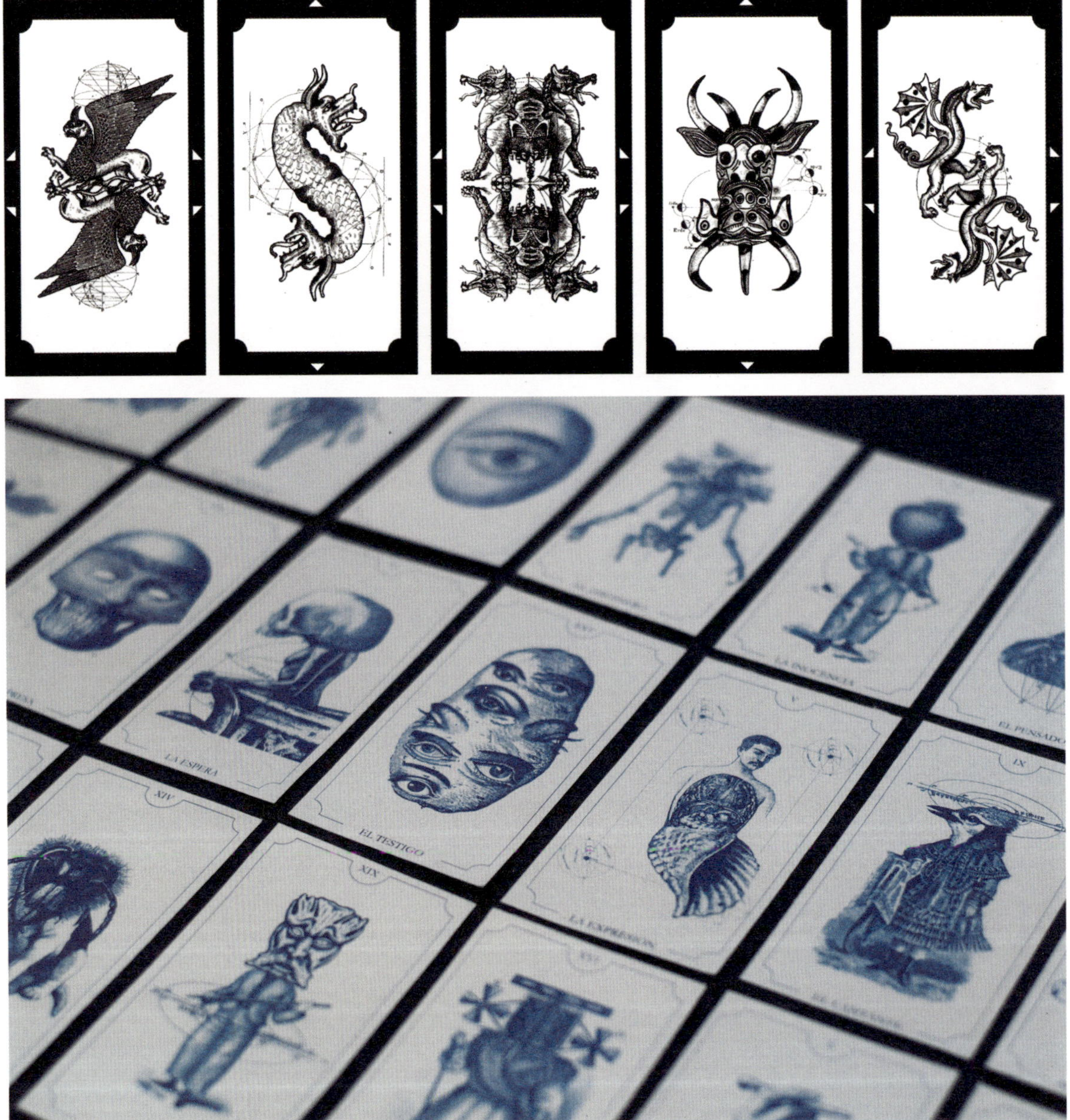

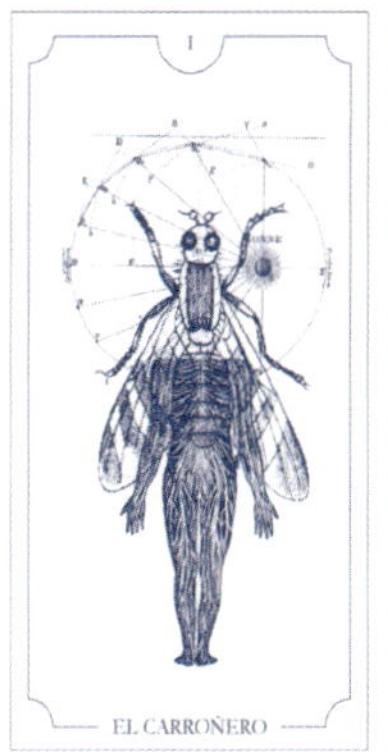
I
EL CARROÑERO
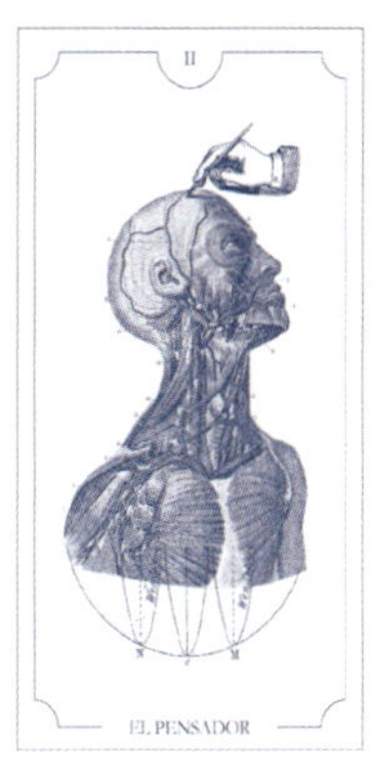
II
EL PENSADOR
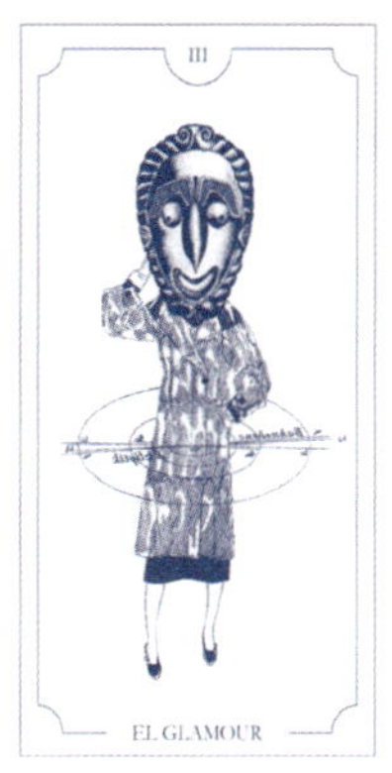
III
EL GLAMOUR
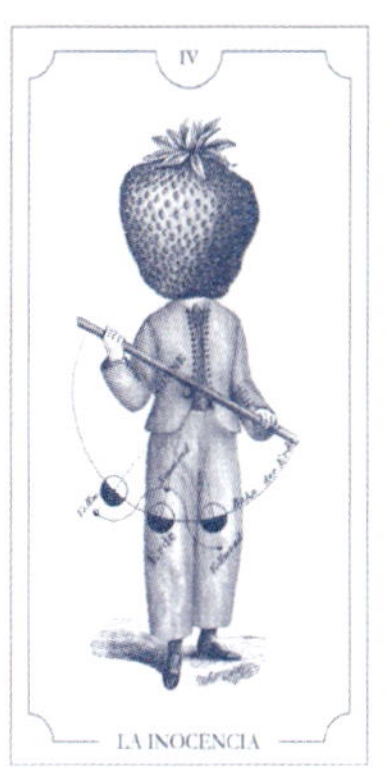
IV
LA INOCENCIA
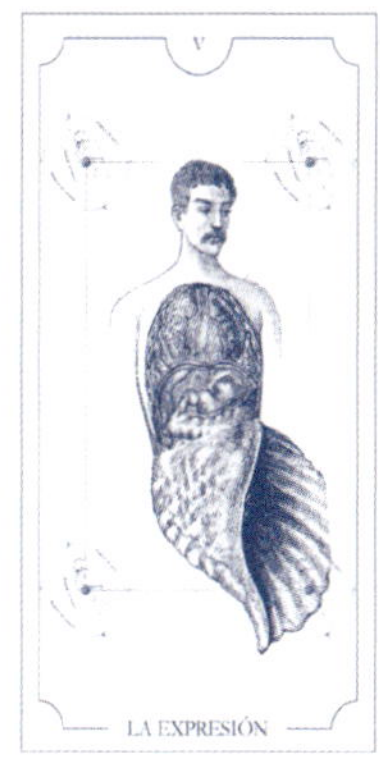
V
LA EXPRESIÓN
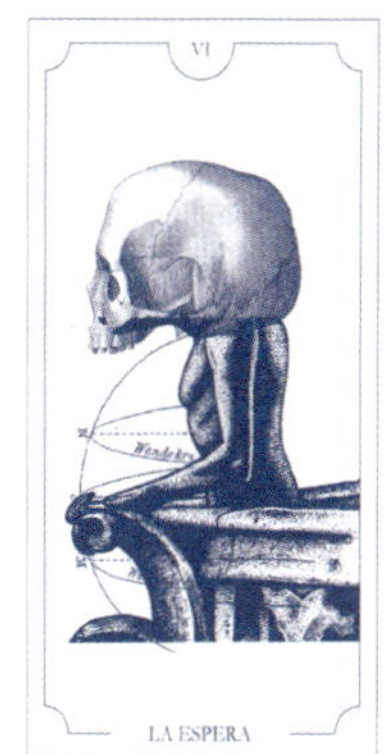
VI
LA ESPERA
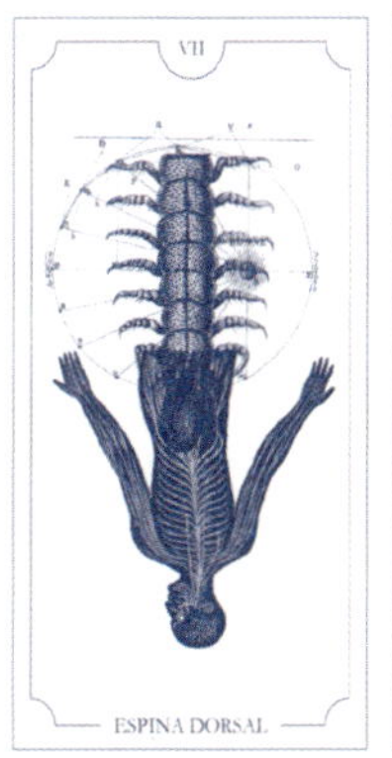
VII
ESPINA DORSAL
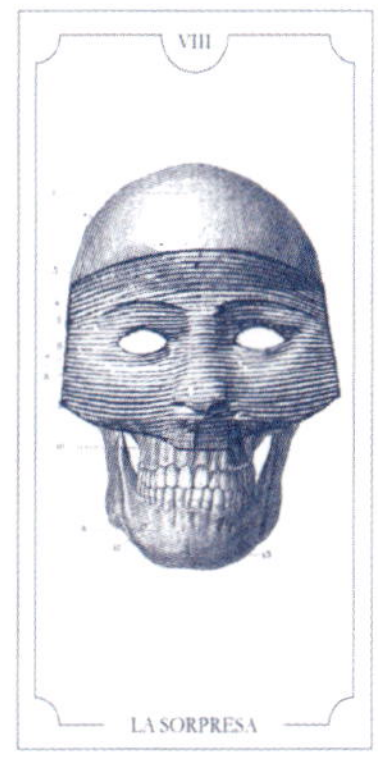
VIII
LA SORPRESA
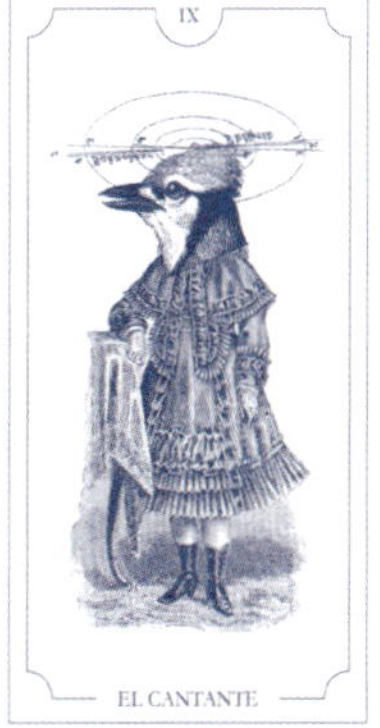
IX
EL CANTANTE
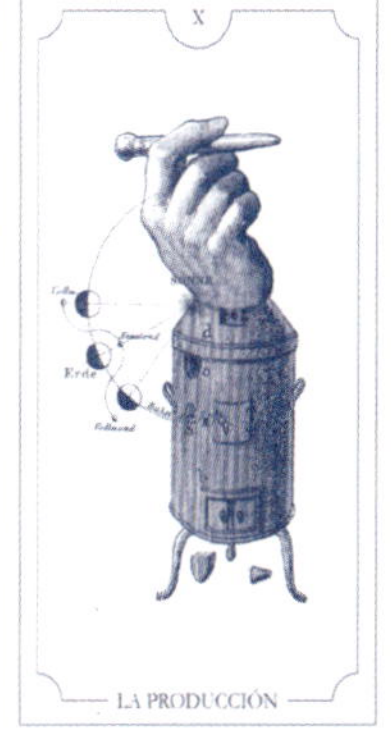
X
LA PRODUCCIÓN
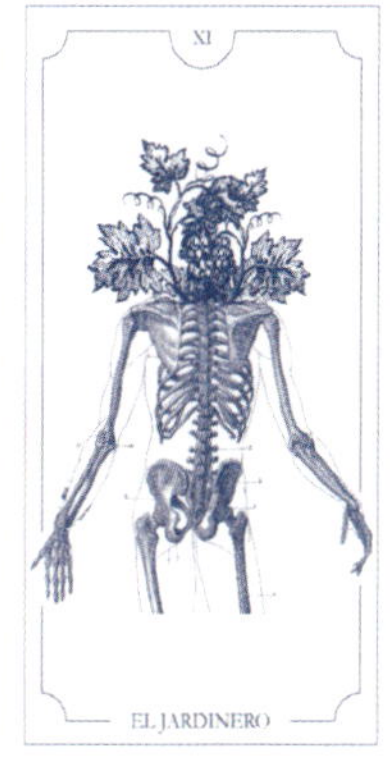
XI
EL JARDINERO
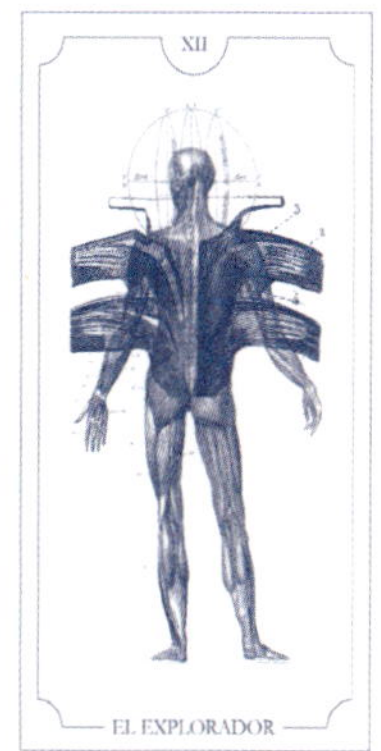
XII
EL EXPLORADOR
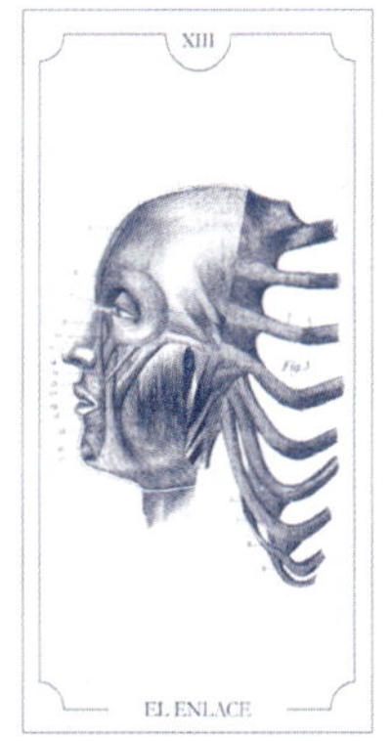
XIII
EL ENLACE
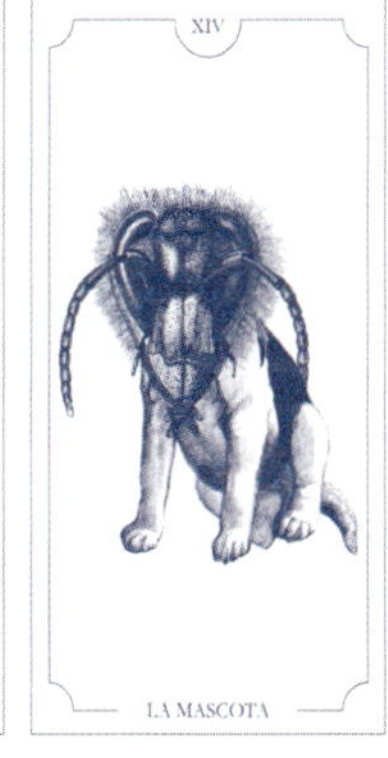
XIV
LA MASCOTA
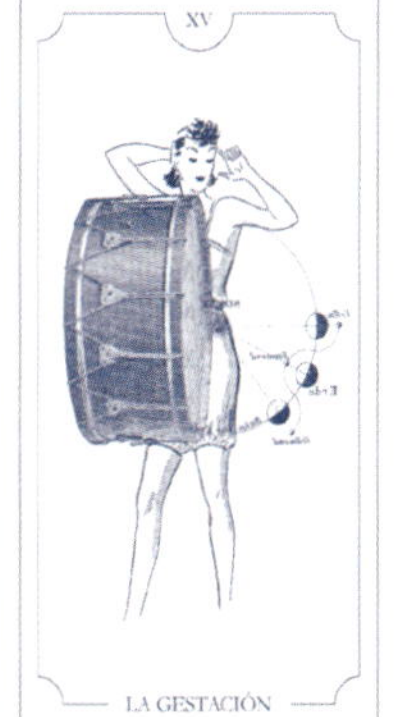
XV
LA GESTACIÓN
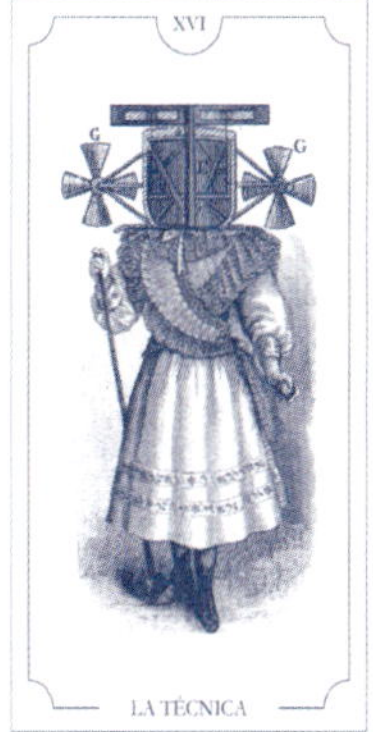
XVI
LA TÉCNICA
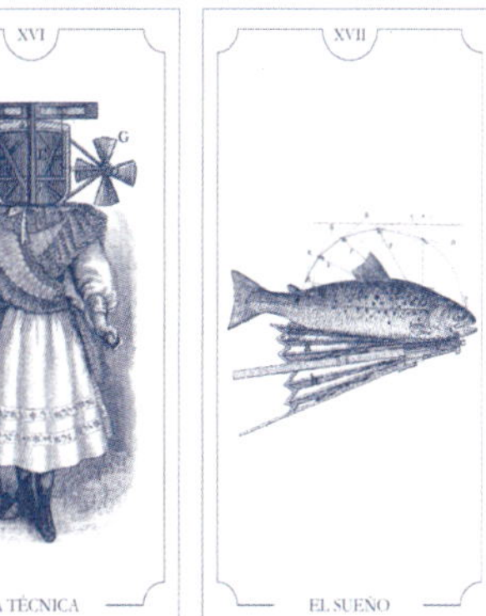
XVII
EL SUEÑO
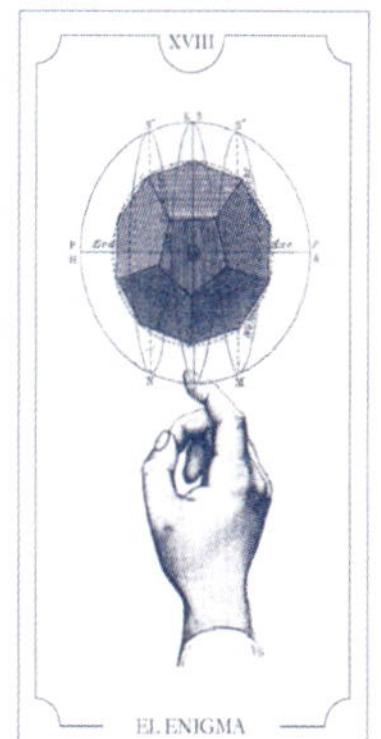
XVIII
EL ENIGMA
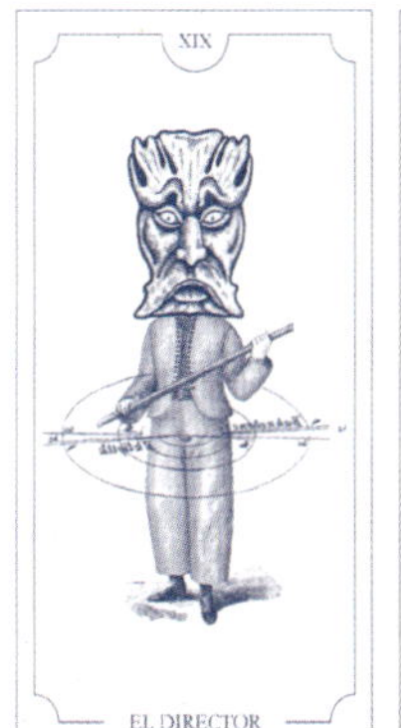
XIX
EL DIRECTOR
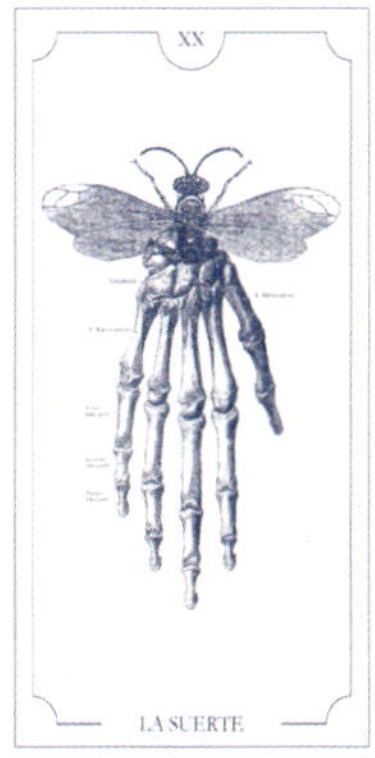
XX
LA SUERTE
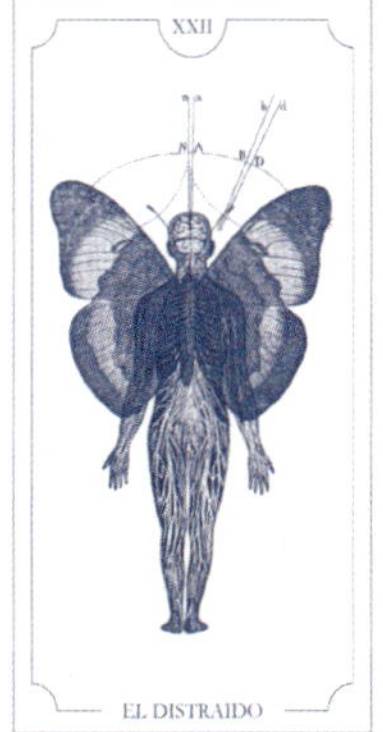
XXII
EL DISTRAIDO
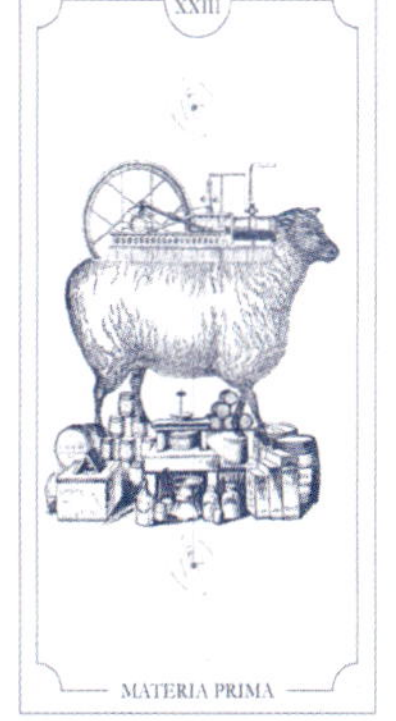
XXIII
MATERIA PRIMA
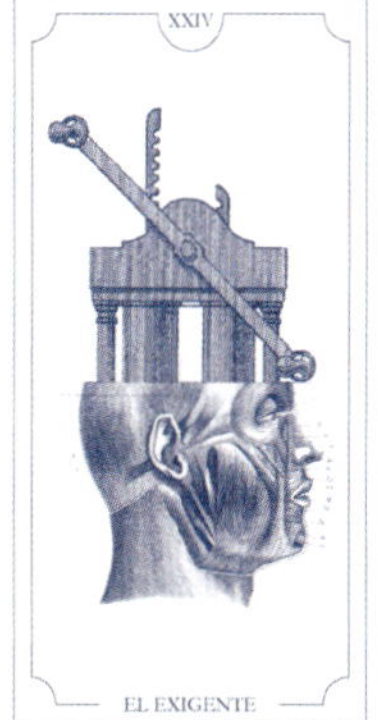
XXIV
EL EXIGENTE
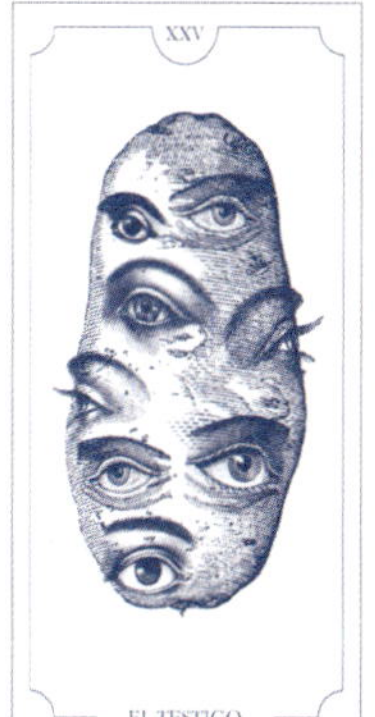
XXV
EL TESTIGO

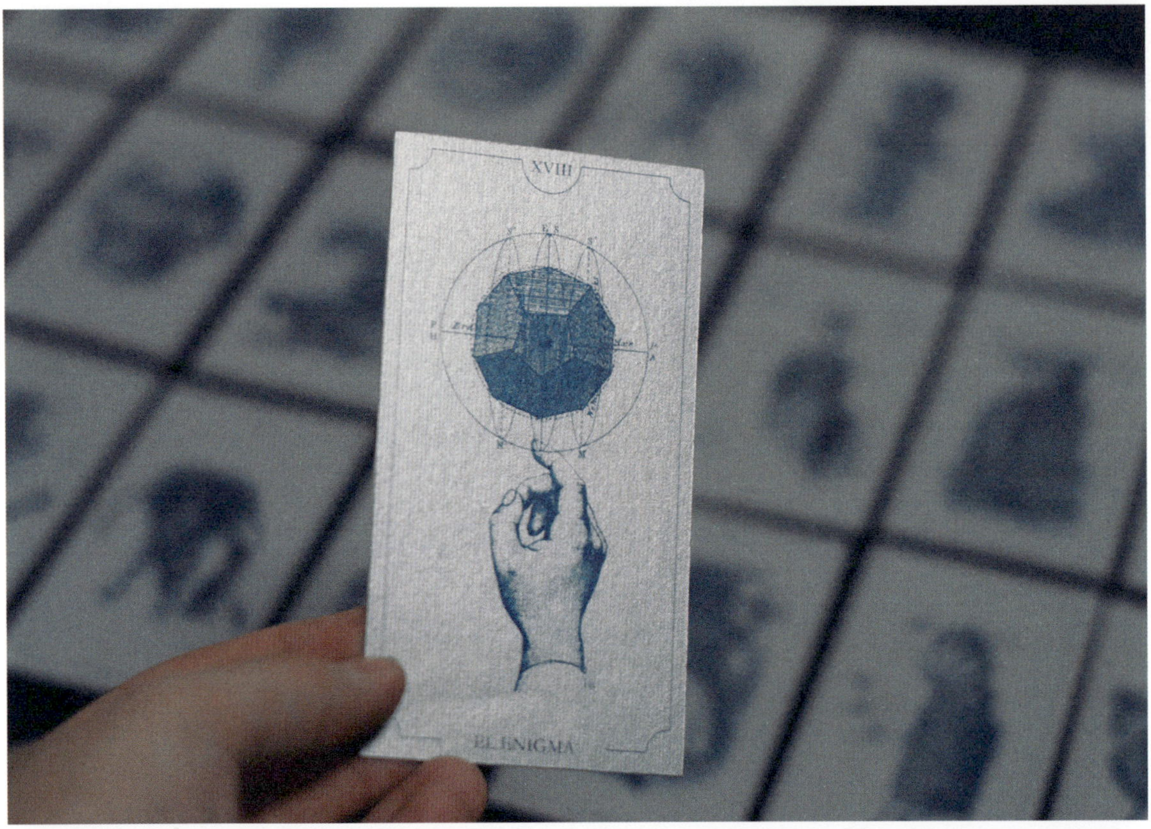
XVIII
EL ENIGMA
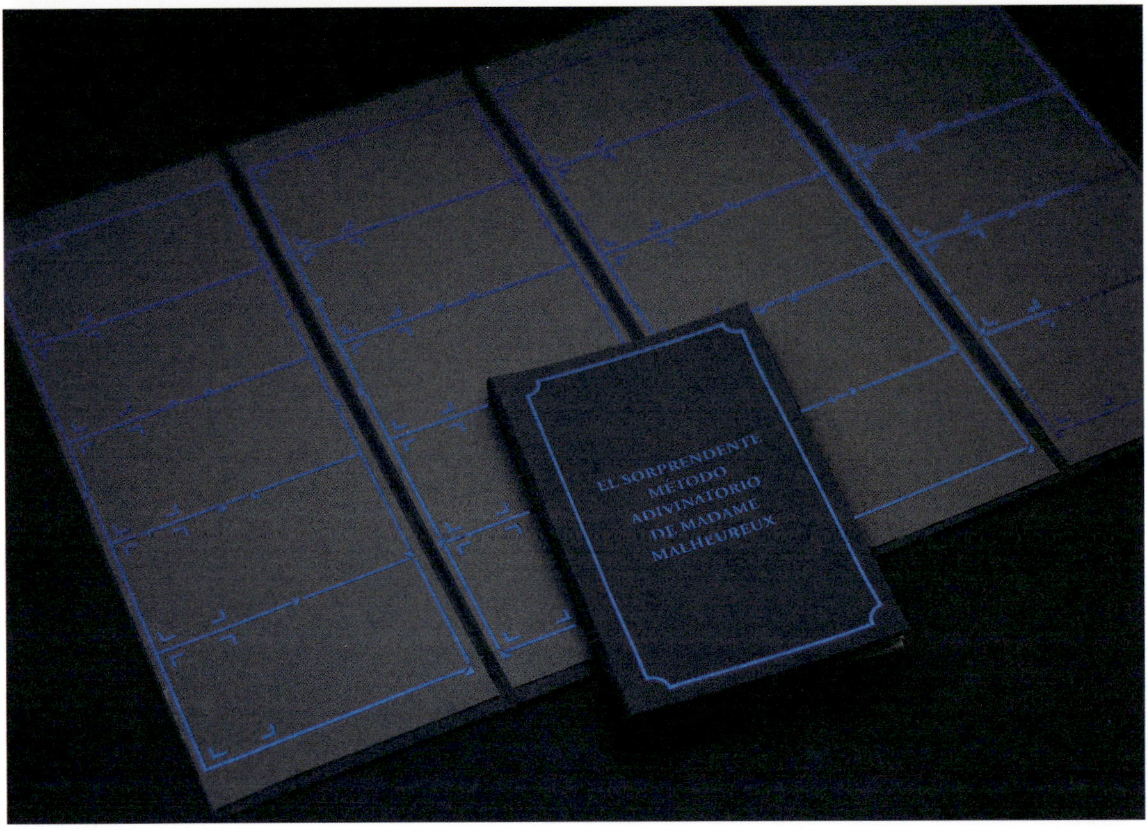
EL SORPRENDENTE
MÉTODO
ADIVINATORIO
DE MADAME
MALHEUREUX

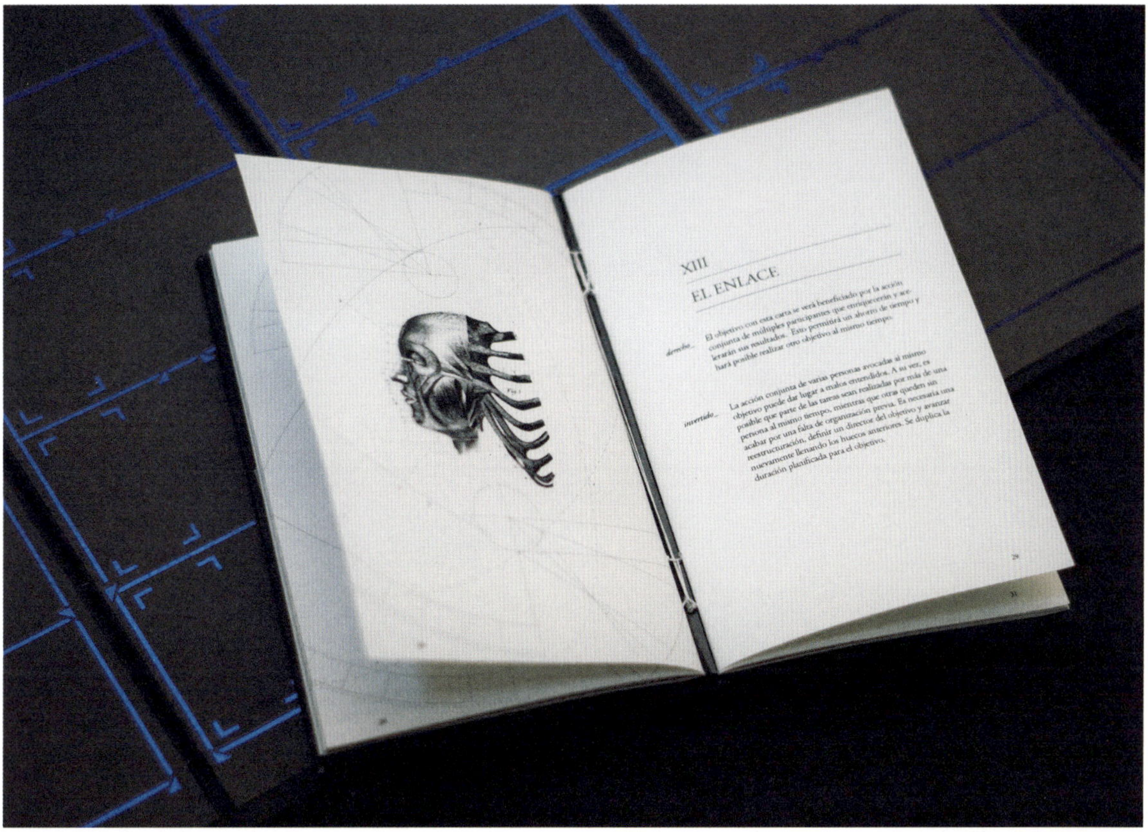

XIII

EL ENLACE

*derecho_* El objetivo con esta carta se verá beneficiado por la acción
conjunta de múltiples participantes que enriquecerán y ace-
lerarán sus resultados. Esto permitirá un ahorro de tiempo y
hará posible realizar otro objetivo al mismo tiempo.

*invertido_* La acción conjunta de varias personas avocadas al mismo
objetivo puede dar lugar a malos entendidos. A su vez, es
posible que parte de las tareas sean realizadas por más de una
persona al mismo tiempo, mientras que otras queden sin
acabar por una falta de organización previa. Es necesaria una
reestructuración, definir un director del objetivo y avanzar
nuevamente llenando los huecos anteriores. Se duplica la
duración planificada para el objetivo.

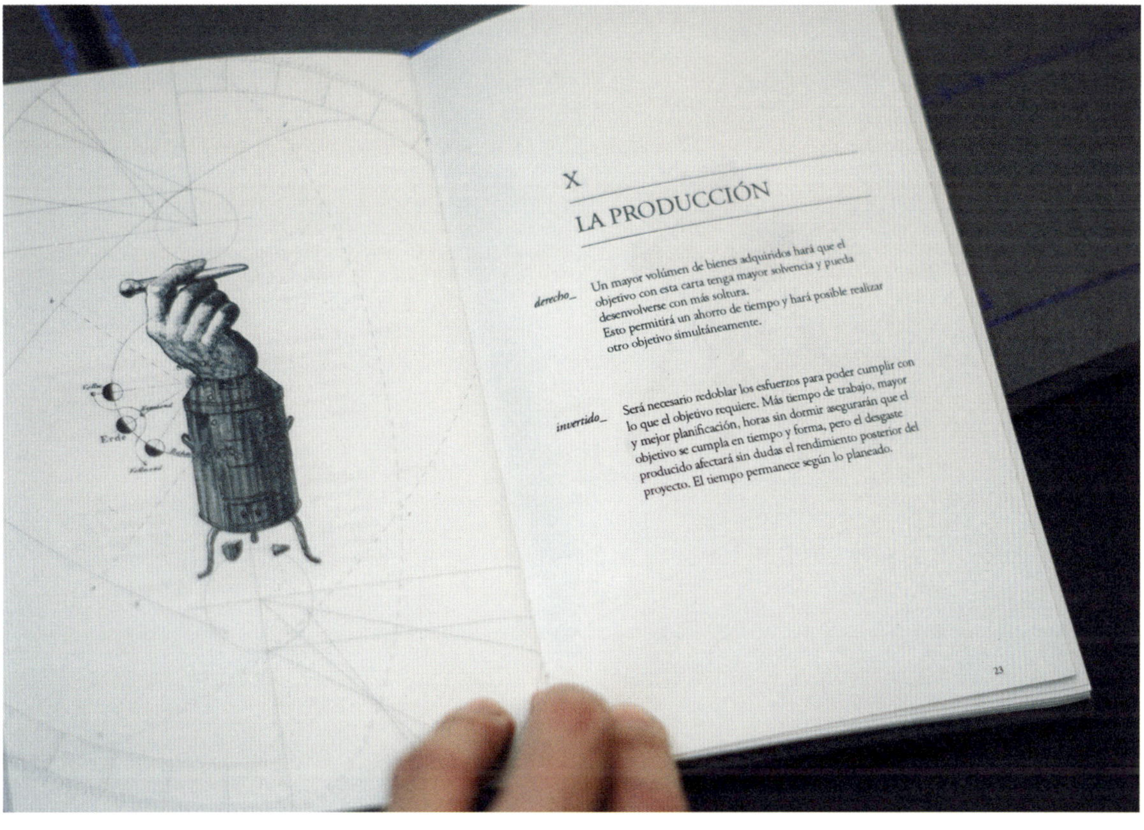

X

LA PRODUCCIÓN

*derecho_* Un mayor volúmen de bienes adquiridos hará que el
objetivo con esta carta tenga mayor solvencia y pueda
desenvolverse con más soltura.
Esto permitirá un ahorro de tiempo y hará posible realizar
otro objetivo simultáneamente.

*invertido_* Será necesario redoblar los esfuerzos para poder cumplir con
lo que el objetivo requiere. Más tiempo de trabajo, mayor
y mejor planificación, horas sin dormir asegurarán que el
objetivo se cumpla en tiempo y forma, pero el desgaste
producido afectará sin dudas el rendimiento posterior del
proyecto. El tiempo permanece según lo planeado.

23

L'ANATOMIE POSTERS

Studio: Caterina Bianchini Studio   Designer: Caterina Bianchini

L'anatomie is a music night based in Edinburgh, Scotland. The nights usually focus on inviting artists from labels like Innervisions and more tech house genre artists. The posters had to reflect the style and feel the nights were trying to create. This series has been developed to include a thick grain overlay and features cell-themed imagery, delivering an out-of-world feeling.

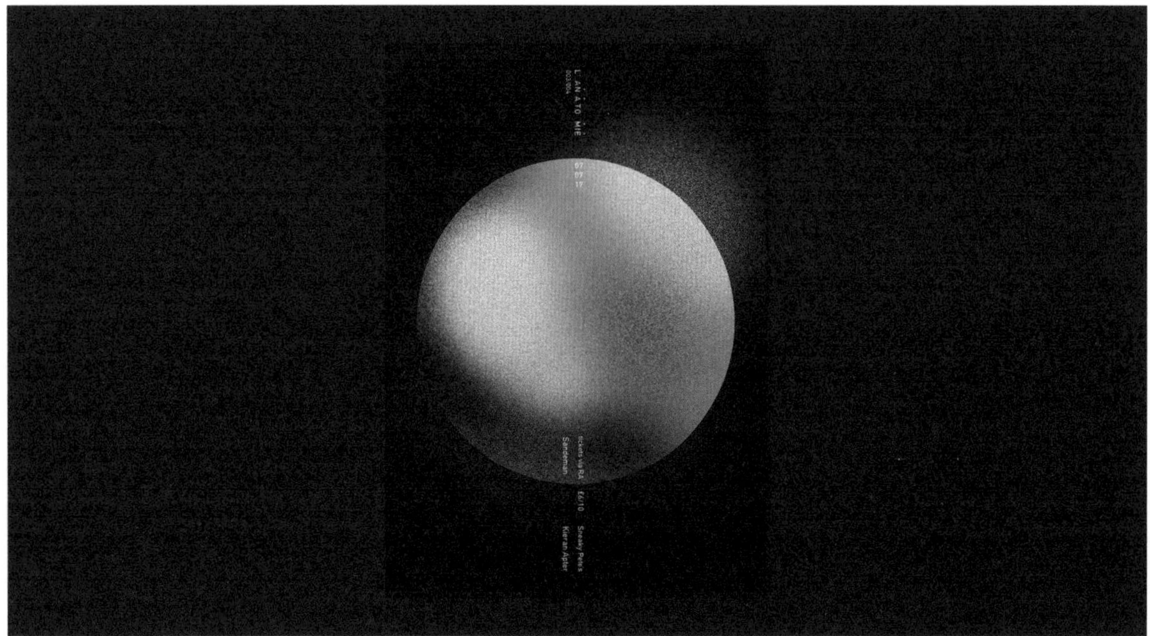

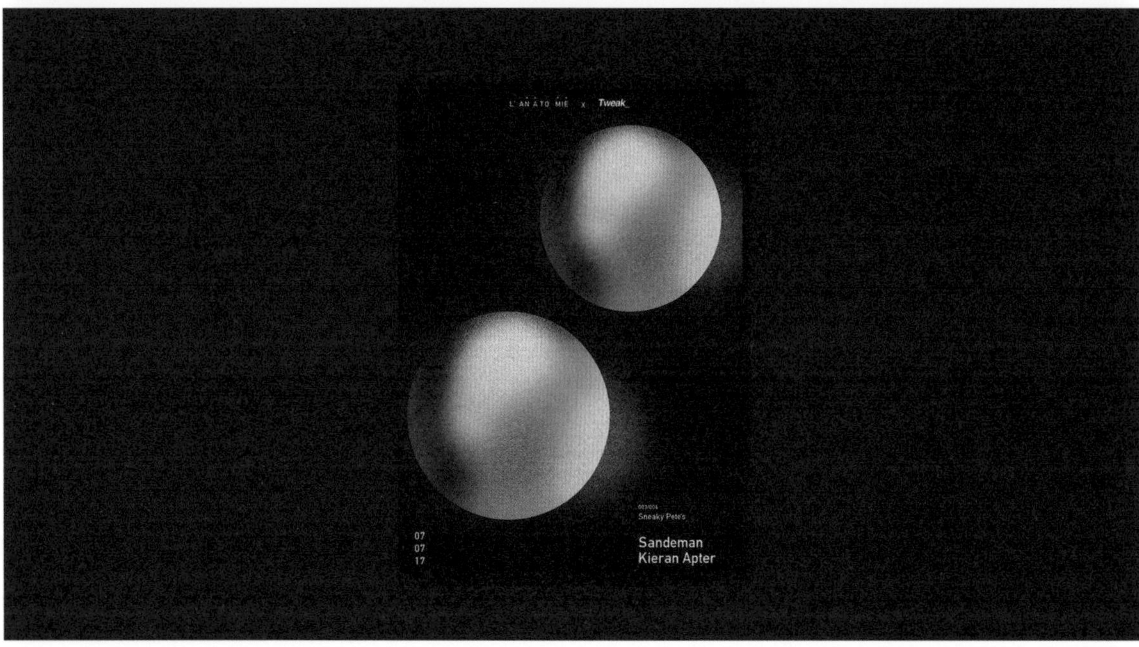

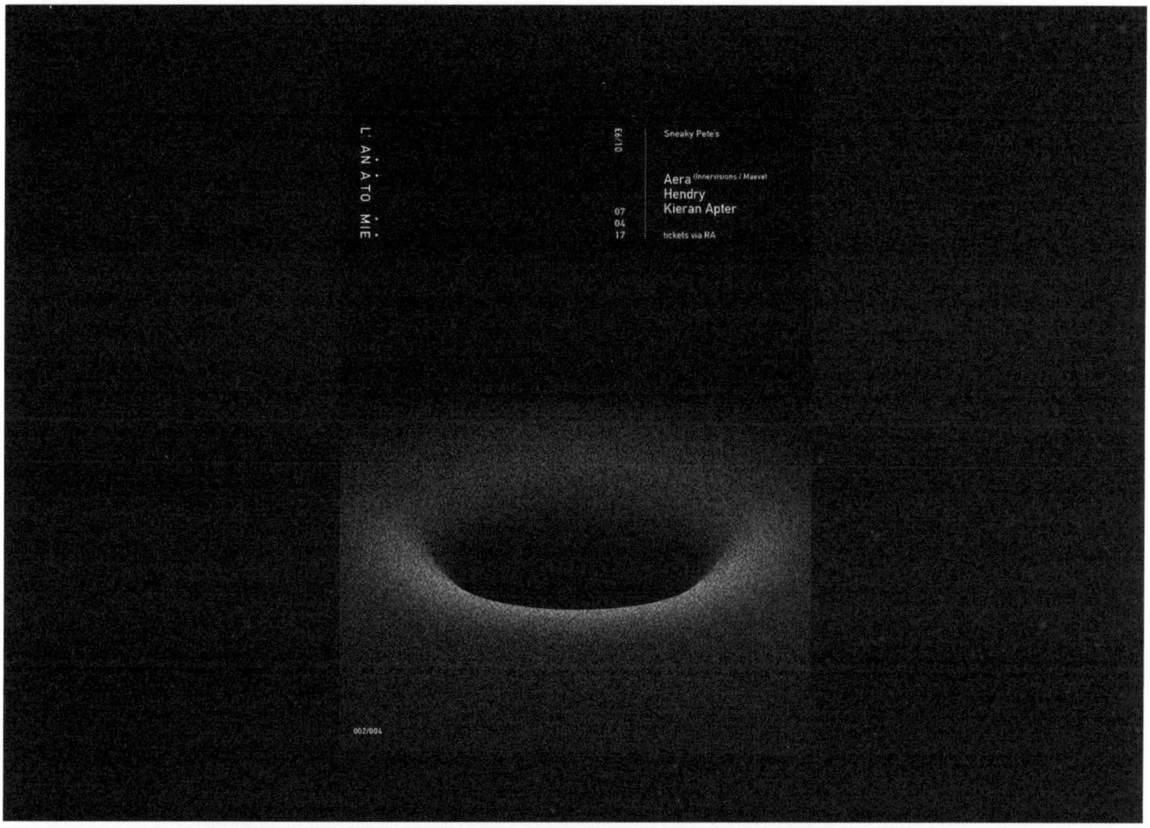

L'ANATOMIE

£6/10

07
04
17

Sneaky Pete's

Aera (Innervisions / Maeve)
Hendry
Kieran Apter

tickets via RA

002/004

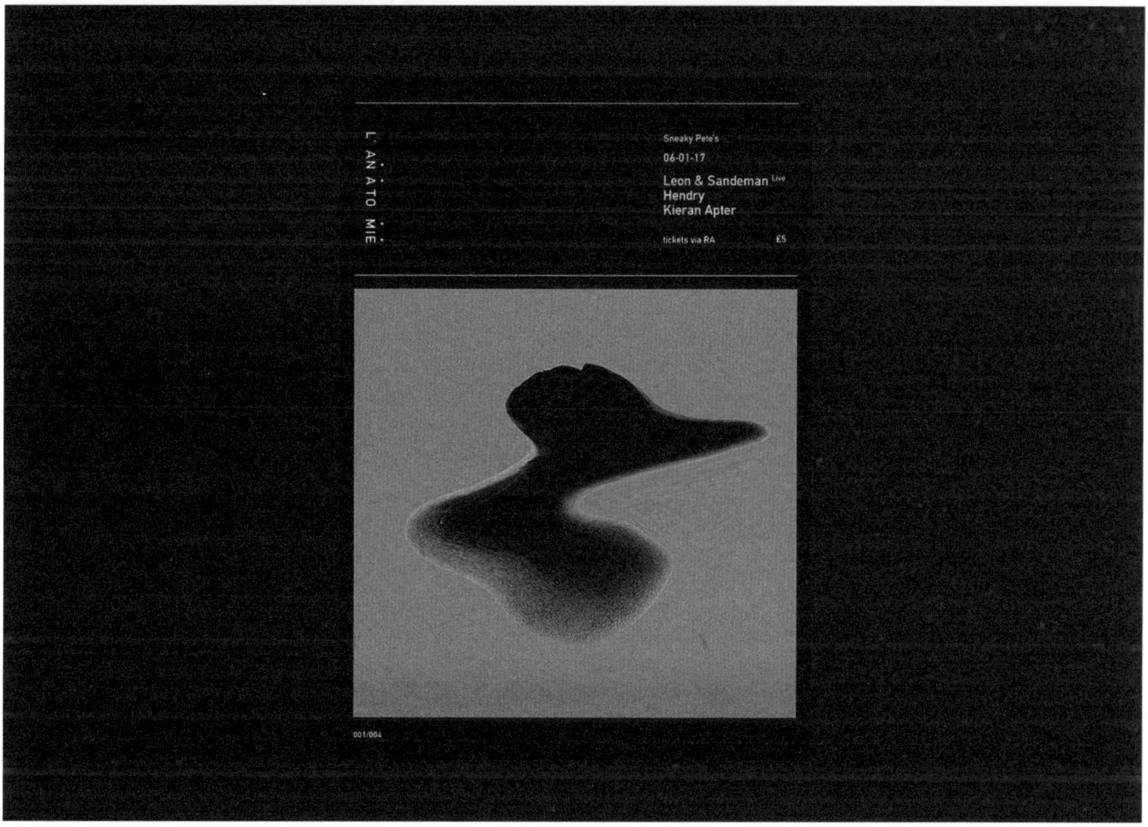

L'ANATOMIE

Sneaky Pete's

06-01-17

Leon & Sandeman Live
Hendry
Kieran Apter

tickets via RA £5

001/004

genre in the horror field—a different phobia. The debut of Phobia will spotlight the fear of the unknown, and its installments will dig deep into the phobias of achluophobia (fear of darkness) and Xenophobia (fear of the unknown), giving its audience a physically and psychologically challenging experience. This comprehensive identity system includes campaign posters, festival website and different interative survival packages (ticket, instruction guide, flashlight, Vinyl of Festival Soundtrack Score).

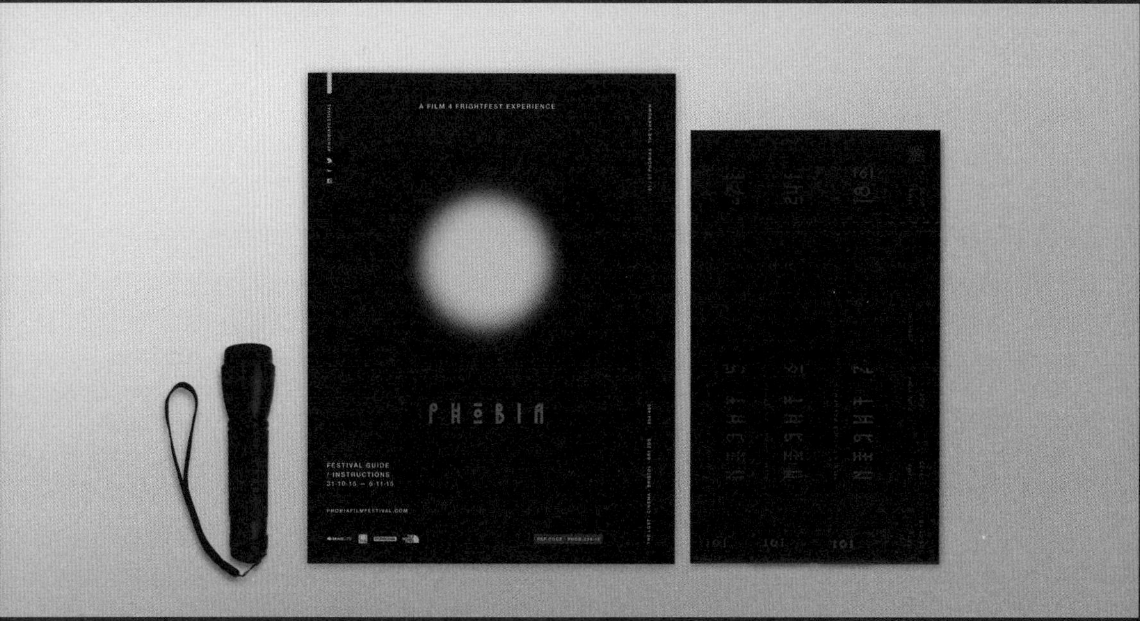

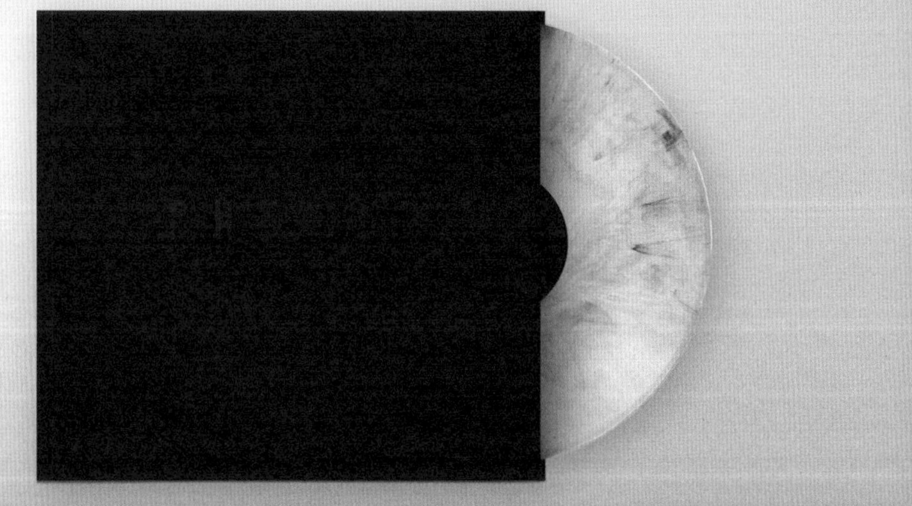

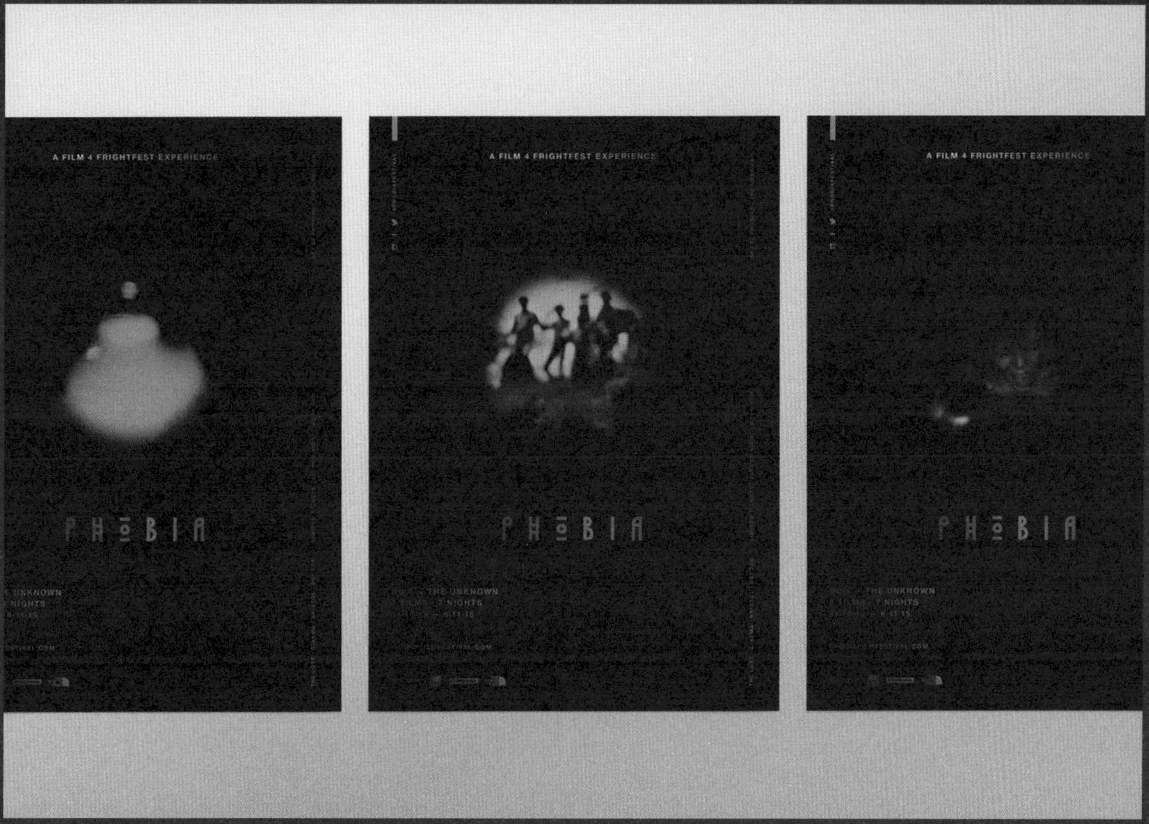

A FILM 4 FRIGHTFEST EXPERIENCE

PHOBIA

A FILM 4 FRIGHTFEST EXPERIENCE

PHOBIA

A FILM 4 FRIGHTFEST EXPERIENCE

PHOBIA

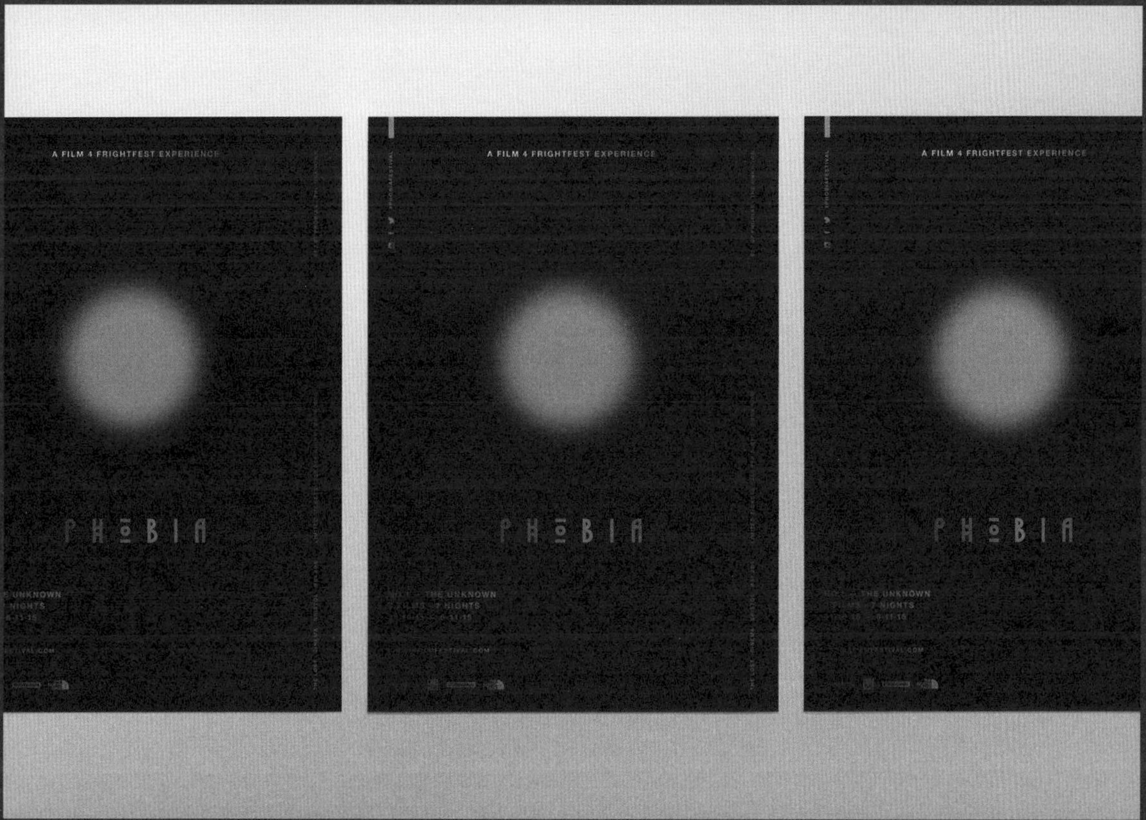

A FILM 4 FRIGHTFEST EXPERIENCE

PHOBIA

A FILM 4 FRIGHTFEST EXPERIENCE

PHOBIA

A FILM 4 FRIGHTFEST EXPERIENCE

PHOBIA

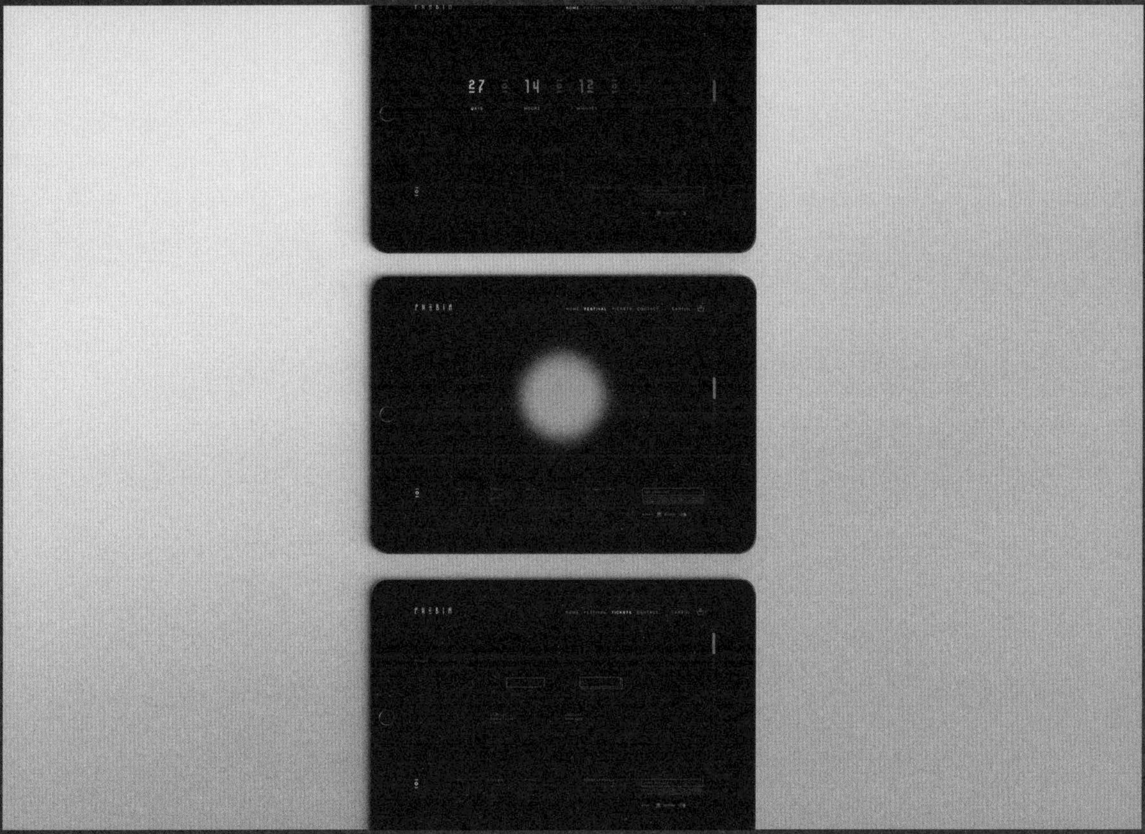

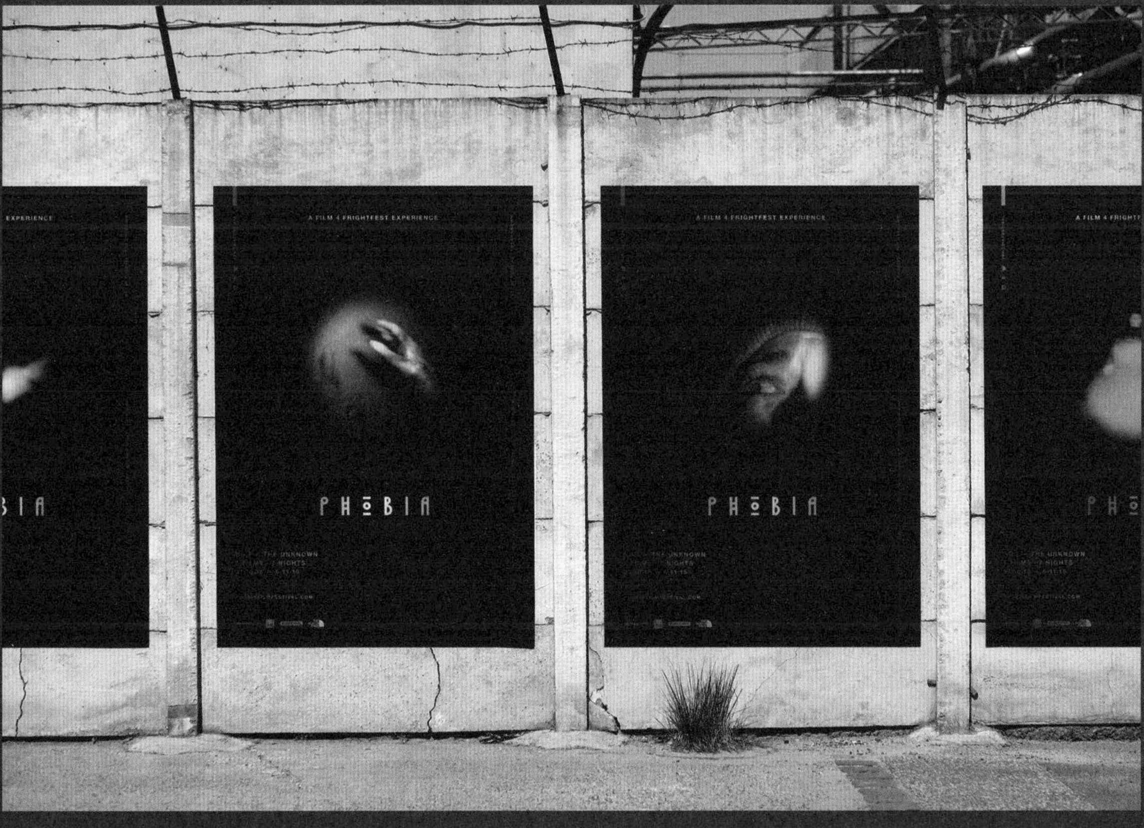

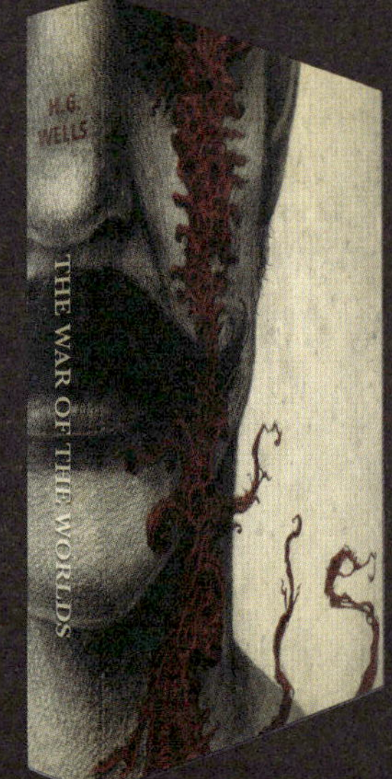

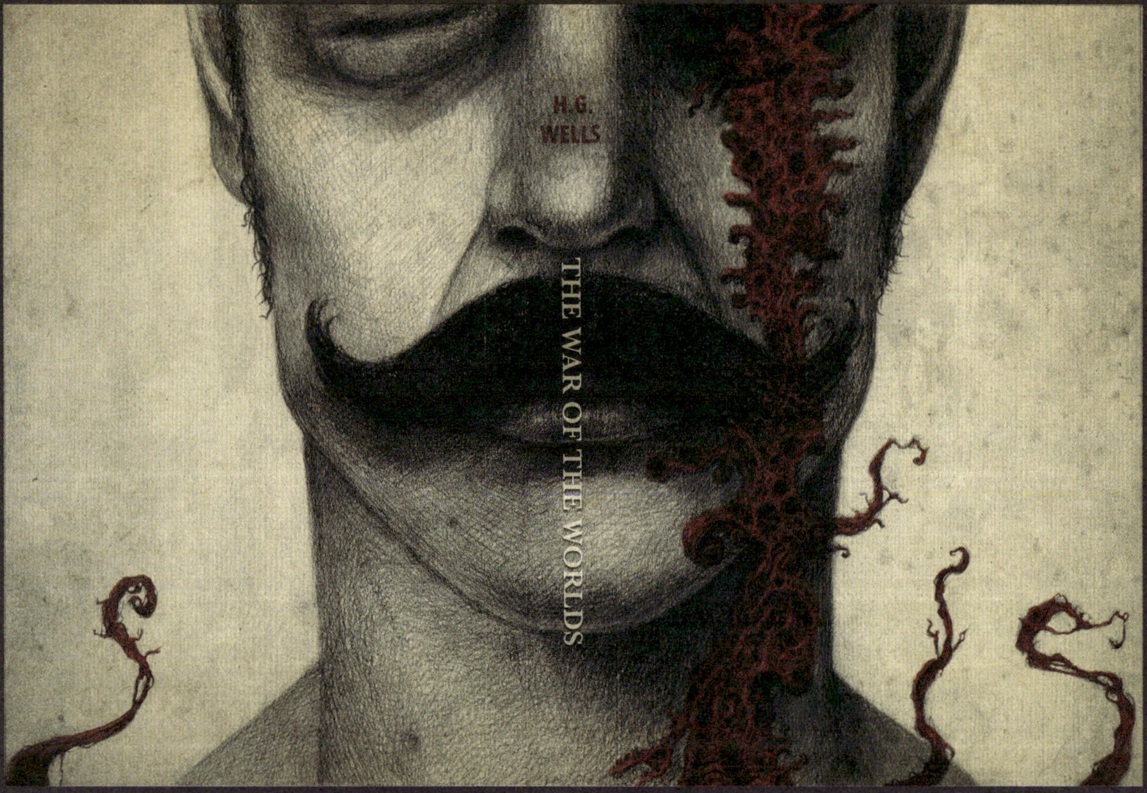

H.G.
WELLS
THE WAR OF THE WORLDS

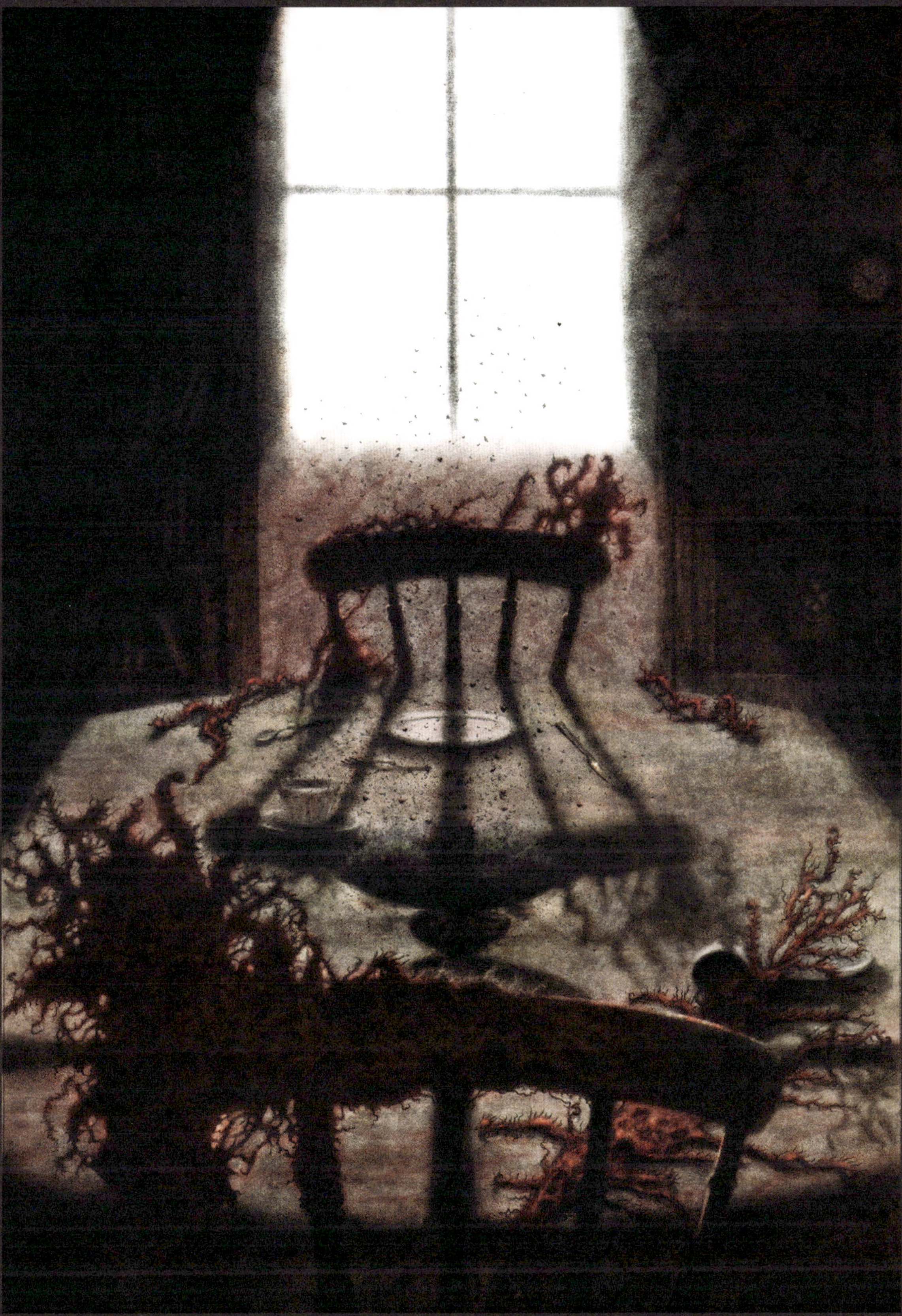

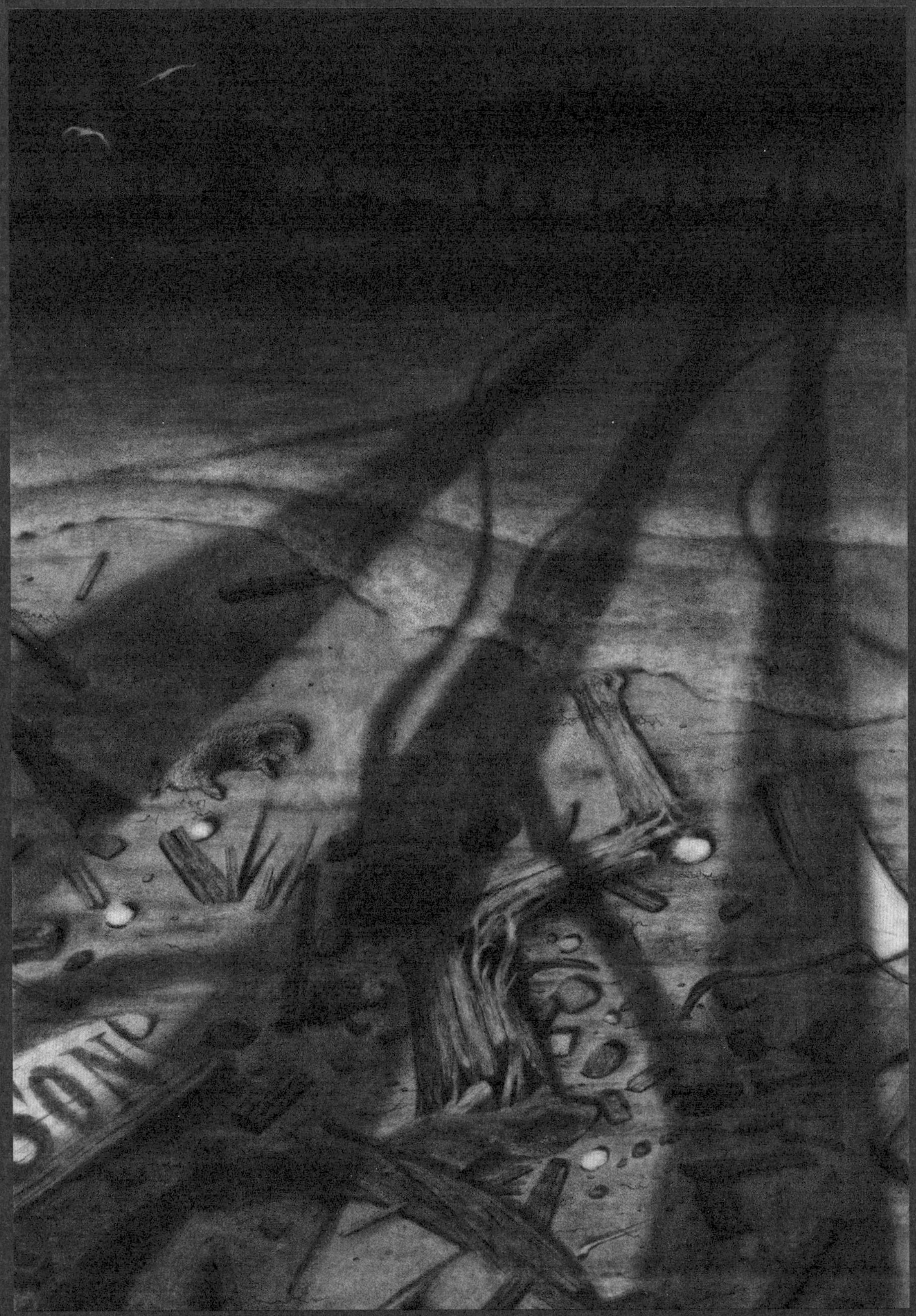

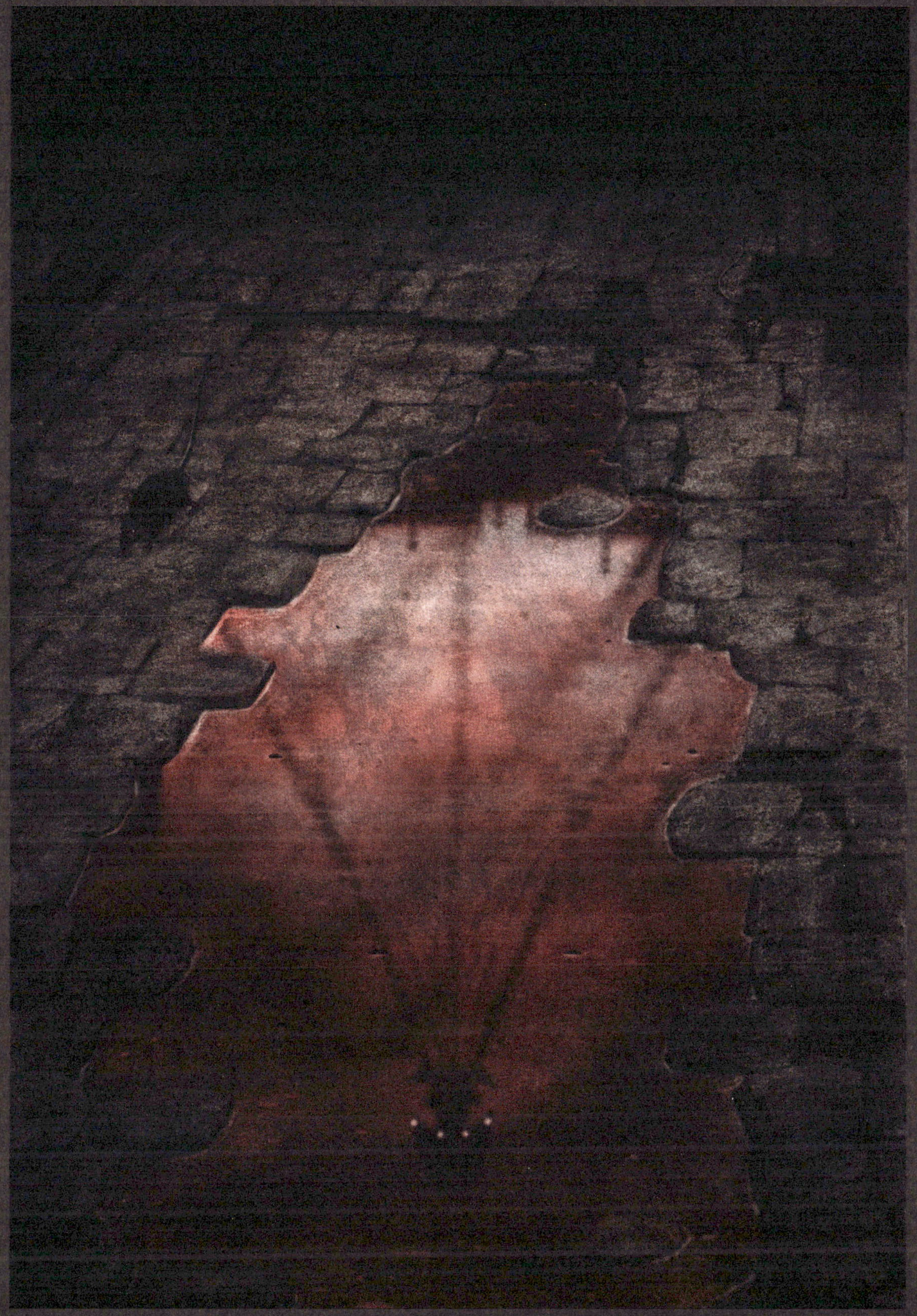

7 DEADLY SINS

Artist: Arkadiusz Jankowski

7 Deadly Sins is a project created in the lithography studio in the Academy of Fine Arts In Warsaw. The intention was to show the sins of today's society. Lithograph was scanned and then printed with risograph.

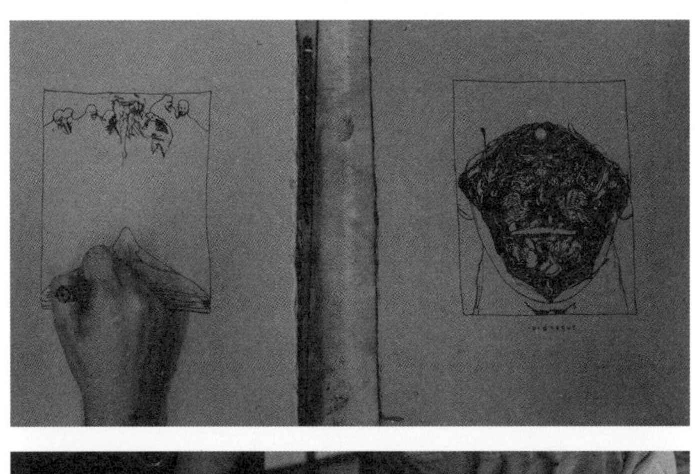

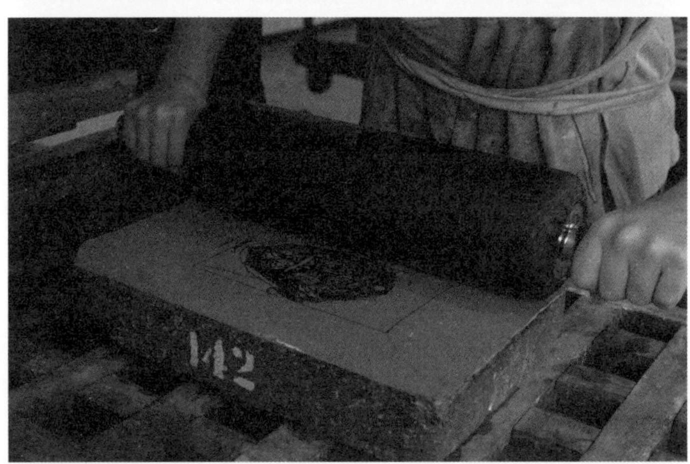

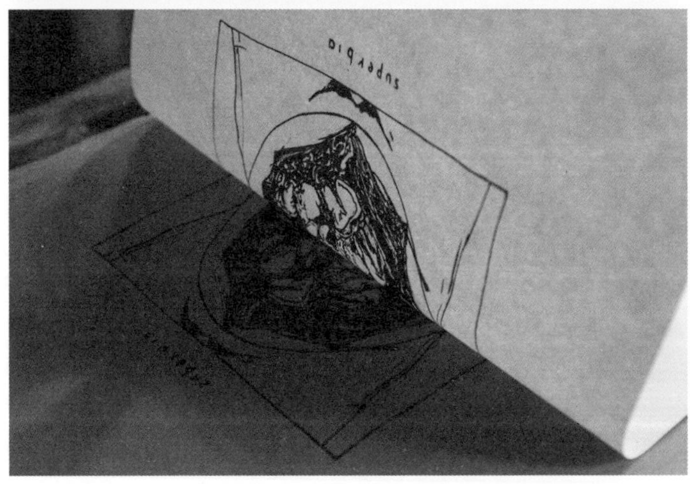

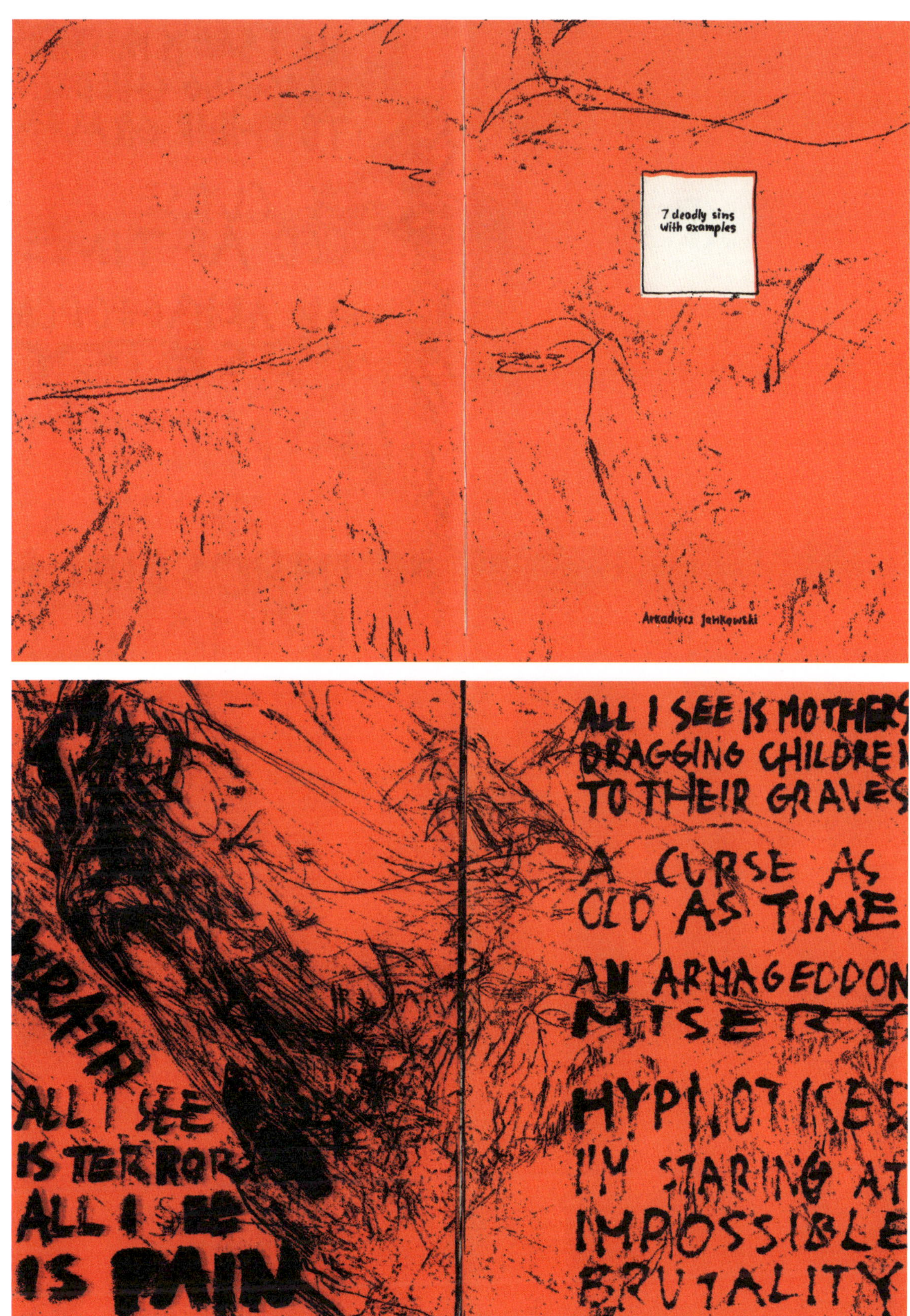
7 deadly sins
with examples
Arkadiusz Jankowski
WRATH
ALL I SEE
IS TERROR
ALL I SEE
IS PAIN
ALL I SEE IS MOTHERS
DRAGGING CHILDREN
TO THEIR GRAVES
A CURSE AS
OLD AS TIME
AN ARMAGEDDON
MISERY
HYPNOTISED
I'M STARING AT
IMPOSSIBLE
BRUTALITY

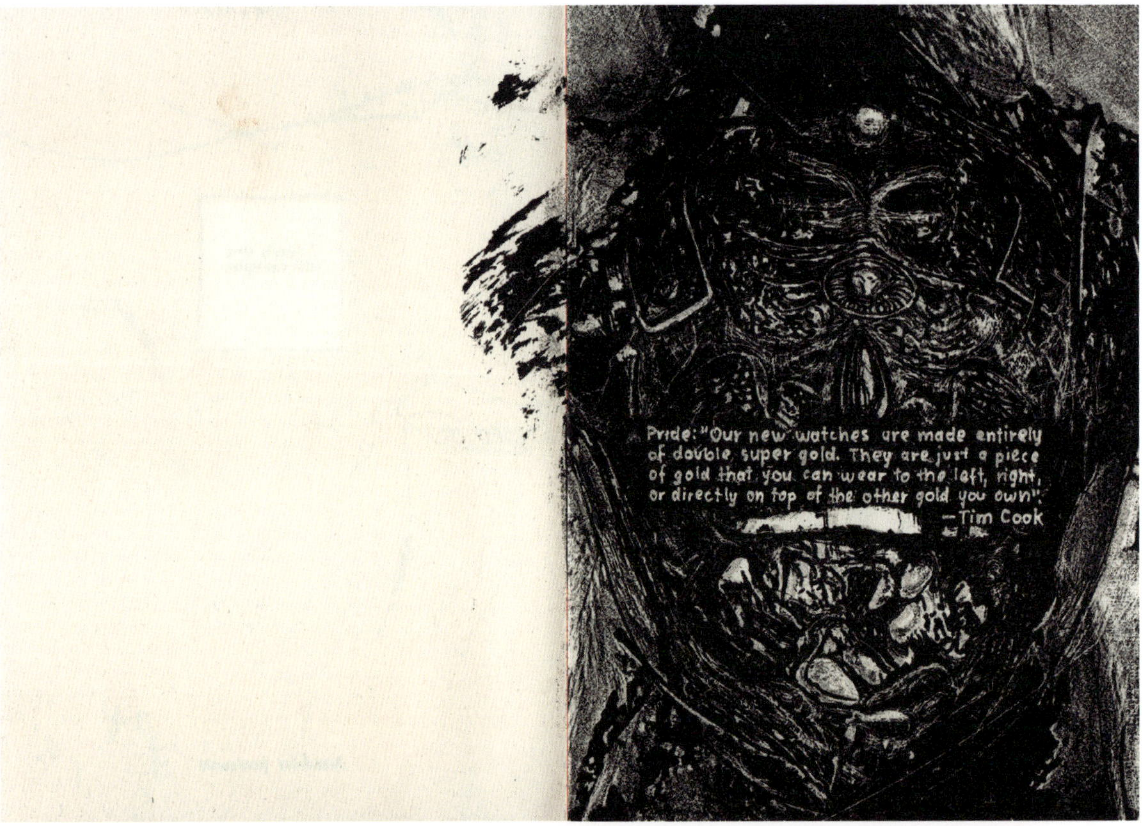

Pride: "Our new watches are made entirely of double super gold. They are just a piece of gold that you can wear to the left, right, or directly on top of the other gold you own".
—Tim Cook

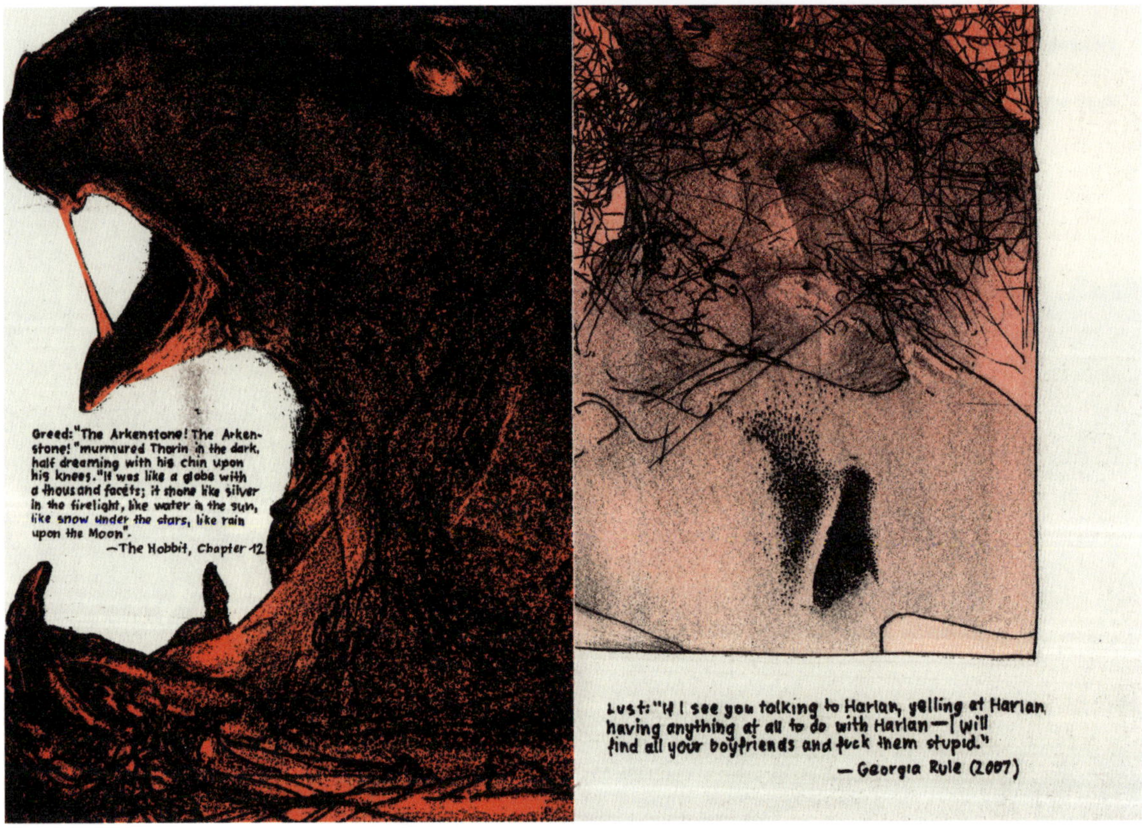

Greed: "The Arkenstone! The Arkenstone!" murmured Thorin in the dark, half dreaming with his chin upon his knees. "It was like a globe with a thousand facets; it shone like silver in the firelight, like water in the sun, like snow under the stars, like rain upon the Moon".
—The Hobbit, Chapter 12

Lust: "If I see you talking to Harlan, yelling at Harlan, having anything at all to do with Harlan—I will find all your boyfriends and fuck them stupid."
—Georgia Rule (2007)

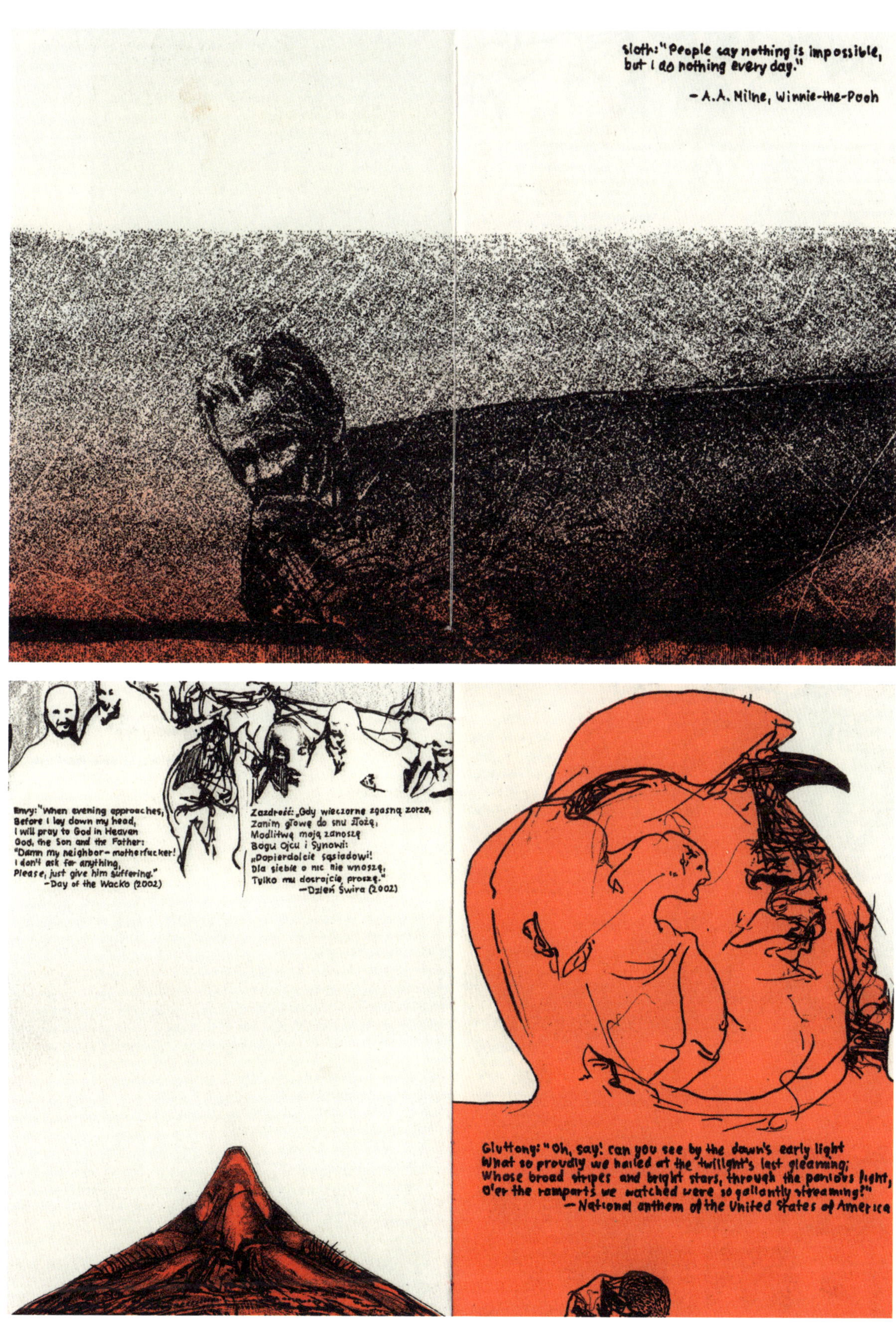

Sloth: "People say nothing is impossible, but i do nothing every day."
– A.A. Milne, Winnie-the-Pooh
Envy: "When evening approaches,
Before I lay down my head,
I will pray to God in Heaven
God, the Son and the Father:
"Damn my neighbor – motherfucker!
I don't ask for anything,
Please, just give him suffering."
–Day of the Wacko (2002)
Zazdrość: „Gdy wieczorne zgasną zorze,
Zanim głowę do snu złożę,
Modlitwę moją zanoszę
Bogu Ojcu i Synowi:
„Dopierdolcie sąsiadowi!
Dla siebie o nic nie wnoszę,
Tylko mu dosrajcie proszę."
–Dzień Świra (2002)
Gluttony: "Oh, say! can you see by the dawn's early light
What so proudly we hailed at the twilight's last gleaming;
Whose broad stripes and bright stars, through the perilous fight,
O'er the ramparts we watched were so gallantly streaming?"
– National anthem of the United States of America

GU DU, LING JIA YU YI QIE

Artist: Bert Chu Chen

This book cover designed for the prose anthology *Gu Du, Ling Jia Yu Yi Qie (Loneliness Reigns)* adopted a bony typeface for the book title to deliver the feeling of loneliness, and the broken structures inside resemble closed windows, symbolizing the dialogue confined to oneself. While mossy spots emblem a journey through which self-awareness grows, the contrast between flying birds with a lonely chair reflects the relationship between the writer and the world: she just sits there watching the drama of life goes on.

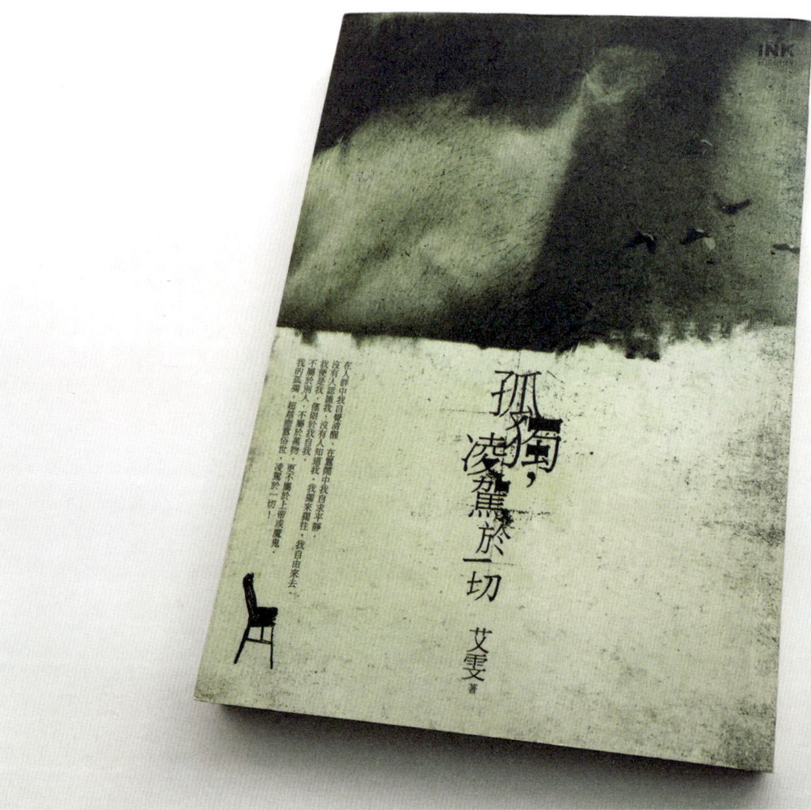

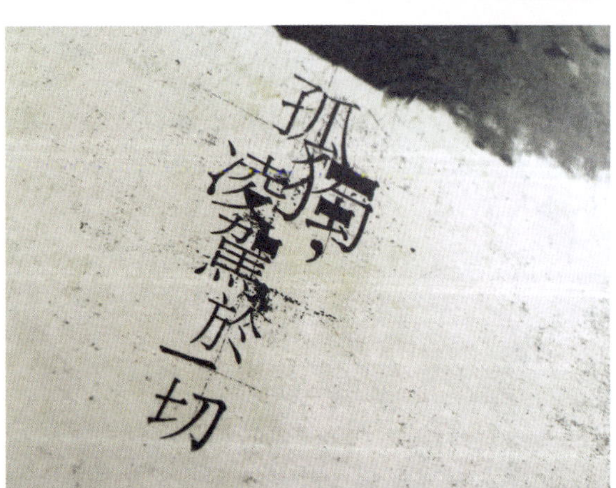

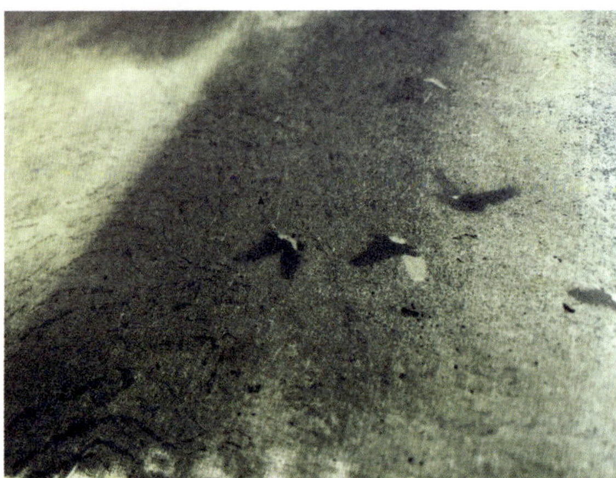

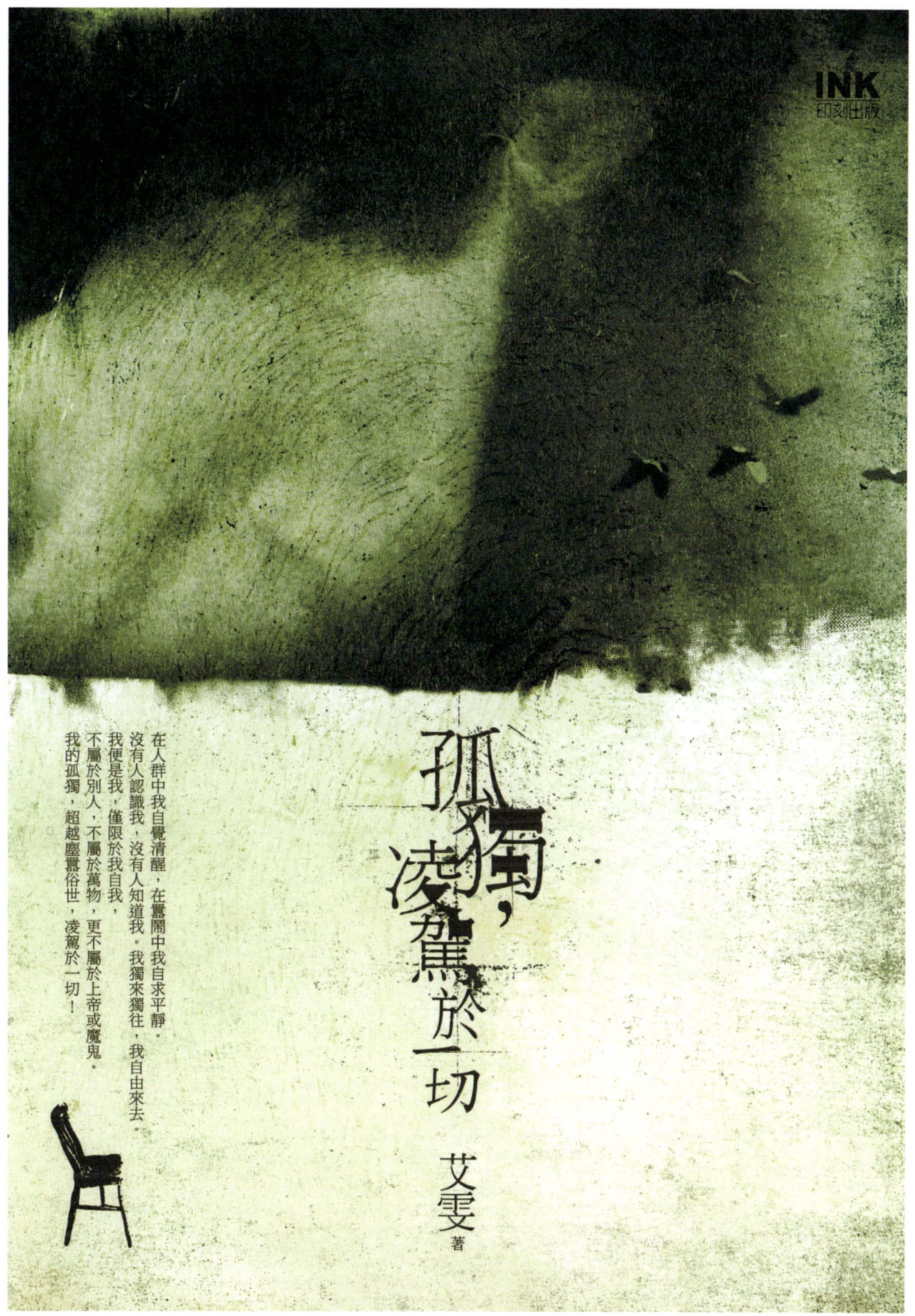
INK
印刻出版
孤獨，凌駕於一切
在人群中我自覺清醒，在囂鬧中我自求平靜。
沒有人認識我，沒有人知道我。我獨來獨往，我自由來去。
我便是我，僅限於我自我，
不屬於別人，不屬於萬物，更不屬於上帝或魔鬼。
我的孤獨，超越塵囂俗世，凌駕於一切！
艾雯
著

NNRA VINYL DESIGN

Designer: Michael Sallit

This design was for the doom-metal band NNRA's self-titled vinyl. In order to highlight the illustrations made by French tattoo artist SM Bousille in a graphic way, the designer assimilated the graphic side with the music side for greater coherence. This work represents a mix of Bauhaus graphic design, French tatouage and industrial elements with a grungy and rugged texture.

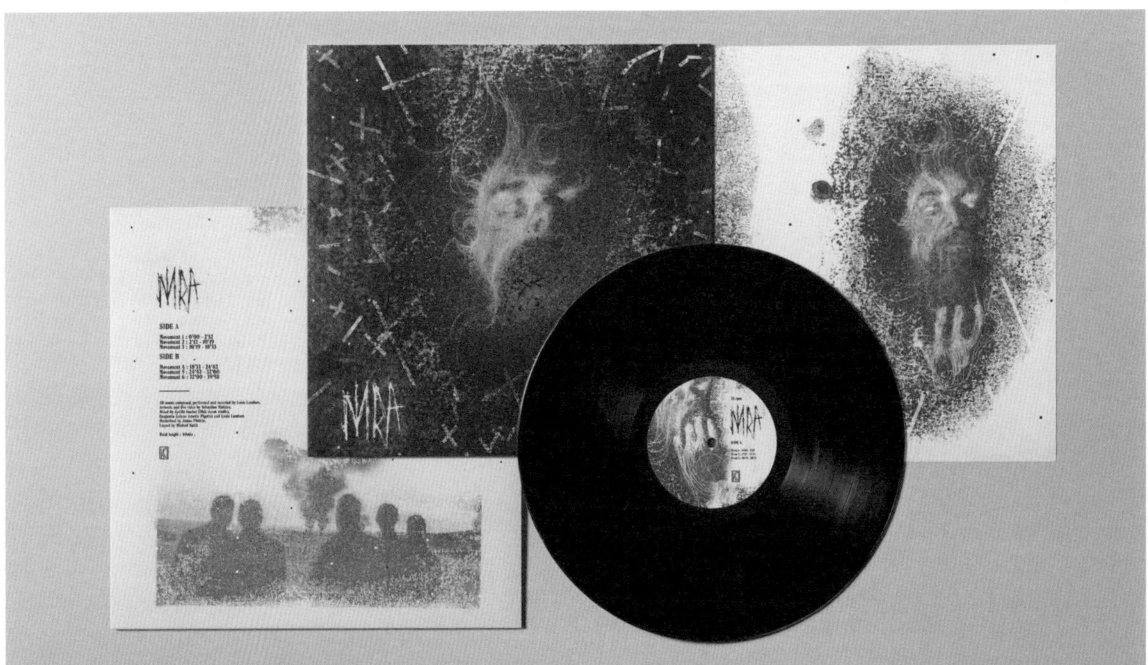

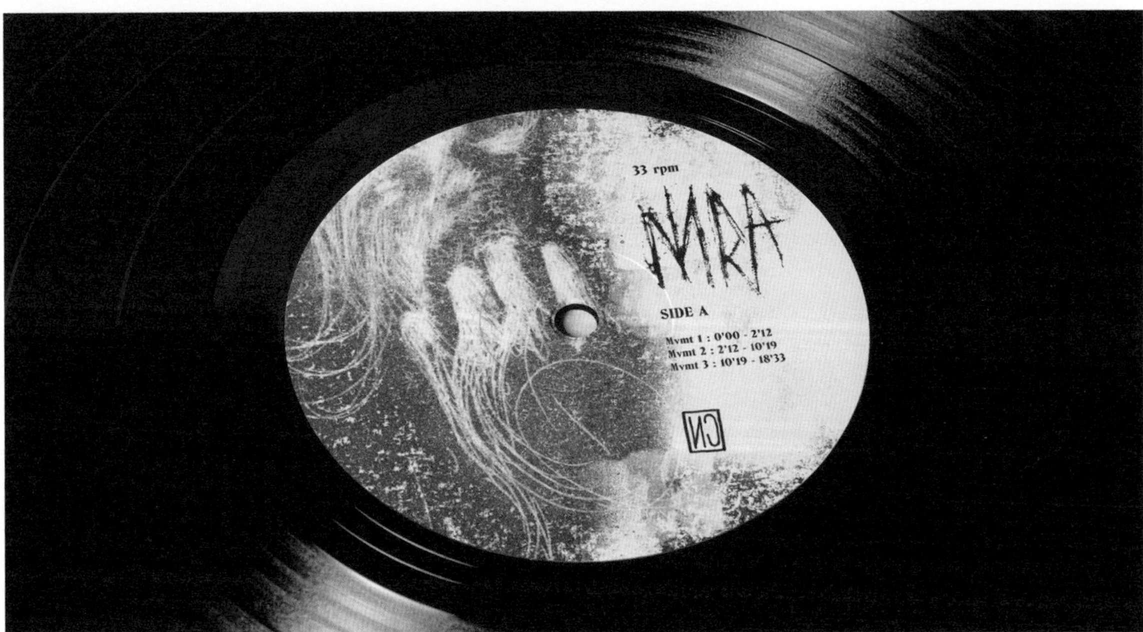

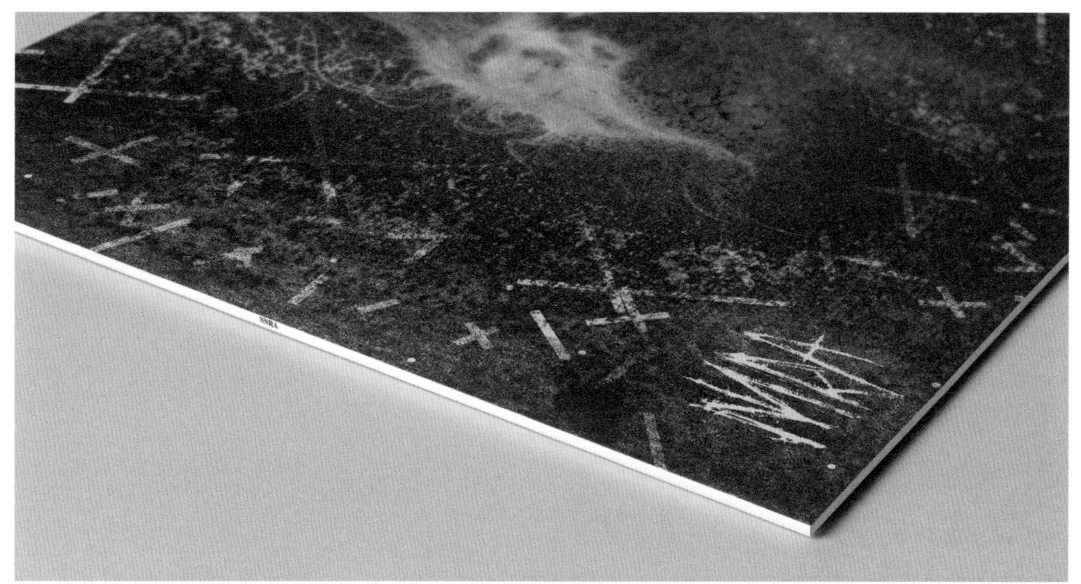

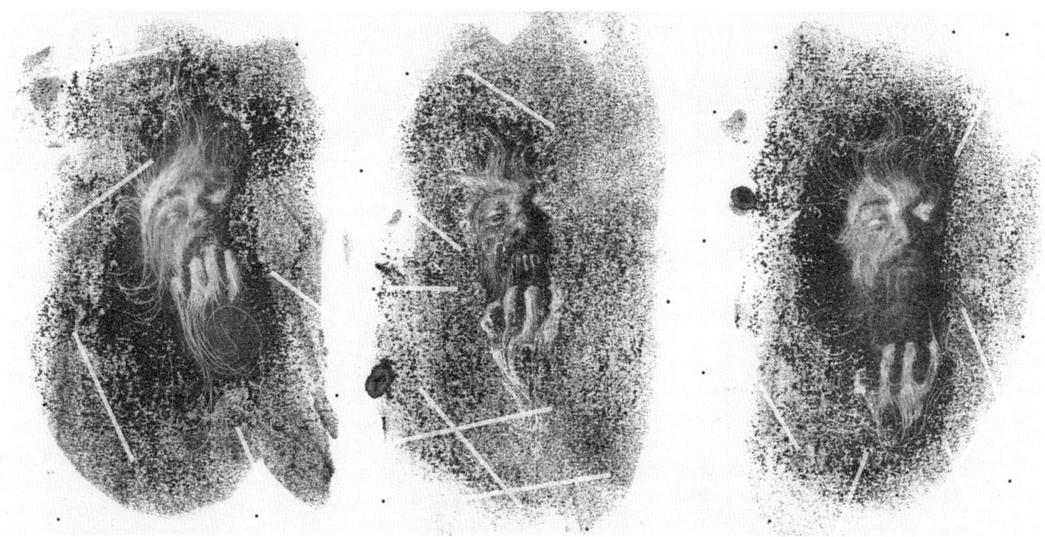

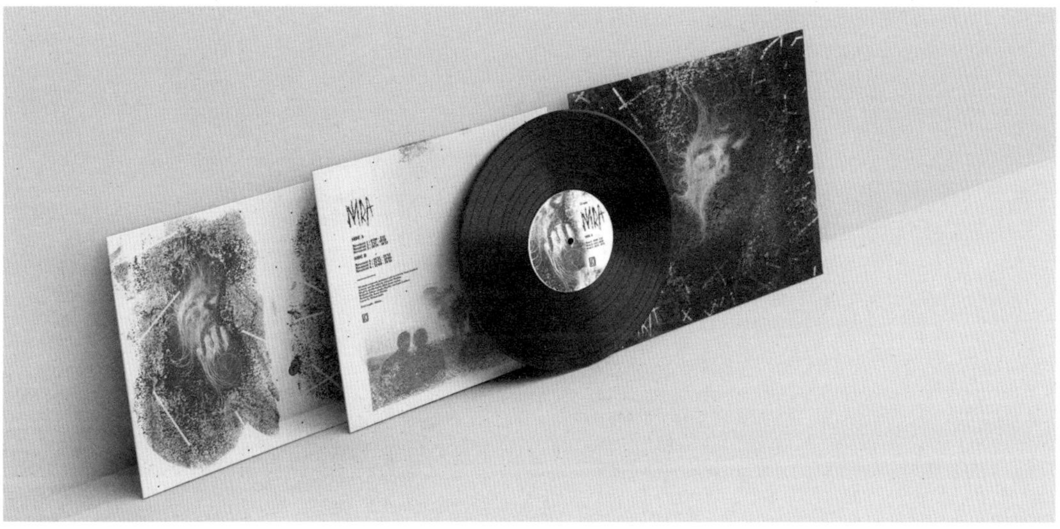

DUELO (MOURNING)

Artist: Miguel A. Cantú García

The series shows the stages of mourning, the painful path from denial to acceptance. It represents the search for acceptance of all the constant changes in the ever changing life, including parts of individual that die and will never return, people that leave, days that are gone.

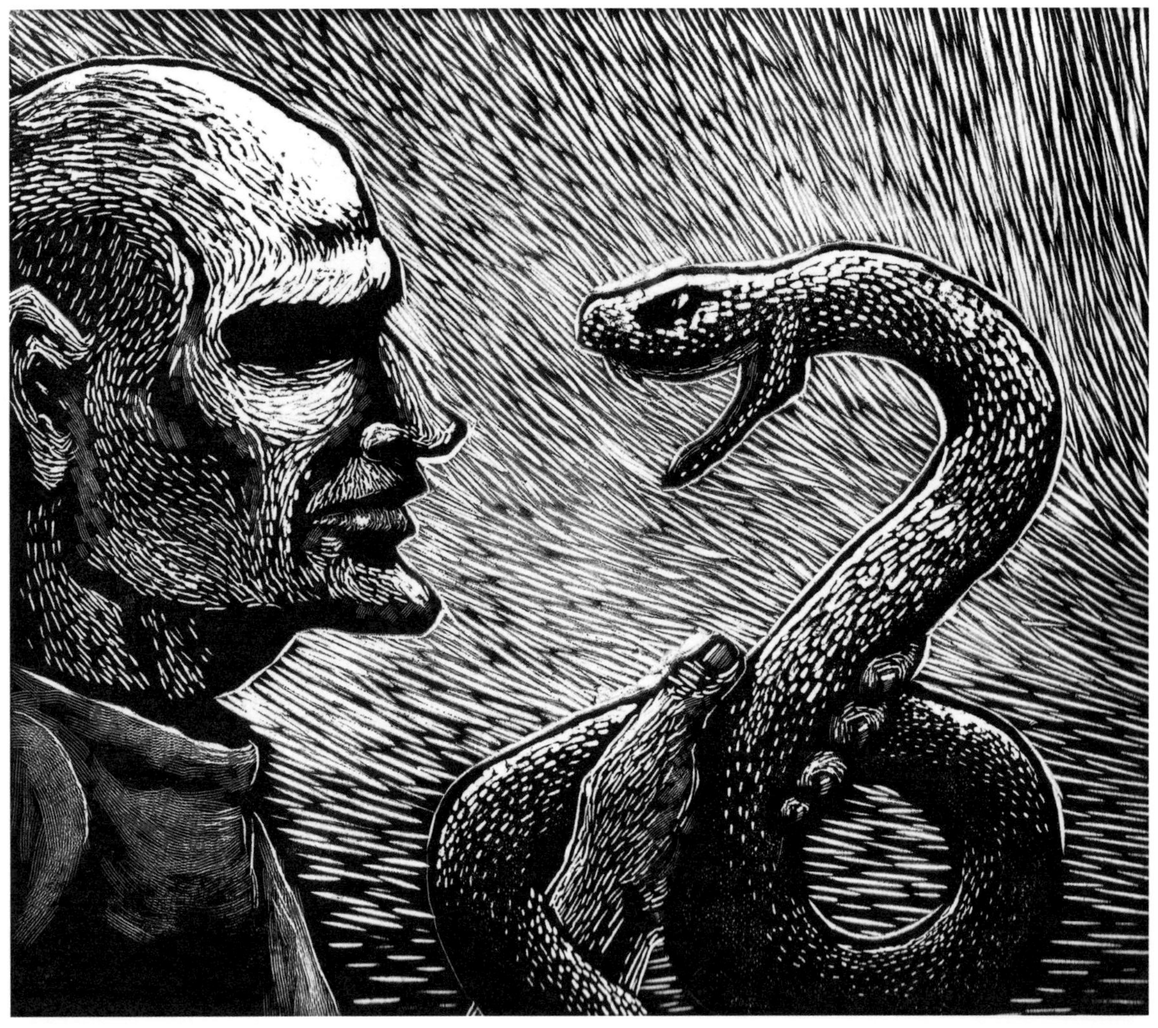

Acceptance

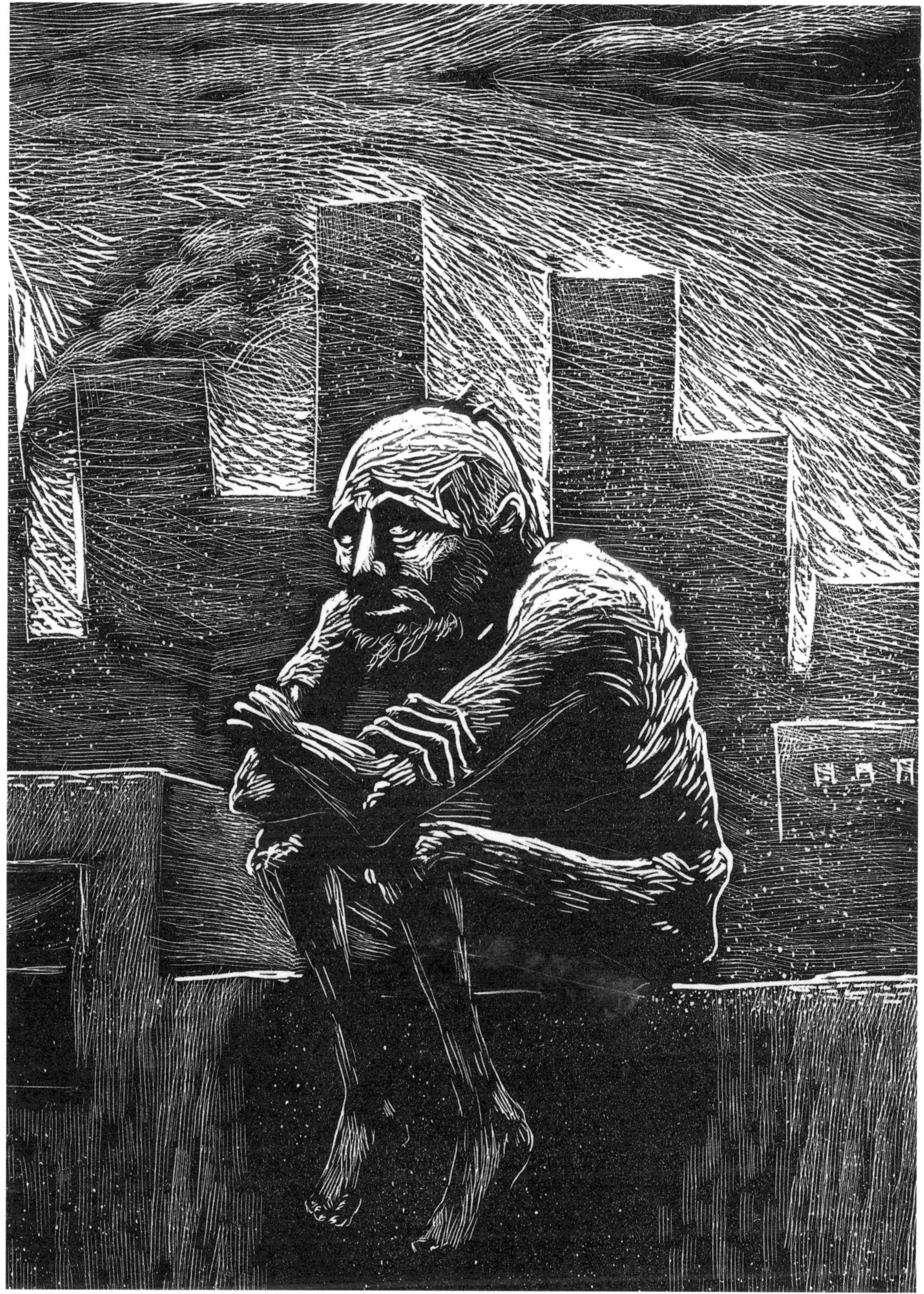

Depression

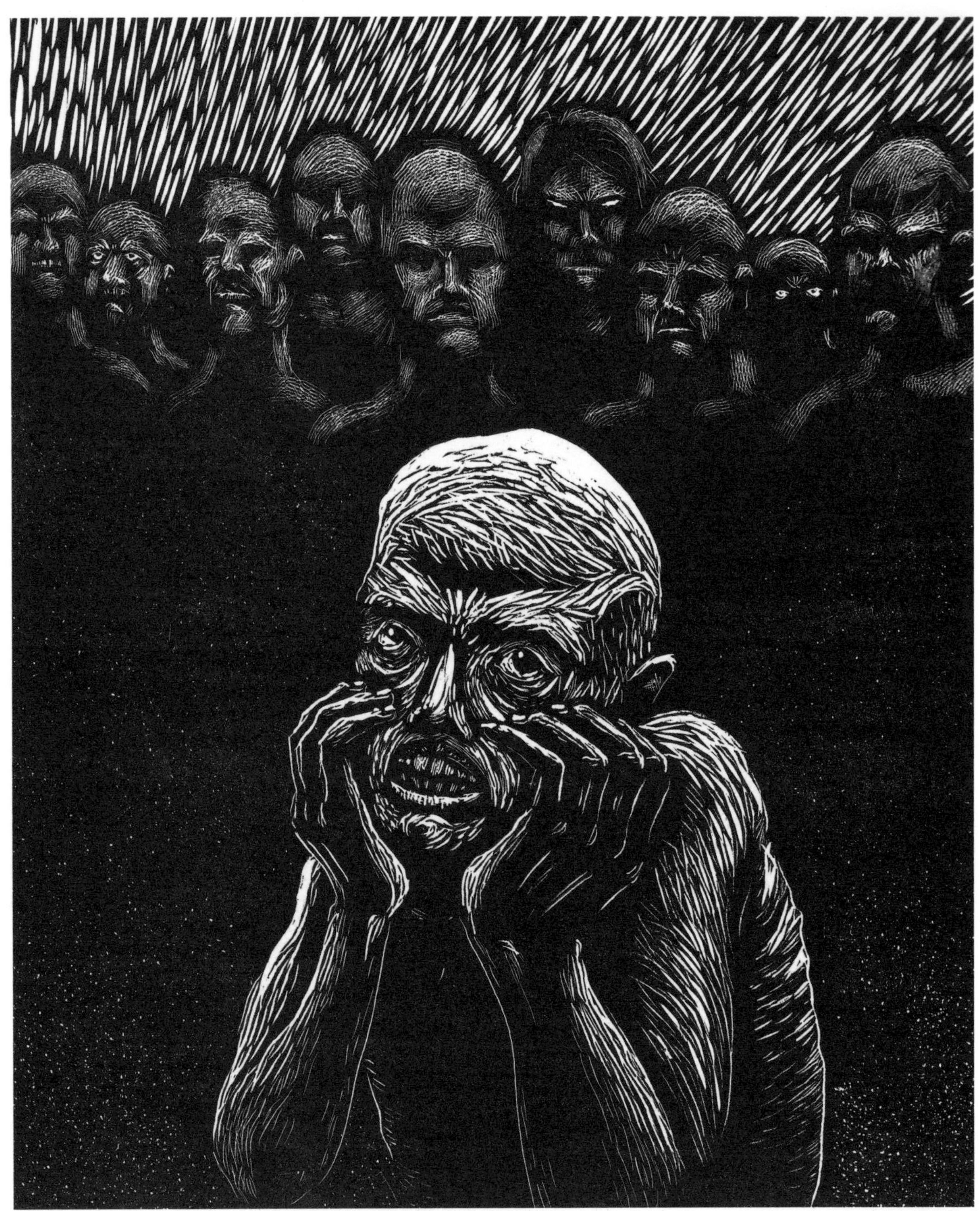

Anger

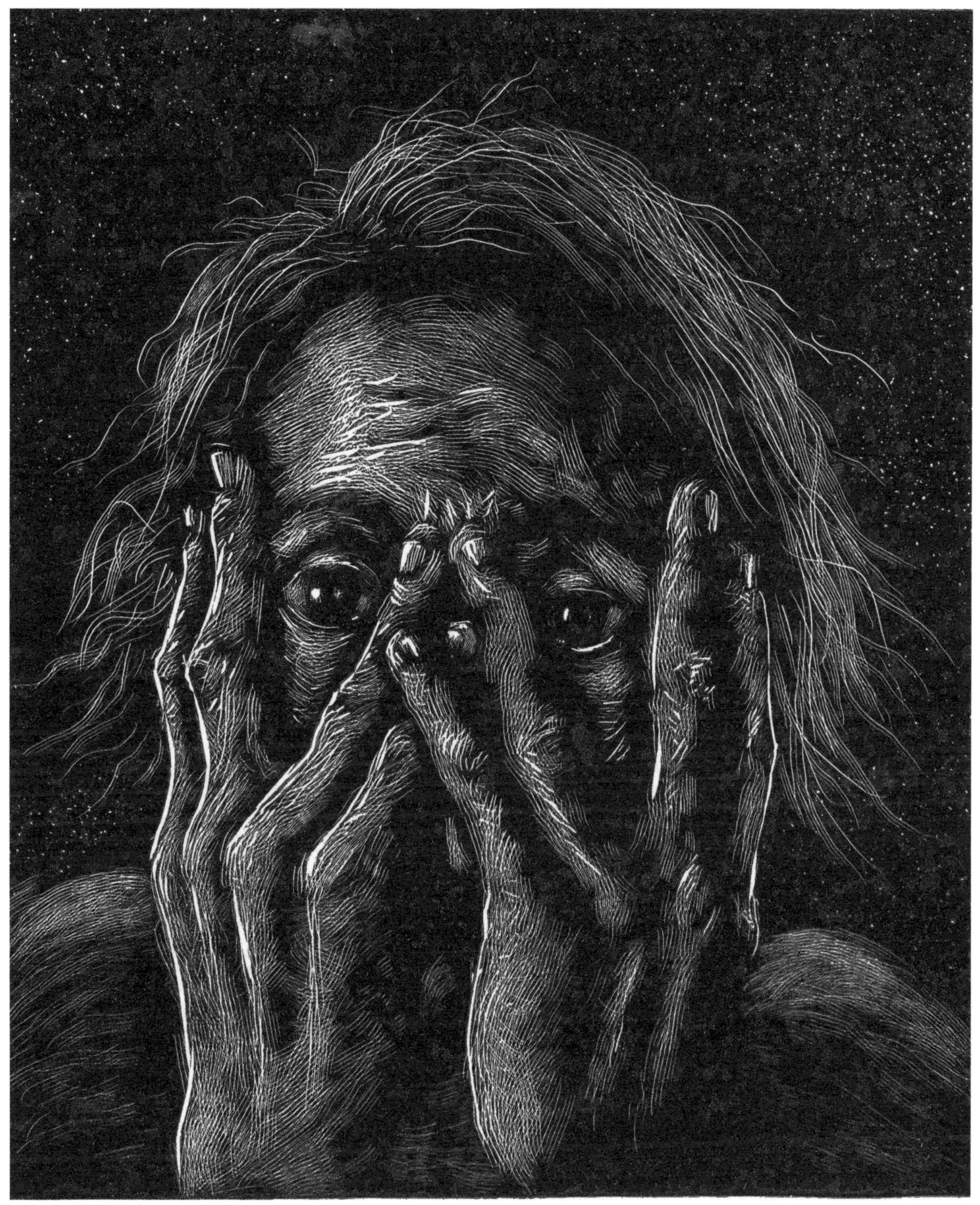

Denial

THEATRE POSTER FOR EL ROSTRO AJENO

Designer: Sonia Bandura

This project features a poster and several postcards for the play "El rostro ajeno (The Face of Another)", which is about a man who seems to become a stranger both to himself and the people who knew him before as he carries another man's face after undergoing a facial transplant surgery due to an accident. The main idea behind the poster is to express the desperate quest for self-knowledge that the main character goes through.

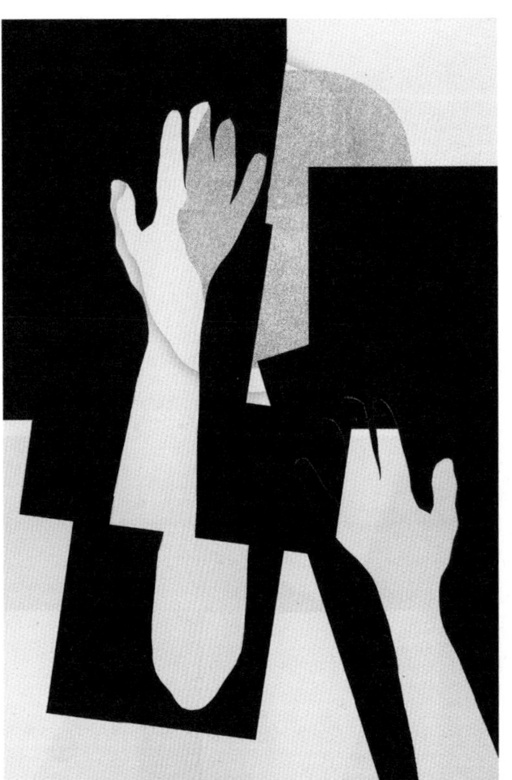

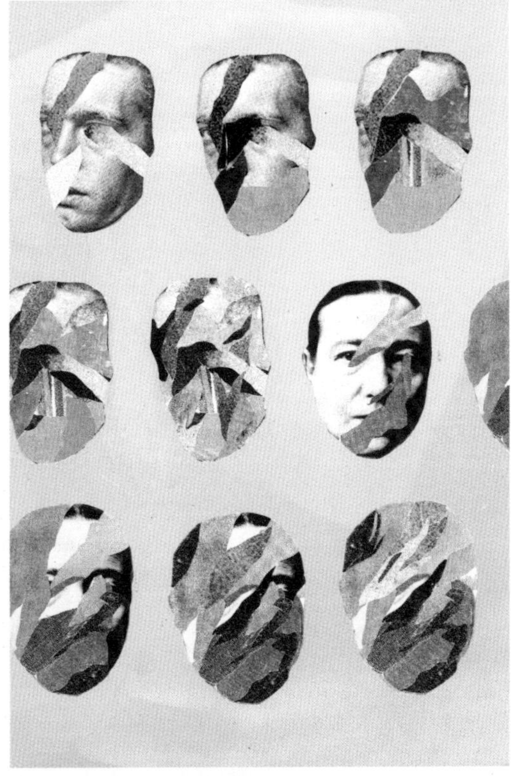

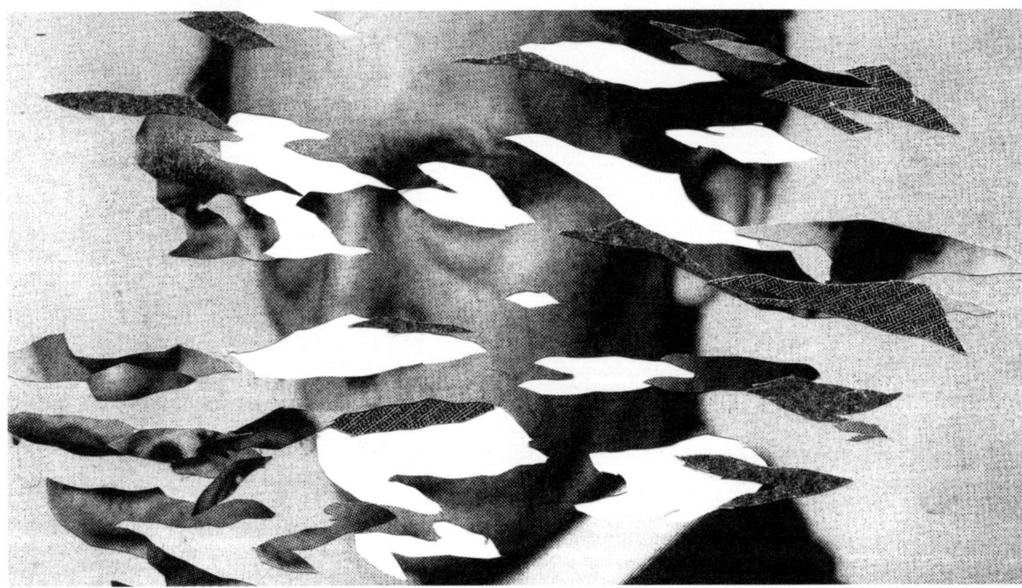

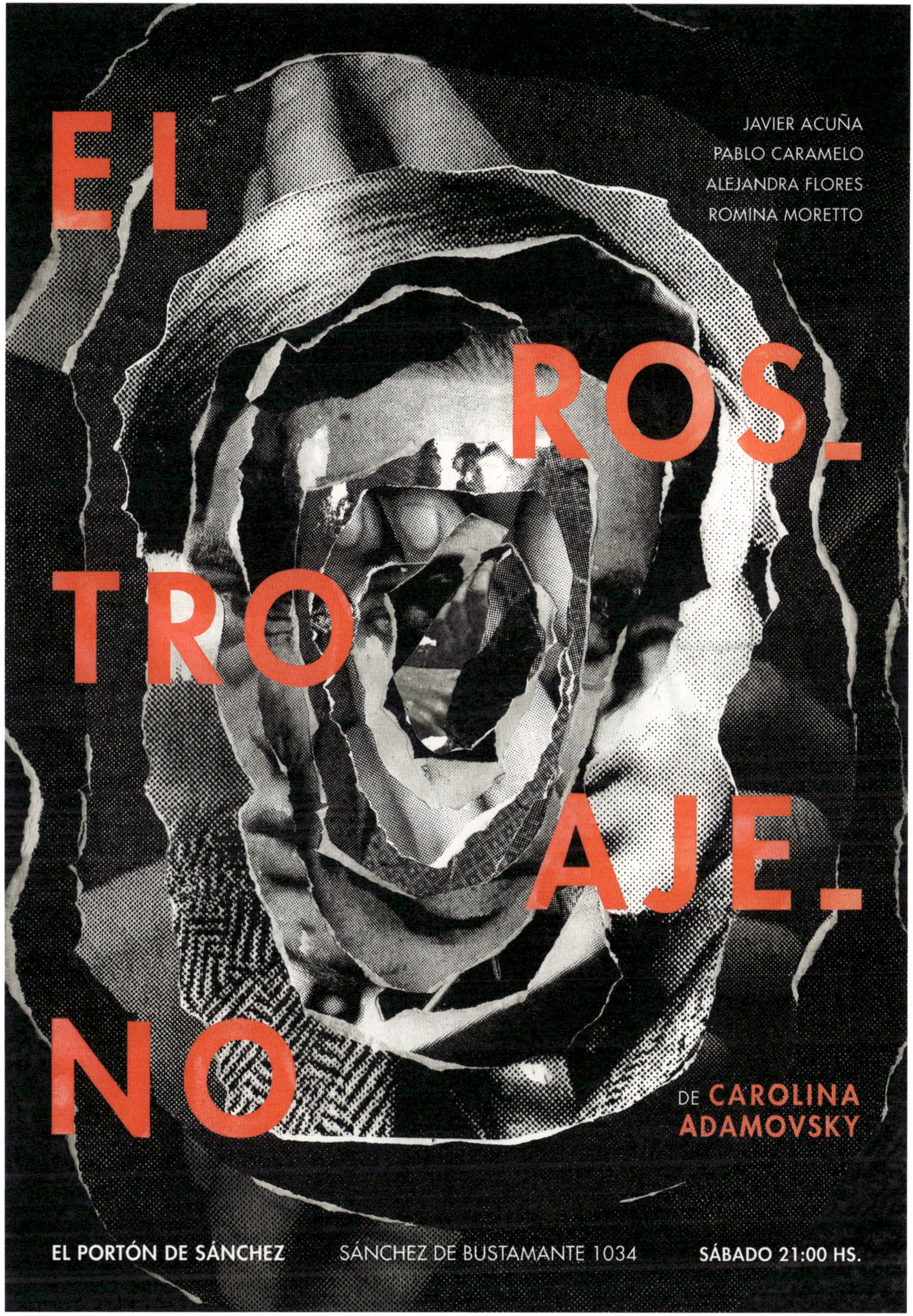
EL
ROS_
TRO
AJE_
NO
JAVIER ACUÑA
PABLO CARAMELO
ALEJANDRA FLORES
ROMINA MORETTO
DE CAROLINA
ADAMOVSKY
EL PORTÓN DE SÁNCHEZ
SÁNCHEZ DE BUSTAMANTE 1034
SÁBADO 21:00 HS.

EDGAR ALLAN POE "THE RAVEN"

Artist: Linas Spurga Jr.

These etching illustrations were created for Edgar Allan Poe's poem "The Raven". The thirteen prints not only picture the text visually, including the white bust of Pallas and the dark raven, but also depict the underlying contrasts deep in the poem's meaning, such as the protagonist's wish to forget and remember at the same time.

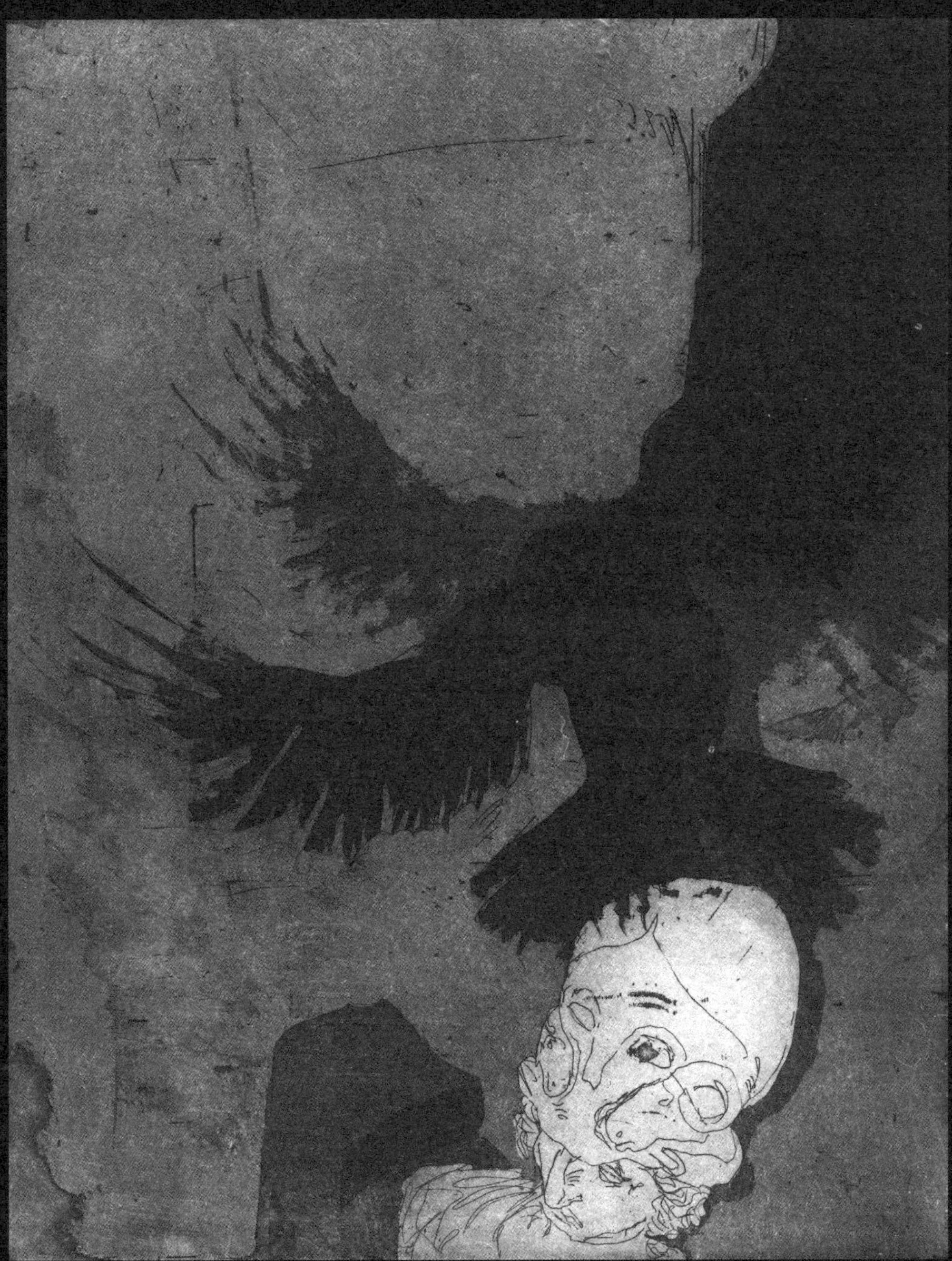

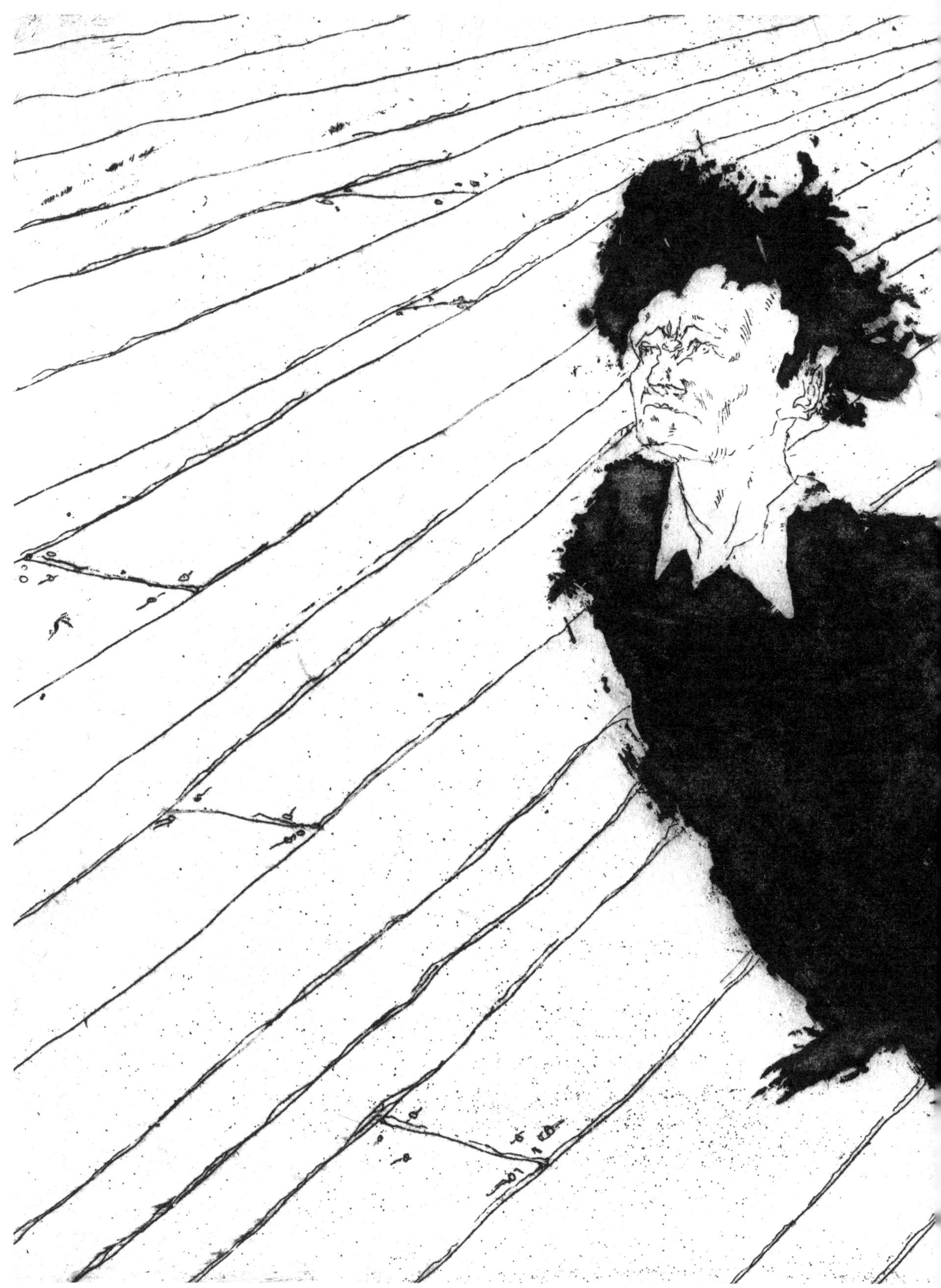

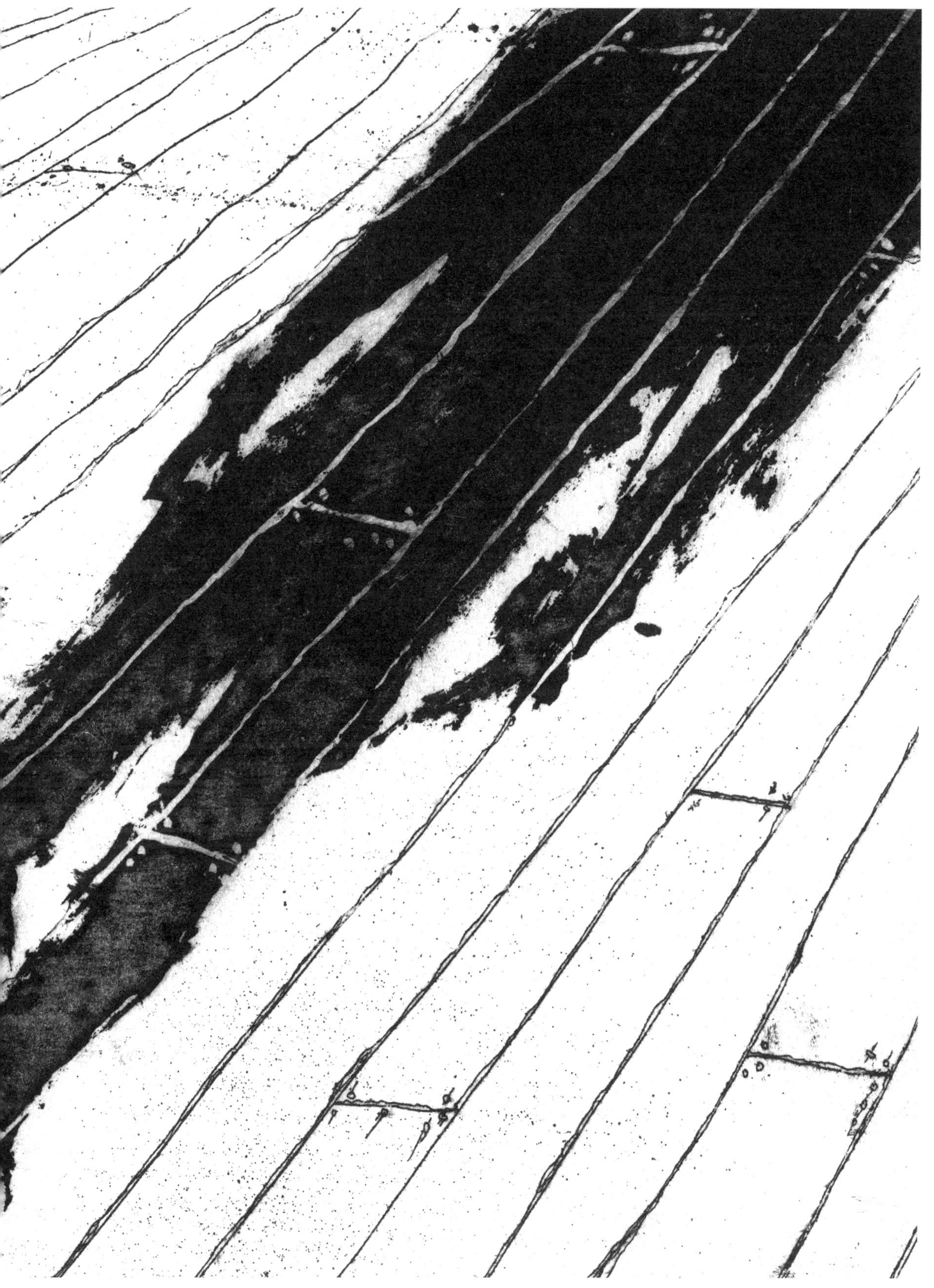

REPRESENTATION

Artist: Patrick Loehr

Through manipulating and re-photographing antique portraits—19th Century tintype photographs purchased from flea markets and online auctions—this series of images set out to explore a distinct topic. Separated from their original owners and descendants by time and circumstances, the identities of their subjects are lost forever. This work examines the desire to be remembered against photograph's inability to assist in the process—while a photograph can represent personal, social, cultural and poetic complexities of human existence, it cannot preserve them.

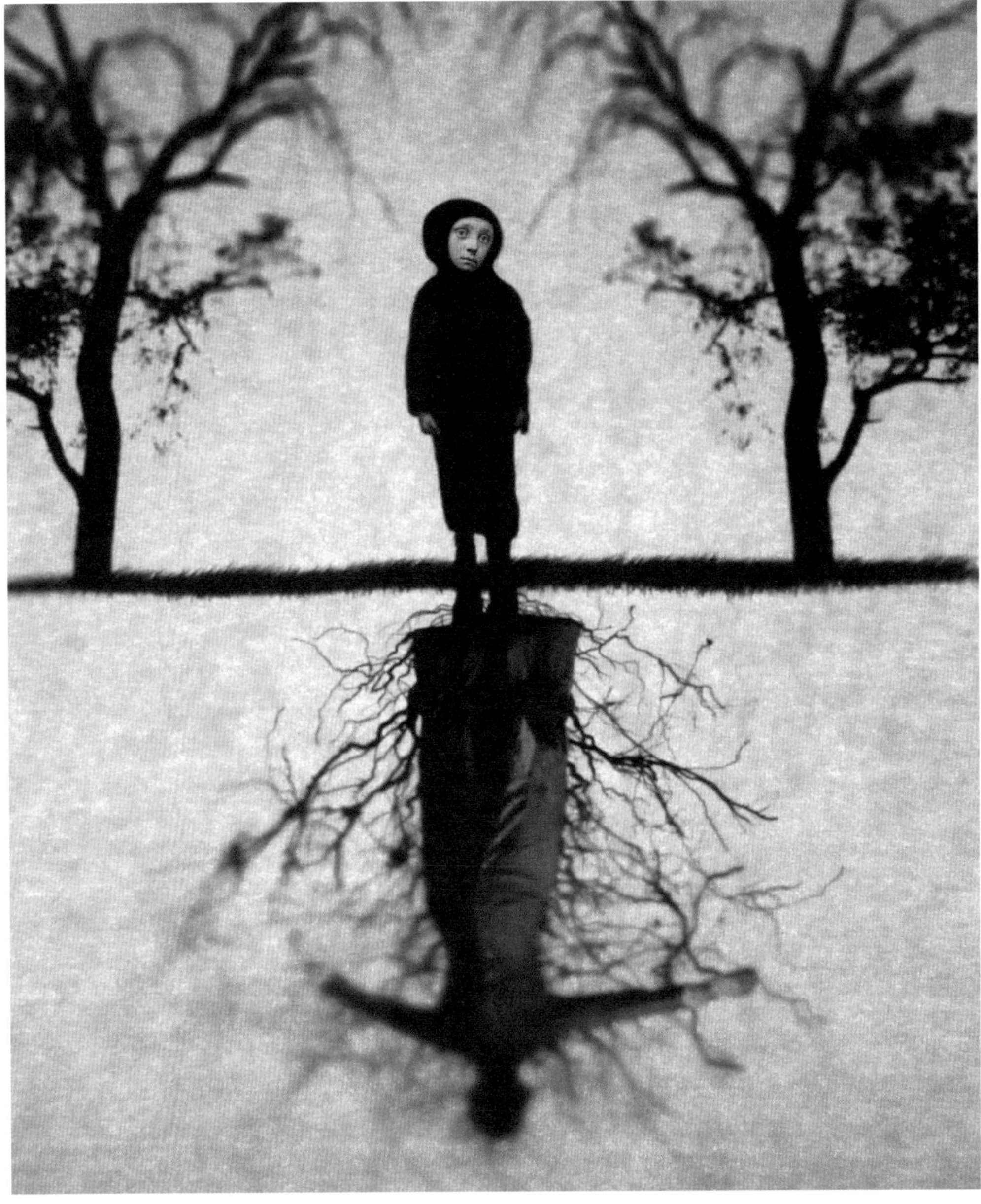

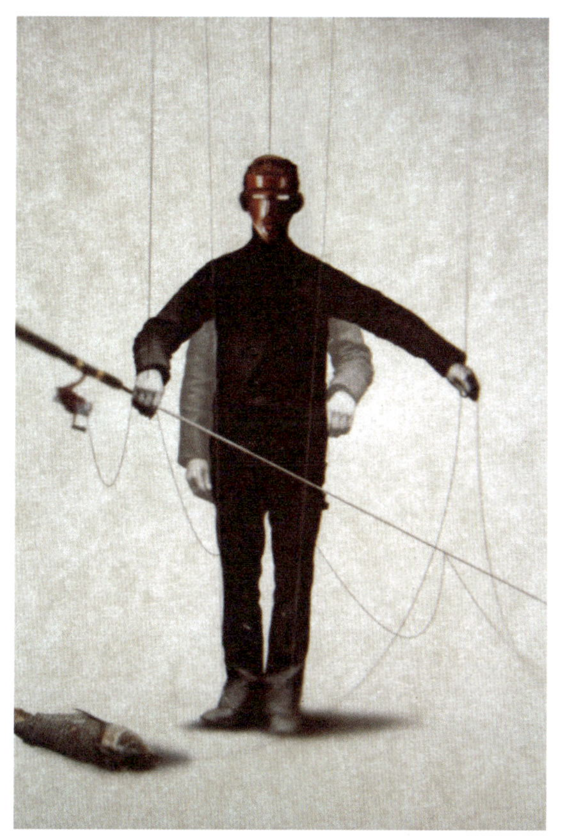

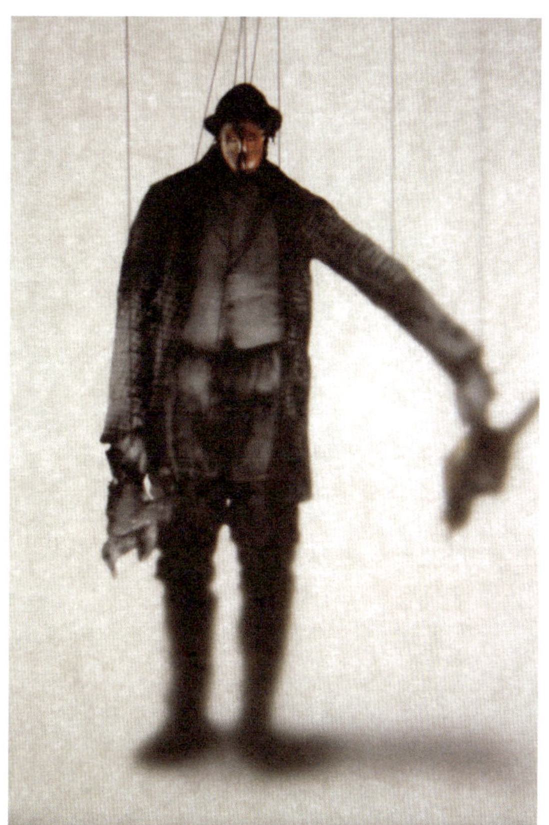

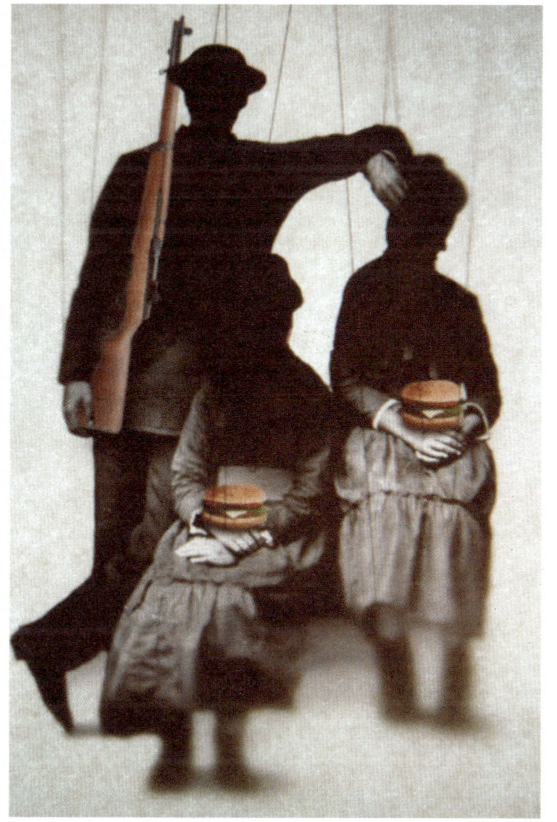

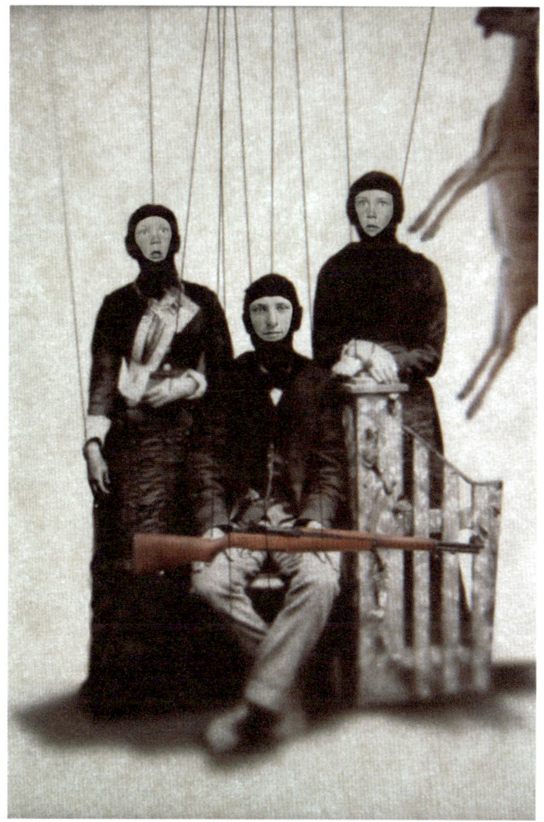

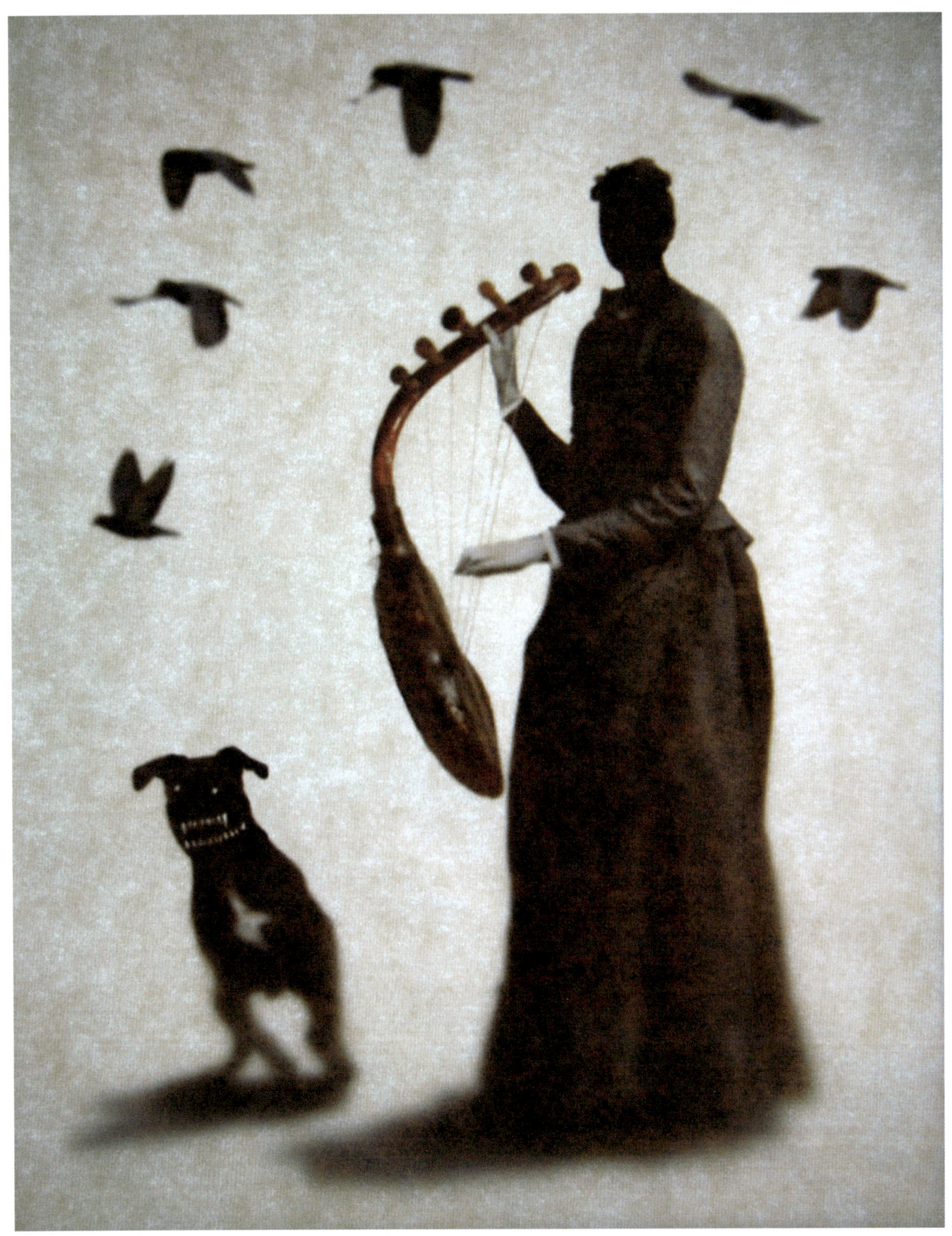

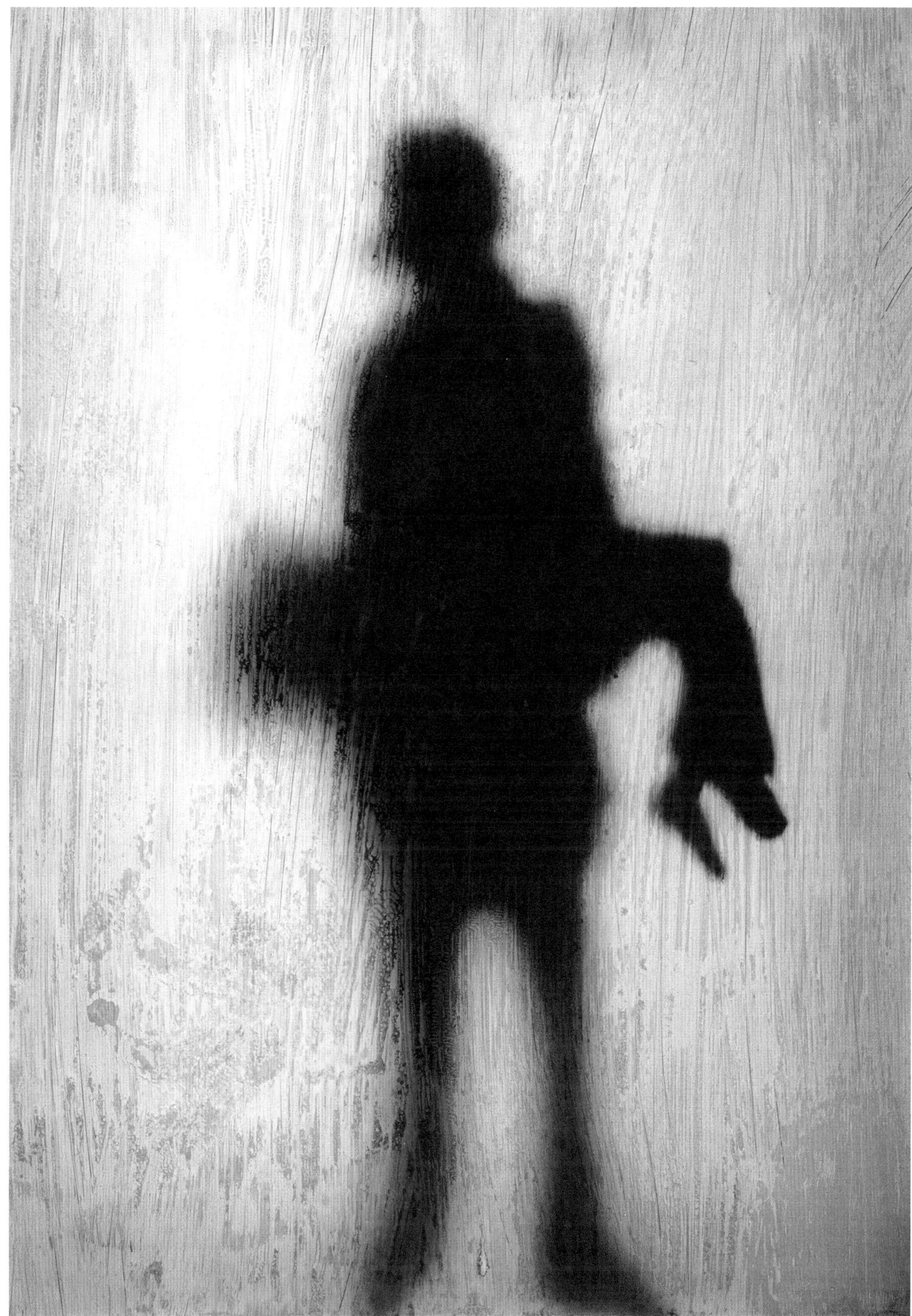

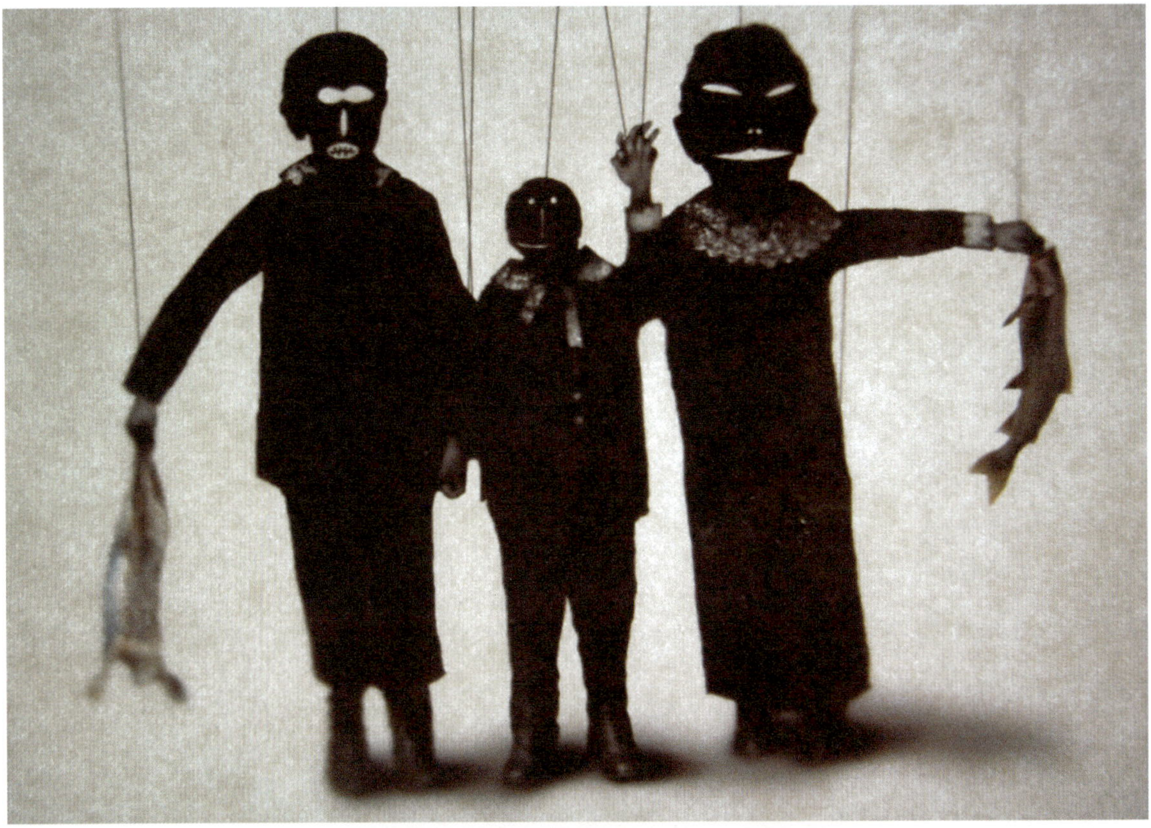

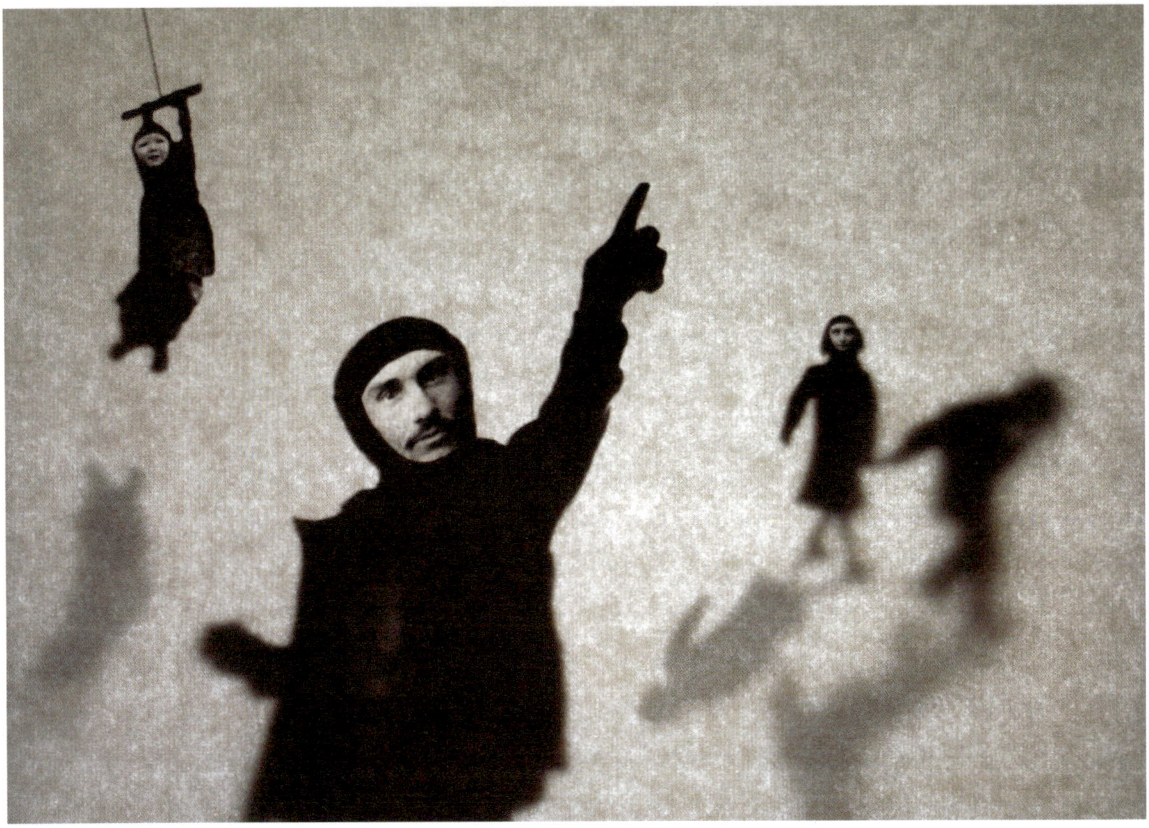

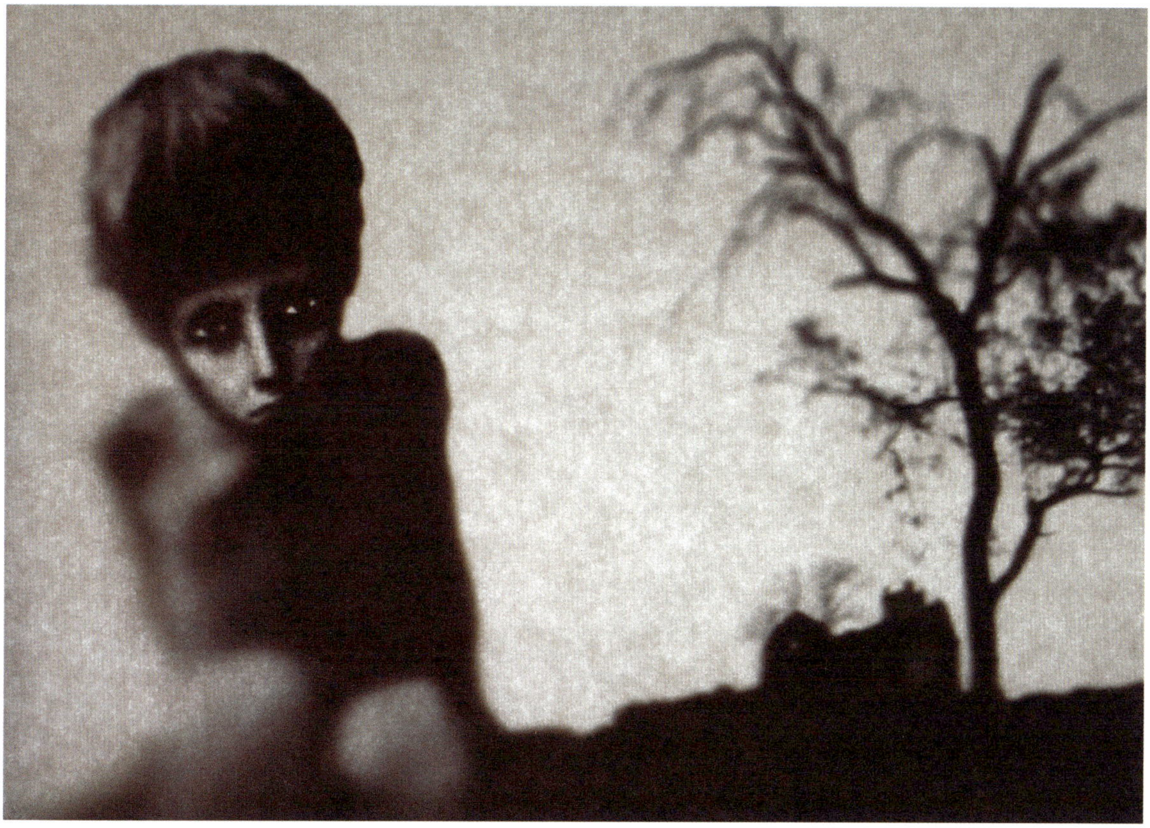

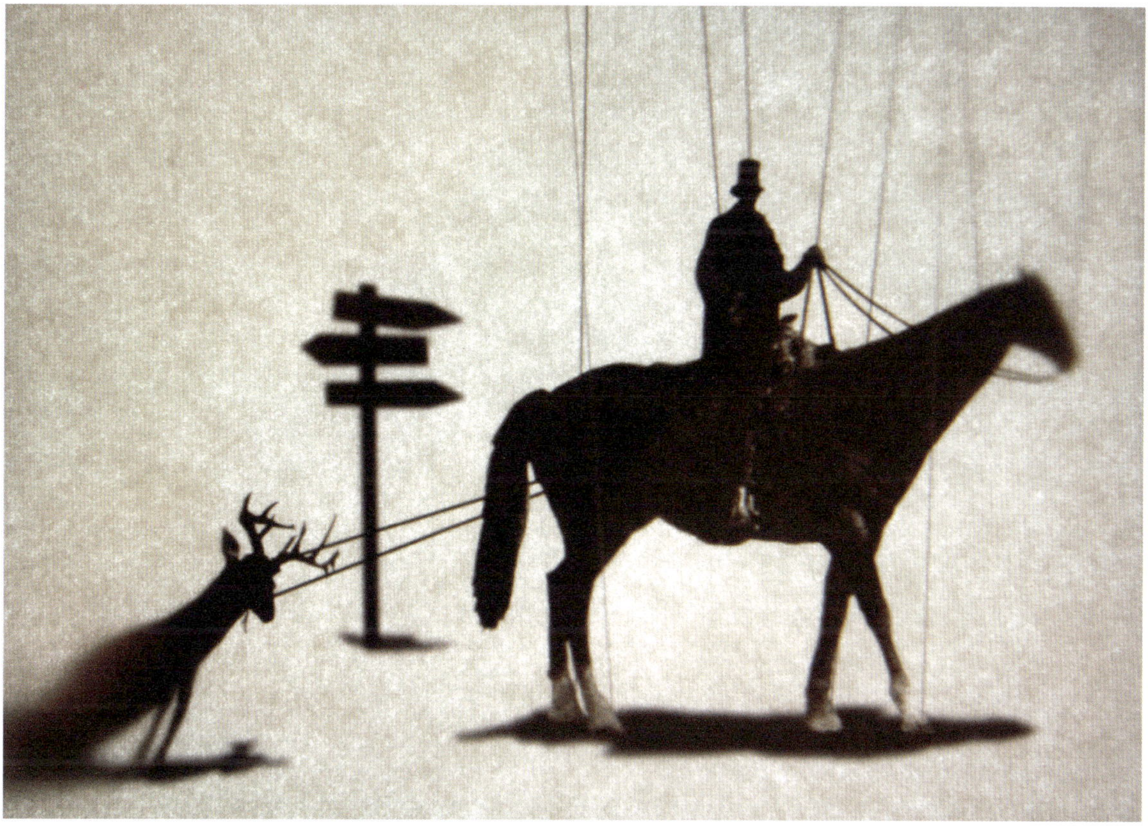

GHOST FAMILY

Artist: EBLTZ

This mixed-media installation consists of numerous collages of vintage photos or paintings. The textile element—the red thread—constitutes the allegory of the signs people will leave after passage. Through the metaphor of "family", the artists tell the fragility of feelings and the failures in human relations.

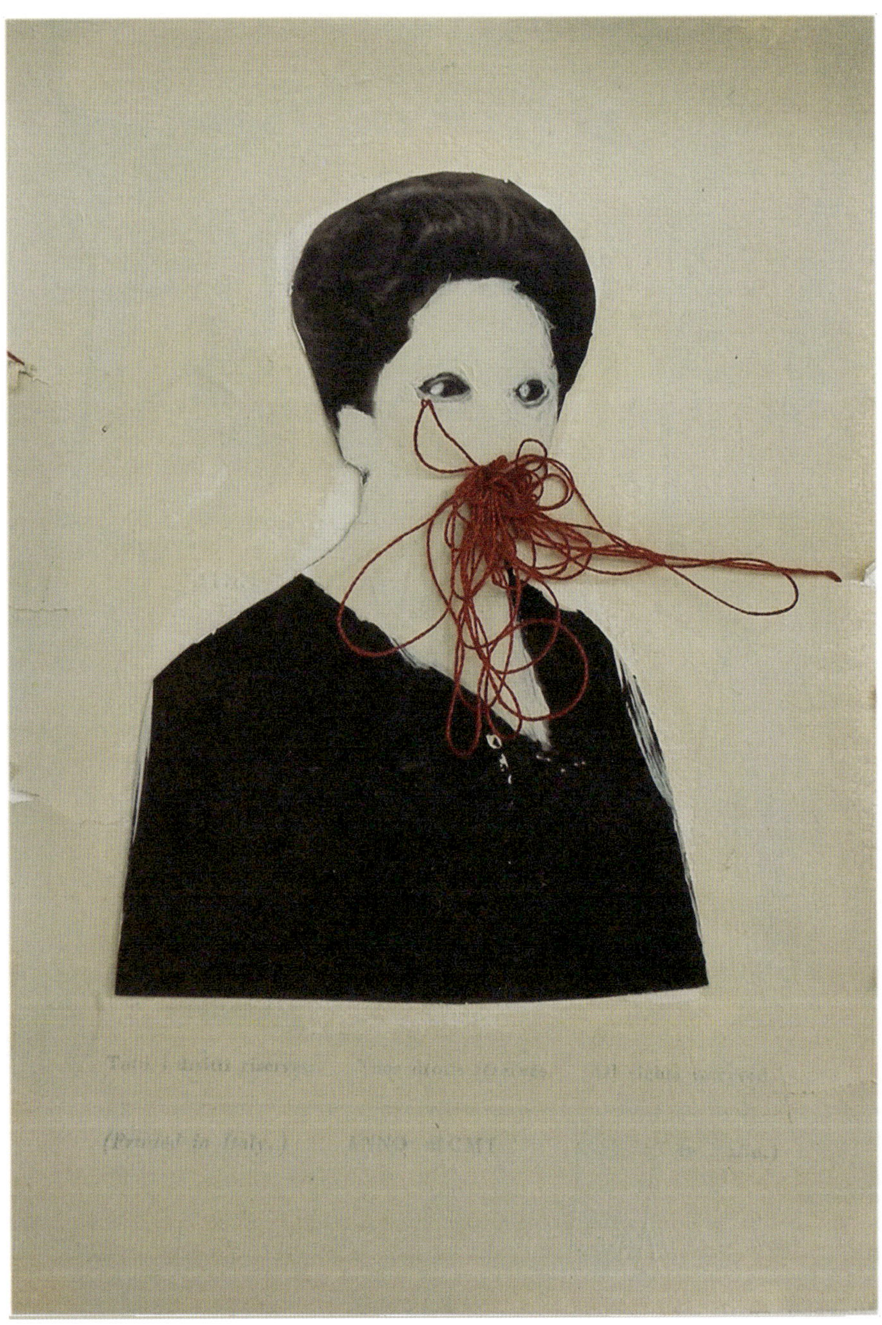

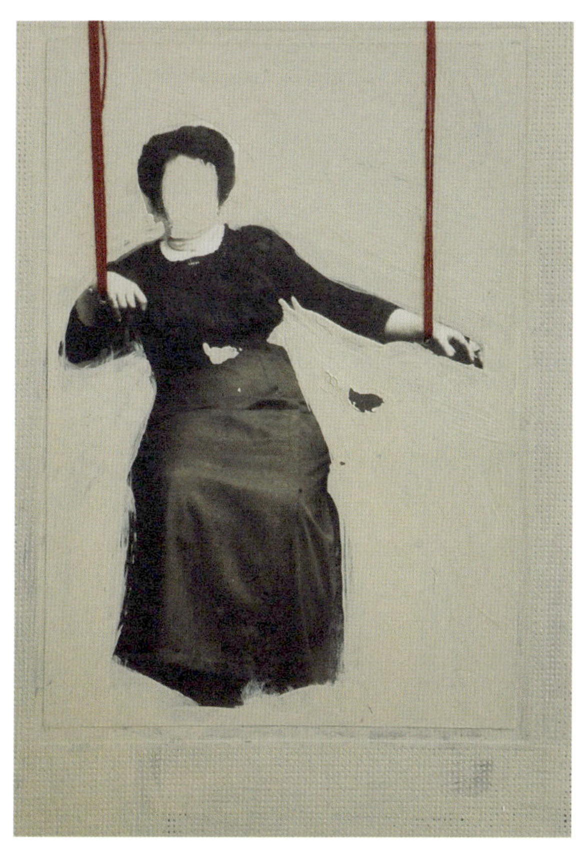
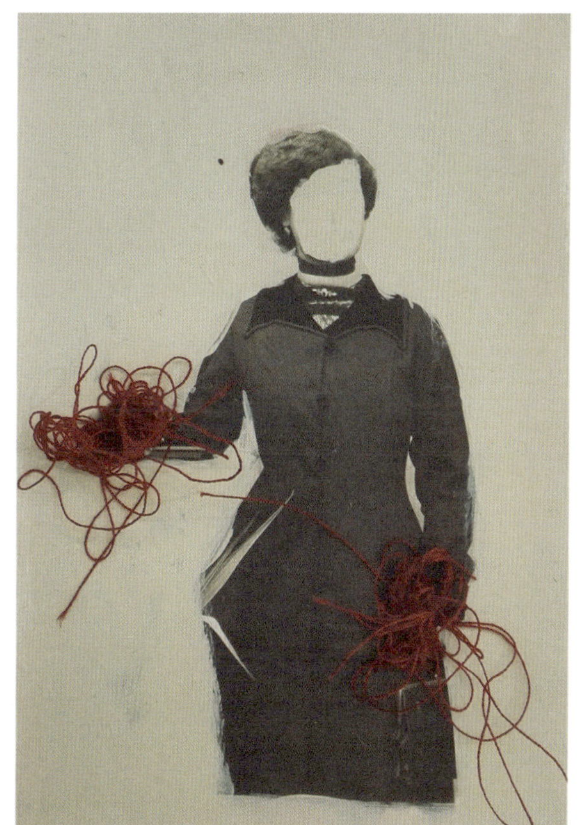
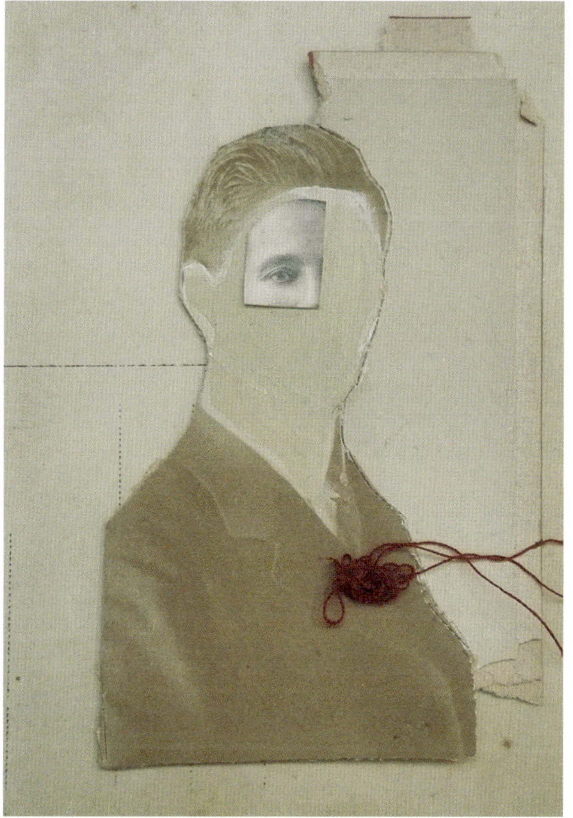
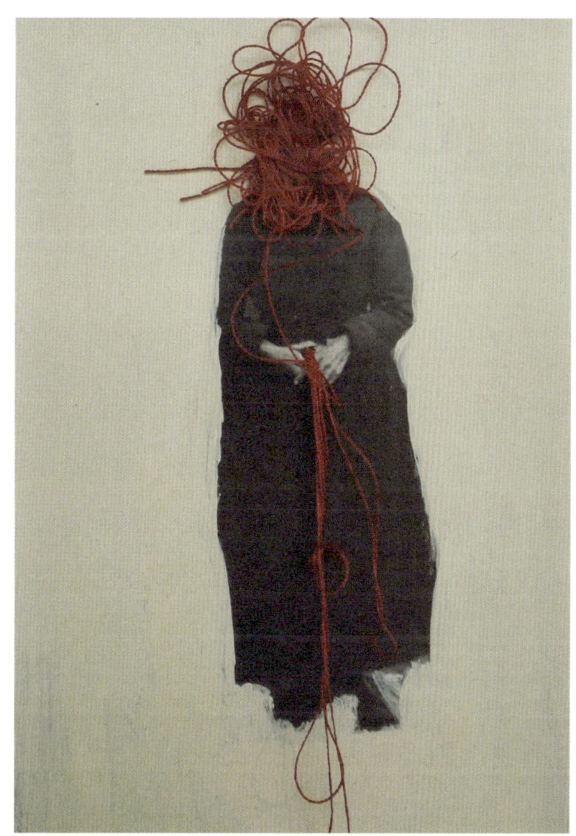

PENCIL DRAWINGS

Artist: Zbigniew Oporski

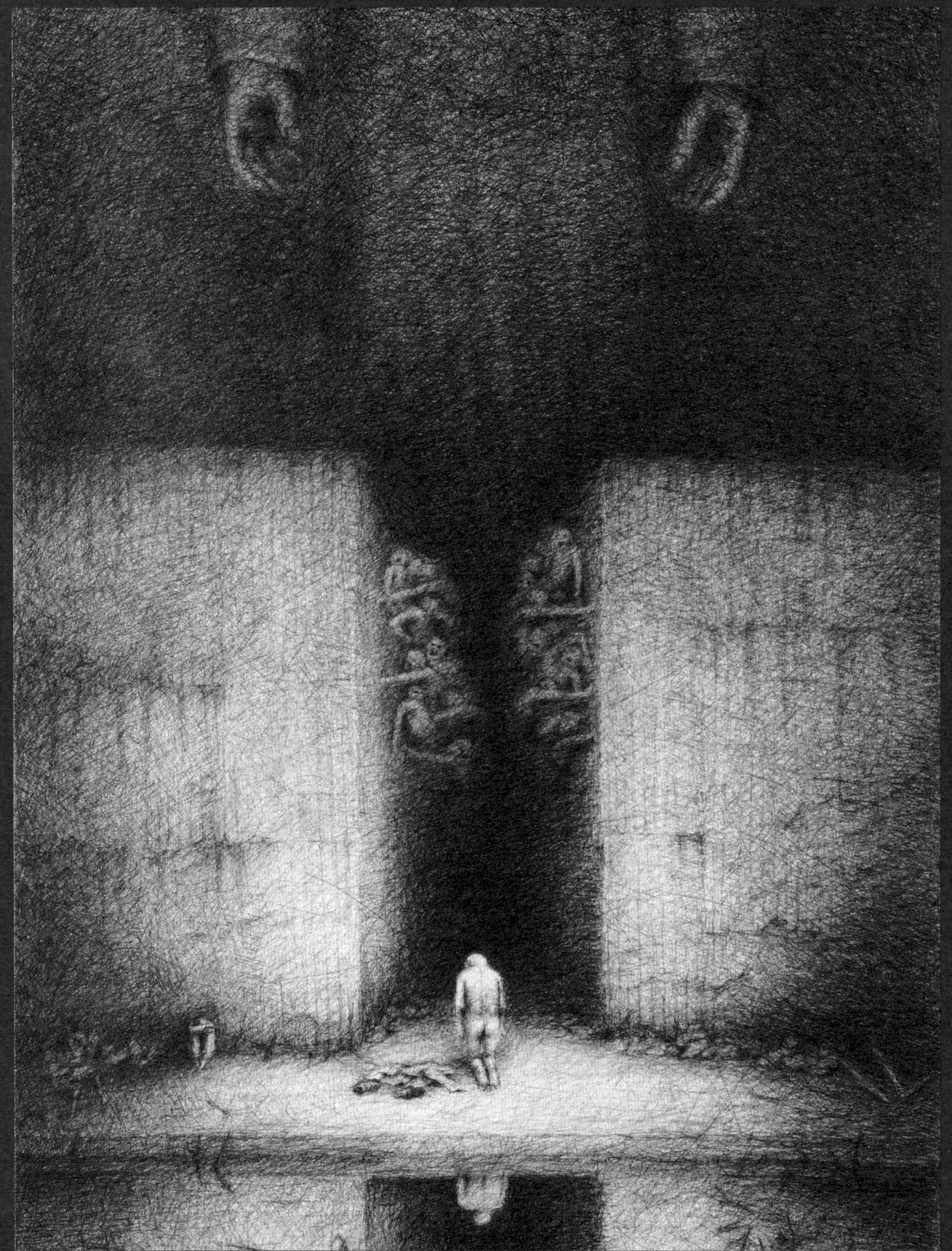

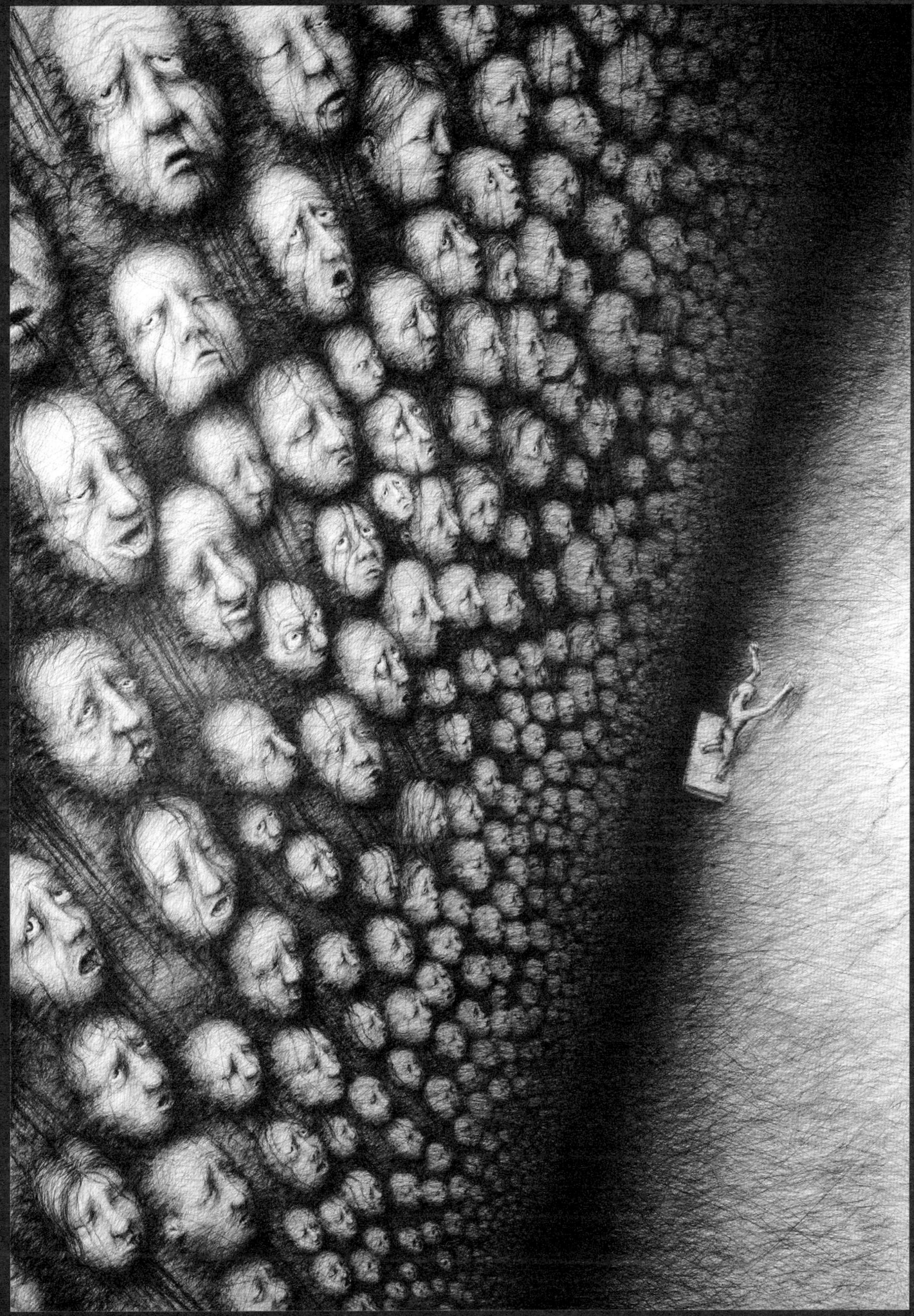

L'ARTE DELLA FUGA

Designer: vacaliebres

L'ARTE DELLA FUGA (The Art of Fugue) was a theatre poster for a show about drug abuse during adolescence for the Associazione Culturale Rizoma in Urbino, Italy. The visual content is a bit disturbing. Through the world of childhood, puppets and toys, the poster tries to express the loss of personality and individuality in the young and display the blurred thin line between childhood and adulthood.

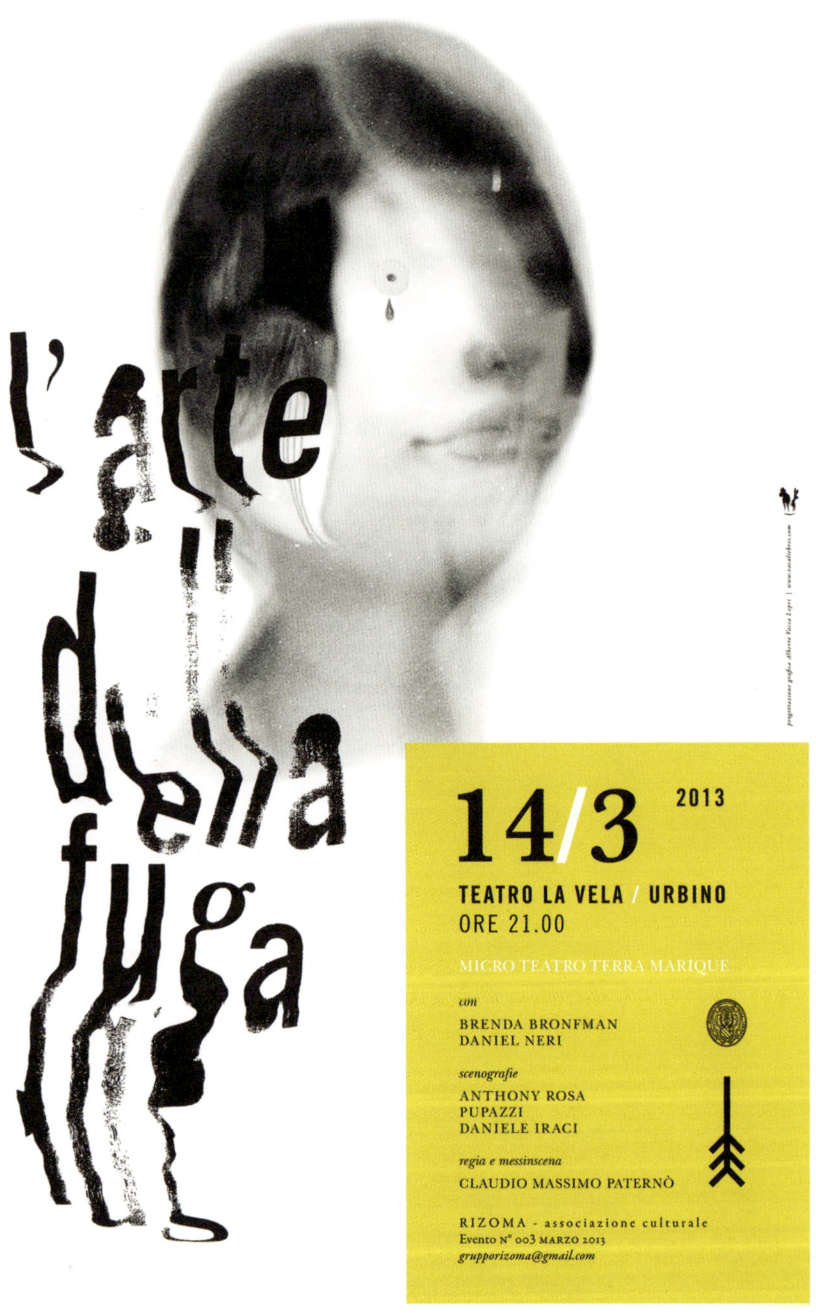

SKIN

Artist: Kebba Sanneh

This is an illustration for the cover of *Science & Health*, an in-house magazine covering scientific discoveries or debates in biomedical research. The theme of this issue was "skin".

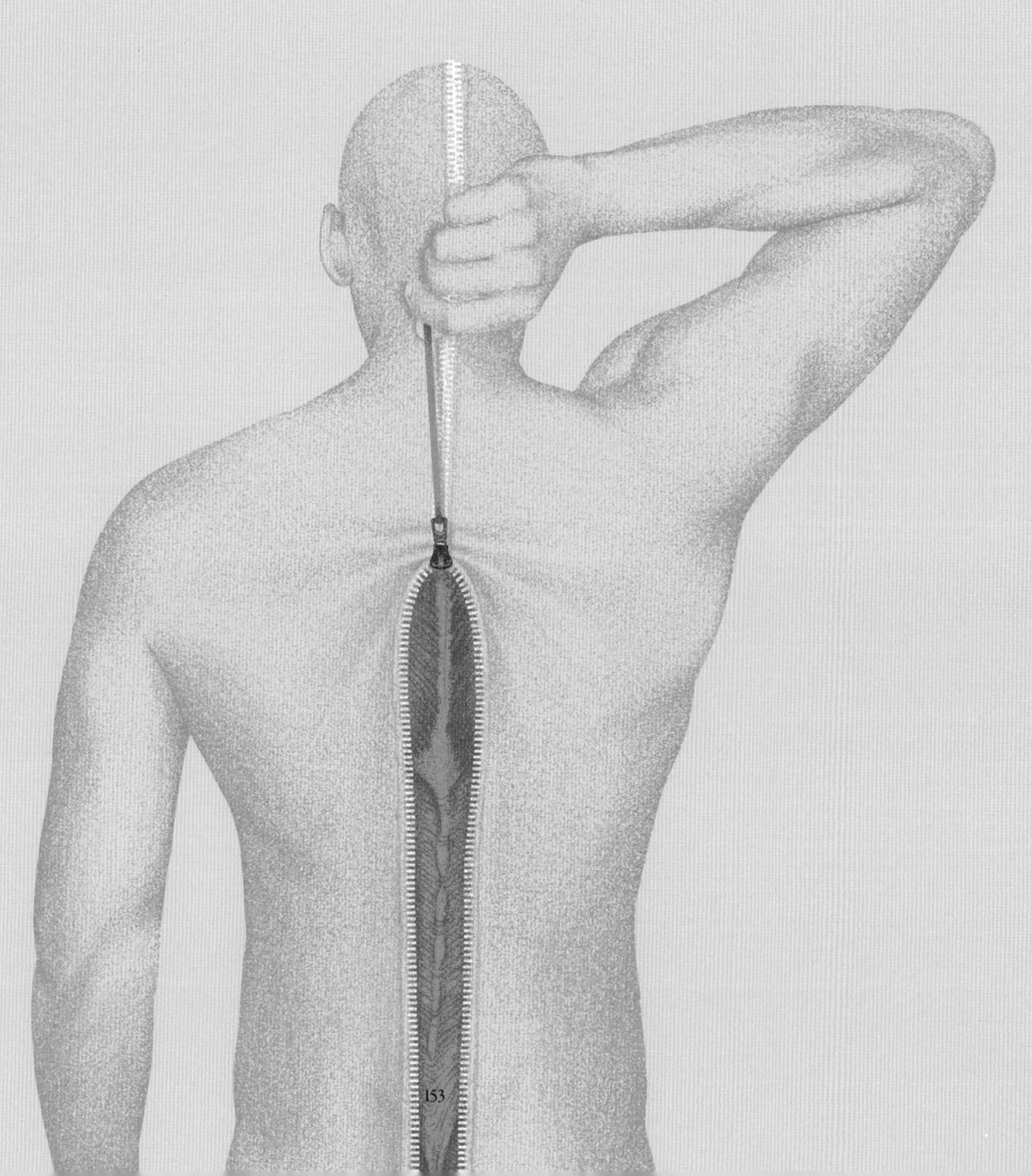

INTRODUCTION

Artist: Kebba Sanneh

This is a personal project: the aim was to explore the different faces people wear in society.

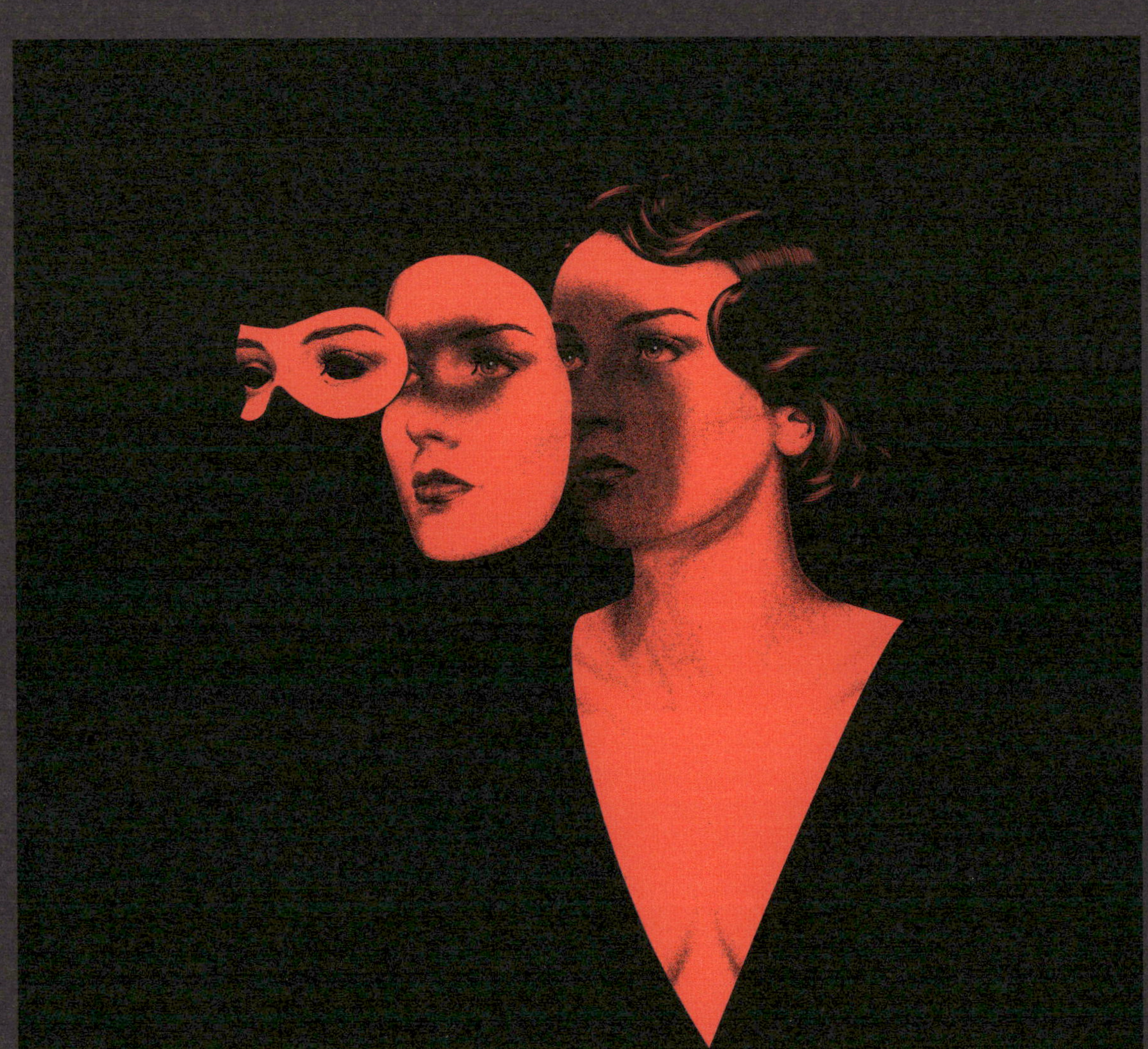

CATE BLANCHETT / CAROL

Artist: Kebba Sanneh

Commissioned by the London-based movie magazine *Little White Lies*, the artist created an illustration of different characters embodied by Cate Blanchett in movie *Carol* for their article.

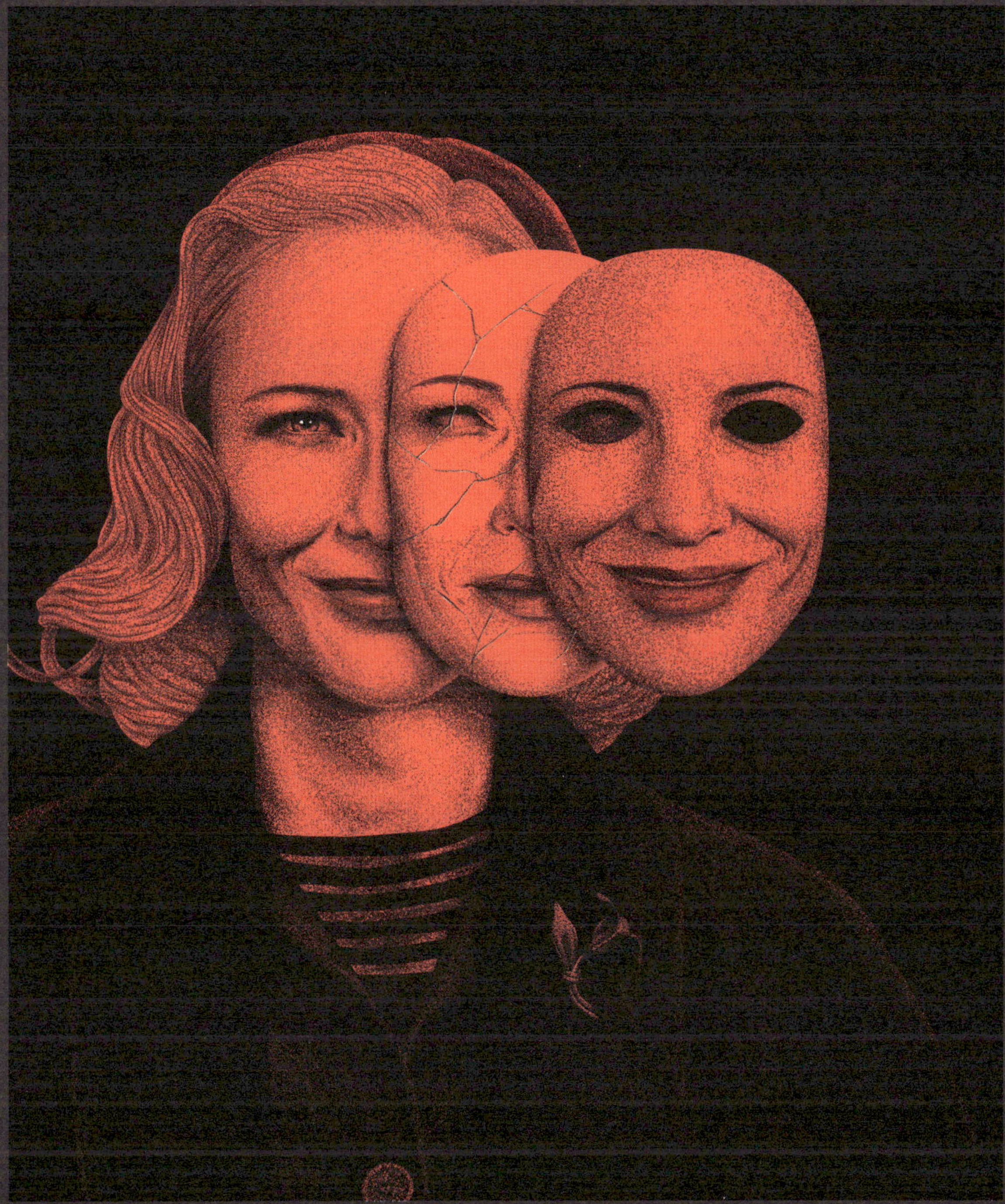

OCEAN MACHINE

Designer: Aleksandar Živanov / Hardworkz

Since getting the CD "Ocean Machine–Biomech" twenty years ago, the designer has been a zealous follower of artist Devin Townsend and his music. The designer is proud to be a part of the landmark in Devin's musical career. On the occasion of the twentieth anniversary of the release of Devin's first album, a special concert was held in the beautiful ambiance of the Roman Theater in Plovdiv (Bulgaria). The designer made the official poster for this event.

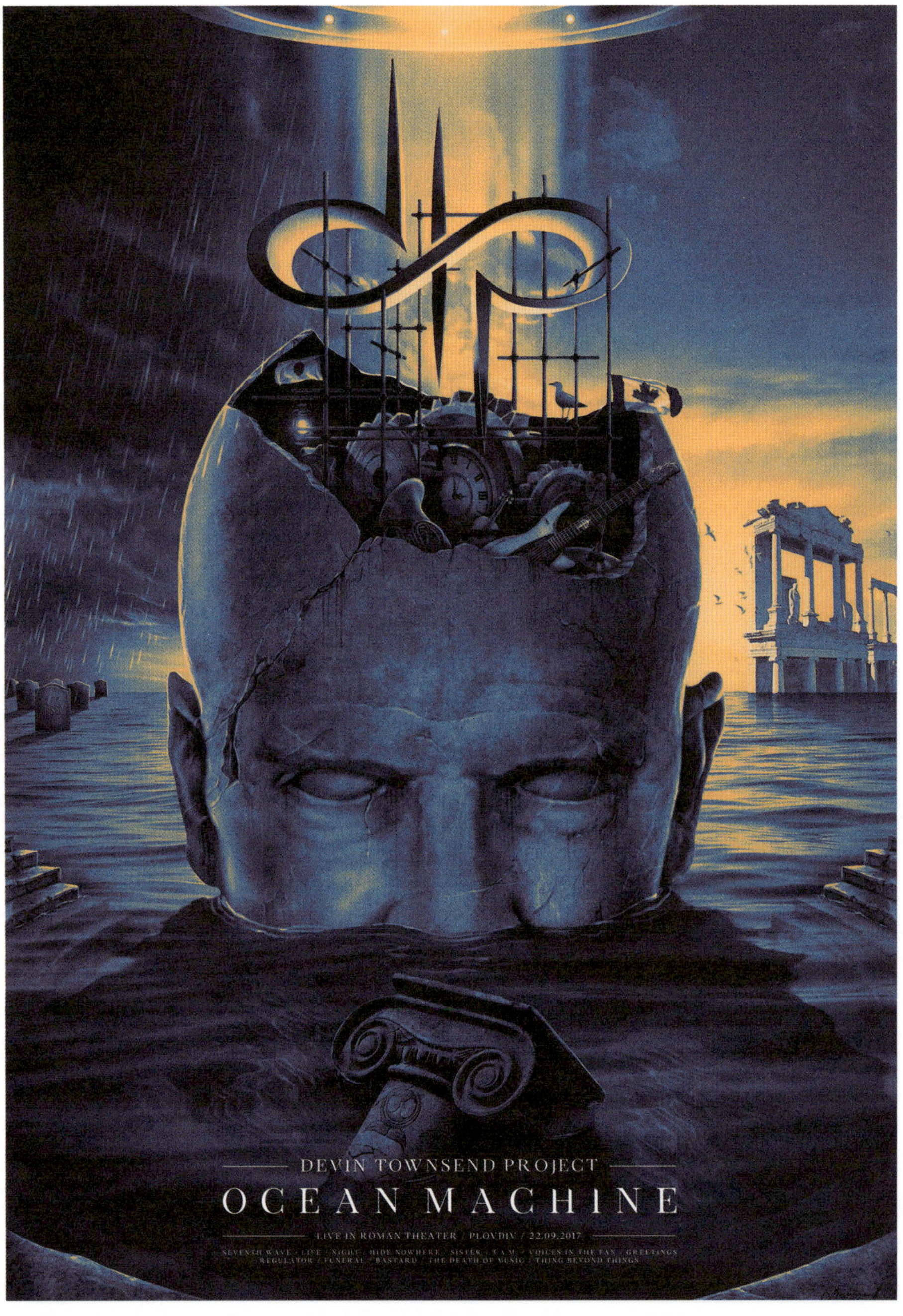

ANXIETY DIARY

Studio: The Royal Studio

This is a part of a self-published visual essay exploring the visual limits of communication on content-less visuals and the general public within the Soireé Graphique 2014 project, a conceptual play on the emptiness of communication exploring new languages and alphabets. The content of each poster is the direct outcome of particular moments that over the course of a particular period triggered anxiety-attack-alike behaviors.

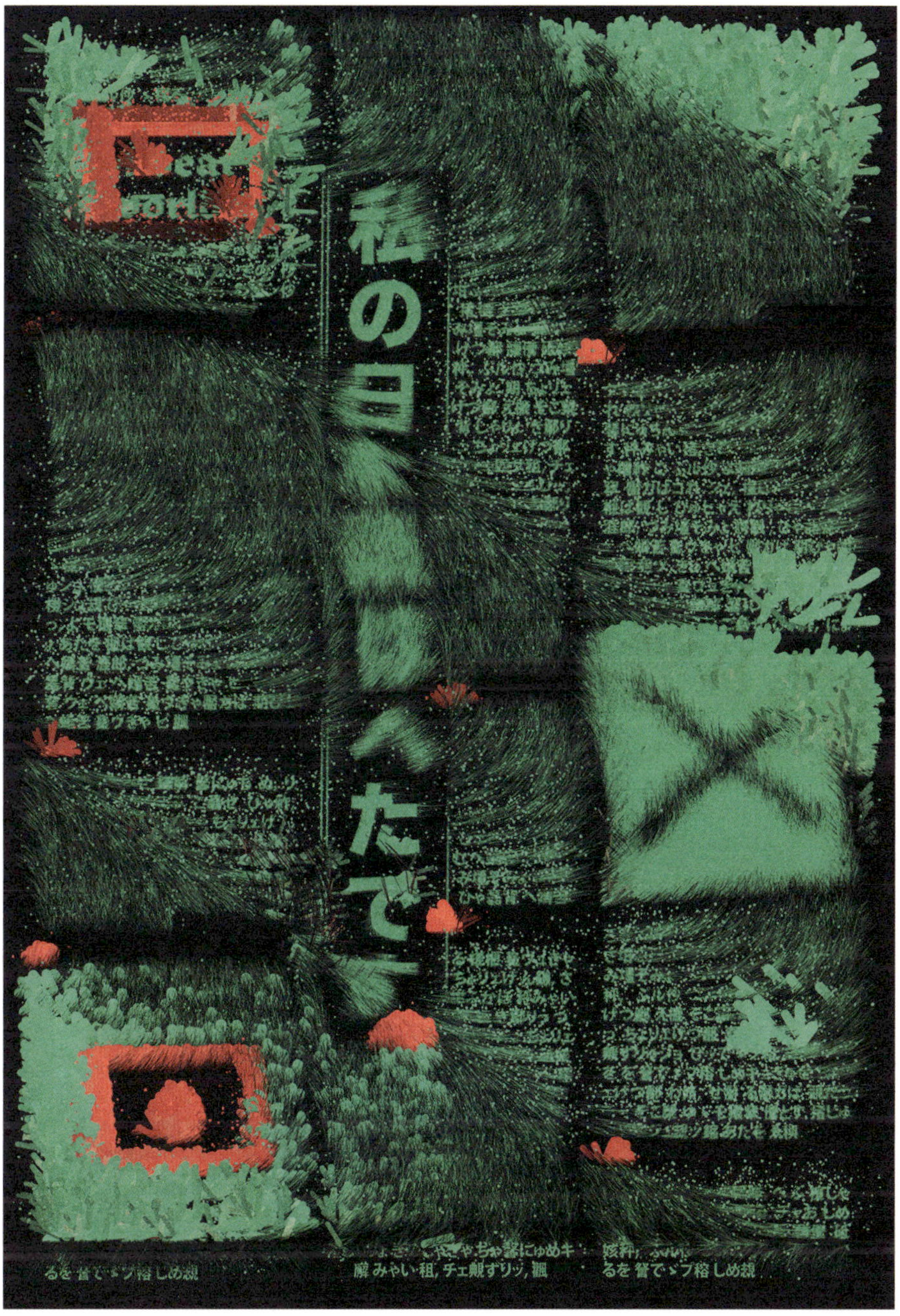

THERE'S SOMETHING DOWNSTAIRS

Artist: Charlie Dixon

This illustration is a personal piece and an exercise in building atmosphere, tension and dread in an otherwise ordinary and recognizable setting. It is expected to be expanded into a series of illustrations that dwell on the dark, the ominous and the paranormal.

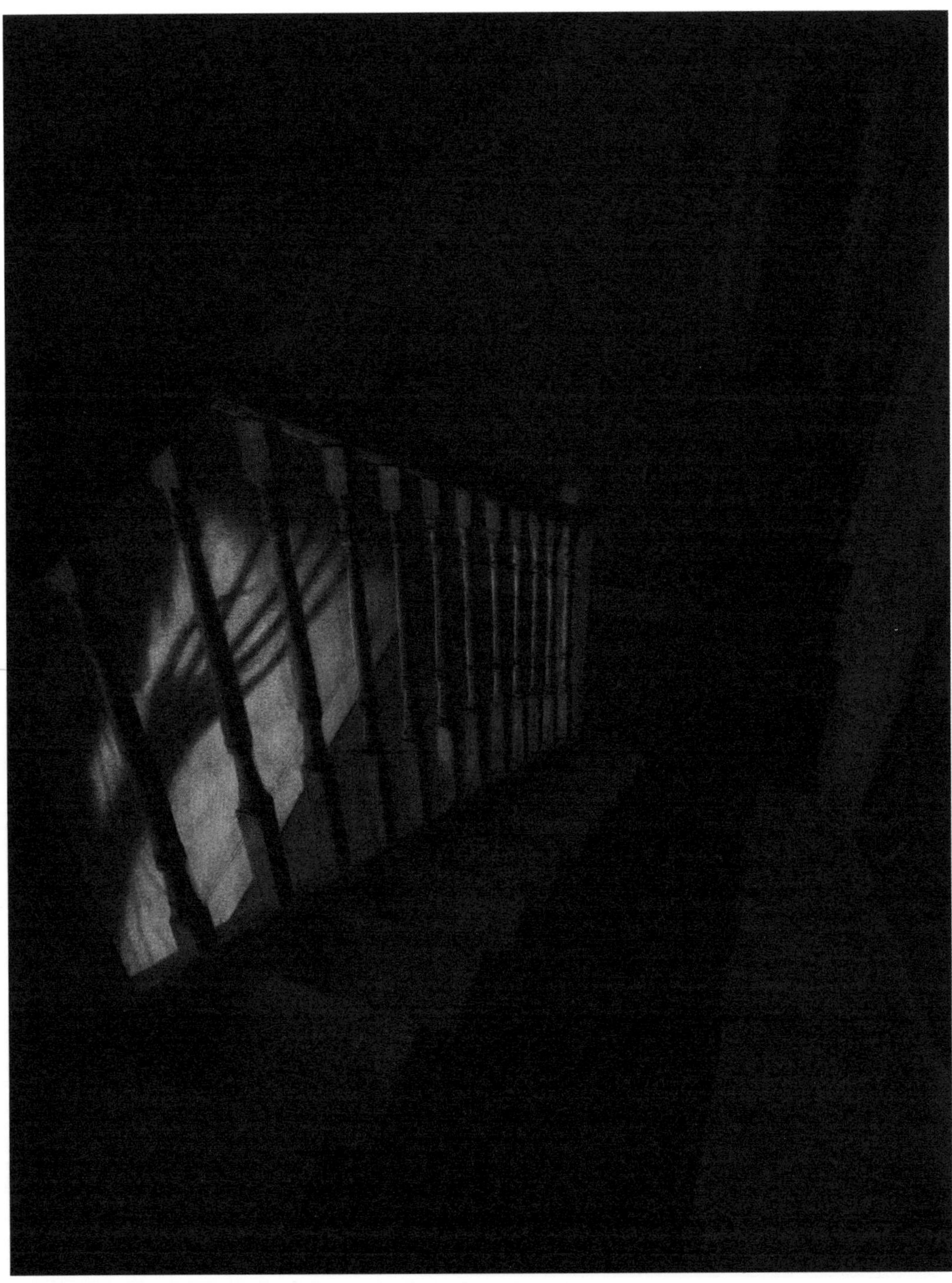

ALIEN

Designer: Cristian Eres

Alien is a screen-printed alternative poster created for a private commission group by Cristian Eres, a Spanish illustrator and image-maker, with influences from sci-fi and fantasy artists from the 70s, specially Jean Giraud, Moebius.

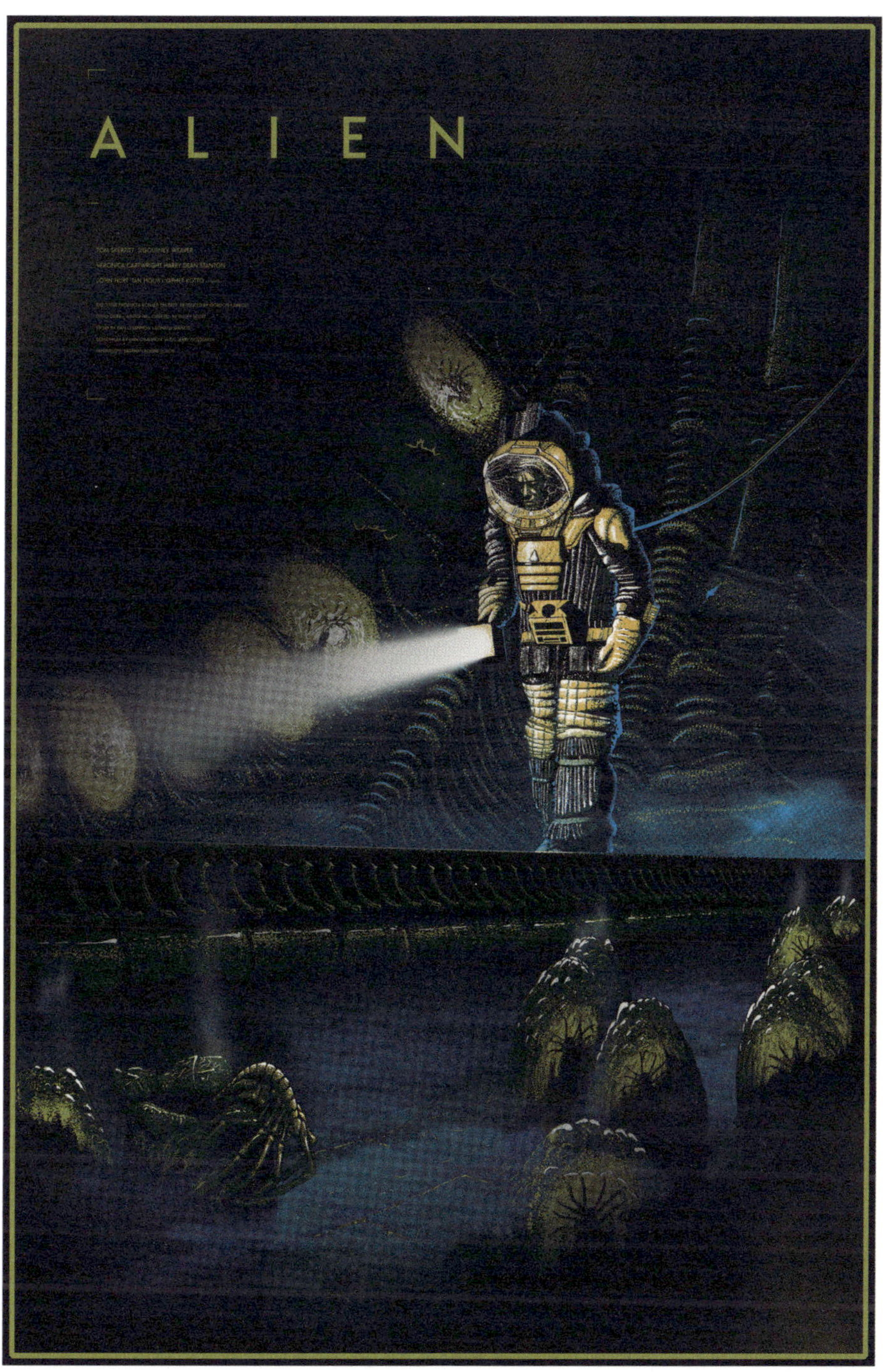

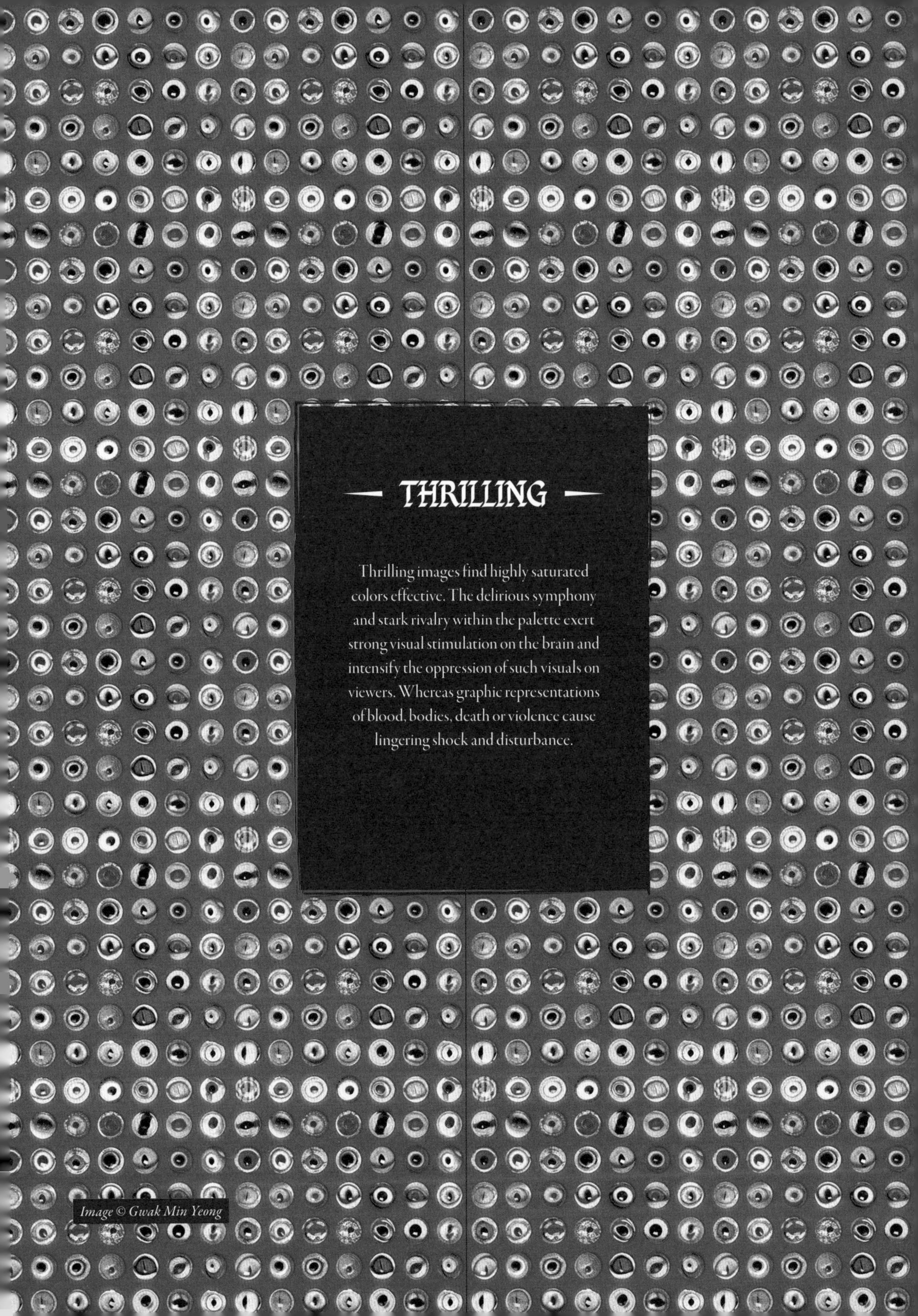

THRILLING

Thrilling images find highly saturated colors effective. The delirious symphony and stark rivalry within the palette exert strong visual stimulation on the brain and intensify the oppression of such visuals on viewers. Whereas graphic representations of blood, bodies, death or violence cause lingering shock and disturbance.

Image © Gwak Min Yeong

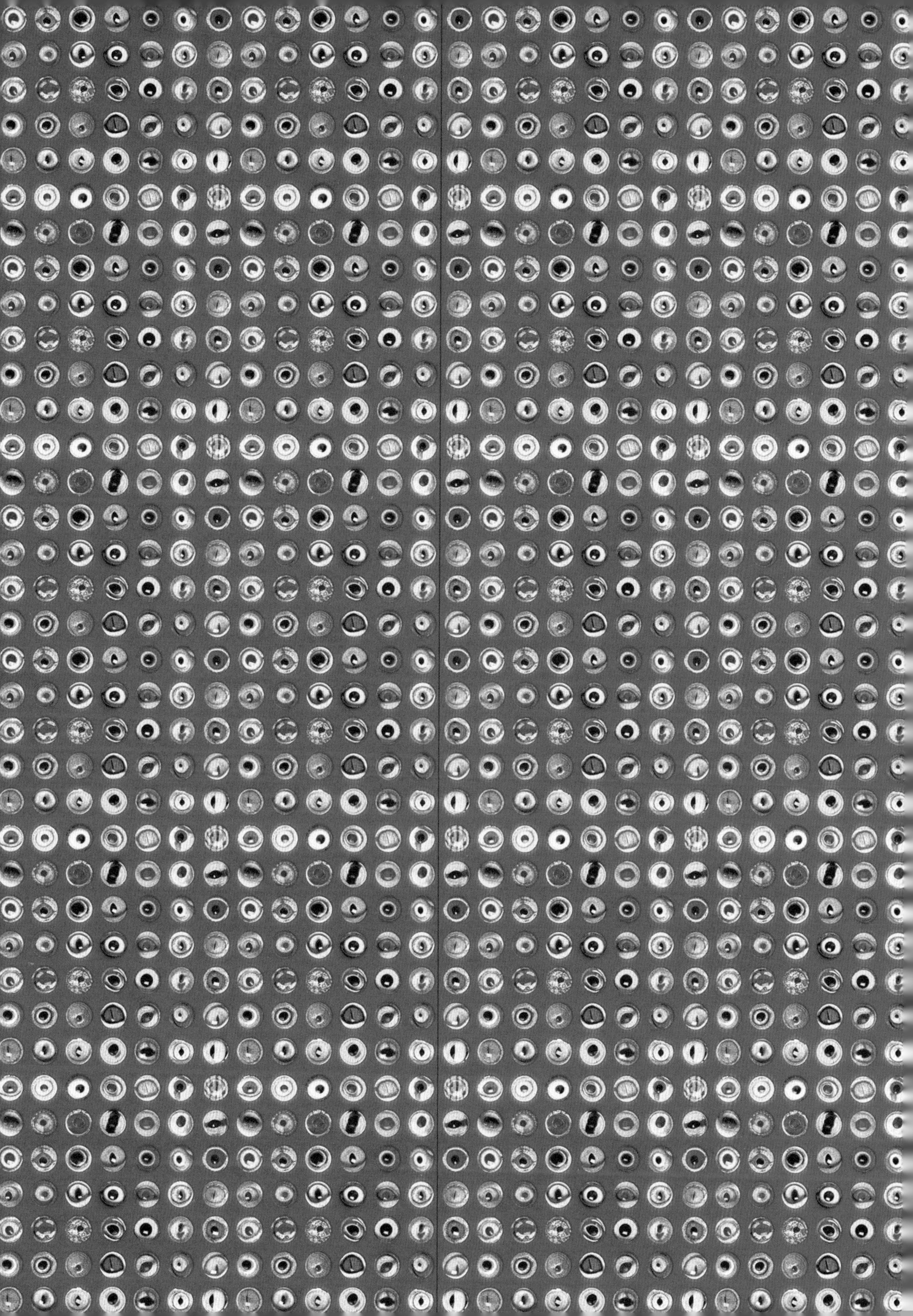

CERITA HANTU MALAYSIA

Designer: Firdaus Mustapa

This poster was designed for the Malaysian horror movie *Cerita Hantu Malaysia*. The subject of a photo from the production house was turned into a horror looking ghost with Photoshop by changing the eye pupils and adding maggots to make it scarier than the original photo.

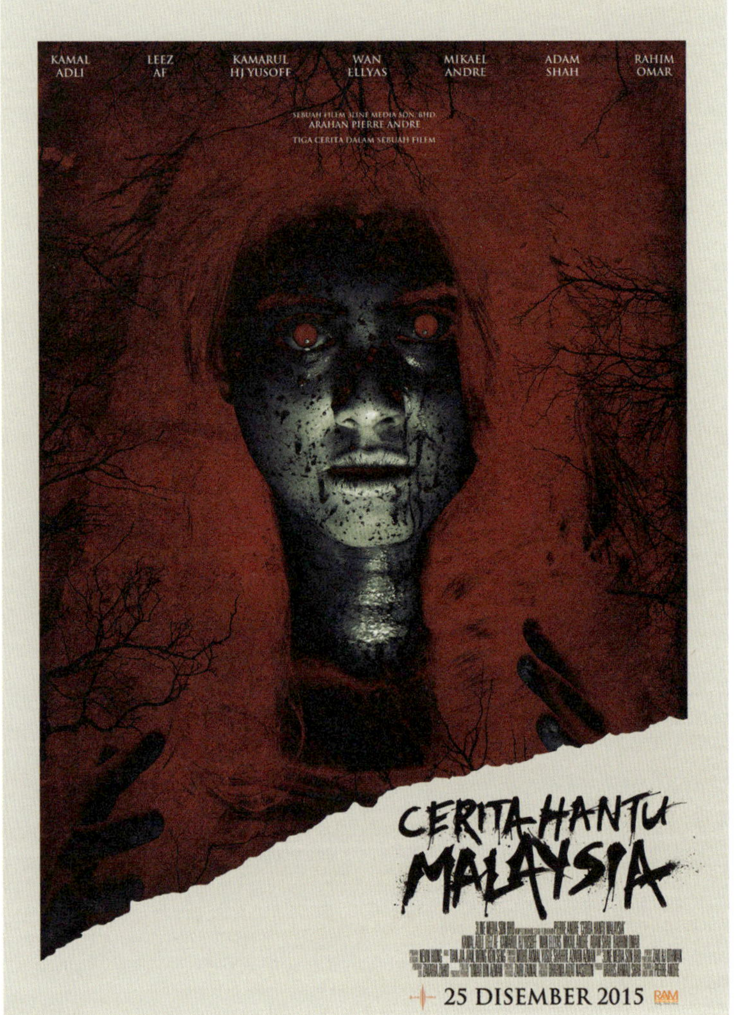

INTERVIEW

Why do you create such fierce visuals?

As I am mainly working in the entertainment advertising business, my task include designing movie posters. I have to come up with eye catching visuals that have the power to market a product, in this case, a movie. For a horror movie, it's a bit challenging yet fun process because it's meant to scare people yet to get their attention to appreciate it and to relate the visuals to the movie. It's challenging because I have to design something that has a story in it while at the same time make sure it is not giving away too much information. The visuals unveil only a little part of a much bigger story.

What are your common approaches to produce a fierce visual effect?

I usually break down ideas by watching an early footage of the film or go through the production or unit photos to see if I can design something out of them. If they're not usable, I will paint the visuals digitally. Also I will go through some references to get the mood or the theme of the visuals that I am about to create. Most of those references are old horror movie posters and dark, obscure photos that I gathered.

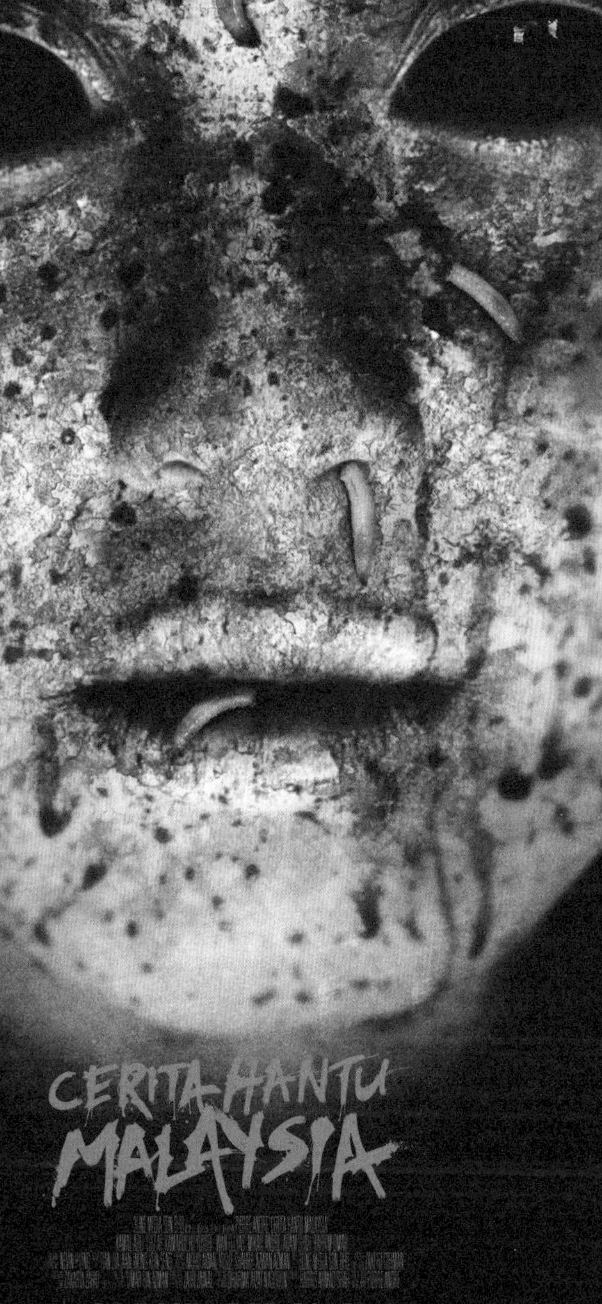
KAMAL ADLI
LEEZ AF
KAMARUL HJ YUSOFF
WAN ELLYAS
MIKAEL ANDRE
ADAM SHAH
RAHIM OMAR
SEBUAH FILEM 3LINE MEDIA SDN. BHD.
ARAHAN PIERRE ANDRE
TIGA CERITA DALAM SEBUAH FILEM
CERITA HANTU MALAYSIA
25 DISEMBER 2015

INSIDIOUS: THE LAST KEY

Designer: Firdaus Mustapa

The digitally painted posters for *Insidious: The Last Key* are immersed in the 1970s and 1980s vibe to relate to the back story of the protagonist's childhood. The designer took a heavy influence from vintage Italian horror movie poster art with the use of red, black and white colors.

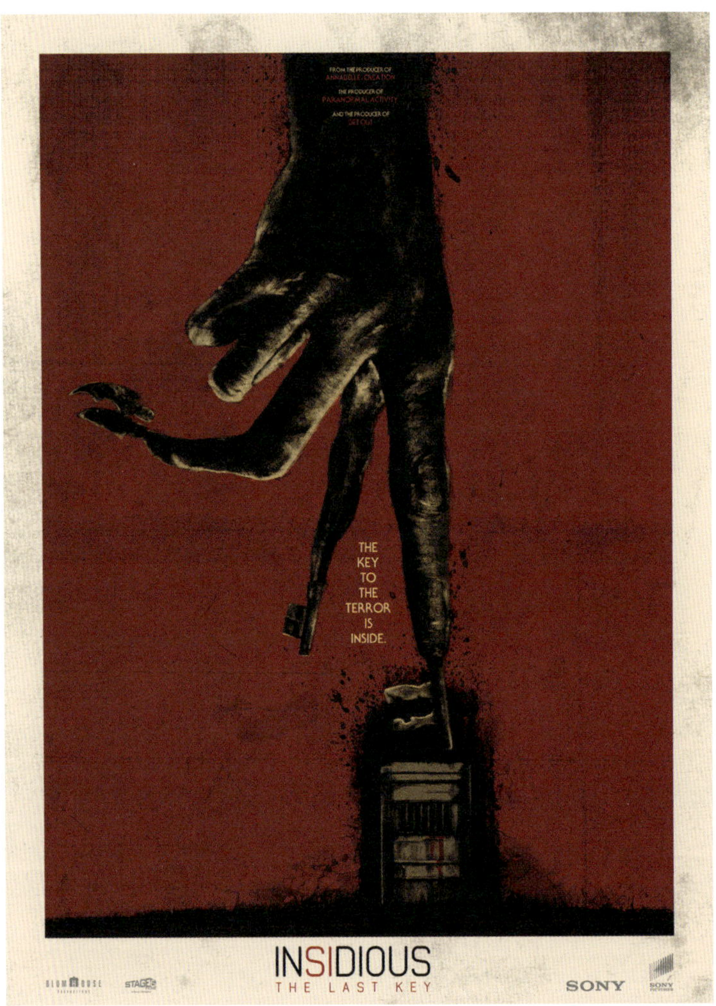

Where do your inspirations come from?

I'm a huge fan of old hand-painted horror movie posters. I love the works of Tom Chantrell, Bill Wiggins, Basil Gogos, Ercole Brini, most of Hammer Horror poster artworks and 1970s Italian horror poster artworks. I could stare at them for hours. For modern day designers, I'm a huge fan of Neil Kellerhouse. He's a master of typography and simplicity. His variation of posters for movie *House of The Devil* is a great nod to old horror movies and his *Antichrist* design work for Criterion collection is amazing. Jay Shaw also did some of the best posters for Mondo. Check out his version of *Suspiria*, it's beyond awesome!

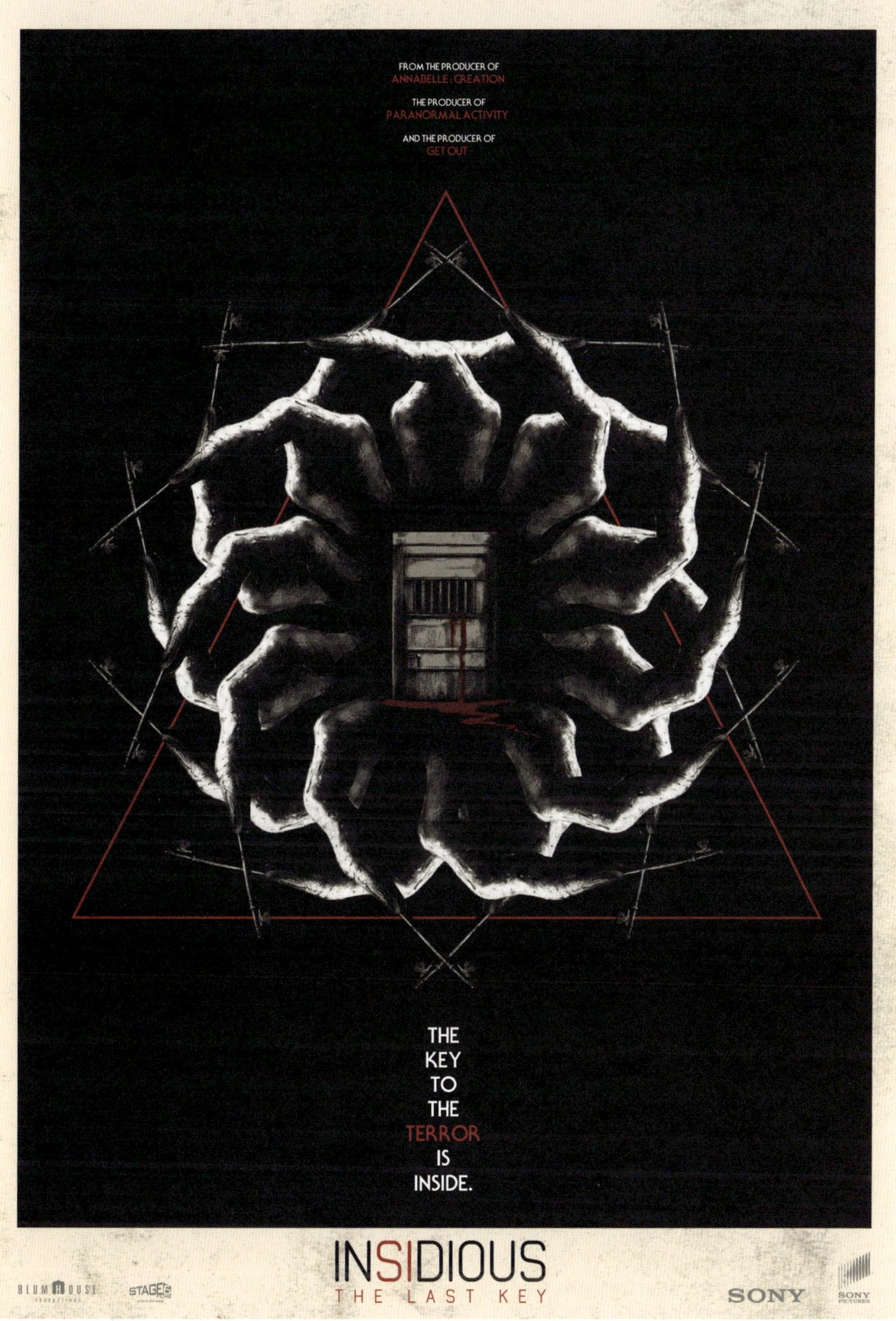
FROM THE PRODUCER OF
ANNABELLE: CREATION
THE PRODUCER OF
PARANORMAL ACTIVITY
AND THE PRODUCER OF
GET OUT
THE
KEY
TO
THE
TERROR
IS
INSIDE.
INSIDIOUS
THE LAST KEY
BLUMHOUSE
STAGE 6
SONY
SONY PICTURES

BITTERFELDT

Designer: Aleksandar Živanov / Hardworkz

This work includes cover illustration, booklet design and layout for German doom metal band bitterfeldt.

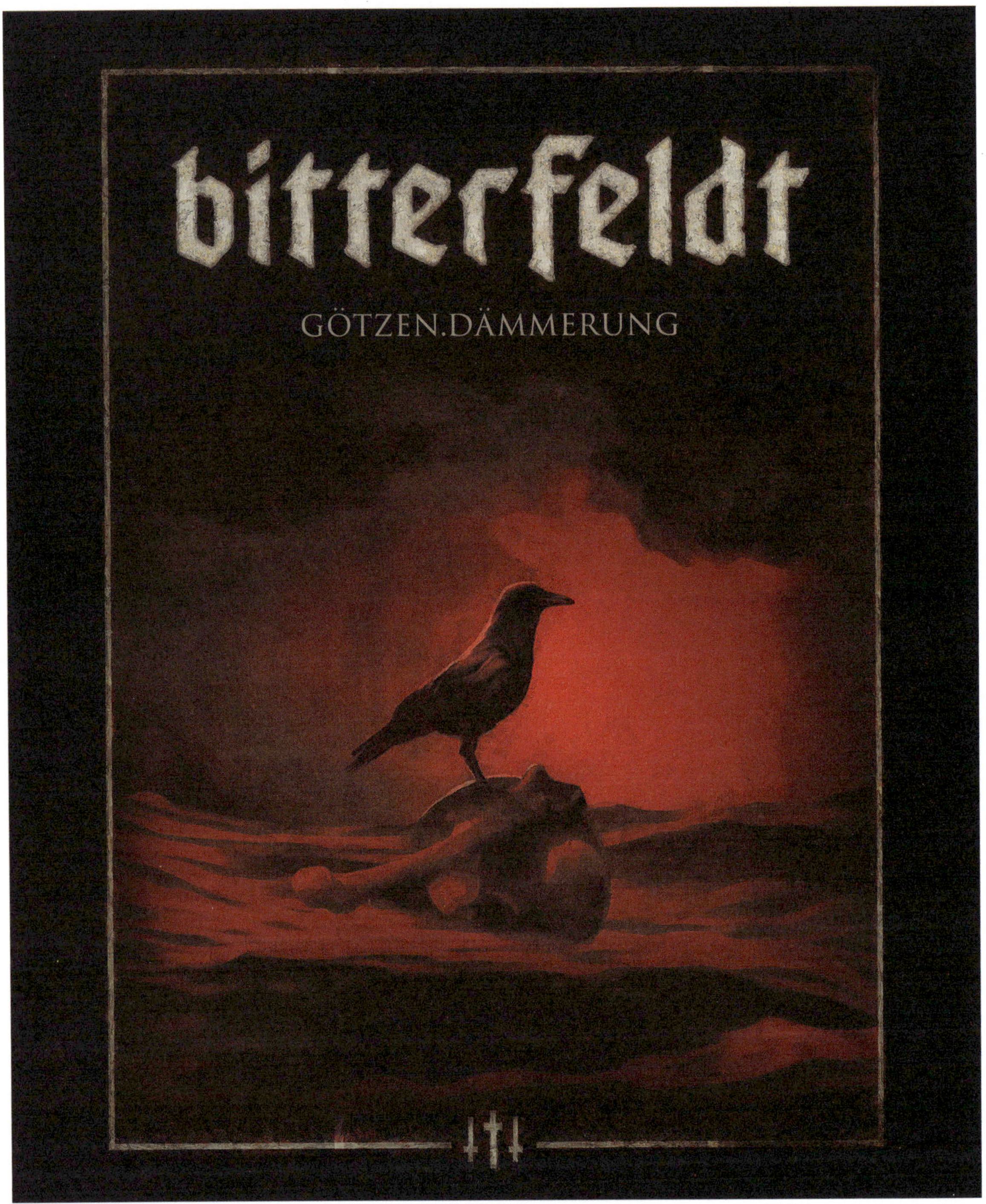

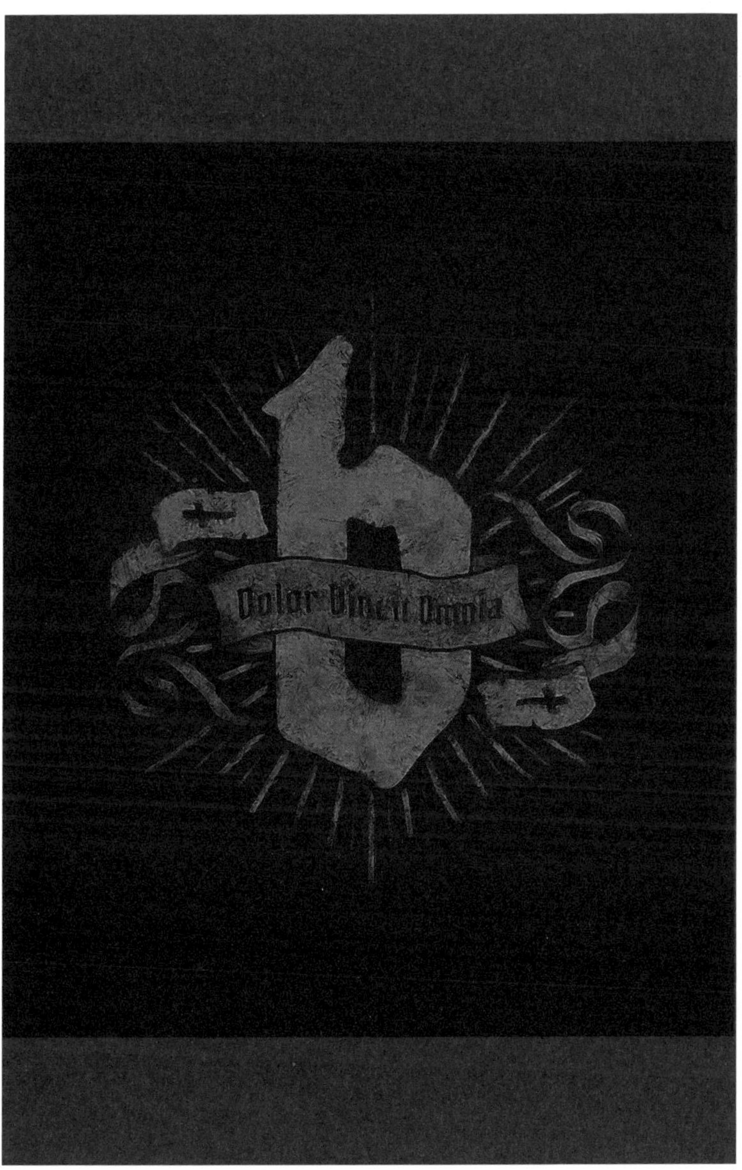

INTERVIEW

Why do you create such fierce visuals?

Since the time I was a teenager I was in love with horror, Sci-Fi, fantasy stuff (movies, books, comics). I also love metal and rock music, a love remains till today unchanged, and it determined the path of my future work. I remember that I had walls full of illustrations and sketches of monsters from LP covers, and my parents always asked me if I can draw or paint something more "beautiful" and not only the horror stuff. But after some time they accept the fact that this is "beautiful" for me...

What are your common approaches to produce a fierce visual effect?

Nothing special, when I get commissioned for the project like CD artwork I usually ask the band to send me some music and lyrics for my inspiration. We will talk about the visual direction and the ideas of the artwork. Many times I come with an almost finished illustration to present to the band/client which I know it's very risky—if they don't like it I will have to do it all over again—fortunately I didn't have this situation so far.

Where do your inspirations come from?

My inspiration mostly comes from metal and rock music. I often read lyrics from my favorite songs and albums and get inspired by that. It comes also from all sci-fi, horror, fantasy related stuff (movies, books, comics). I follow many artists on social networks and get inspired by their works and styles too.

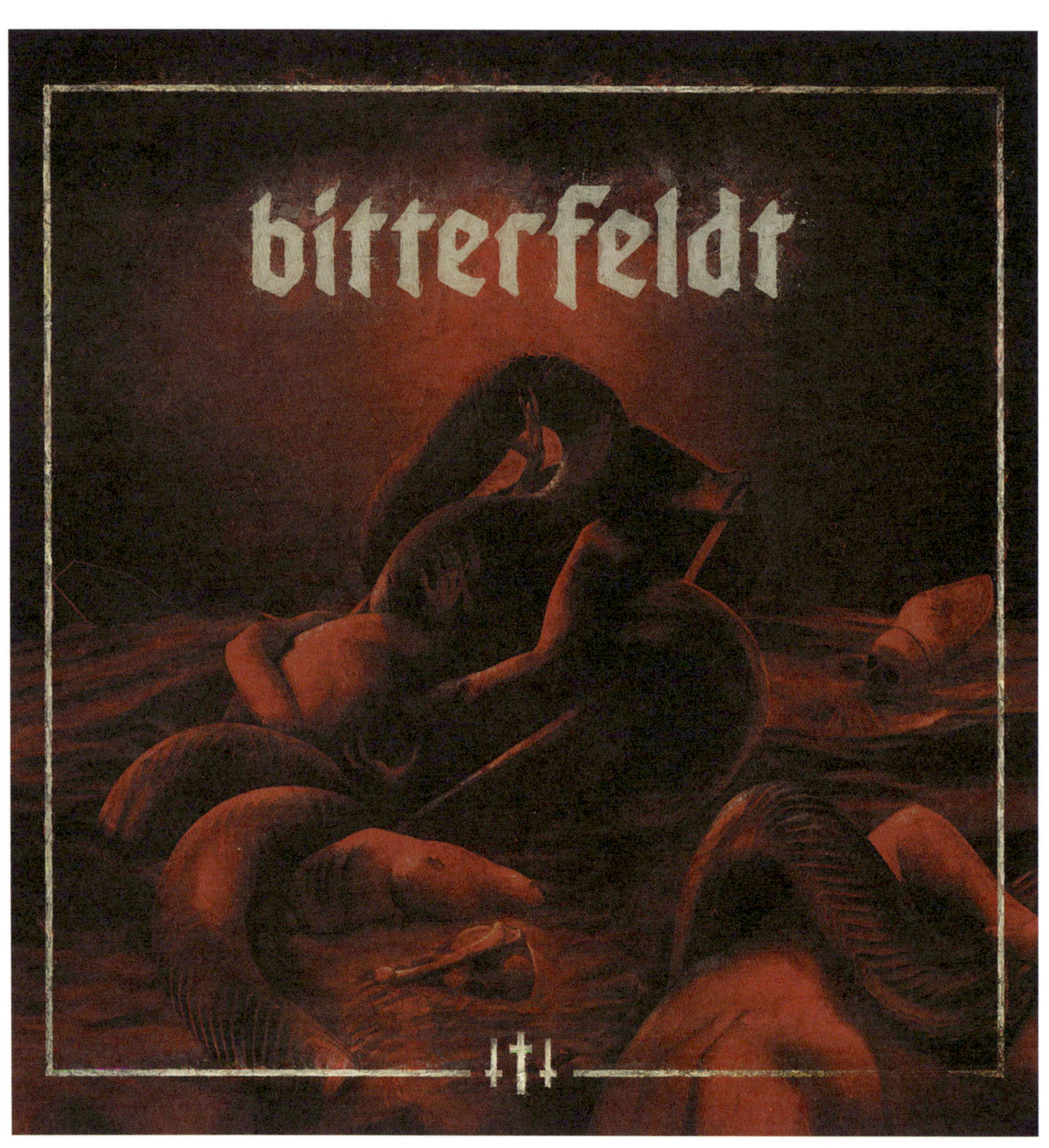
bitterfeldt

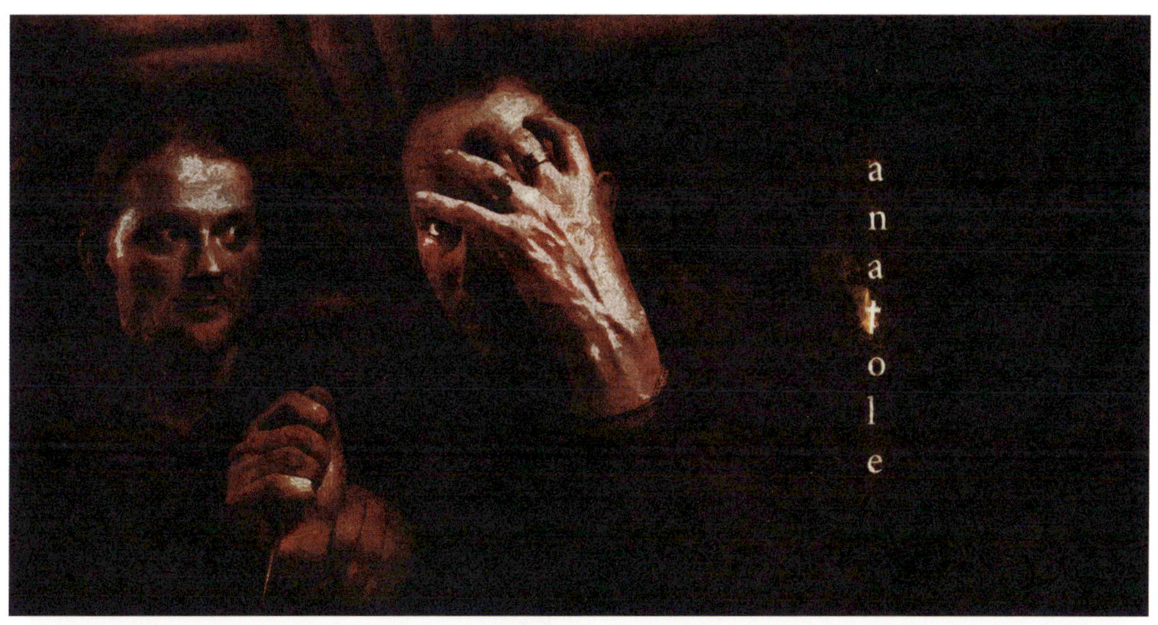
anatole

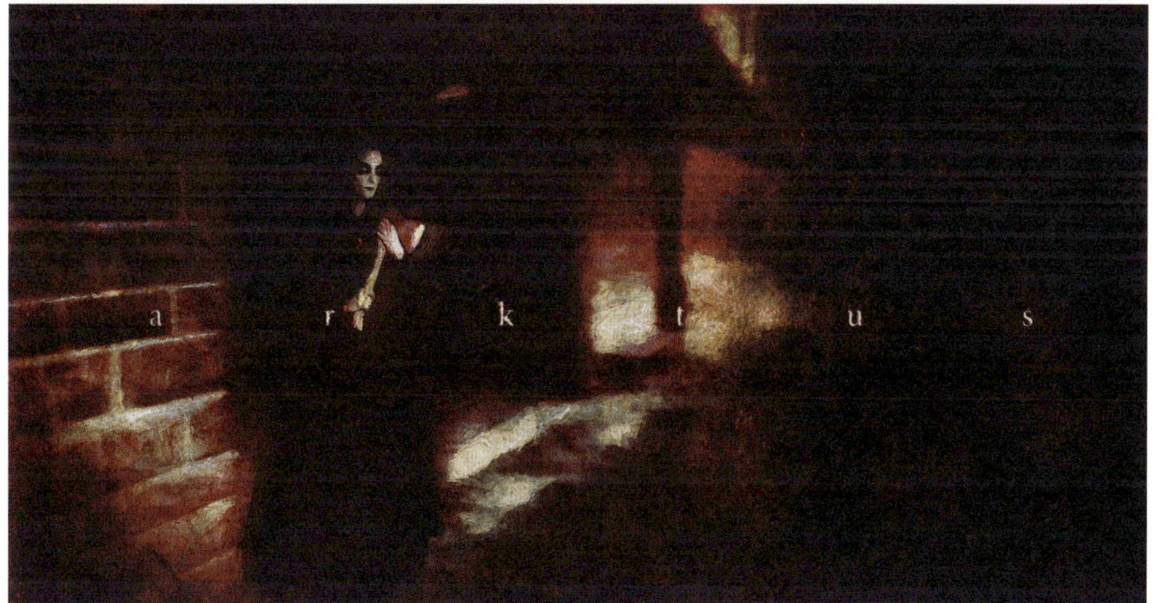
arktus

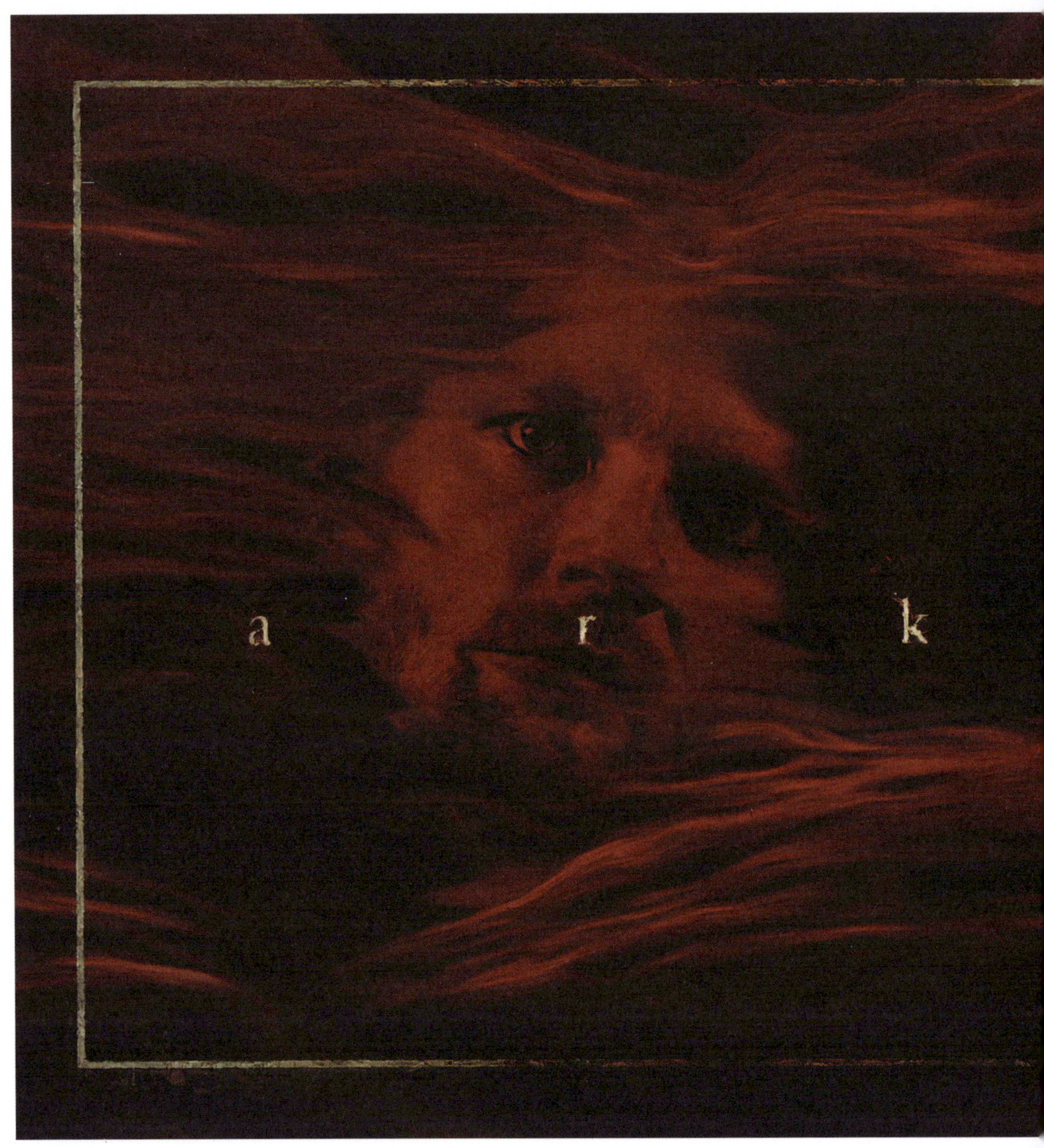
a r k

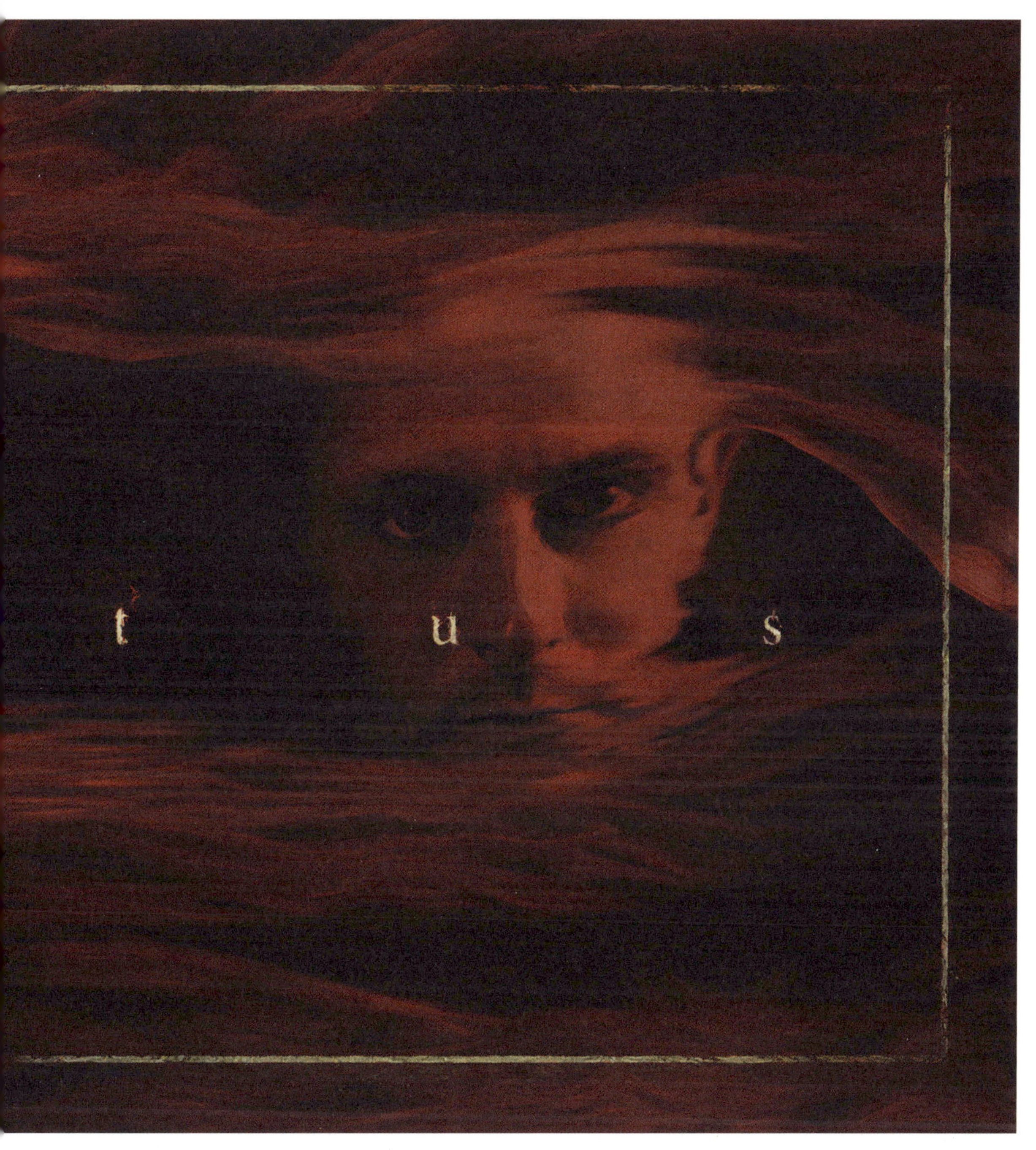
t u s

ALESKA

Designer: Alexandre Goulet

This project features album artworks created for the French post-metal band Aleska. It soon became one of the designer's favourite projects ever. All the details and complexity reflected very well what the band tried to deliver with his music—a deep shade of despair.

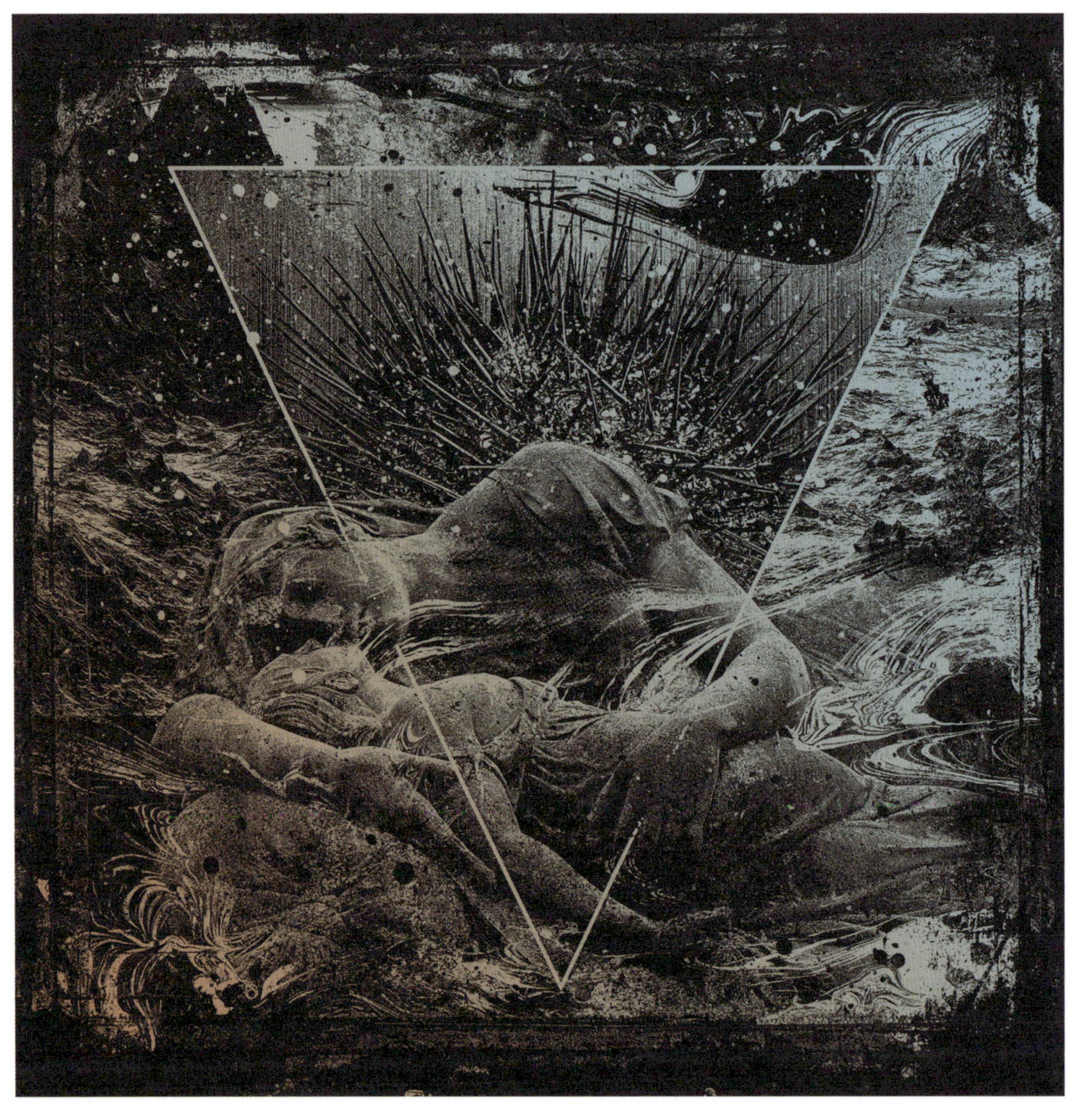

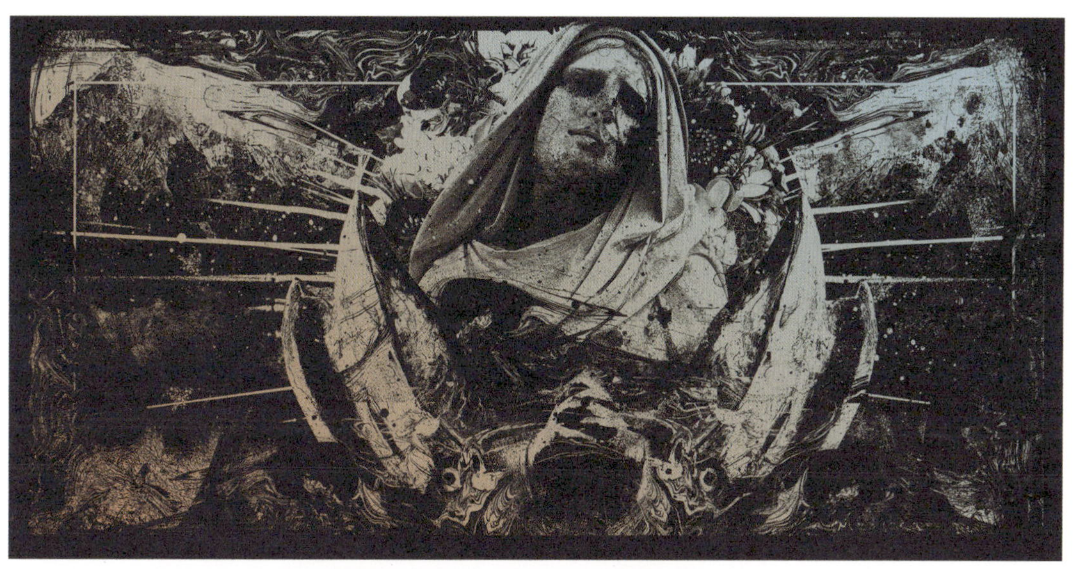

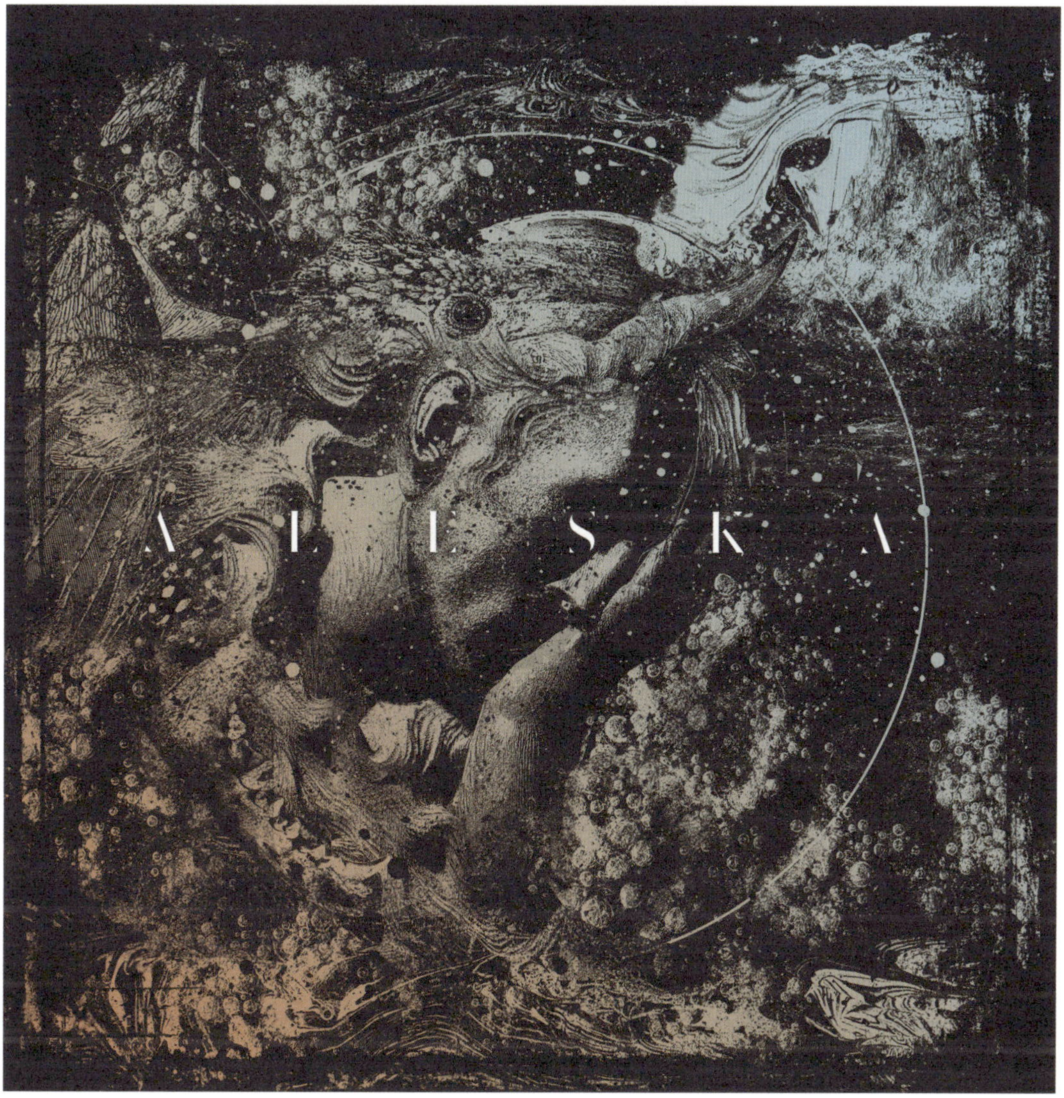

ABUSE EXHIBITION

Designer: Gwak Min Yeong

The Abuse Exhibition set out to reveal the degeneration and the ending of humans who once ruled at the top of the food chain. Their predominance in the food chain and their behavior of abusing animals for their own benefit and convenience are against the natural order. The food chain symbolizes the natural law of survival, under which the lives and deaths of all living things, from invisible microorganisms to the warriors of all things, are interconnected. A balanced food chain keeps the world of lives healthy, and if at some point the connection is cut off, there will be great confusion in the ecosystem. This exhibition, from the point of view of Anthroposophy, examines human's fall caused by their selfishness and arrogance and prophesies the end of such a violent world.

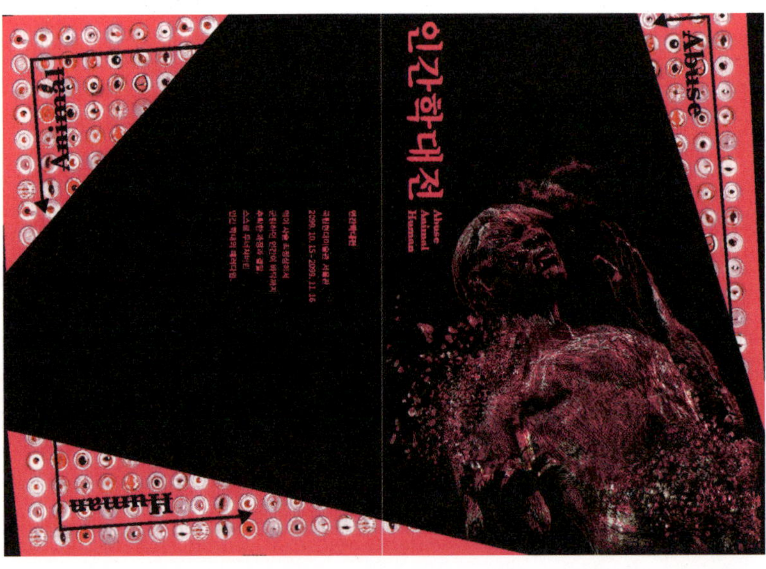

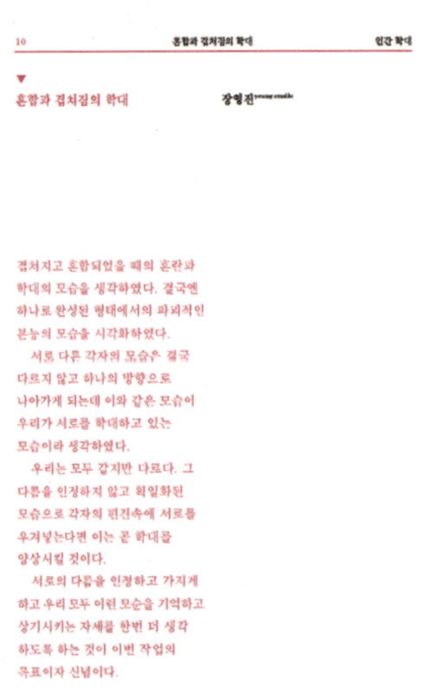

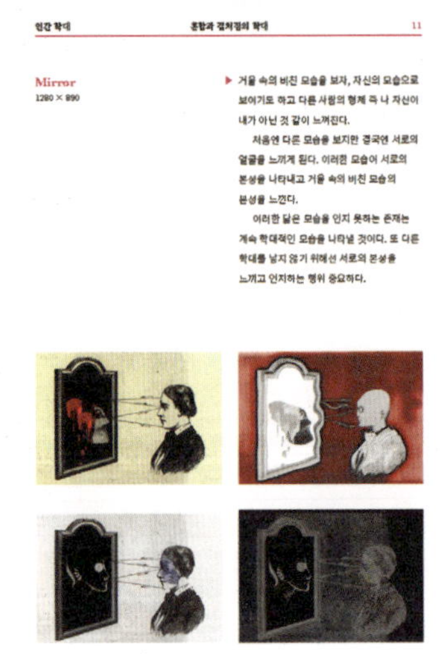

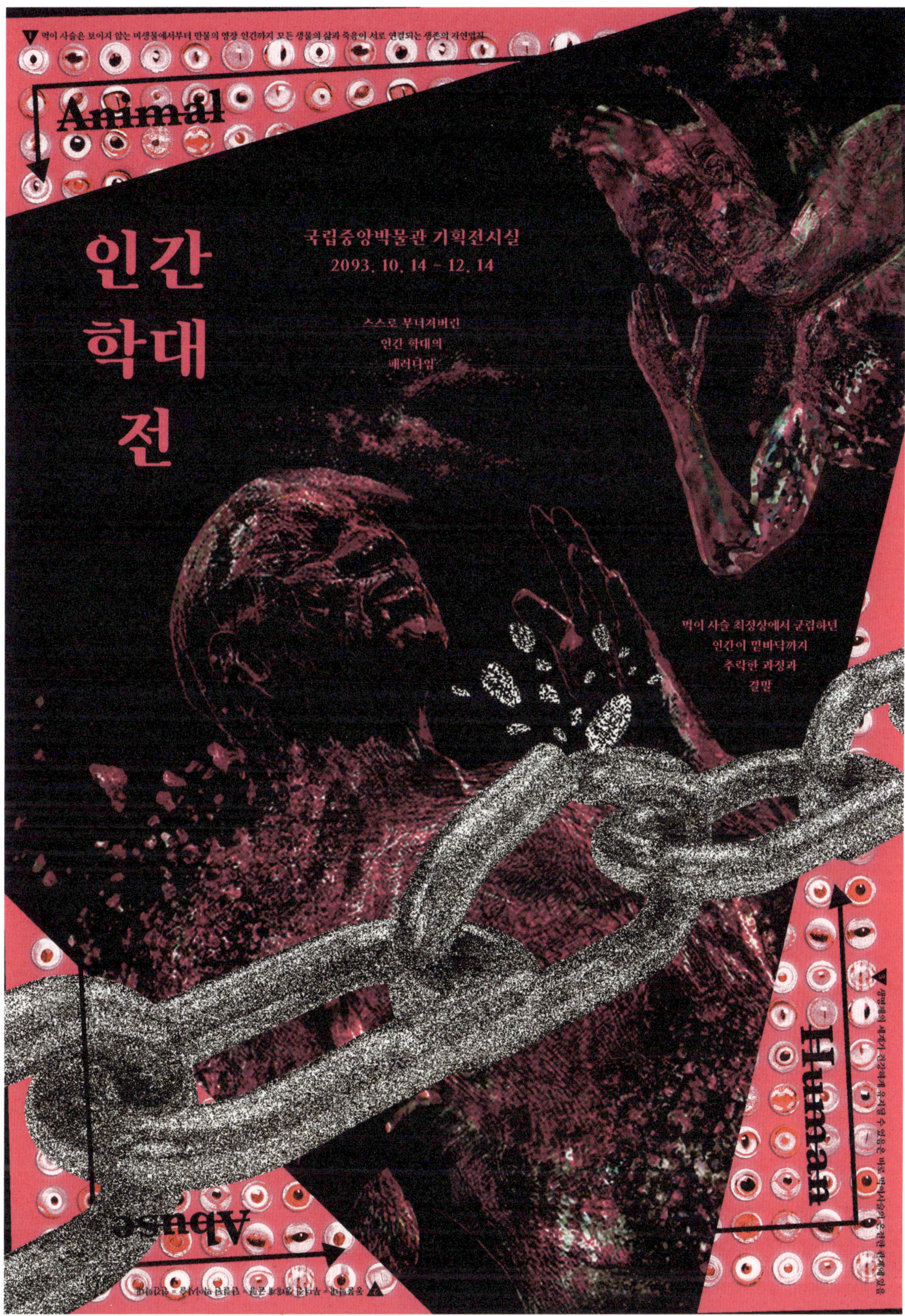
1 먹이 사슬은 보이지 않는 미생물에서부터 만물의 영장 인간까지 모든 생물의 삶과 죽음이 서로 연결되는 생존의 자연법칙
Animal
인간
학대
전
국립중앙박물관 기획전시실
2093. 10. 14 - 12. 14
스스로 무너져버린
인간 학대의
패러다임
먹이 사슬 최정상에서 군림하던
인간이 밑바닥까지
추락한 과정과
결말
Human
3 생명계의 세계가 건강하게 유지될 수 있음은 바로 먹이사슬의 온전한 관계에 있음
Abuse

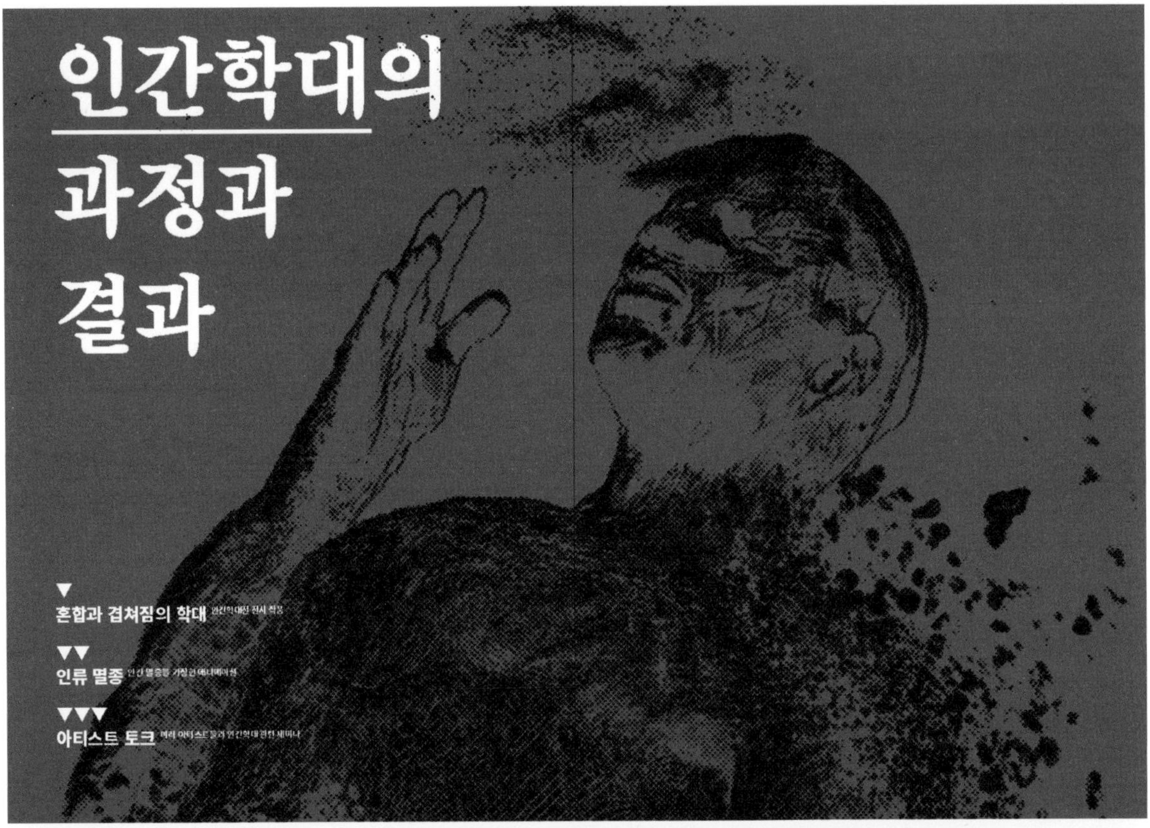

인간학대의 과정과 결과

▼
혼합과 겹쳐짐의 학대 인간학대전 전시 작품

▼▼
인류 멸종 인간 멸종을 가정한 애니메이션

▼▼▼
아티스트 토크 여러 아티스트들과 인간학대 관련 세미나

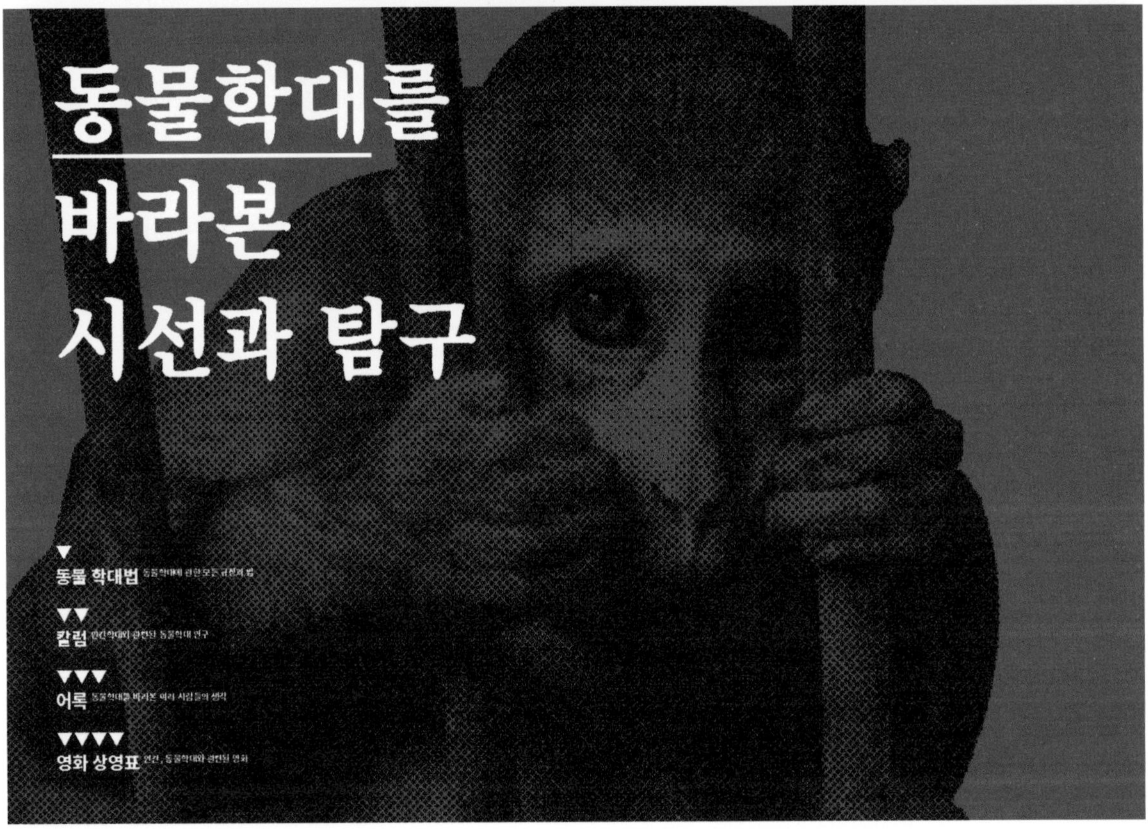

동물학대를 바라본 시선과 탐구

▼
동물 학대법 동물학대에 관한 모든 규정과 법

▼▼
칼럼 인간학대와 관련된 동물학대 연구

▼▼▼
어록 동물학대를 바라본 여러 사람들의 생각

▼▼▼▼
영화 상영표 인간, 동물학대와 관련된 영화

12 혼합과 겹쳐짐의 학대 인간 학대

Born
594 × 1158

▶ 인간들은 태어날 때부터 자신의 모습은 어떠한 모습의 본성일까라는 고민을 한다. 아기 때부터 이런 본성의 고민을 시작해서 각자의 모습으로 변화되어 가는 모습을 보여주고자 하였다.

결국의 한사람의 최종 본능은 다른이의 모습으로 변화 된 모습이다. 본성에 대한 모습의 결과는 결국 다른이의 파괴적인 모습처럼 태어난다.

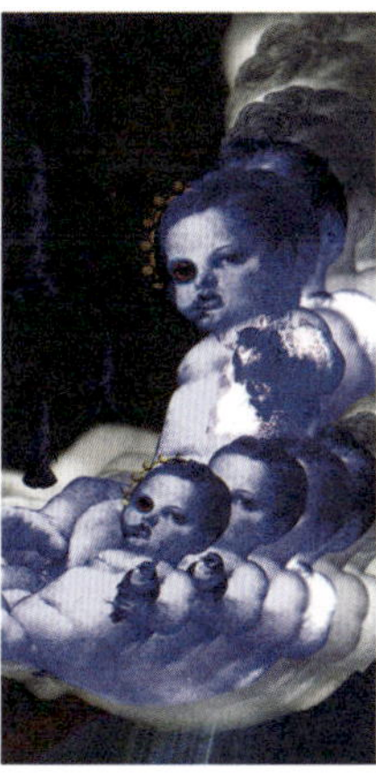
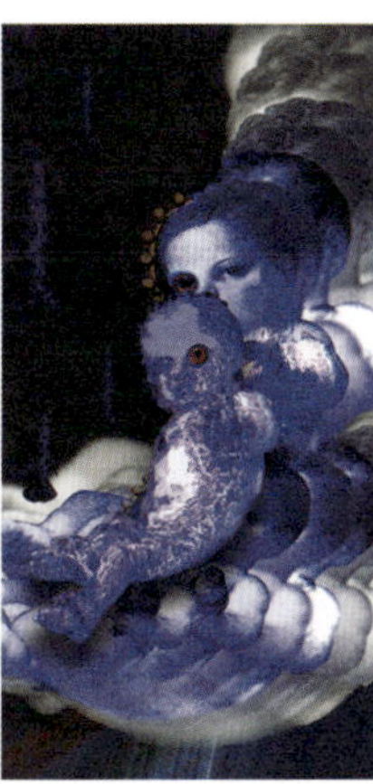

인간 학대 혼합과 겹쳐짐의 학대 13

Destroyed
990 × 1985

▶ 인간은 단순하다. 자신의 입장이 주가 되며 그러한 입장에서 합리화를 시작한다. 하나의 공존이라기보다는 서로의 파괴를 시사한다. 이러한 행동은 결국엔 서로의 학대로 이어지게 되는 모순이 생긴다.

그들의 정신적 의식이 파괴되었을 때 나타나는 형상을 담았다. 파괴는 또 다른 파괴를 낳는다 그리고 학대는 더욱 더 커진다.

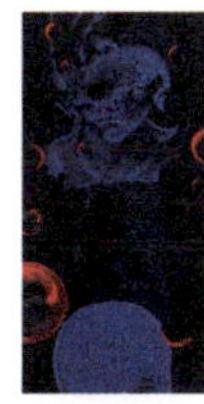
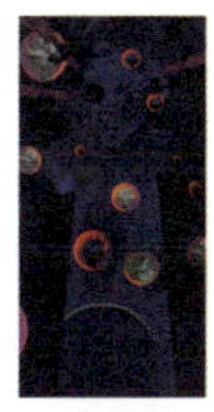
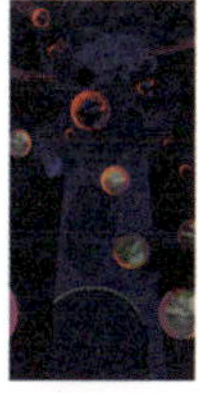
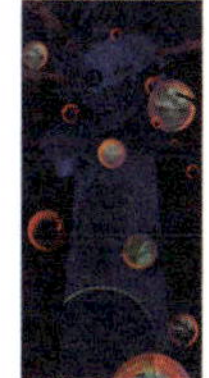
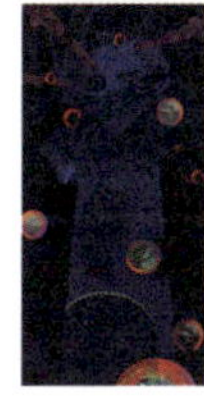
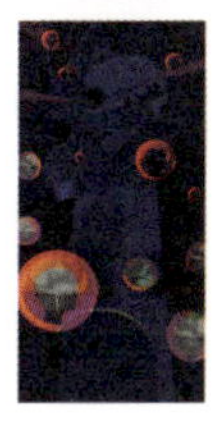
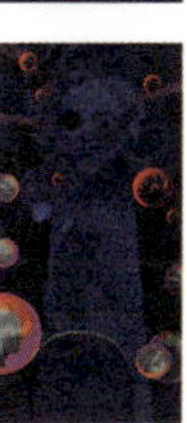

14 혼합과 겹쳐짐의 학대 인간 학대

Target
2231 × 4113

▶ 한 인간의 타겟이 된 인간은, 결국 그들을 저격하며 이러한 저격으로 서로의 파괴적 행동을 나타낸다.

서로의 학대를 통해 이러한 타겟의 입장은 언제든지 바뀔 수 있다. 결국은 타겟의 행하는 자와 당하는 자의 입장차는 없다. 무의미한 행위를 반복할 뿐이다.

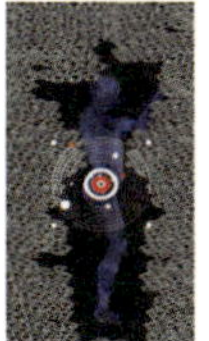
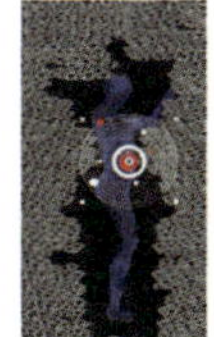
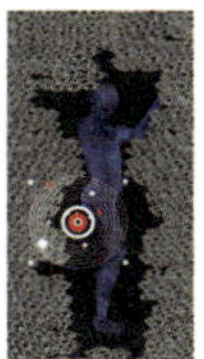
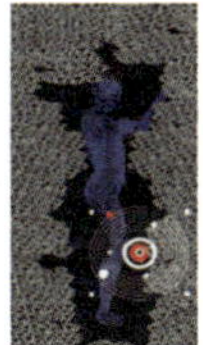
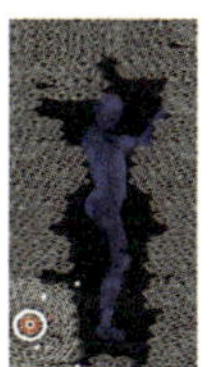
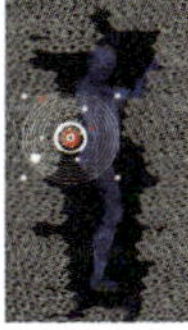

인간 학대 혼합과 겹쳐짐의 학대 15

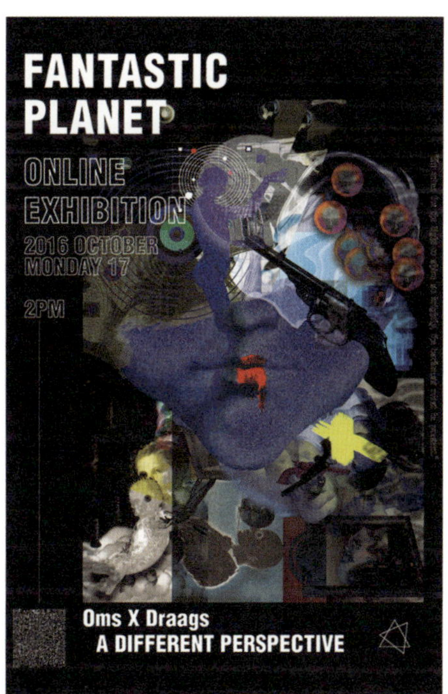

GEGEN BERLIN–FLYER SERIES

Designer: Stefan Fähler

The 3 posters, Gegen Innocence, Gegen Birth and Gegen Family, belong to an ongoing flyer series for "Gegen Berlin", one of the most liberal and inclusive queer parties emerging from Berlin's vibrant underground scene, which takes place every other month at the city's infamous Kit Kat Club.

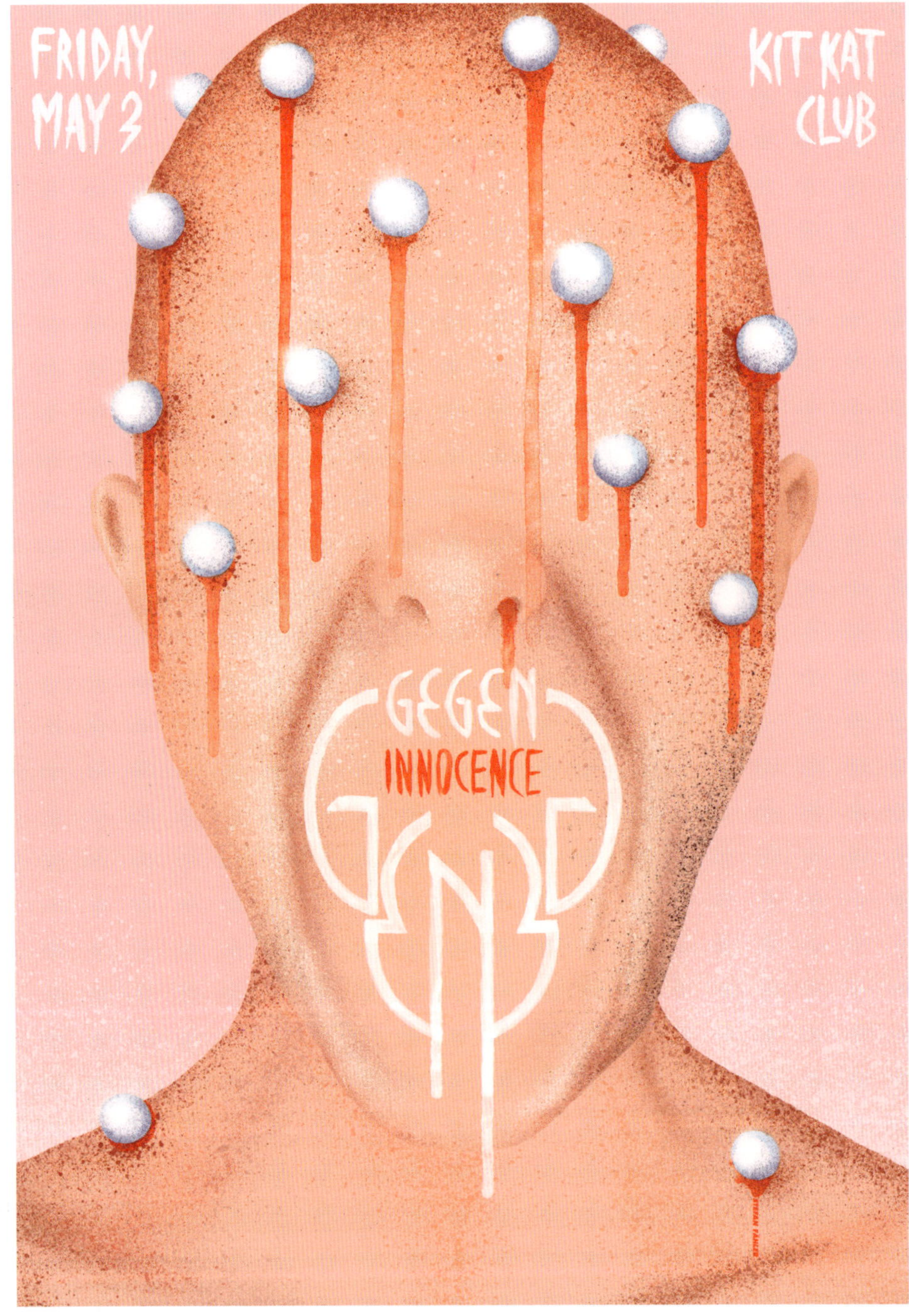

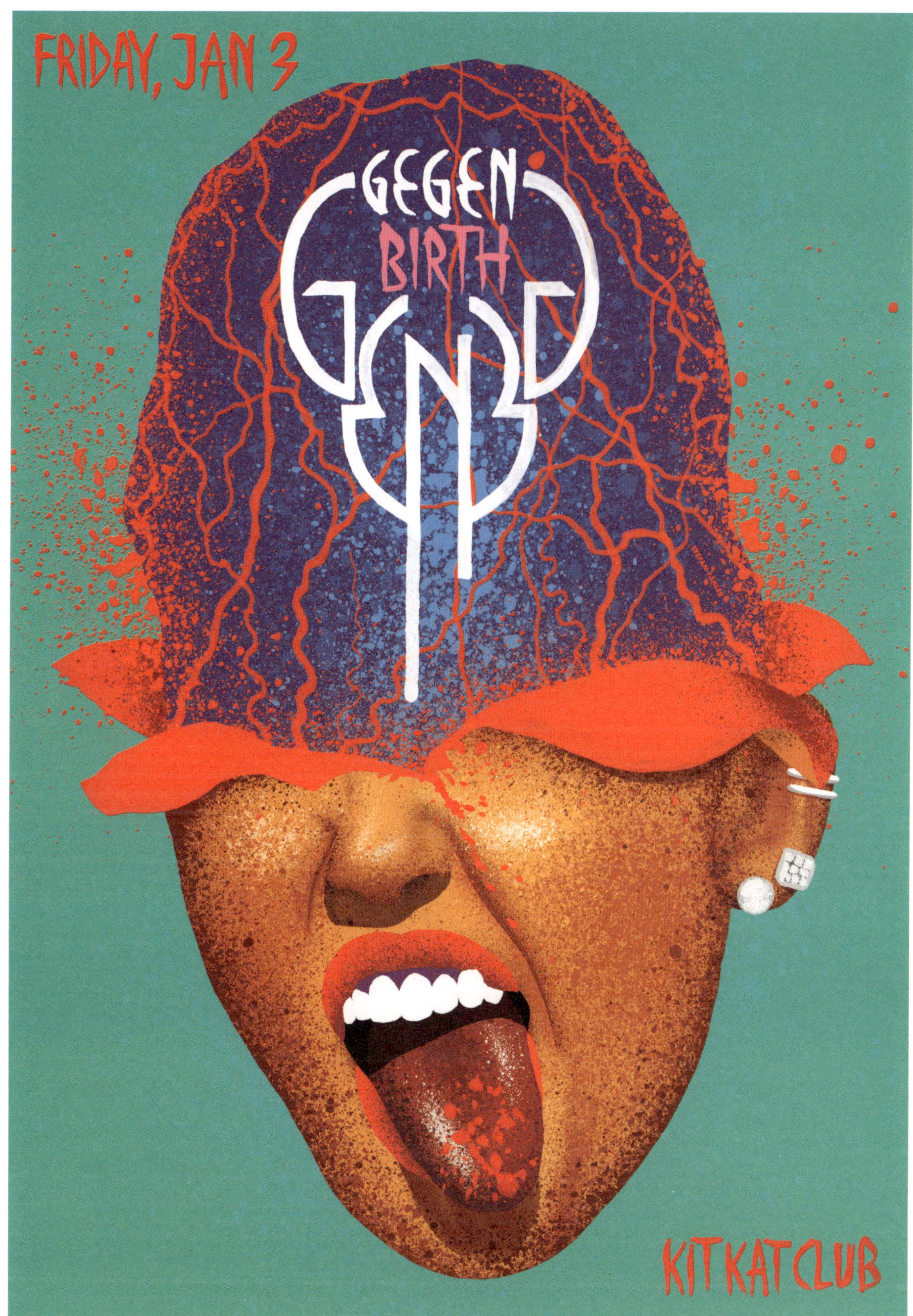
FRIDAY, JAN 3
GEGEN
BIRTH
KIT KAT CLUB

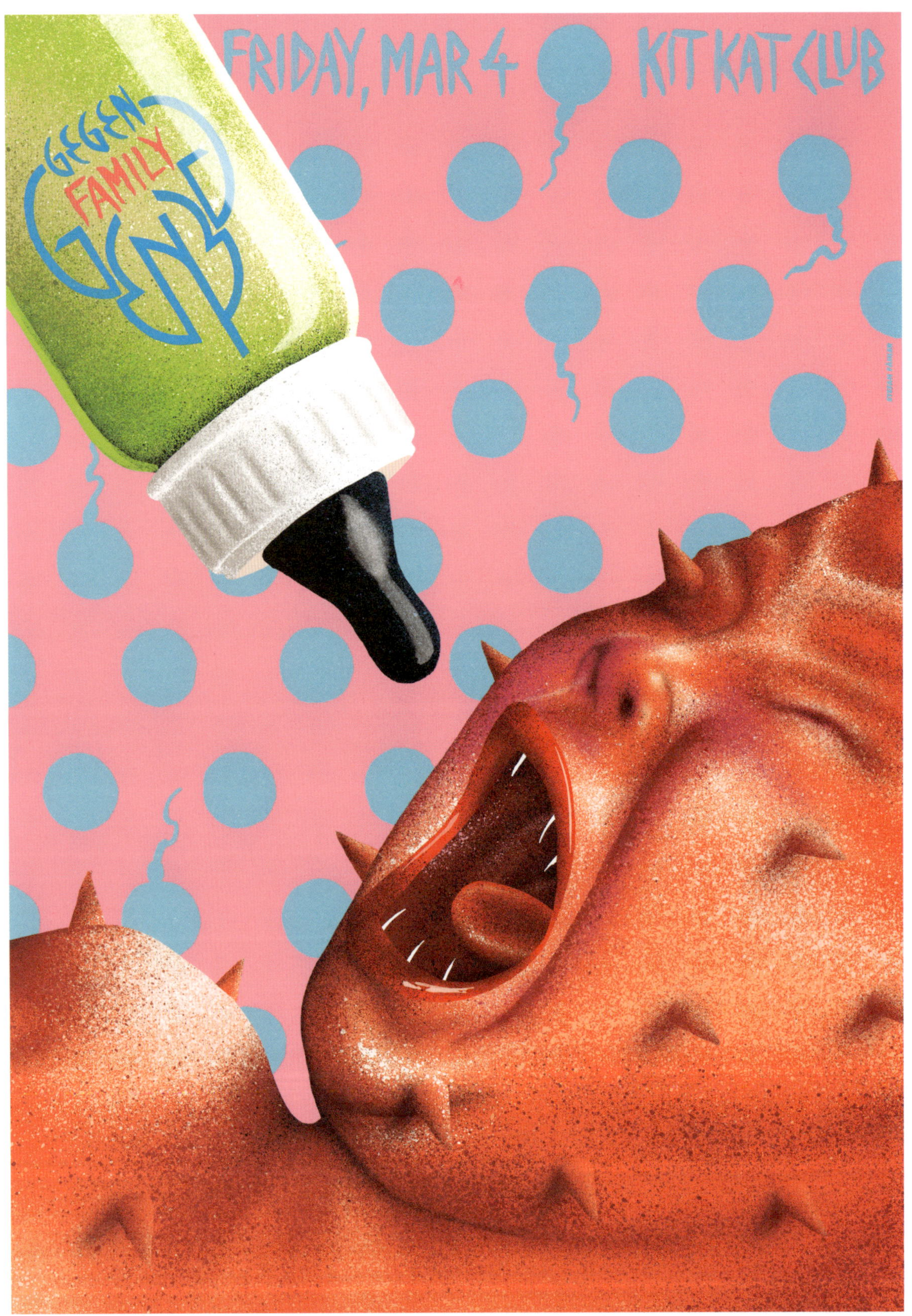
FRIDAY, MAR 4
KIT KAT CLUB
GEGEN-
FAMILY

SYDNEY UNDERGROUND FILM FESTIVAL

Designer: Stefan Fähler

This is a poster for Sydney Underground Film Festival 2015, an alternative film festival which is held once every year in Sydney.

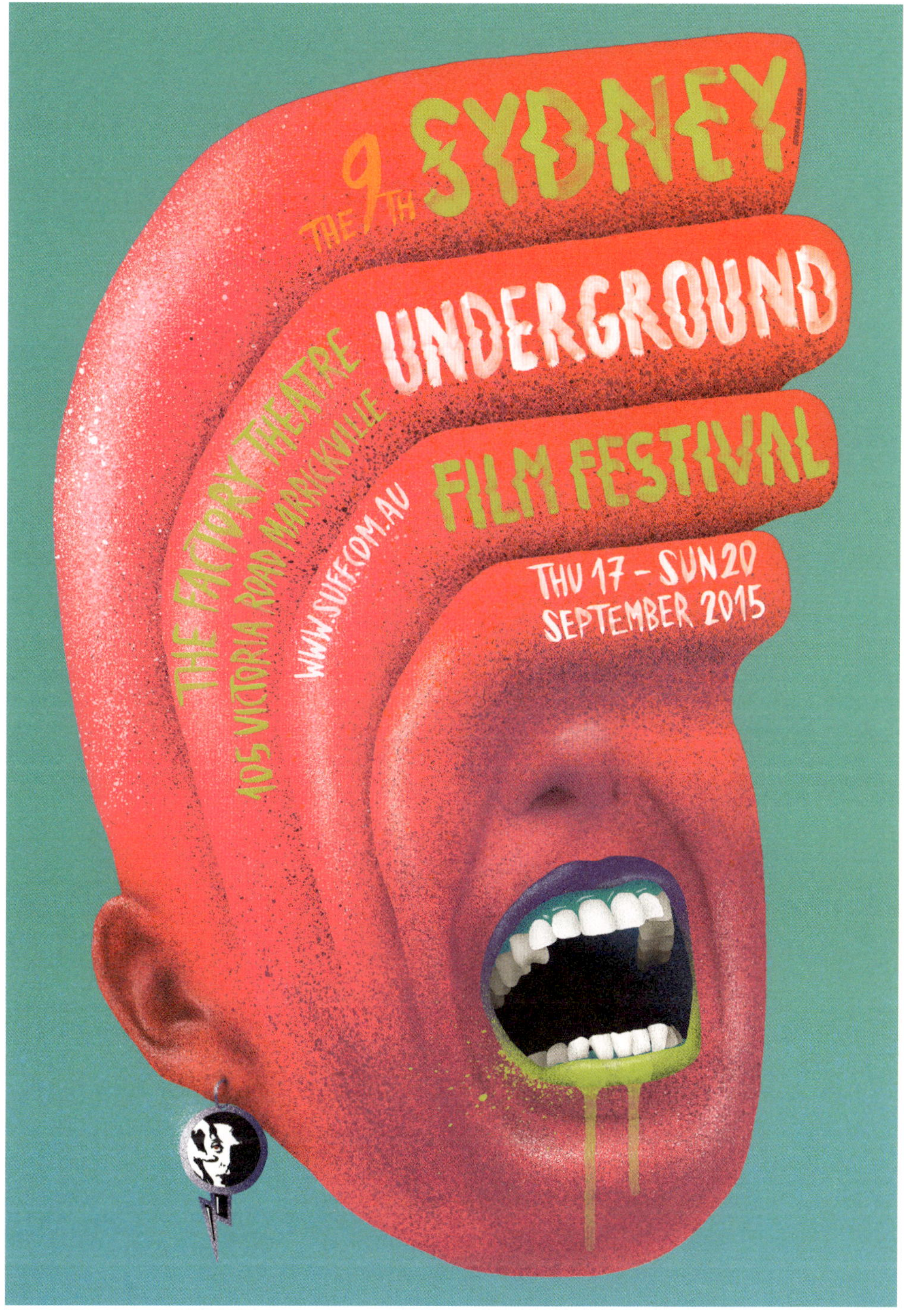

LAUSANNE UNDERGROUND FILM FESTIVAL

Studio: Automatico Studio Designer: Demian Conrad

For the ninth edition of the Lausanne Underground Film & Music Festival, which had the vocation of demonstrating the panoply of music creation and cinematography left in the shadow of the mainstream culture, the designer started the creative work based on the concept of the management, the method of direction and engagement. Following a critical and provocative view, the whole campaign has been created with a second message, which will be reveled with the help of a pair of glasses with red filters. Thus the team of managers have been featured in this campaign in which their identity of being monsters will be revealed with a second reading.

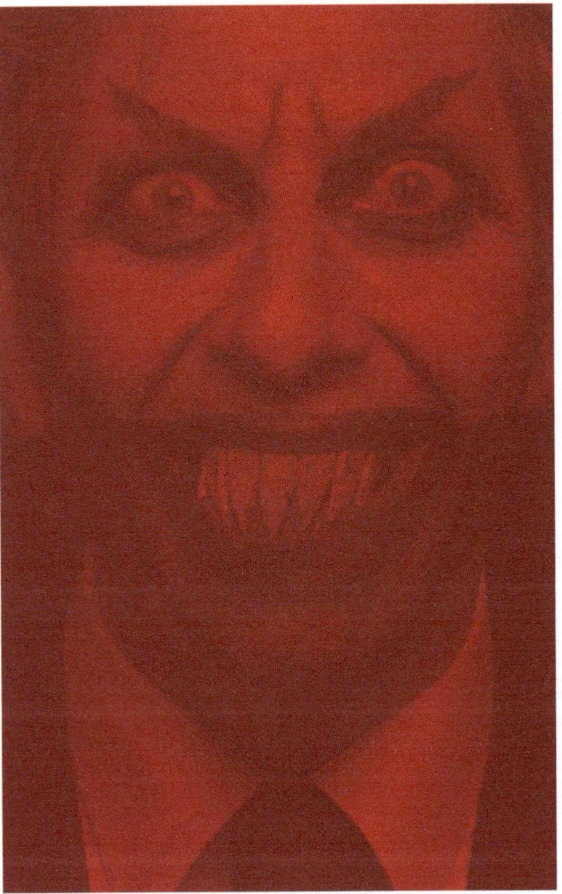

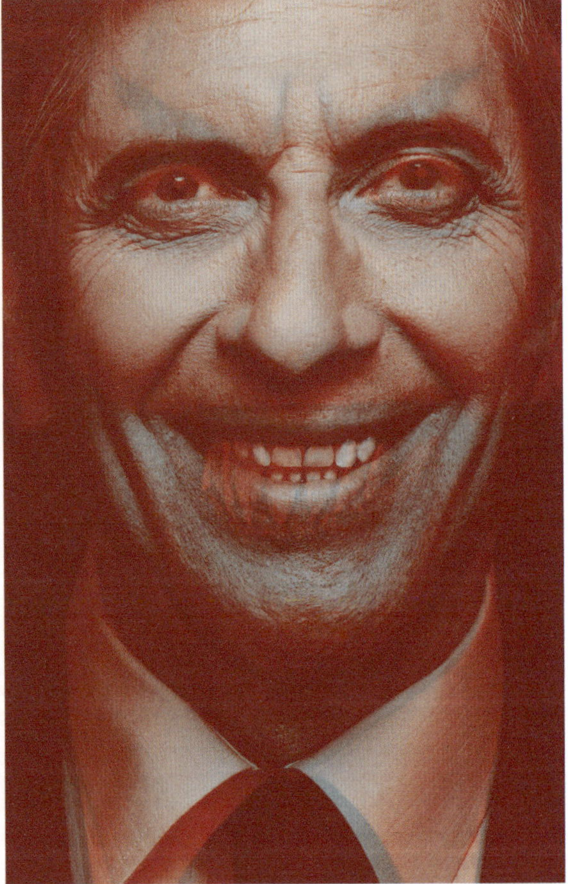

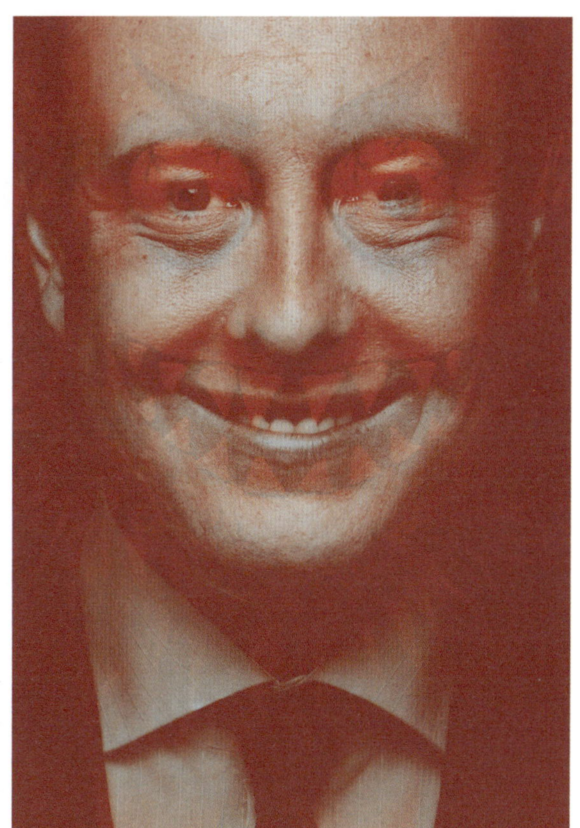
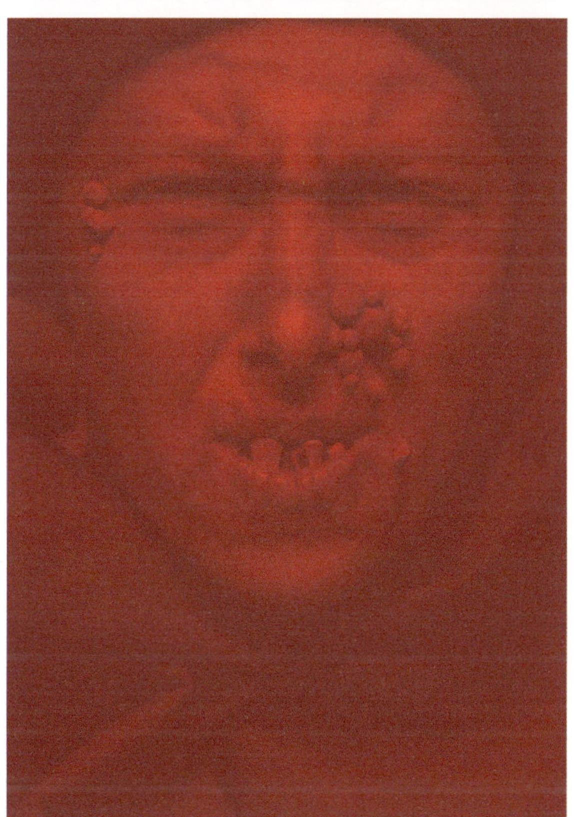
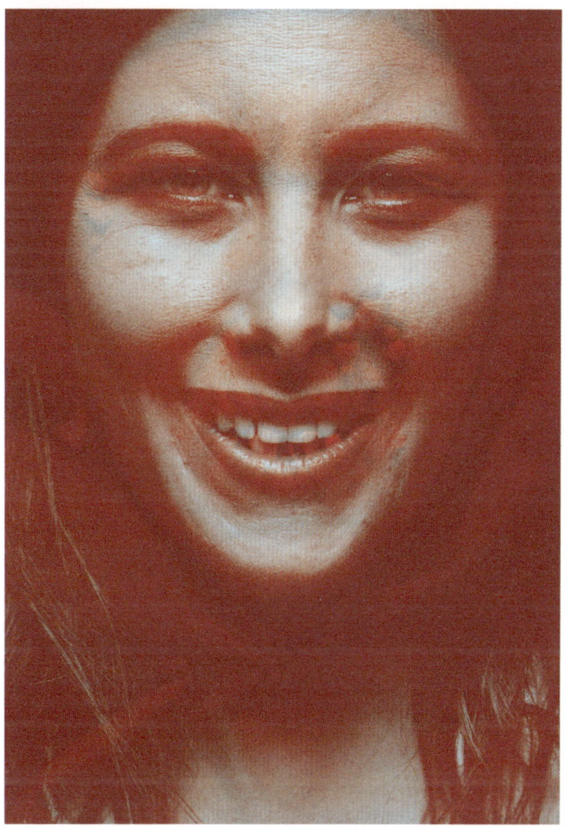

THE EXHIBITION "CONSTRUCTOR FOR ADULTS"

Designer: Peter Bankov

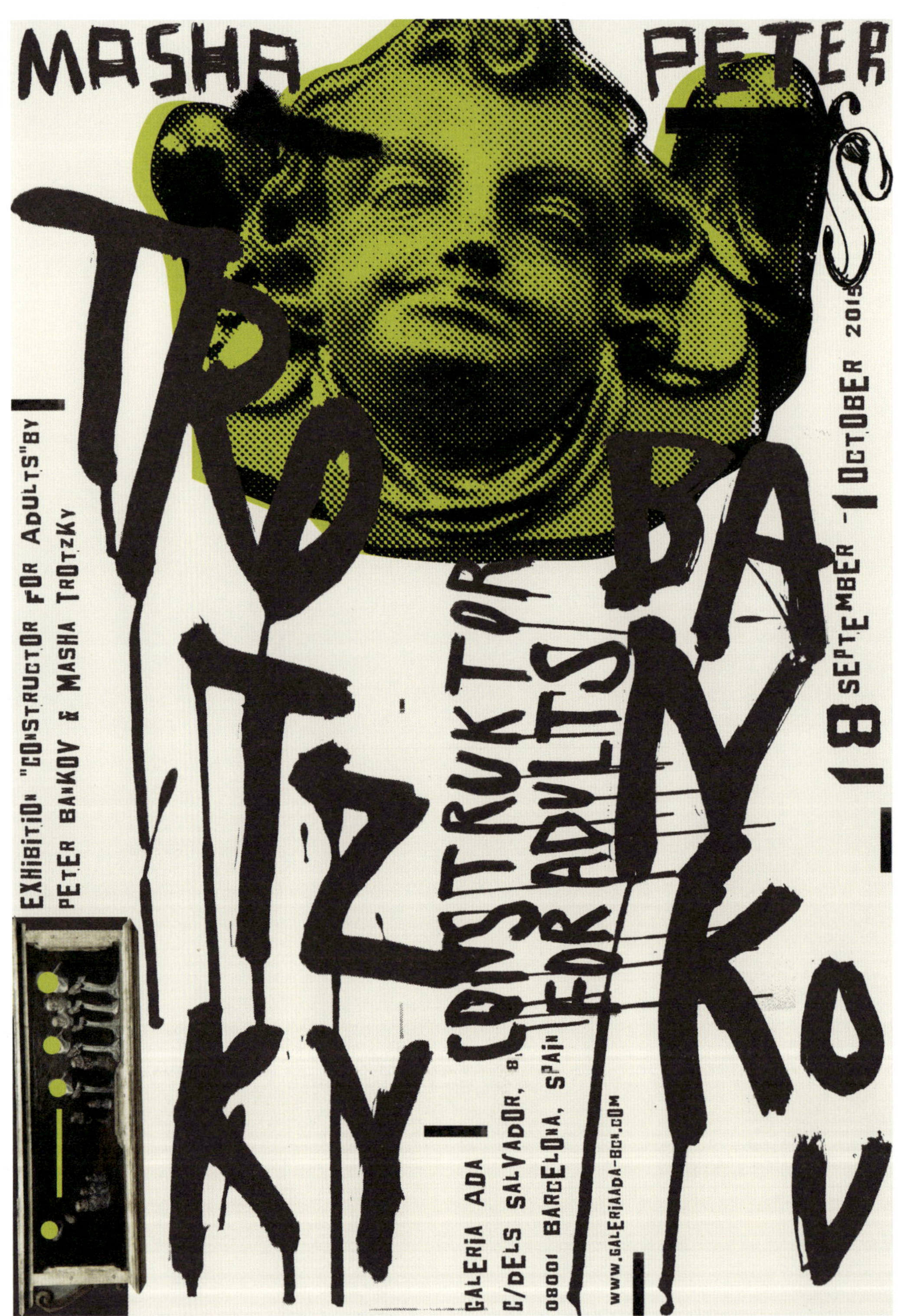

A PLAY "AN ORDINARY STORY"

Designer: Peter Bankov

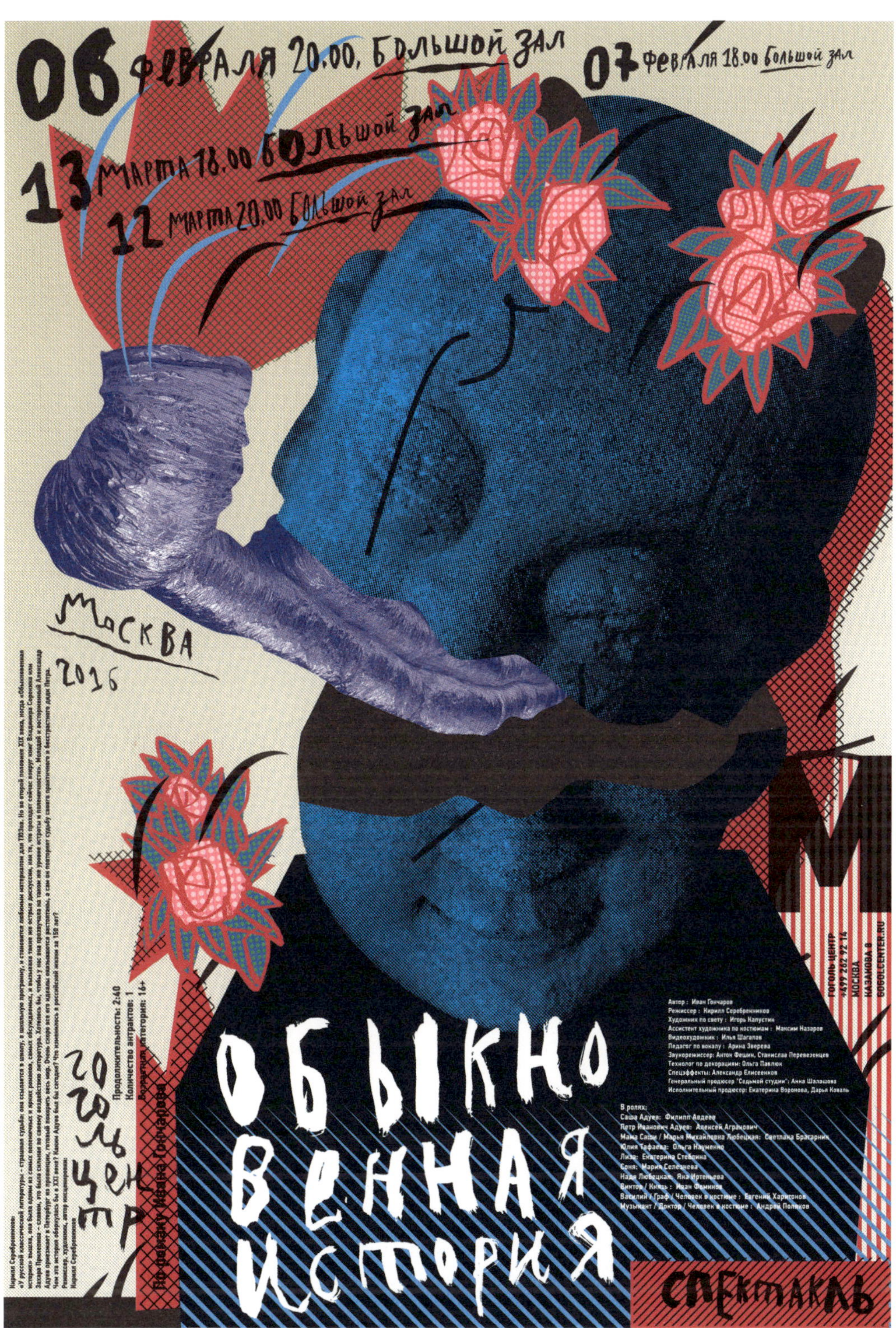

DEMONS

Designer: Katarzyna Zapart

This poster is for a play in Craow's STU Theatre based on *Demons*, a book by the 19th century Russian writer Fiodor Dostoyevsky. The book starts with a Bible quote about a group of demons, who left a possessed man and asked Jesus to let them enter a herd of pigs before running towards the chasm and got killed. Its story depicts, allegorically, how a charismatic conspirator orchestrated a failed revolution and led others to a catastrophe. To reflect the story, the designer decided to show a head full of demons, shown as pigs, in the poster.

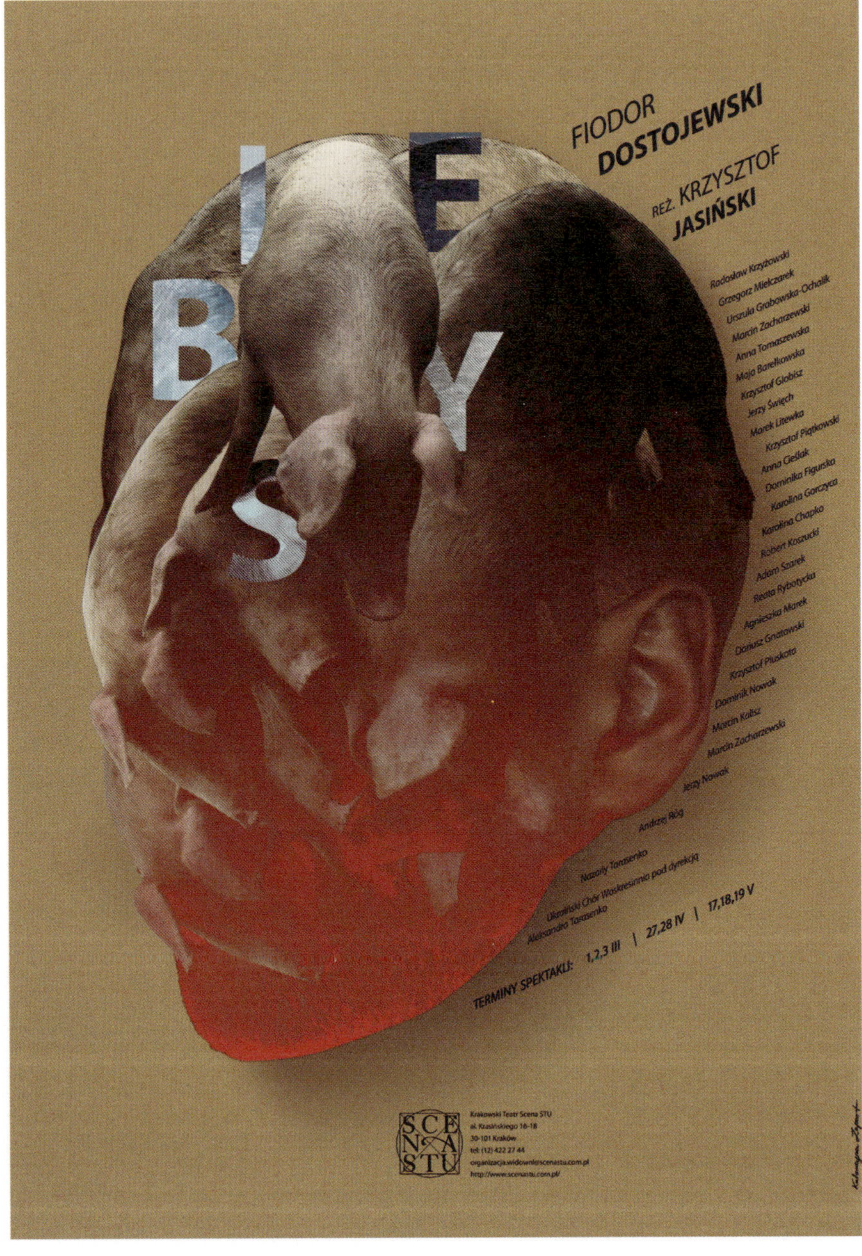

PASIVNO PUSENJE (PASSIVE SMOKING)

Designer: Ana Pesic

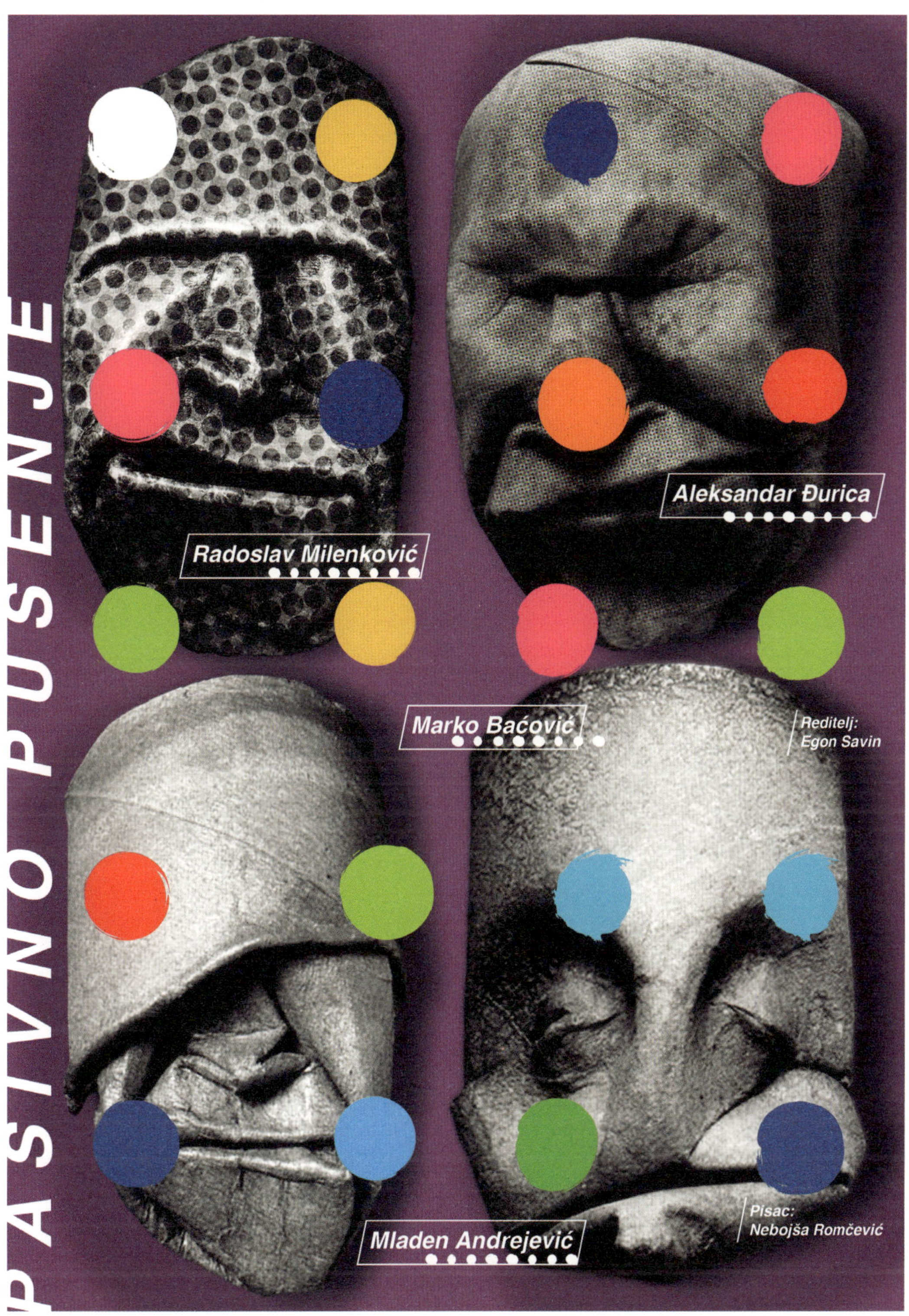

KINO

Designer: Krzysztof Iwanski

These two poster are from School Cinema series.

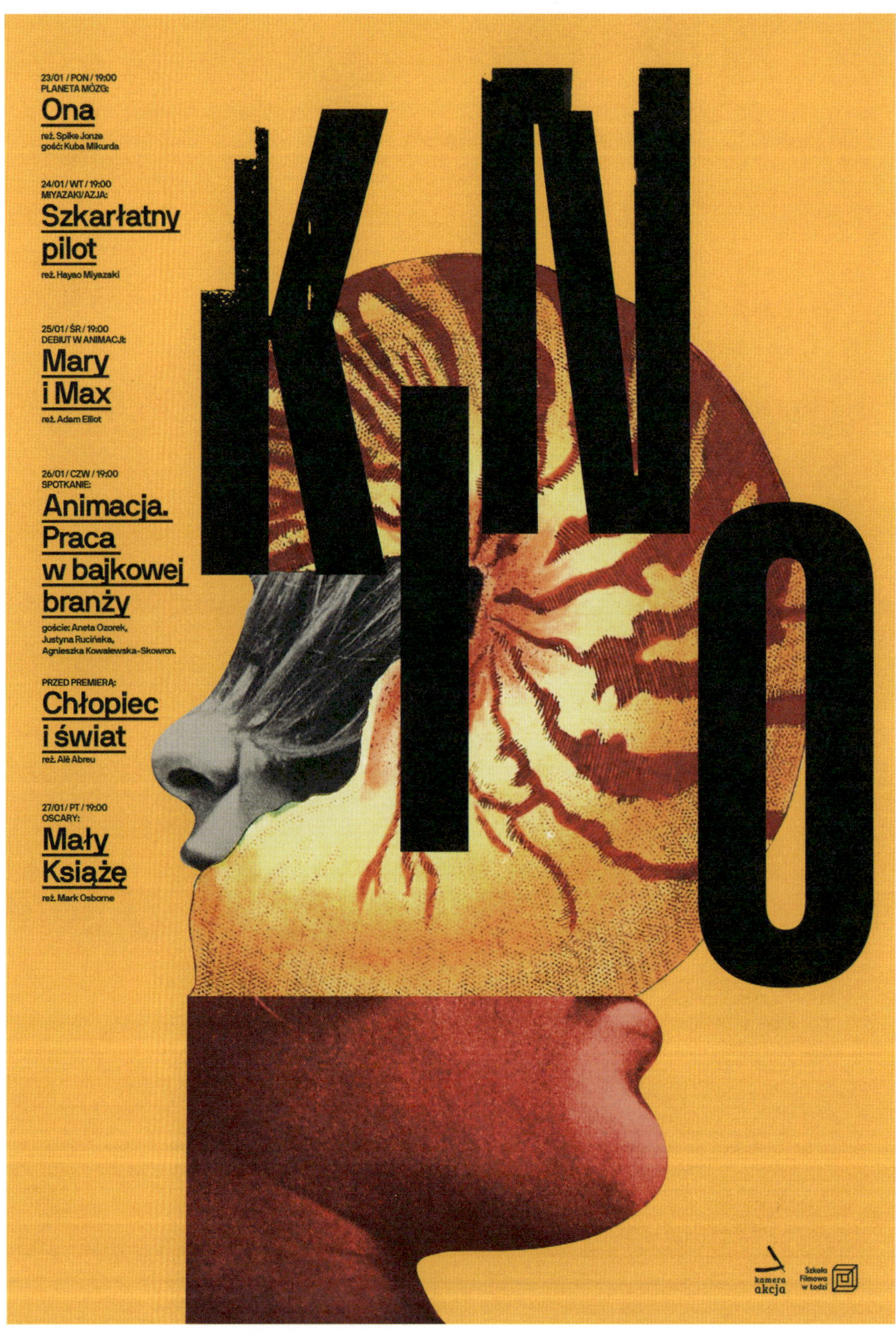

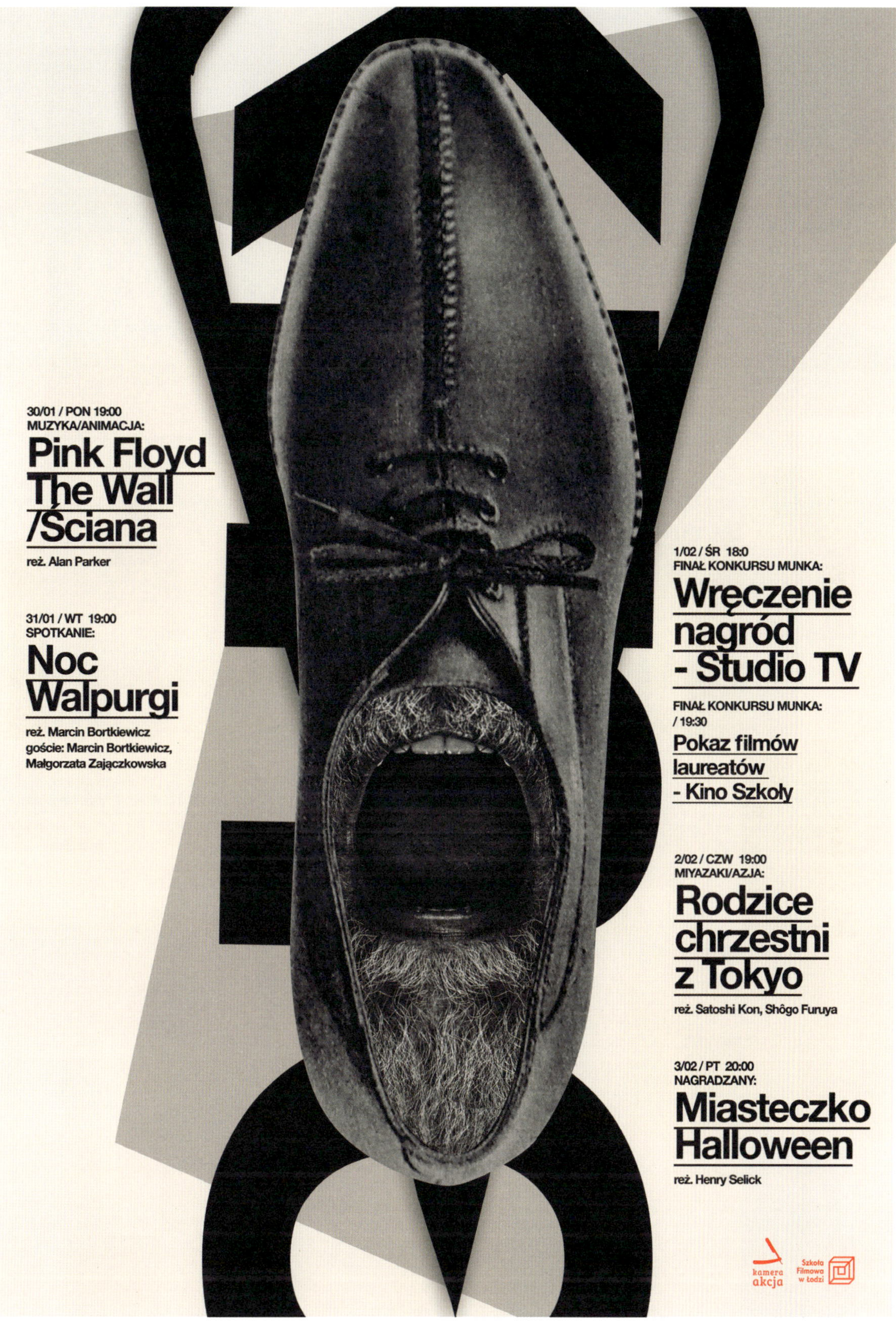
30/01 / PON 19:00
MUZYKA/ANIMACJA:
Pink Floyd The Wall /Ściana
reż. Alan Parker
31/01 / WT 19:00
SPOTKANIE:
Noc Walpurgi
reż. Marcin Bortkiewicz
goście: Marcin Bortkiewicz, Małgorzata Zajączkowska
1/02 / ŚR 18:0
FINAŁ KONKURSU MUNKA:
Wręczenie nagród - Studio TV
FINAŁ KONKURSU MUNKA:
/ 19:30
Pokaz filmów laureatów - Kino Szkoły
2/02 / CZW 19:00
MIYAZAKI/AZJA:
Rodzice chrzestni z Tokyo
reż. Satoshi Kon, Shôgo Furuya
3/02 / PT 20:00
NAGRADZANY:
Miasteczko Halloween
reż. Henry Selick
kamera akcja
Szkoła Filmowa w Łodzi

PEOPLE NO ONE WILL EVER MISS

Designer: Katarzyna Zapart

People No One Will Ever Miss is a two-poster project for a film which is about ecological disaster and individuals' often self-inflicted tragedies by Ivan Robles from Frankfurt. The posters show the main characters merged with scenes of ecological disasters. A hand-made and jaggy typography corresponds with the messed up lives showed in the film.

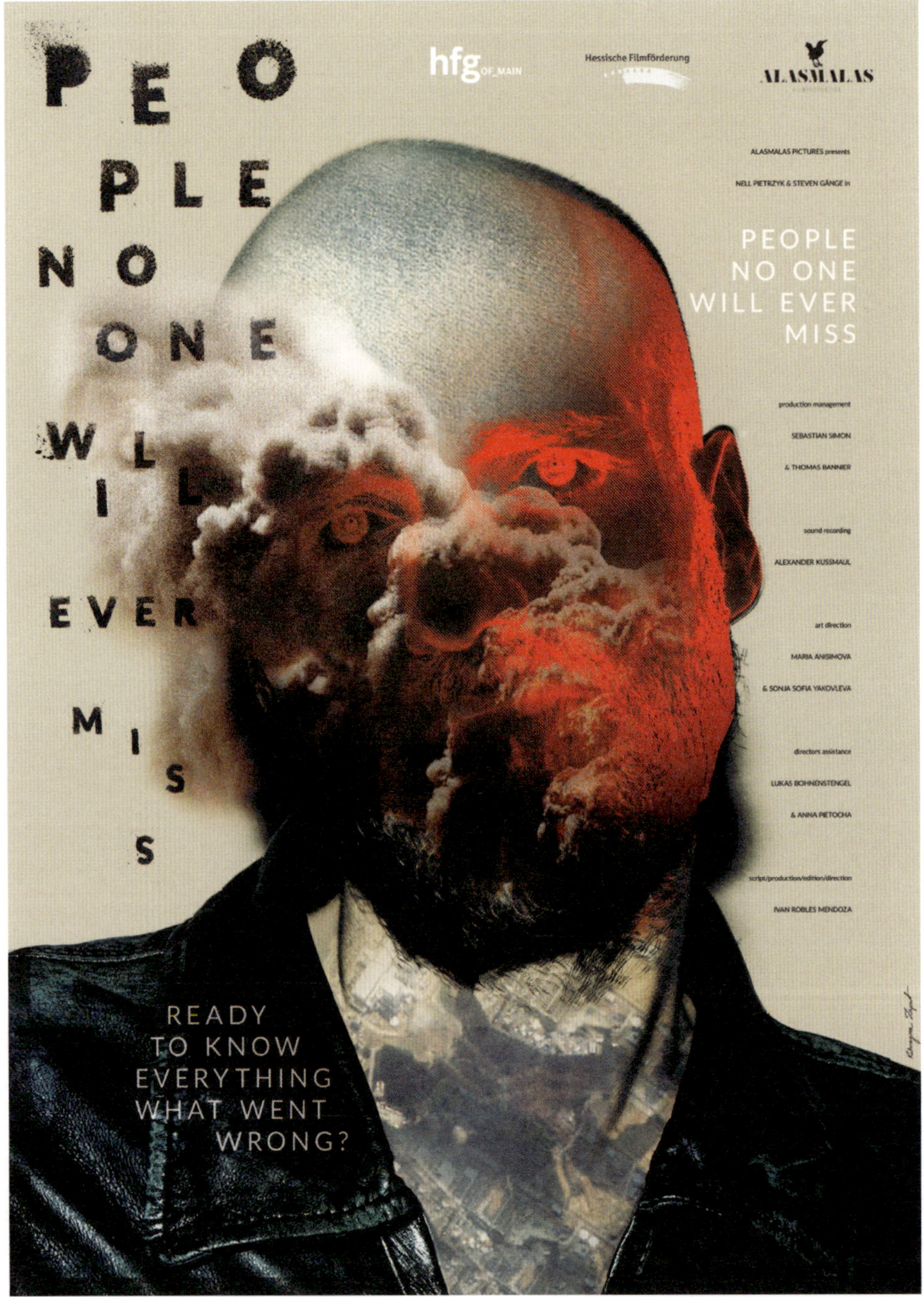

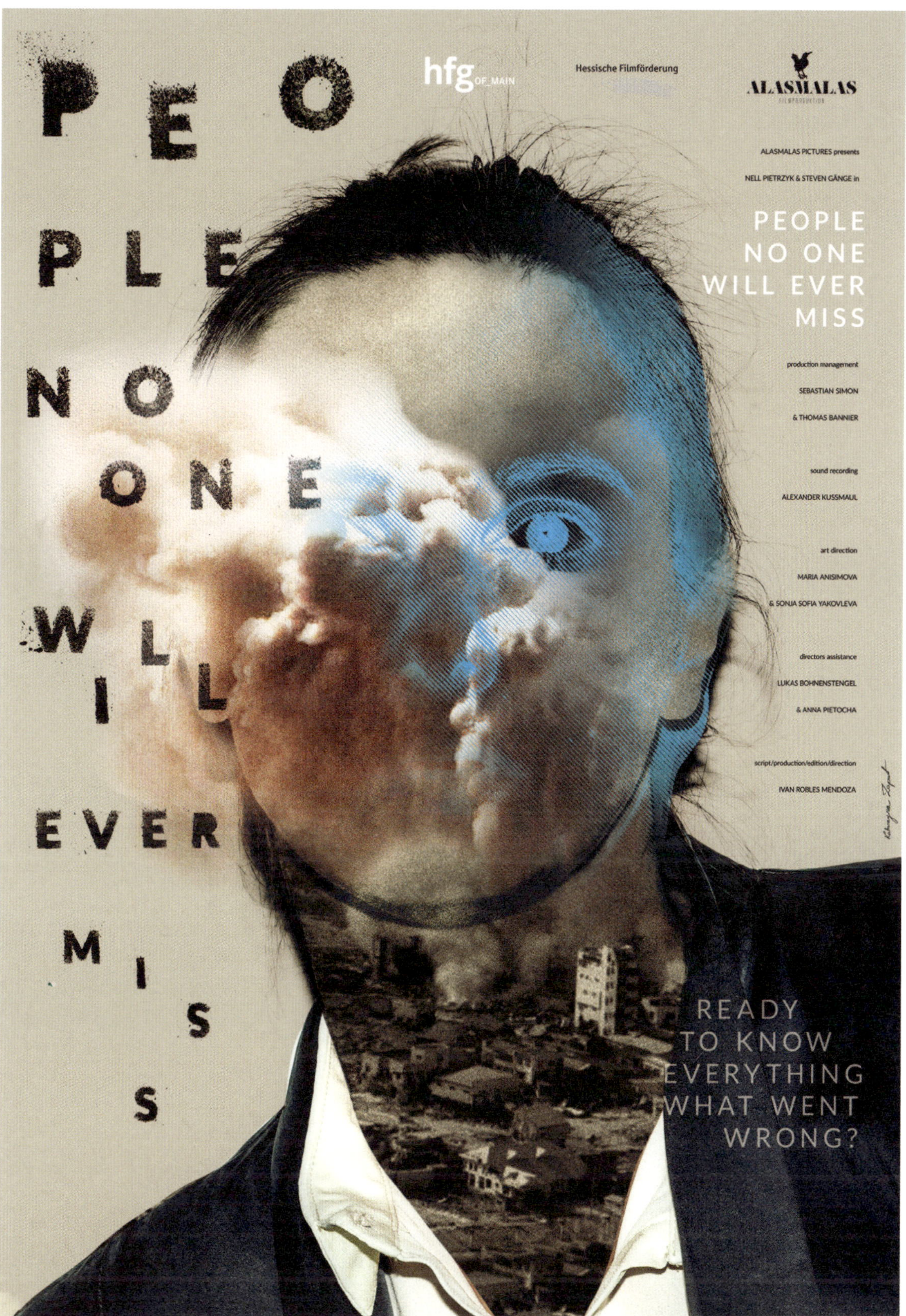
PEO
PLE
NO
ONE
WILL
EVER
MIS
S
hfg OF_MAIN
Hessische Filmförderung
ALASMALAS
ALASMALAS PICTURES presents
NELL PIETRZYK & STEVEN GÄNGE in
PEOPLE
NO ONE
WILL EVER
MISS
production management
SEBASTIAN SIMON
& THOMAS BANNIER
sound recording
ALEXANDER KUSSMAUL
art direction
MARIA ANISIMOVA
& SONJA SOFIA YAKOVLEVA
directors assistance
LUKAS BOHNENSTENGEL
& ANNA PIETOCHA
script/production/edition/direction
IVAN ROBLES MENDOZA
READY
TO KNOW
EVERYTHING
WHAT WENT
WRONG?

LADY M

Designer: Krzysztof Iwanski

This is a poster for *Lady M*, a play performed in theater of Gdynia Glowna.

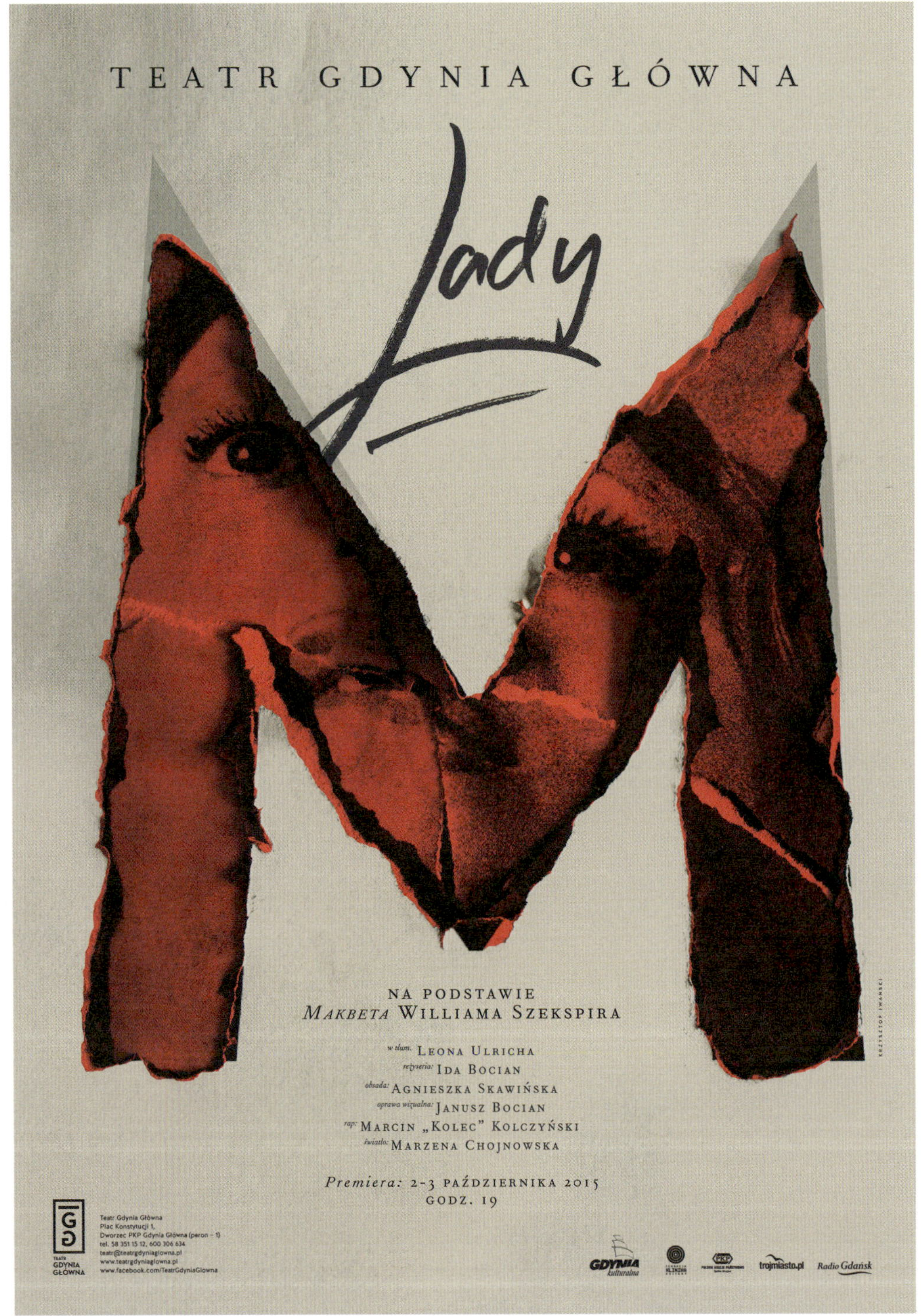

SOKIN I BOSINA (SOKIN AND BOSINA)

Designer: Ana Pesic

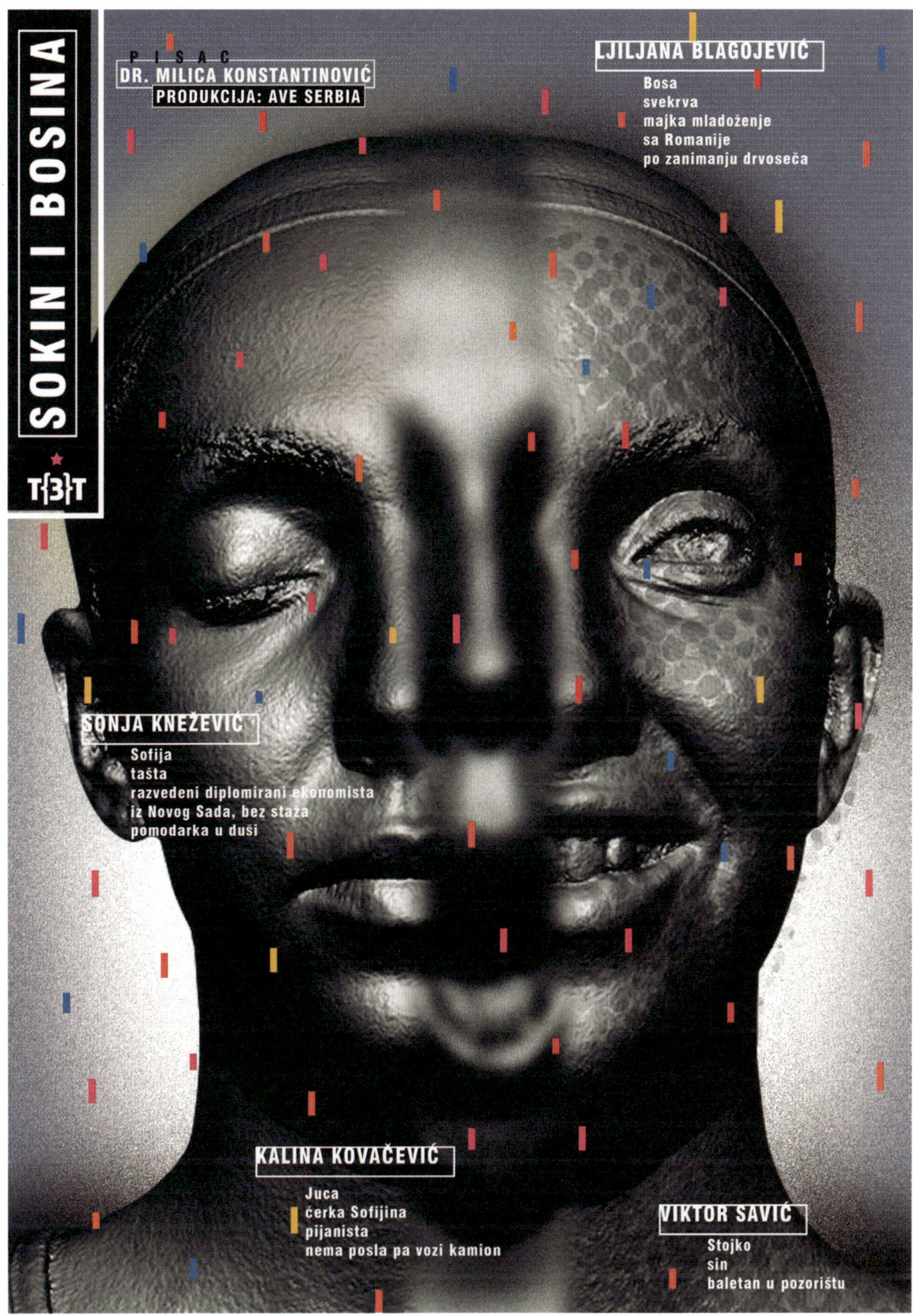

PAPUN 1113 CONCERT

Designer: FKWU Illustrator: Chili Chang

This Identity for band PAPUN's 1113 concert aimed to voice the resolution to march onward bravely despite unknown and unimaginable challenges ahead. It is about the increasing awareness of one's responsibilities for society, work, families and relationship as one grows up.

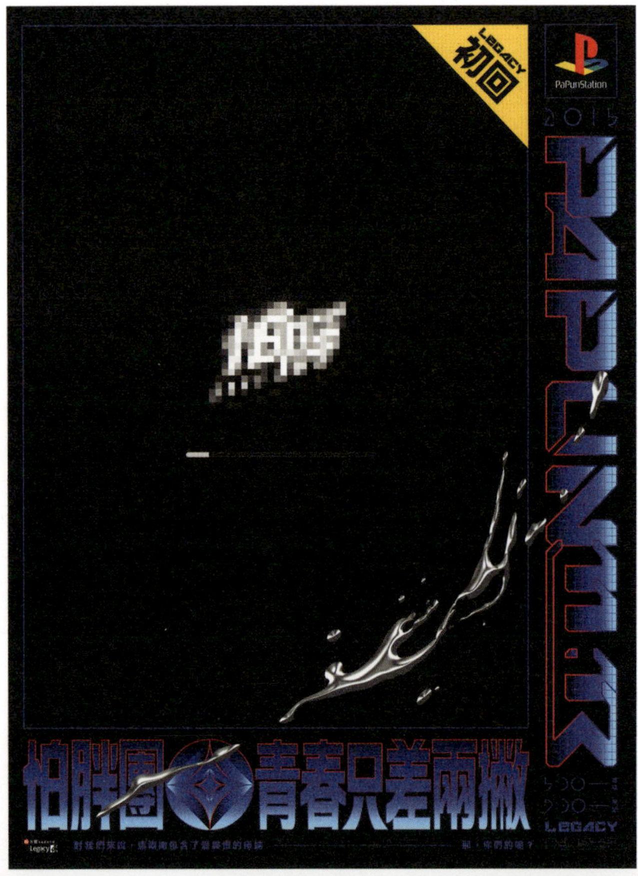

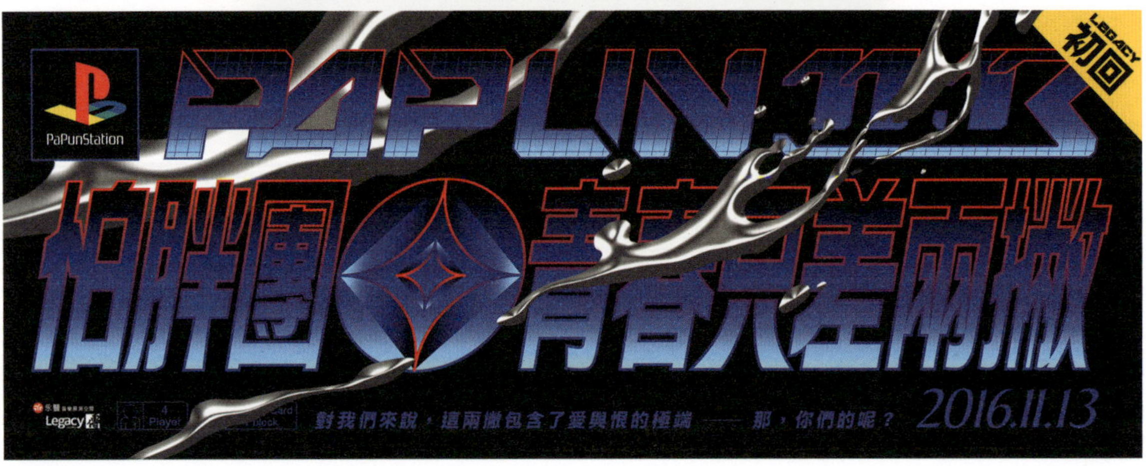

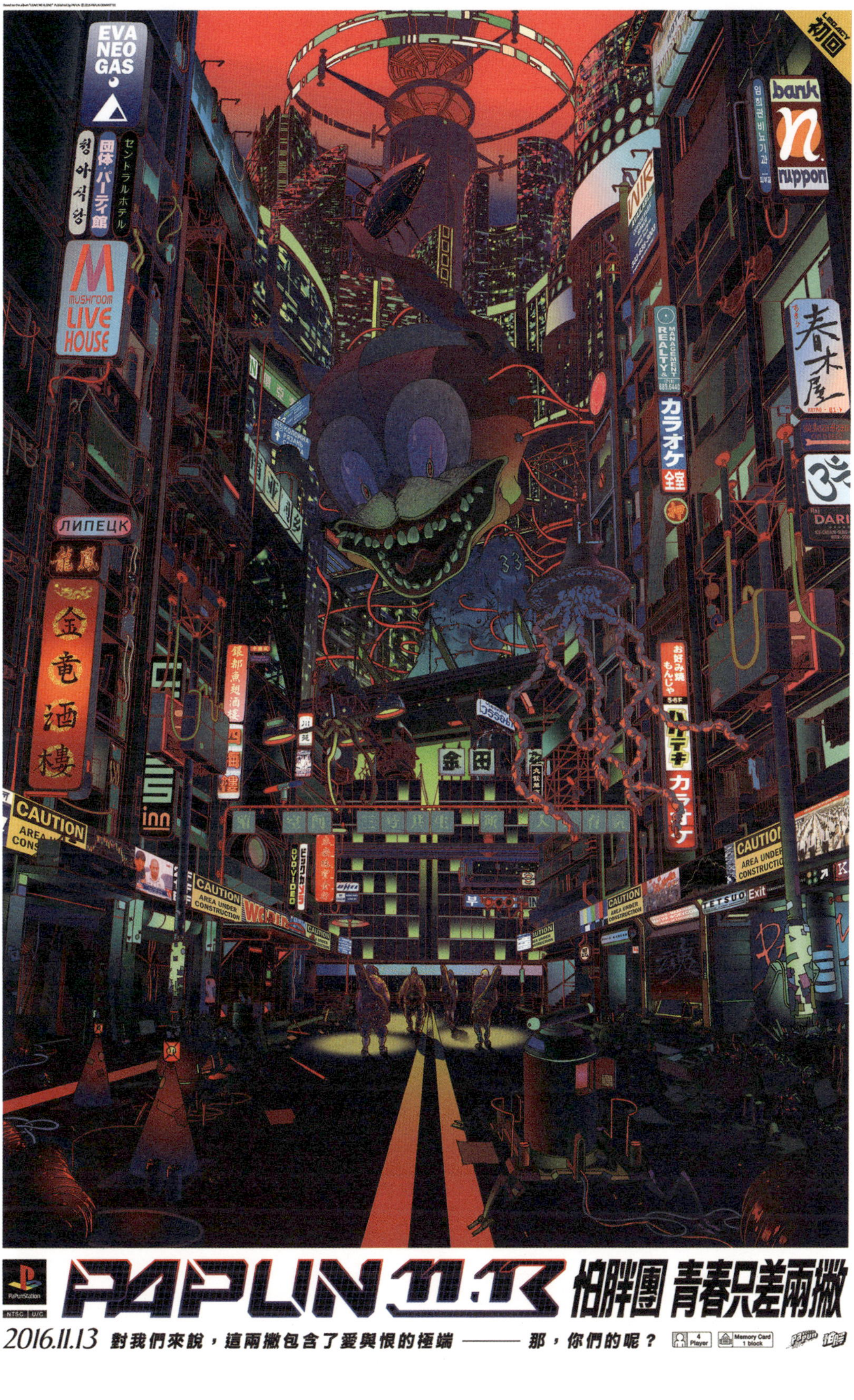

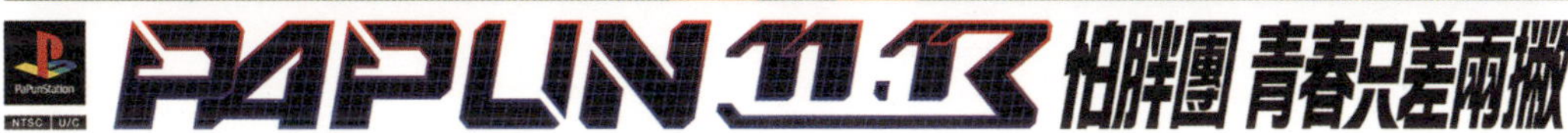
PaPunStation
NTSC U/C
PAPUN 11.13
帕胖團 青春只差兩撇
2016.11.13 對我們來說，這兩撇包含了愛與恨的極端 ——— 那，你們的呢？
4 Player
Memory Card 1 block

MUTILATION!

Designer: Juan Bautista Espíndola

"MUTILACION!" is an event held at the General San Martín Cultural Centre in Buenos Aires to pay tribute to the master of horror movies: John Carpenter. Its identity consists of a main poster, a brochure and a series of postcards. Since the beginnings, John Carpenter was not a stranger to the culture of self-publishing. As fanzine being the most faithful equivalent to self-publishing in the graphic industry, the creation is based on the 4 foundations of fanzine: cutting, pasting, writing and repeating.

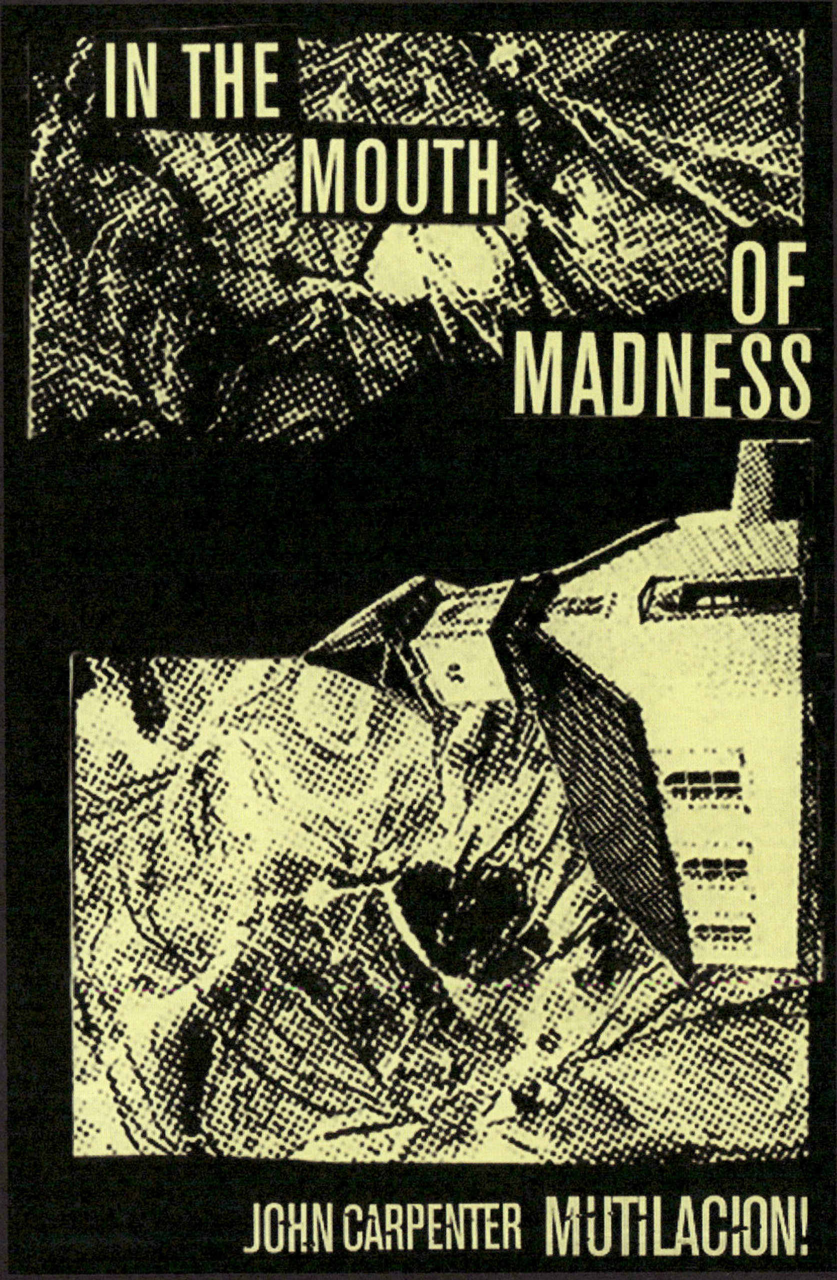

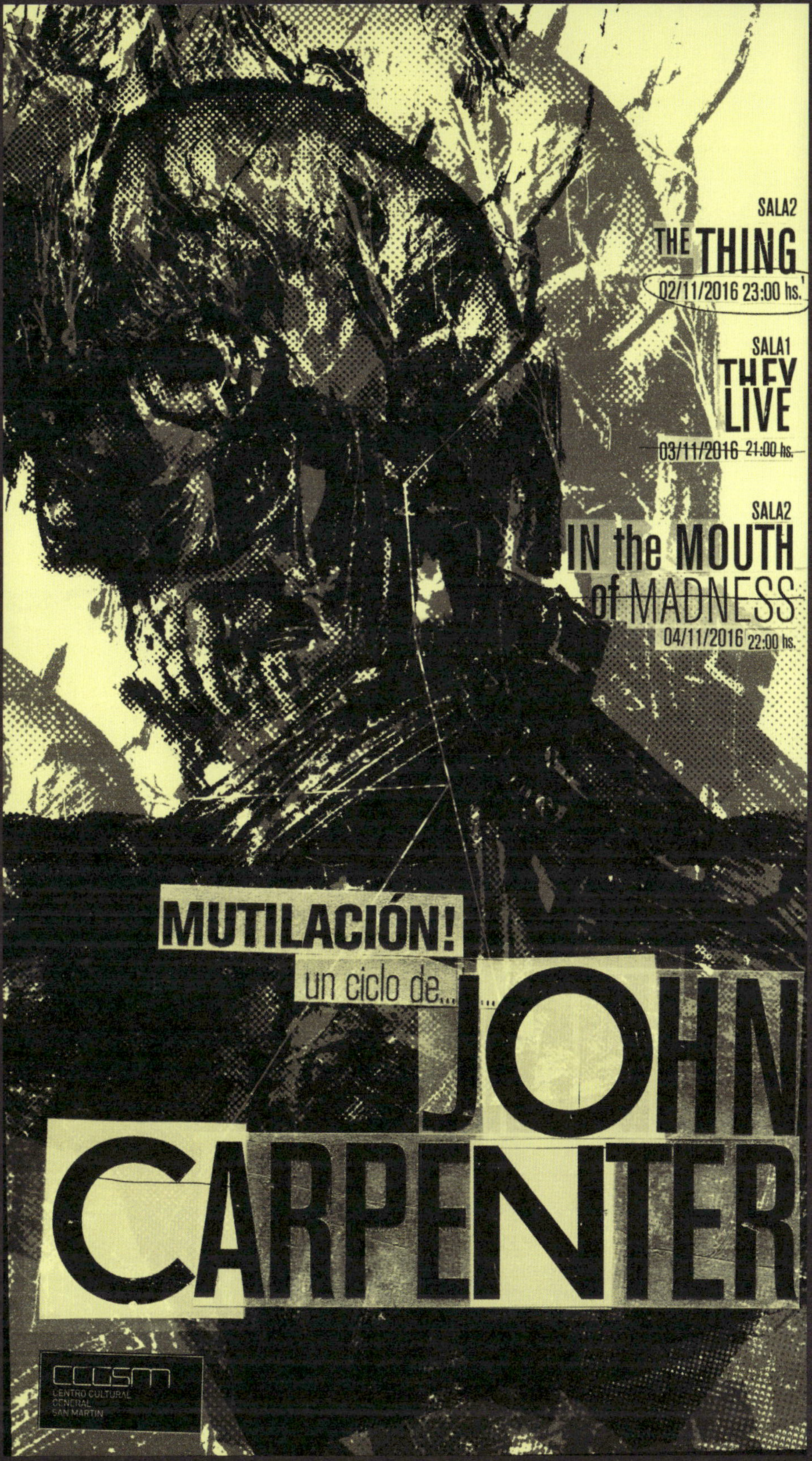

SALA2

THE THING

02/11/2016 23:00 hs.

SALA1

THEY LIVE

03/11/2016 21:00 hs.

SALA2

IN the MOUTH of MADNESS

04/11/2016 22:00 hs.

MUTILACIÓN!

un ciclo de...

JOHN CARPENTER

CCGSM

CENTRO CULTURAL GENERAL SAN MARTIN

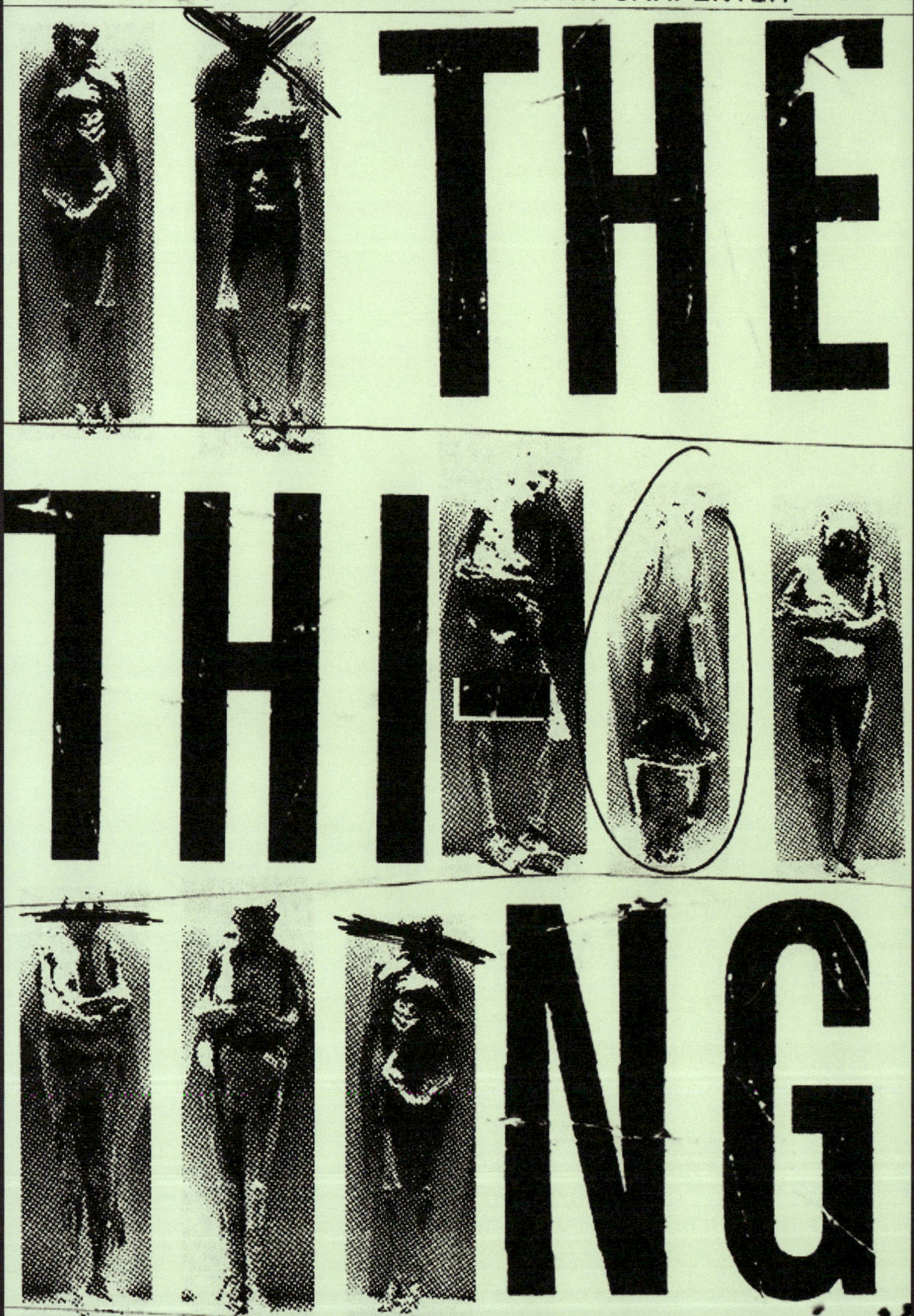
N CARPENTER CICLO MUTILACIÓN JOHN CARPENTER CICLO
THE
THING

THEY LIVE

CICLO

MUTILACIÓN!

JOHN CARPENTER

JOHN CARPENTER

Director, músico y guionista nacido en Carthage, New York, en 1948. Desde temprano la prometedora carrera de su hijo en el cine quedó marcada al ganar, con sólo 22 años, el Oscar al mejor cortometraje por **La resurección de Bronco Billy.**
Su primer largometraje: **Dark Star** (1974), que realizó en estrecha colaboración con Dan O'Bannon, coguionista de Alien.

Fue **Halloween** (1978), la que lanzó a la fama al director, tanto en lo que a taquilla se refiere como en el respeto que la crítica empezó a profesarle. En el remake **The Thing** (1982), Carpenter combinó el suspense y los efectos especiales para crear una atmósfera de pánico.

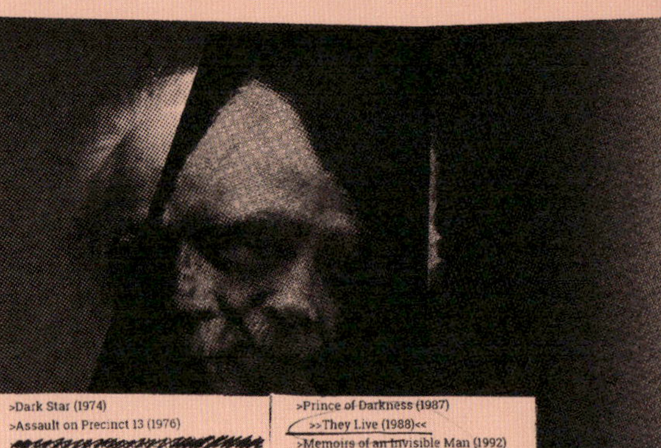

>Dark Star (1974)
>Assault on Precinct 13 (1976)
>Halloween (1978)
>The Fog (1980)
>Escape from New York (1981)
>>The Thing (1982)<<
>Christine (1983)
>Starman (1984)
>Big Trouble in Little China (1986)
>Prince of Darkness (1987)
>>They Live (1988)<<
>Memoirs of an Invisible Man (1992)
>Body Bags (1993)
>>In the Mouth of Madness (1994)<<
>Village of the Damned (1995)
>Escape from L.A. (1996)
>Vampires (1998)
>Ghosts of Mars (2001)
>The Ward (2010)

THE THING
Miércoles 2 de noviembre, 23:00 hs.
Sala 1

THEY LIVE!
Jueves 3 de noviembre, 21:00 hs.
Sala 2

IN THE MOUTH OF MADNESS
Viernes 4 de noviembre, 22:00 hs.
Sala 1

CCGSM
CENTRO CULTURAL GENERAL SAN MARTIN

Sarmiento 1551 (C1042ABC) 4374
www.centroculturalsanmartin.co

>>j carpenter _021116 2300:_ sil _031116 2100:_ SI _041116 2200 SII

>ciC MUTLACION

>01 >_the >_thing_ >>>krt RUSsell

>02 >_they- >_live} _roddypipper

>03 >_inthe >_mouth:of_ _ssendam SAM >_neill_

ccgsm> _nvmbr1:6 ba_

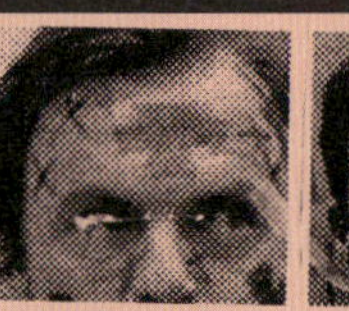
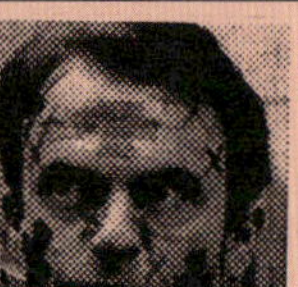
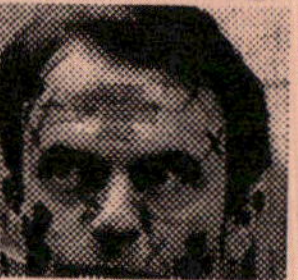
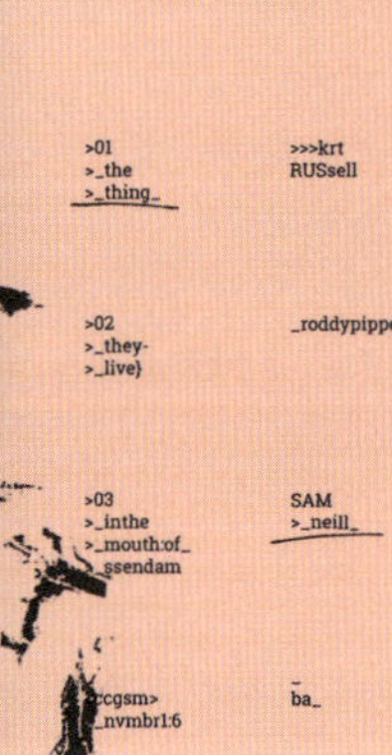
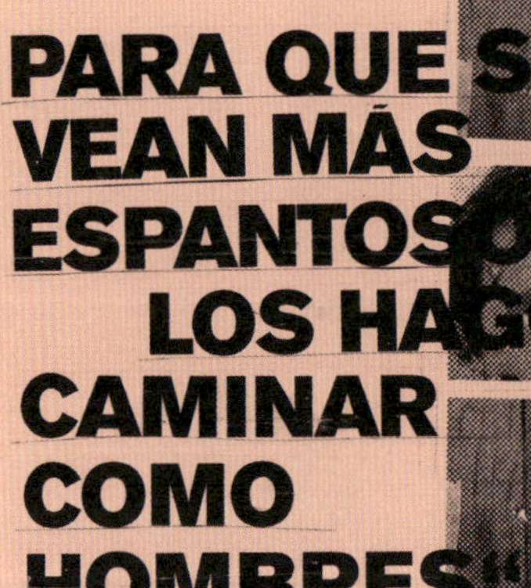

PARA QUE SE VEAN MÁS ESPANTOSOS LOS HAGO CAMINAR COMO HOMBRES"

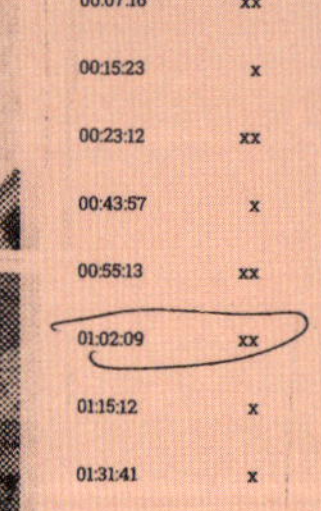

00:07:16	xx
00:15:23	x
00:23:12	xx
00:43:57	x
00:55:13	xx
01:02:09	xx
01:15:12	x
01:31:41	x

THE THING- 1982

La obra maestra de John Carpenter, el artesano del cine del Terror, que rechazada en su momento tanto por la crítica como por el público, poco a poco, con el paso de los años, se ha ganado el sitial que se merece: **una de las mejores películas de suspenso de la historia del Cine.**

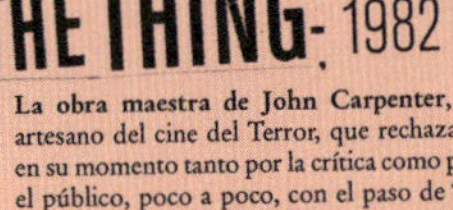

"La mejor remake de todos los tiempos"

La nieve, la aridez glacial y unos personajes equidistantes entre el asombro y la demencia conforman una trama tan simple como adictiva. Todo complementado con un gran nivel técnico, una estupenda dirección y la **sobresaliente banda sonora de Ennio Morricone.** Sin duda, The Thing es **todo un ejemplo del mejor cine de género de los fructíferos años ochenta.**
Una pesadilla espeluznante que deja huella en el espectador.

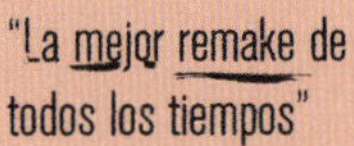

~~CLARK~~
~~BENNINGS~~
~~FUCHS~~
~~NORRIS~~
~~PALMER~~
~~COPPER~~
~~WINDOWS~~
GARRY
CHILDS
MCREADY

01the thing
02they live
03in the mouth of madness

MUTIL-ACION

—UN CICLO DE

JOHN CARPENTER

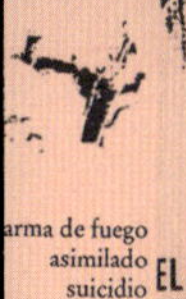

arma de fuego
asimilado
suicidio
asimilado
asimilado
desangrado
asimilado
asimilado

EL HOMBRE ES EL LUGAR
MÁS CALIDO PARA ESCONDERSE

1982
109min.
rtng ****
kurt russell

1988
97min.
rtng ***'
roddy pipper

1994
97min.
rtng***'
sam neill

THEY LIVE - 1988

Ver They Live representa una experiencia conflictiva. Es una singular combinación de mensajes reveladores con actuaciones

"...están apoderando de nosotros,
...s están convirtiendo en esclavos..."

deslucidas, potentes comentarios sociales con efectos especiales de cintas de serie B de los 1950 y una cautivante sátira con extrañas frases de remate. Provocando que

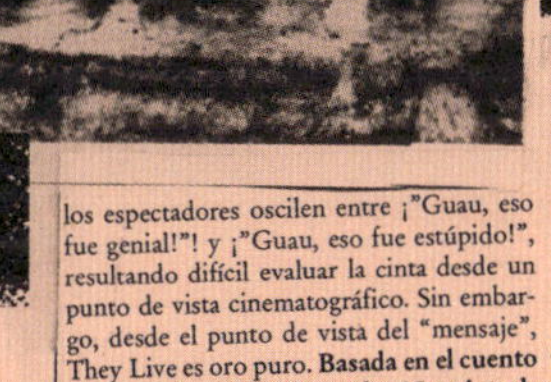

los espectadores oscilen entre ¡"Guau, eso fue genial!"! y ¡"Guau, eso fue estúpido!", resultando difícil evaluar la cinta desde un punto de vista cinematográfico. Sin embargo, desde el punto de vista del "mensaje", They Live es oro puro. **Basada en el cuento corto Eight O'Clock in the Morning de Ray Nelson,** la película es una de esas raras historias subversivas que fuerzan al espectador a cuestionar su mundo y lo que lo rodea.

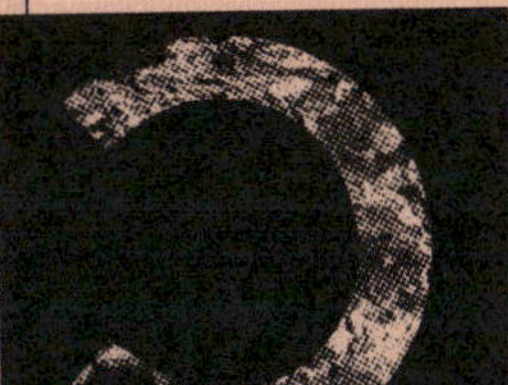

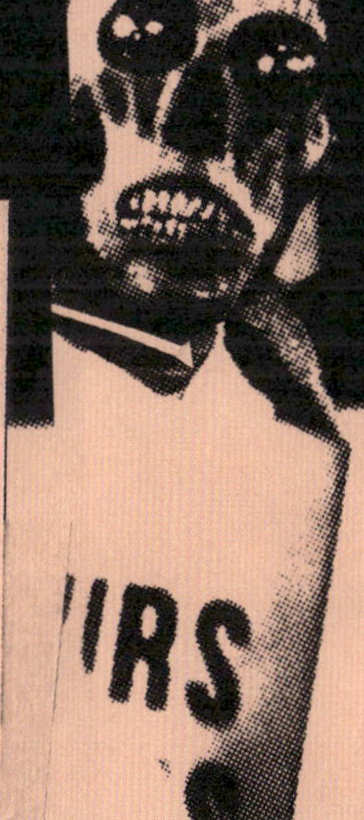

IN the MOUTH of MADNESS - 1994

Una película que para algunos significa un esfuerzo menor dentro de la filmografía de Carpenter, pero que para otros, **es una prueba más de su gran talento narrativo,** de su estimulante sentido del humor y de su (muchas veces negadas, de manera incomprensible) gran inteligencia, astucia y sutilidad. Un cine más basado en el terror, que en el horror o en el susto fácil, que nunca oculta su condición de cine de género, pero **que le sirve como excusa a Carpenter para hablar de muchas de sus obsesiones e inquietudes,** las mismas que ya llevaba cerca de veinte años deslizando furtivamente por debajo de las trepidantes o espeluznantes historias que nos contaba.

MAKING HORROR

Studio: Anagrama

Making horror is a Hong Kong based new film label that focuses on horror and thriller films. With components relating to crime scenes, the brand identity tells a story through a forensic detective's eyes, hinting at an atmosphere of terror and mystery. The logo portrays the fine line between order and madness with a structured typeface which has been distorted inconsistently to form different variations throughout print and video. Incorporating the characteristics of horror film and thriller, repeating lines and typos are adopted in the stationery to deliver a psychotic personality. The identity communicates the studio's cinematic expertise in the horror film industry while offering a memorable experience.

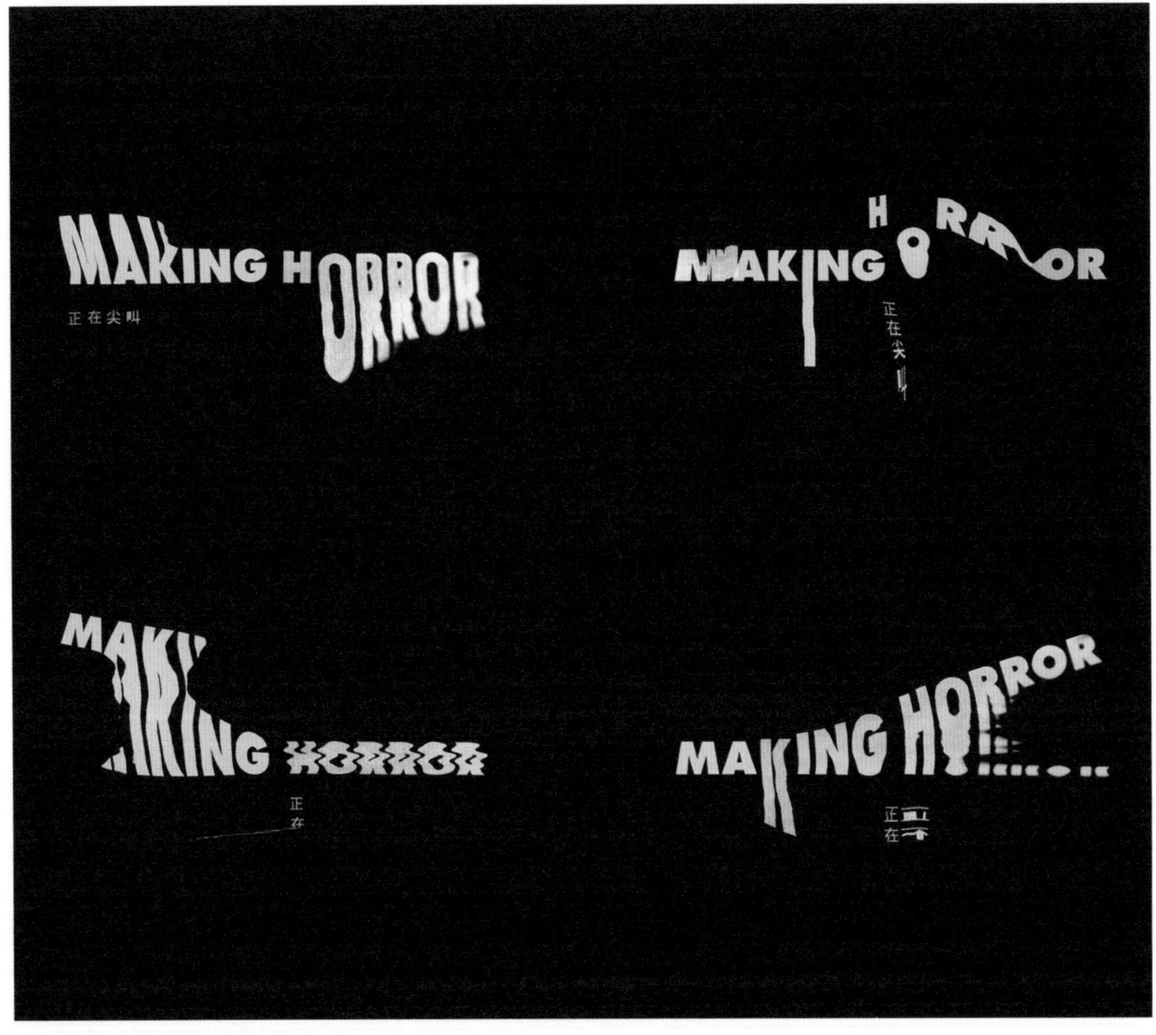

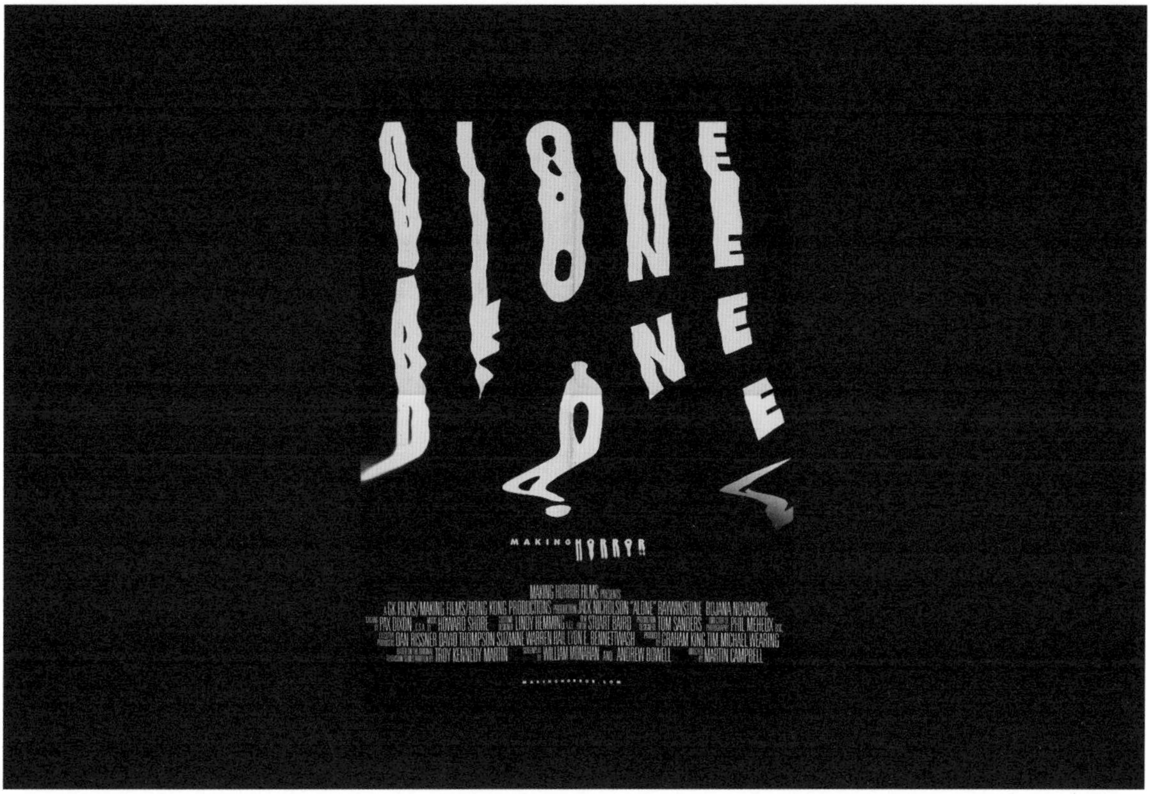
MAKING HORROR
MAKING HORROR FILMS PRESENTS
A GK FILMS/MAKING FILMS/HONG KONG PRODUCTIONS JACK NICHOLSON "ALONE" RAYWINSTONE BOJANA NOVAKOVIC
PAX DIXON HOWARD SHORE LINDY HEMMING STUART BAIRD TOM SANDERS PHIL MEHEUX
DAN RISSNER DAVID THOMPSON SUZANNE WARREN HAL LYON E. BENNETWASH GRAHAM KING TIM MICHAEL WEARING
TROY KENNEDY MARTIN WILLIAM MONAHAN AND ANDREW BOWELL MARTIN CAMPBELL

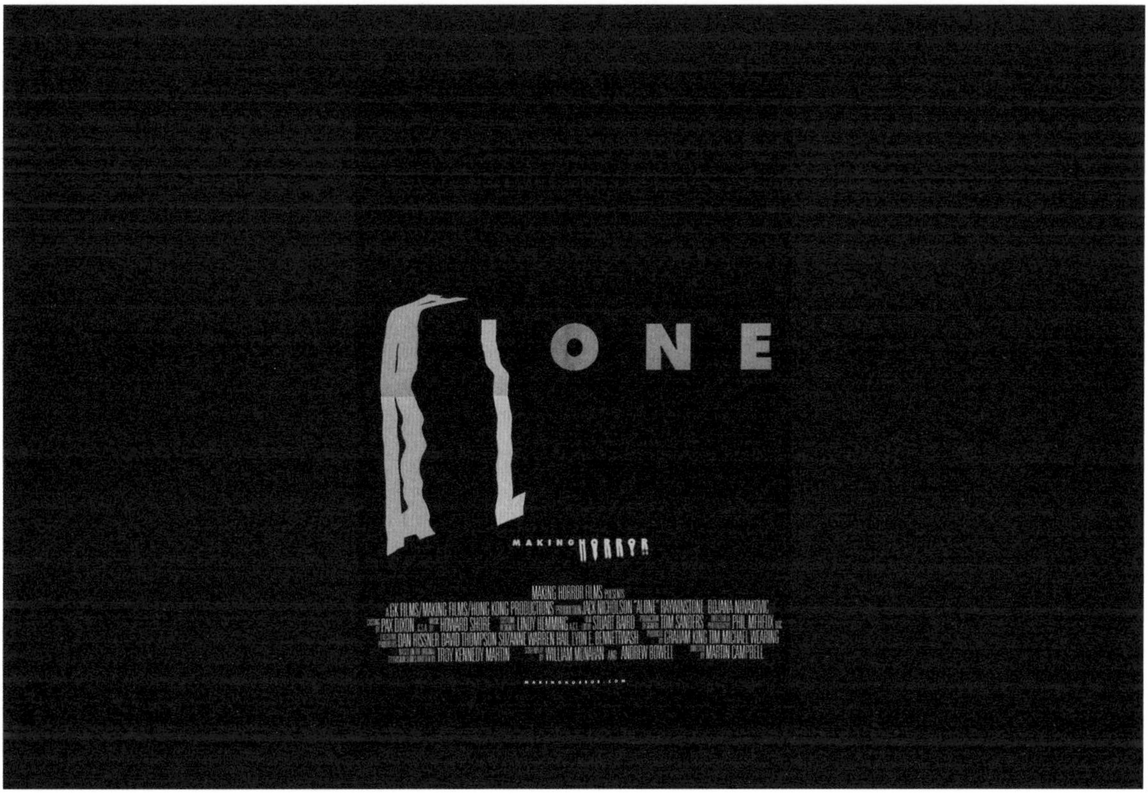
ONE
MAKING HORROR
MAKING HORROR FILMS PRESENTS
A GK FILMS/MAKING FILMS/HONG KONG PRODUCTIONS JACK NICHOLSON "ALONE" RAYWINSTONE BOJANA NOVAKOVIC
PAX DIXON HOWARD SHORE LINDY HEMMING STUART BAIRD TOM SANDERS PHIL MEHEUX
DAN RISSNER DAVID THOMPSON SUZANNE WARREN HAL LYON E. BENNETWASH GRAHAM KING TIM MICHAEL WEARING
TROY KENNEDY MARTIN WILLIAM MONAHAN AND ANDREW BOWELL MARTIN CAMPBELL

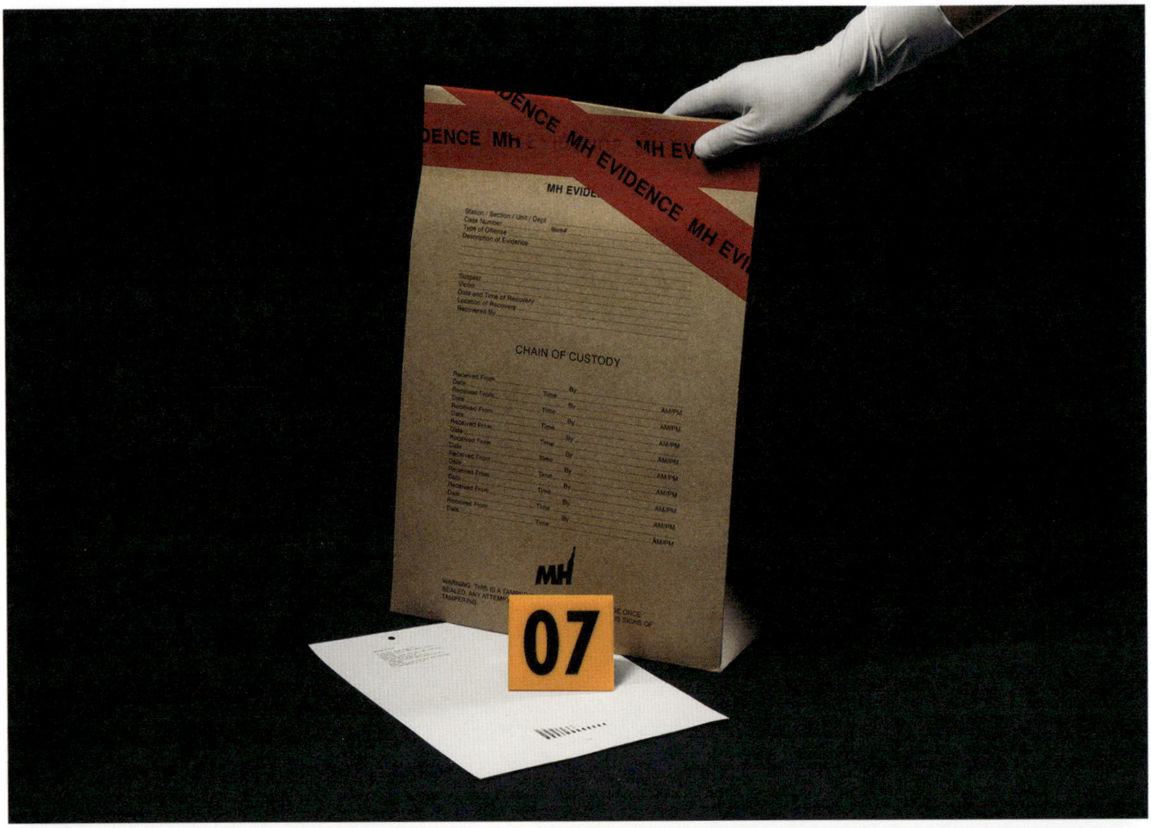
MH EVIDENCE
CHAIN OF CUSTODY
07

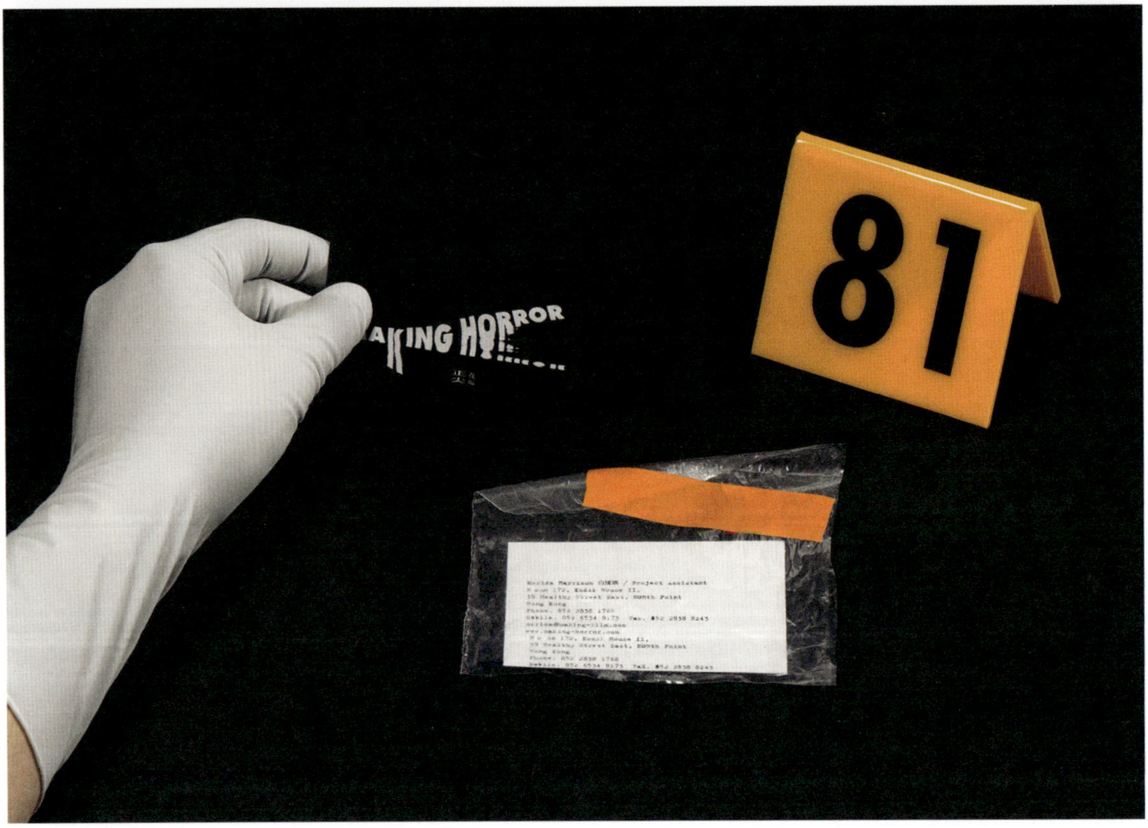
81

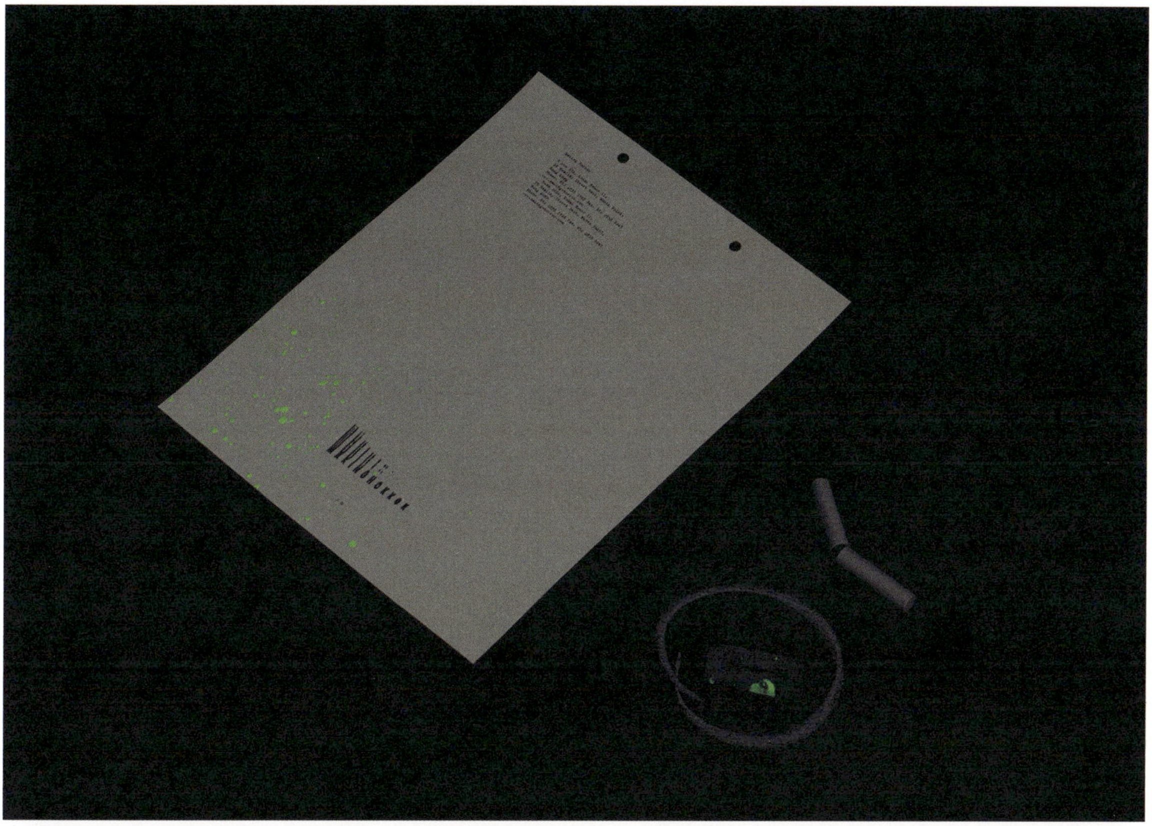

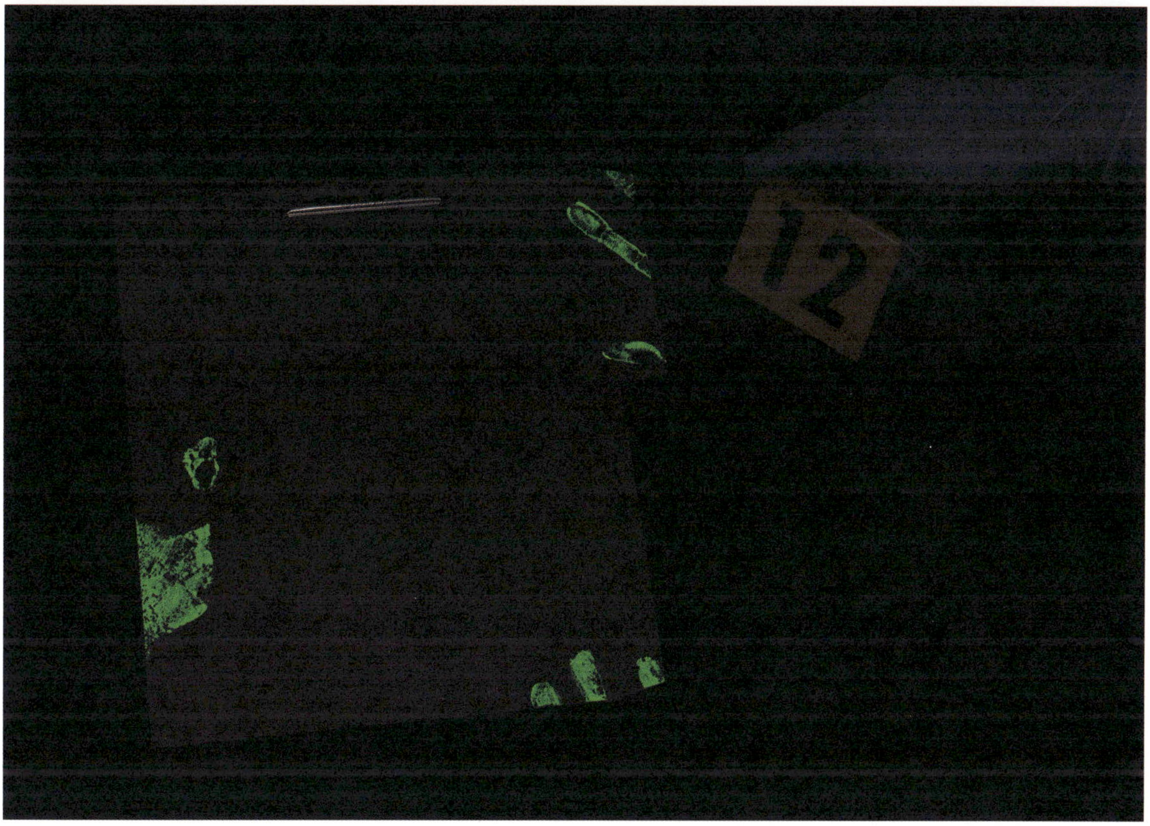

PLANET

Artist: BANG SANG-HO

With curiosity about the invisible things, the artist works mostly to establish unknown worlds of planets while describing landscapes and living things in it through Media Art such as illustrations, graphics, and videos. In this work, he captures the changing scenes of evolution of living things during the growth of a planet, which basically is a totally separate universe from reality. It will mainly go through 4 stages: creation, connection, explosion and changes. Though it seems like a simple cycle, the changes in there will bring new stories to this world and another planet that might be connected to it.

Everything to be created, exploded, and mated is very primitive and free on the planet. The many holes on the planet connect to the unknown world with sizes nor locations unrecognizable. When looking into these holes, one can see other worlds same with many holes. The artist hoped that people can imagine this planet with him.

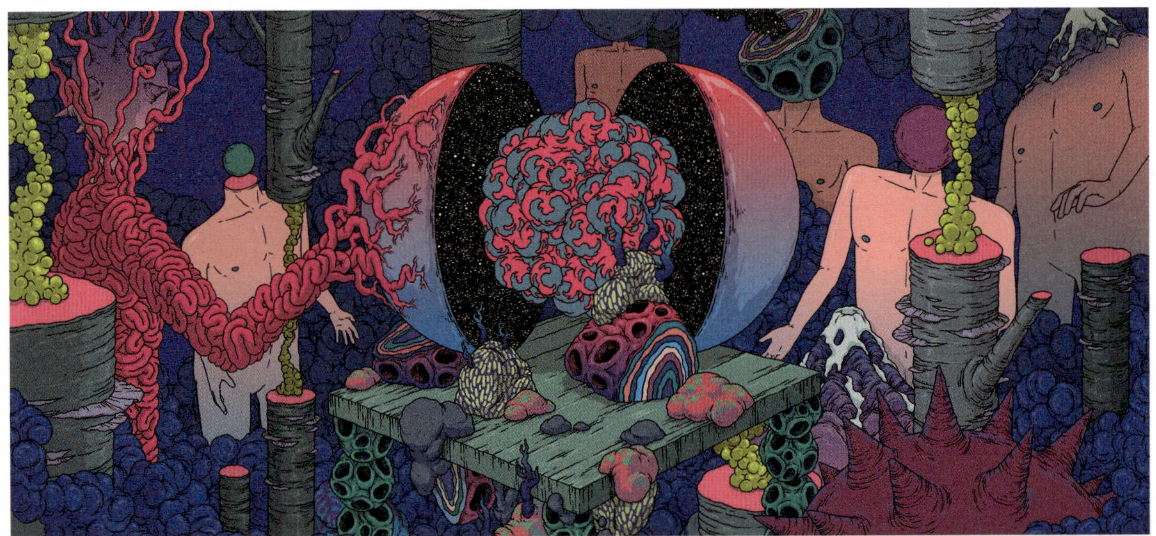

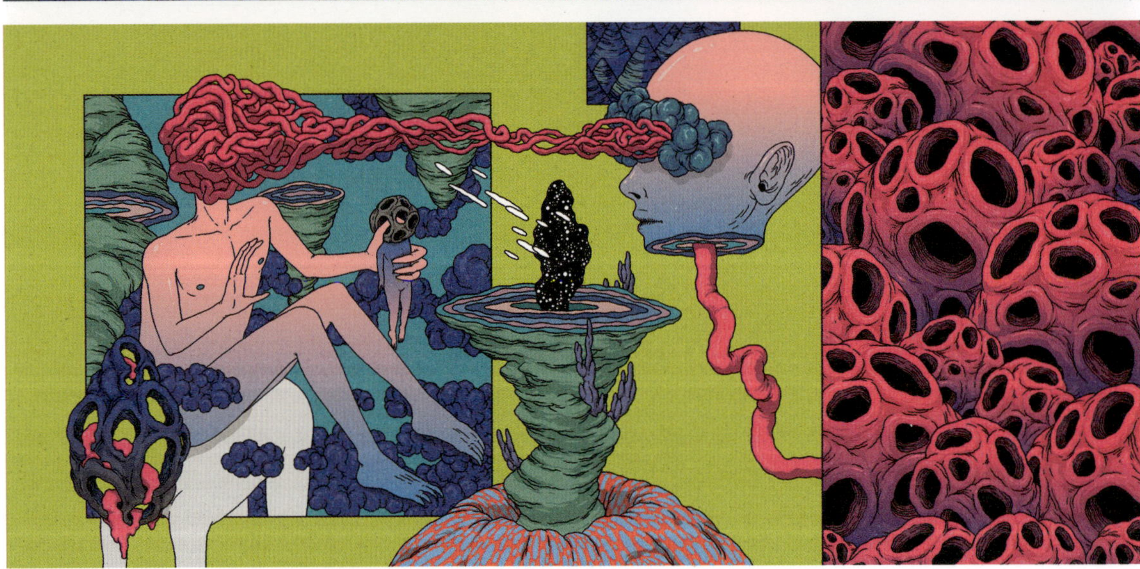

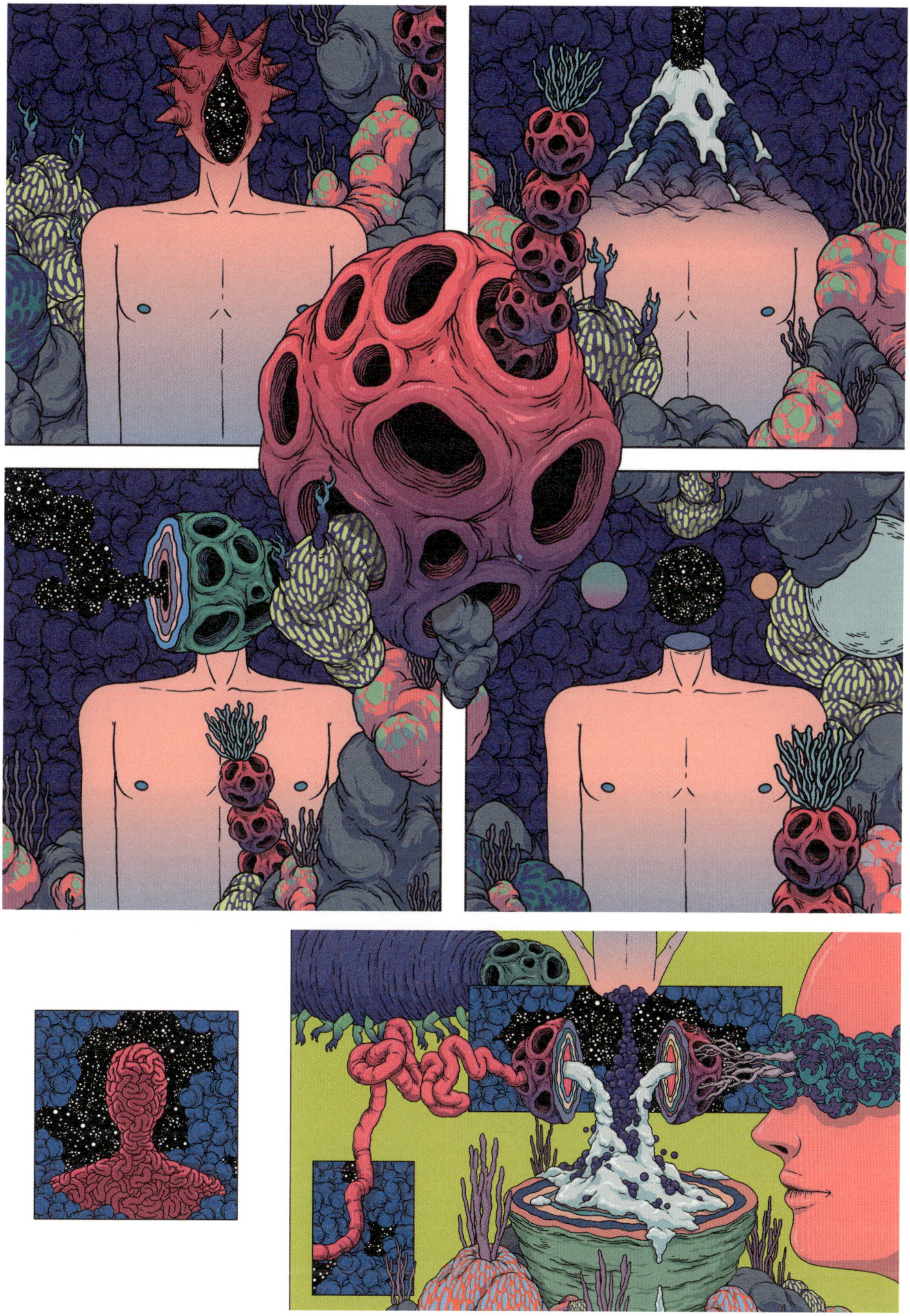

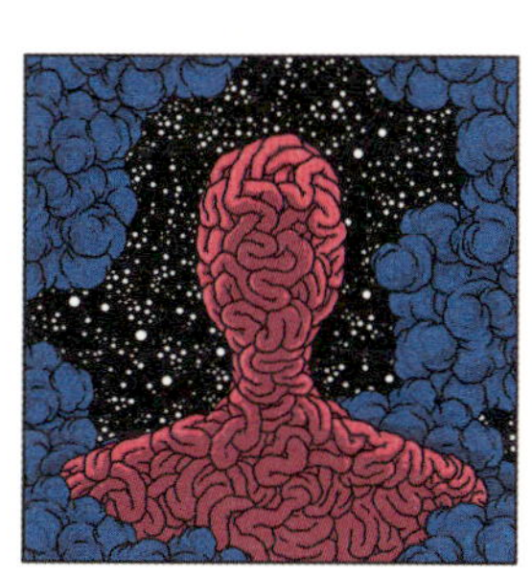

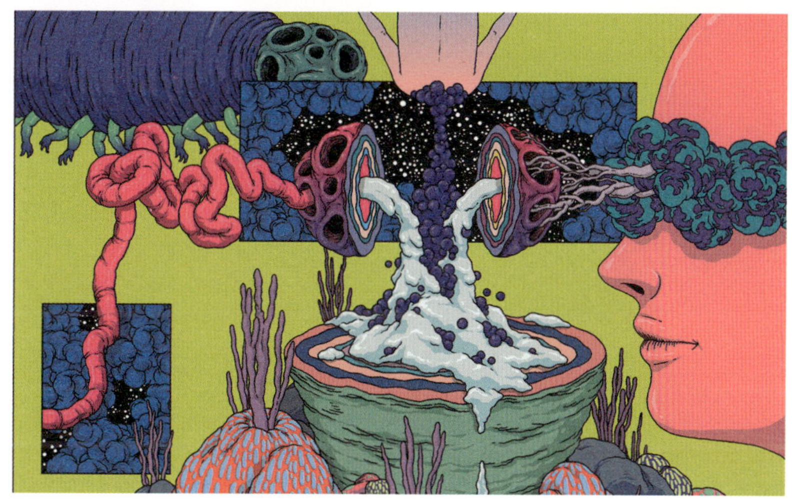

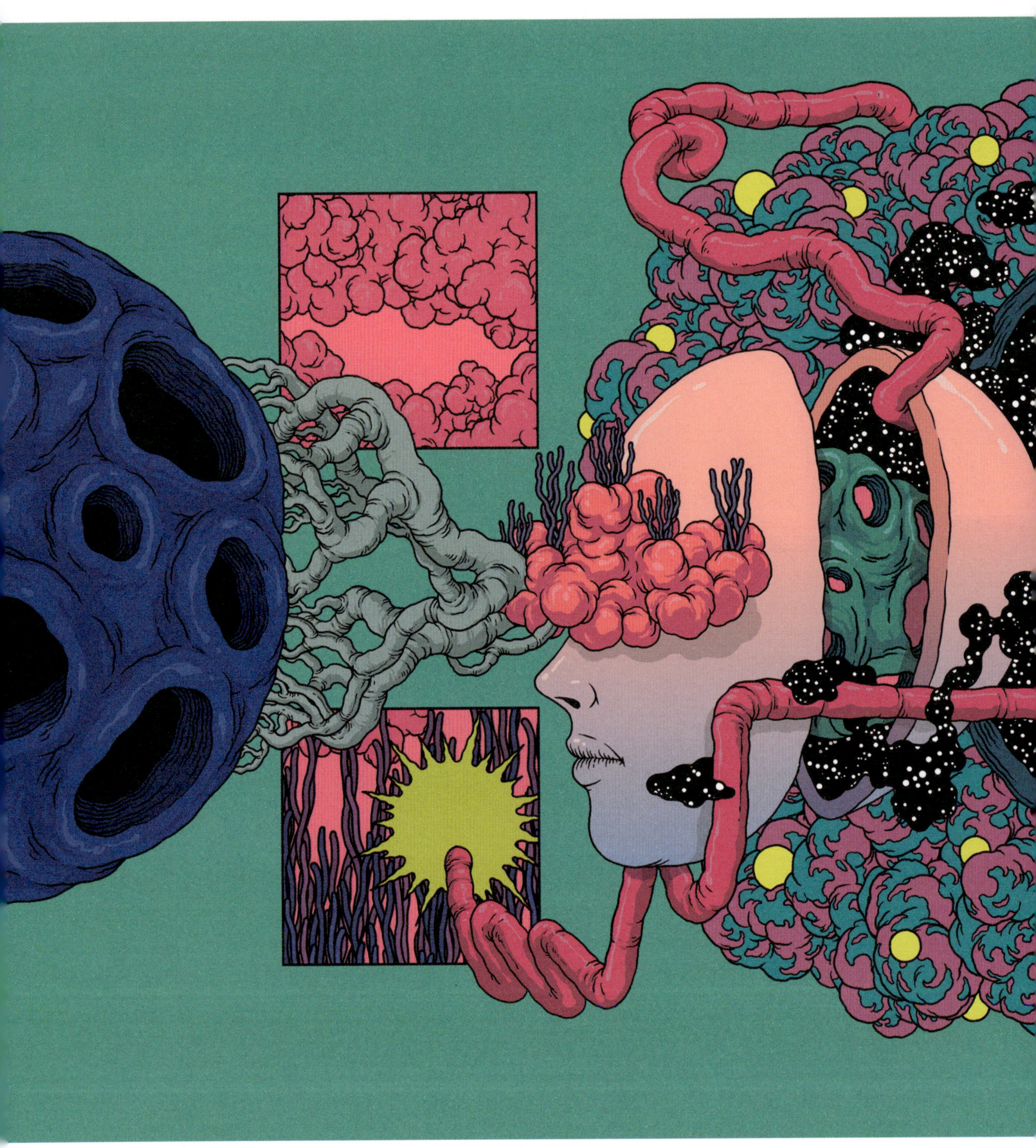

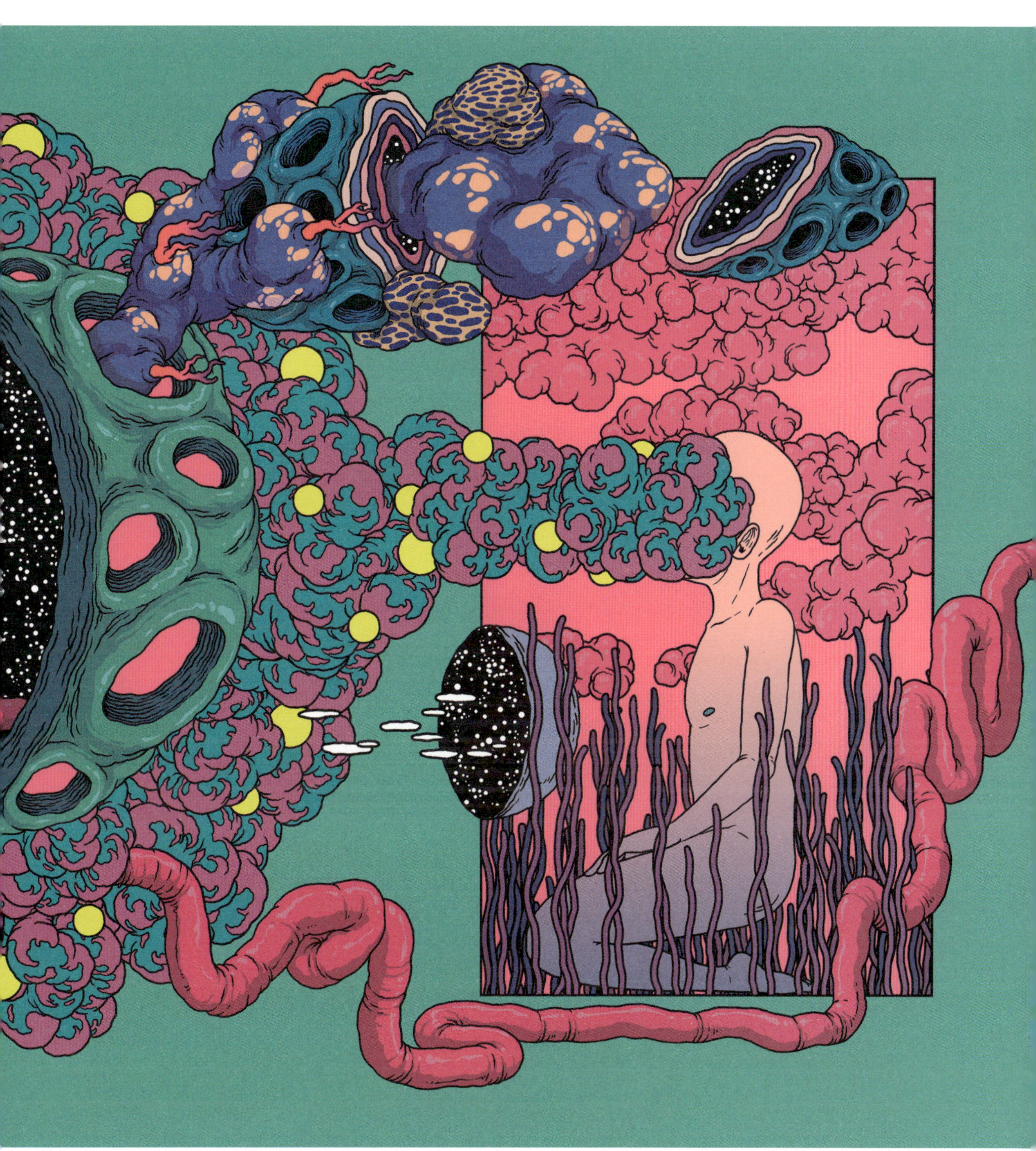

CHIEFINSPECTOR

Artist: Mario Pegas

Inspired by the cult horror films of John Carpenter and David Cronenberg from the 1970s and 1980s, the artist created this illustration series portraying the study of body horror genre, the manipulation of flesh and human anatomy. The series is comprised of three pieces, featuring different characters in different stages or actions of cannibalism.

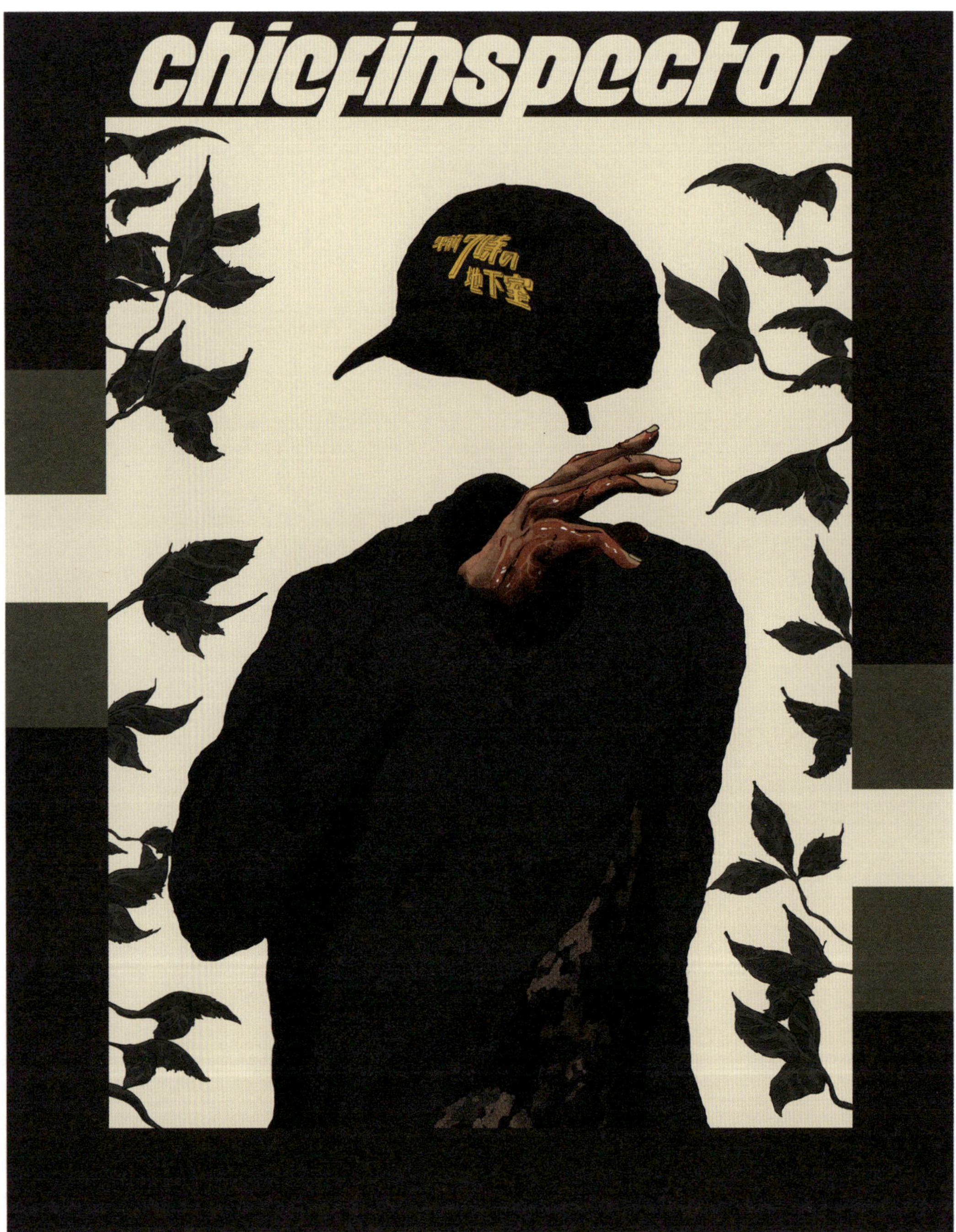

VISIT US

Artist: Mario Pegas

Inspired by the local culture of Indonesia, the artist illustrated an artificially augmented scene in which symbols of Wayang kulit had been used as the face of android devices and A.I. of tourist sites, picturing a Westworld–like twist for Indonesian tourism in the future. This illustration also performed as a satire for the incompetence to appreciate the beauty of Indonesian tourism resources of its own people.

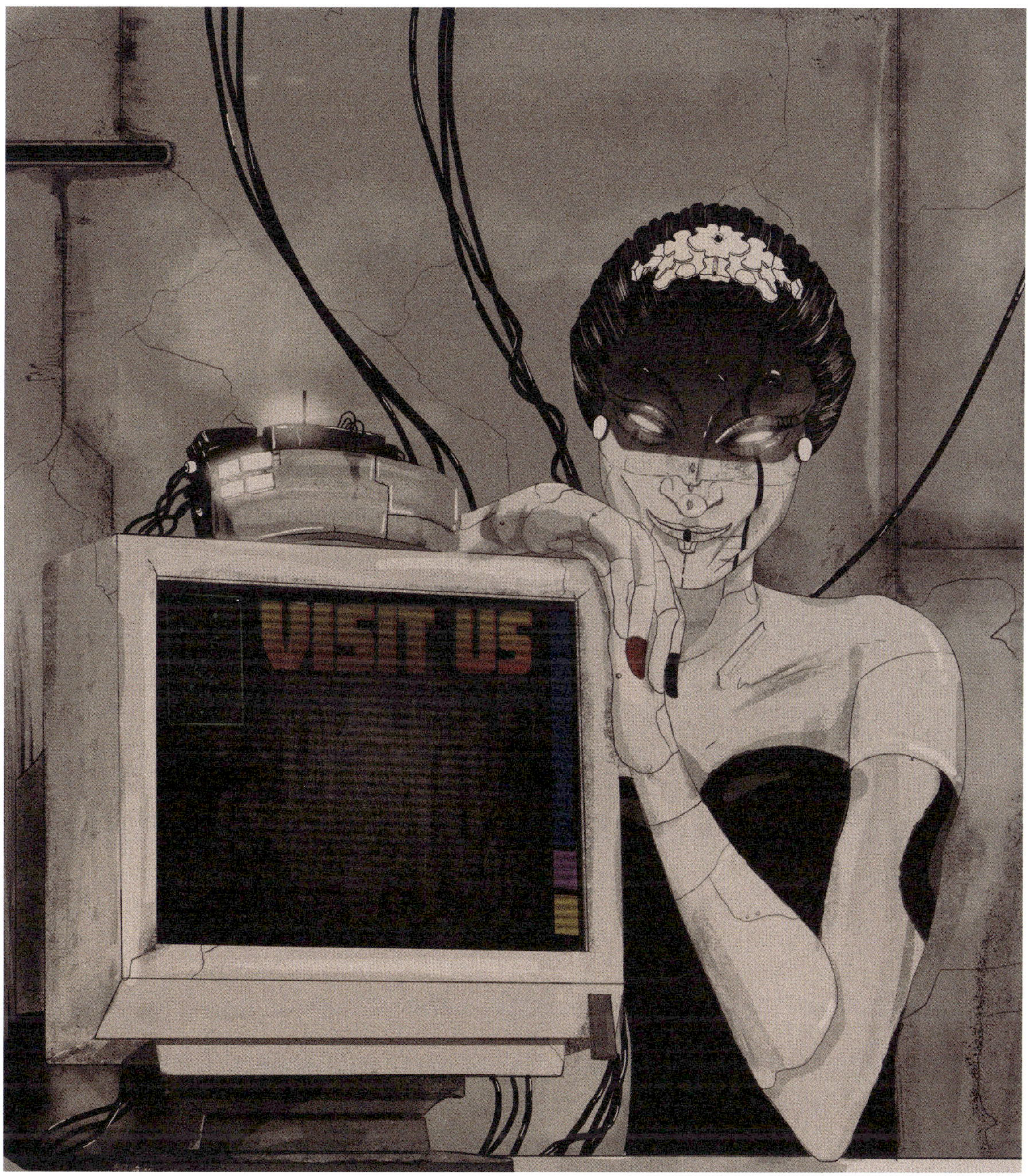

SCREAM

Artist: Mario Pegas

Inspired by the fear of technology that grows in line with the advancement, the artist created this illustration picturing the cybernetic hell. The scene has a blend of science fiction with horror, expressing artist's concern about the challenges posted to people's psychological and mental states along with the development of artificial intelligence and supporting technologies.

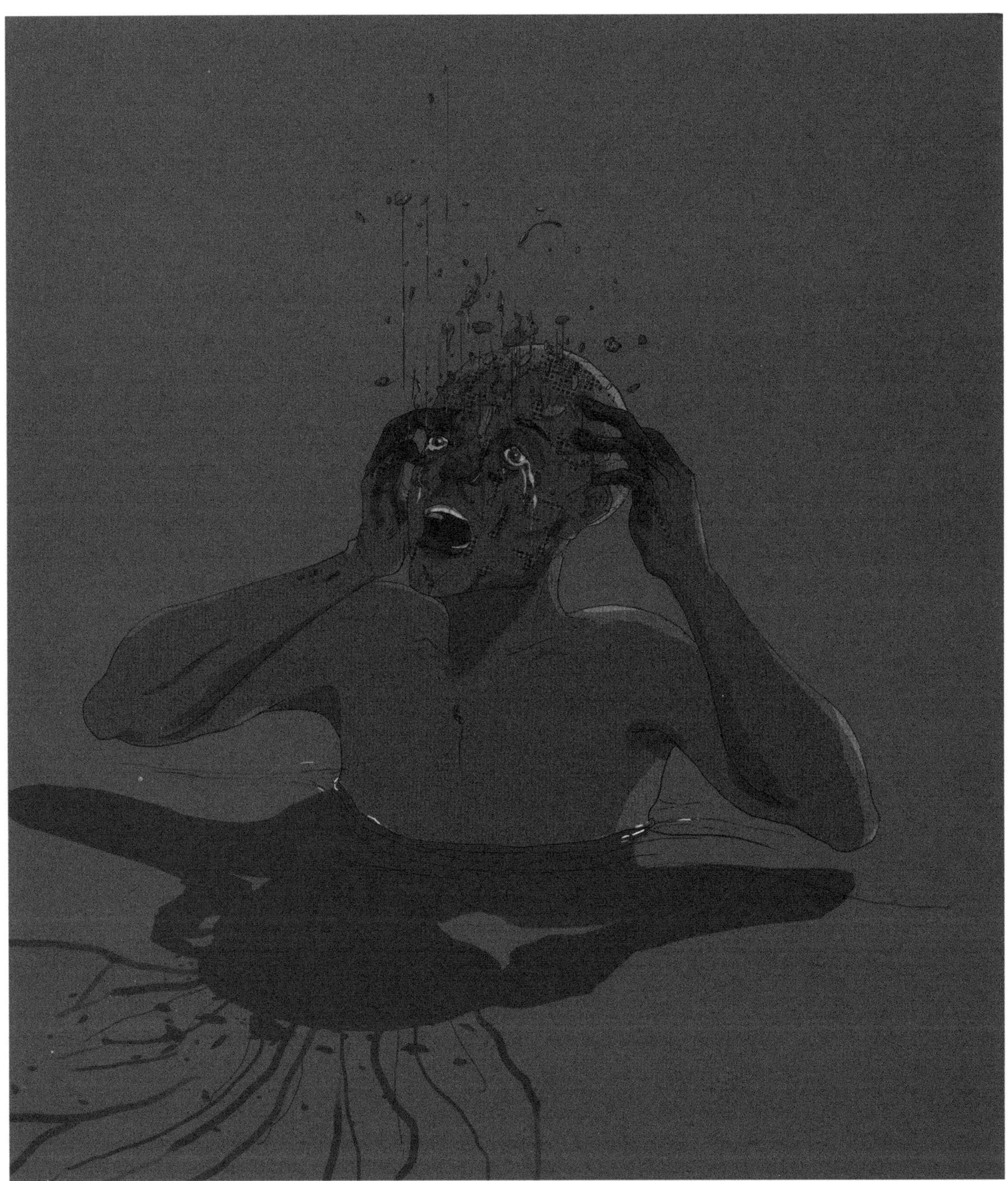

HARKONNEN-BLOOD REDUX

Artist: Mario Pegas

An imaginary future magazine named HARKONNEN was created with inspiration from Frank Herberts' science fiction *Dune*. The HARKONNEN tracks the evolution of human race and explores technological and scientific development in the future. For the 80th issue, the theme is about the controversial medical treatment, Blood Redux, which can be utilised to regenerate cyber-augmented bodies and born-authentic human bodies for extended lifespan, and to manipulate any known diseases the body has ever experienced.

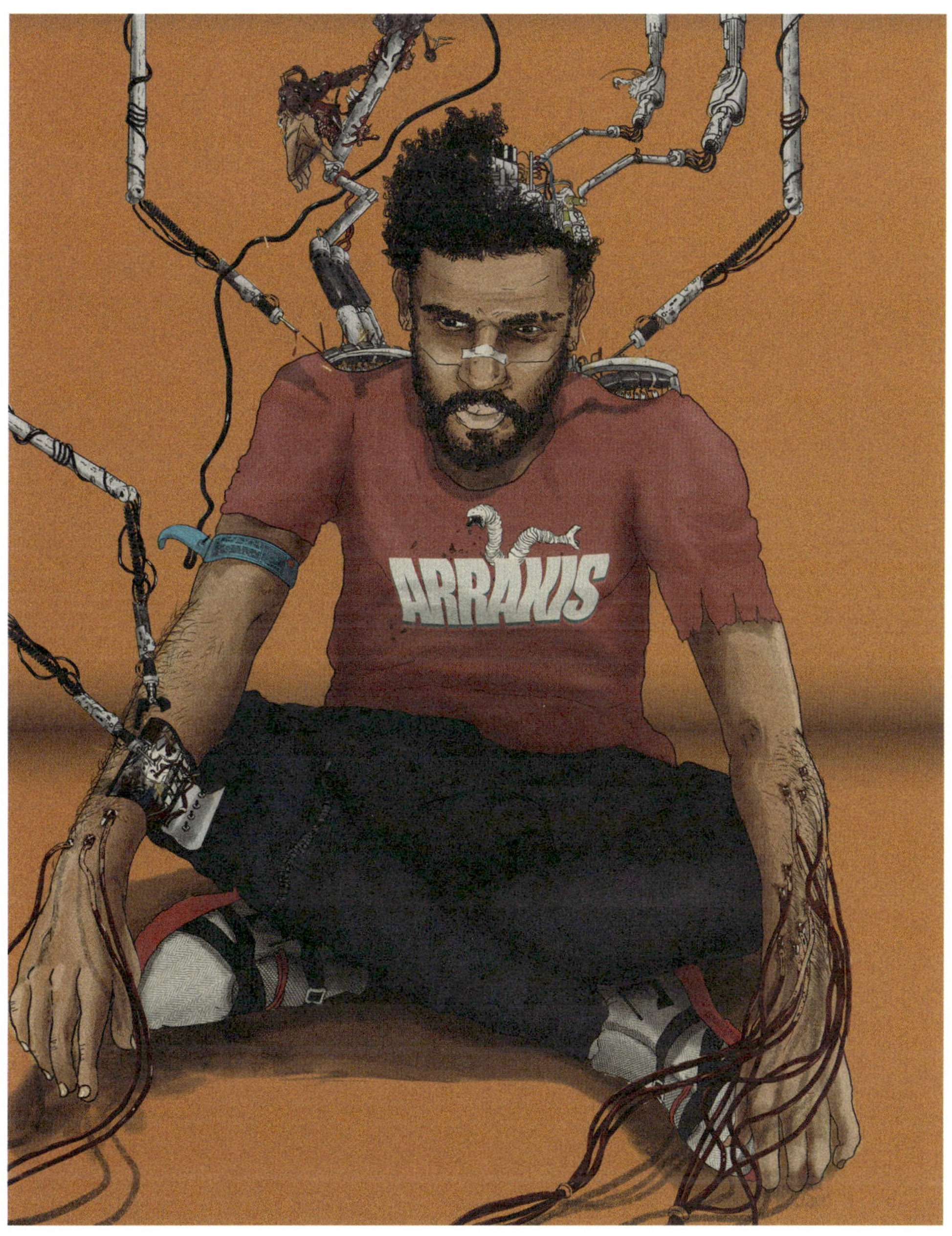

EL CORAZÓN DELATOR DE EDGAR ALLAN POE

Designer: Hermes Mazali

The work was to illustrate a selected fragment of *The Tell Tale Heart* by Edgar Allan Poe using typography as a resource. After analyzing the story, the designer decided to rely on the nerves suffered by the narrator, who at the end confessed his crime out of unbearable burden of guilt. The main objective was to reflect of the conflict between the narrator's obsession with his murder and his need of confession. Based on anatomy of human body, the designer hand-drew the typography with reference to a selected typeface to communicate the murder. The typeface evolves as tension increased.
The book was made in vertical format and bound by hand after digital printing.

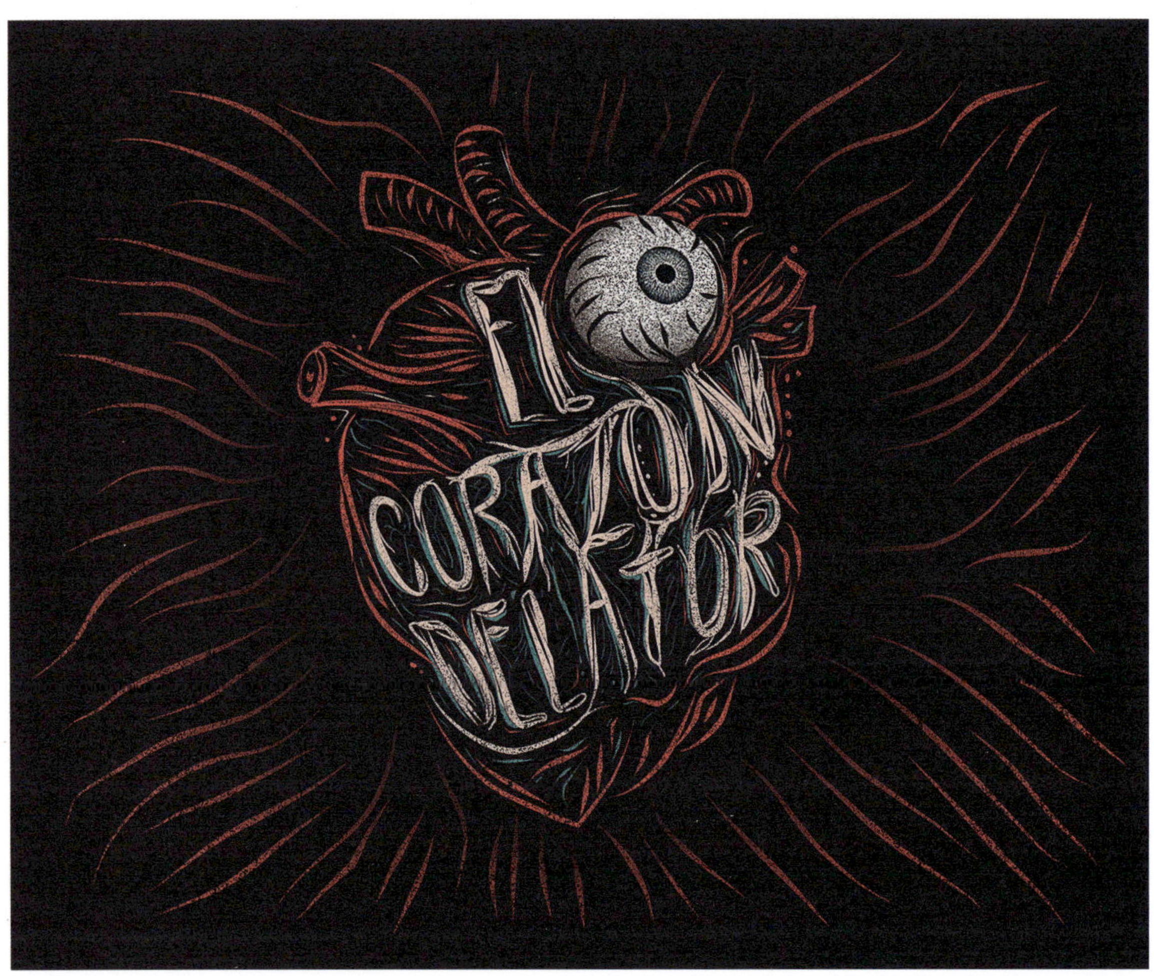

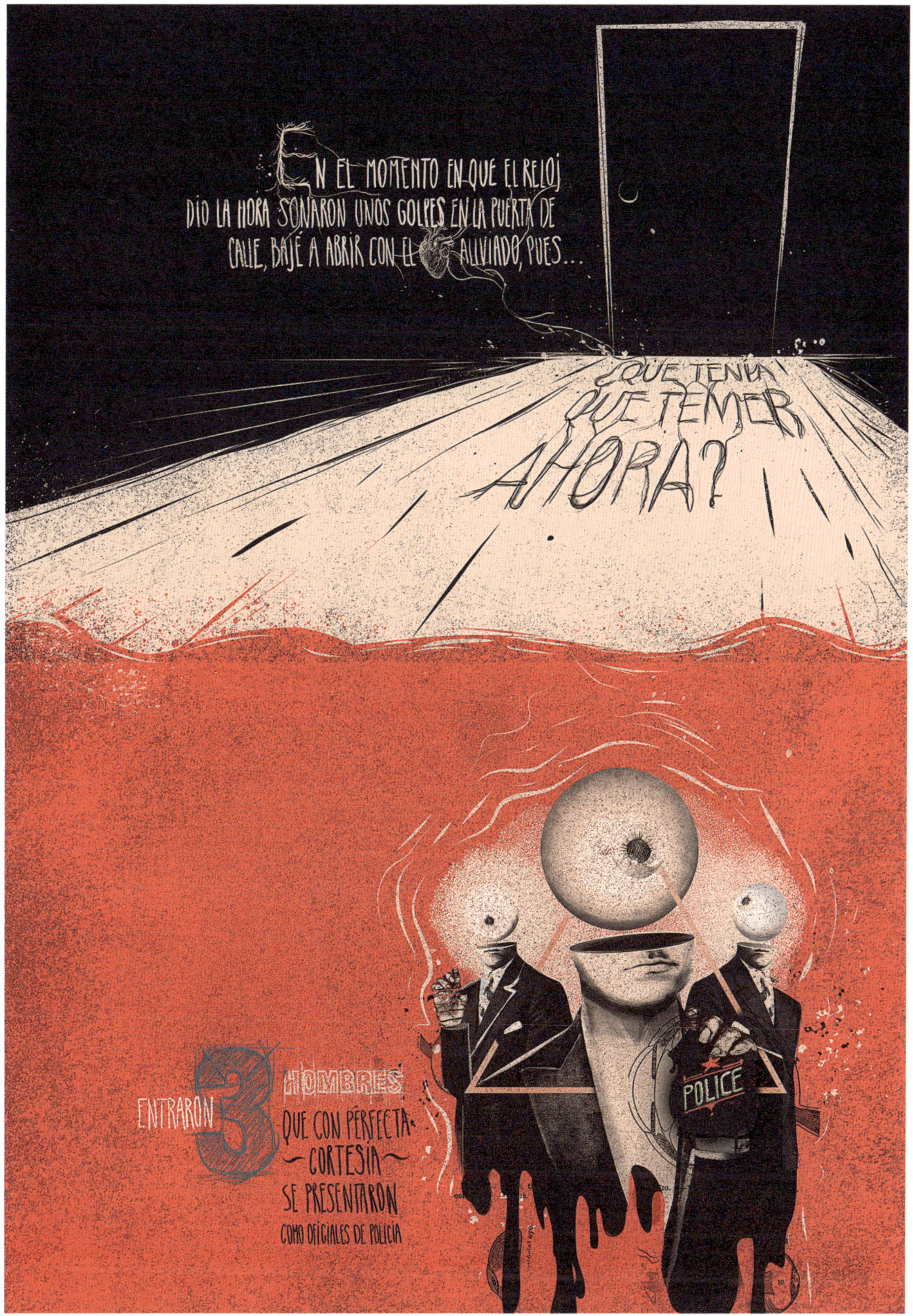
En el momento en que el reloj dio la hora sonaron unos golpes en la puerta de calle, bajé a abrir con el alliviado, pues...
¿Qué tenía que temer ahora?
Entraron 3 hombres que con perfecta ~cortesía~ se presentaron como oficiales de policía
POLICE

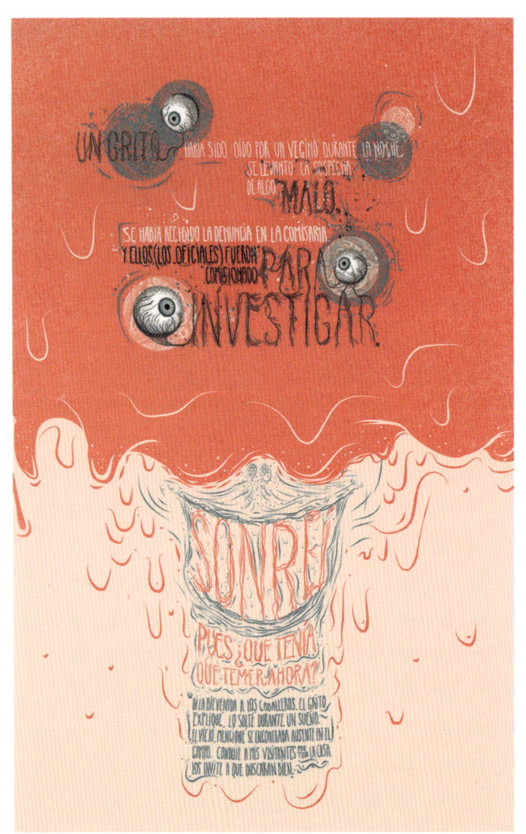
UN GRITO HABIA SIDO OIDO POR UN VECINO DURANTE LA NOCHE
SE LEVANTO LA SOSPECHA
DE ALGO MALO.
SE HABIA RECIBIDO LA DENUNCIA EN LA COMISARIA
Y ELLOS (LOS OFICIALES) FUERON COMISIONADO PARA INVESTIGAR.
SONREÍ
PUES ¿QUE TENIA QUE TEMER AHORA?
DI LA BIEVENIDA A LOS CABALLEROS. EL GRITO EXPLIQUÉ, LO SOLTÉ DURANTE UN SUEÑO. EL VIEJO, MENCIONÉ SE ENCONTRABA AUSENTE EN EL CAMPO. CONDUJE A MIS VISITANTES POR TODA LA CASA. LOS INVITÉ A QUE BUSCARAN BIEN.

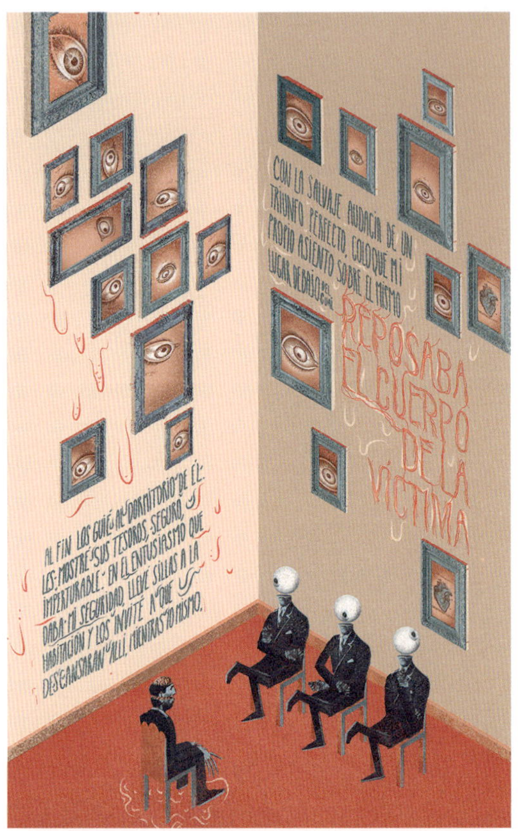
CON LA SALVAJE AUDACIA DE UN TRIUNFO PERFECTO, COLOQUÉ MI PROPIO ASIENTO SOBRE EL MISMO LUGAR DEBAJO DEL CUAL
REPOSABA EL CUERPO DE LA VÍCTIMA
AL FIN LOS GUIÉ AL DORMITORIO DE ÉL. LES MOSTRÉ SUS TESOROS, SEGURO, IMPERTURABLE. EN EL ENTUSIASMO QUE DABA MI SEGURIDAD, LLEVÉ SILLAS A LA HABITACIÓN Y LOS INVITÉ A QUE DESCANSARAN ALLÍ, MIENTRAS YO MISMO,

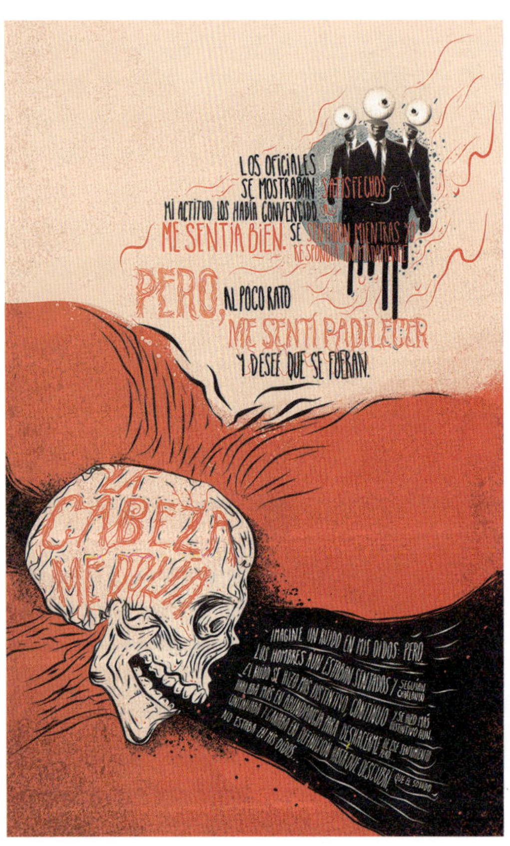
LOS OFICIALES SE MOSTRABAN SATISFECHOS
MI ACTITUD LOS HABÍA CONVENCIDO
ME SENTÍA BIEN. SE SENTARON MIENTRAS YO RESPONDÍA ANIMADAMENTE
PERO, AL POCO RATO ME SENTÍ PADILECER Y DESEÉ QUE SE FUERAN.
LA CABEZA ME DOLÍA
IMAGINE UN RUIDO EN MIS OIDOS: PERO LOS HOMBRES AUN ESTABAN SENTADOS Y SEGUÍAN CHARLANDO
EL RUIDO SE HIZO MAS DISTINTIVO, CONTINUO Y SE HIZO MÁS DISTINTIVO AUN.
HABLABA MÁS EN ABUNDANCIA PARA DESHACERME DE ESE SENTIMIENTO PERO CONTINUABA Y GANABA EN DEFINICIÓN HASTA QUE DESCUBRÍ QUE EL SONIDO NO ESTABA EN MIS OIDOS.

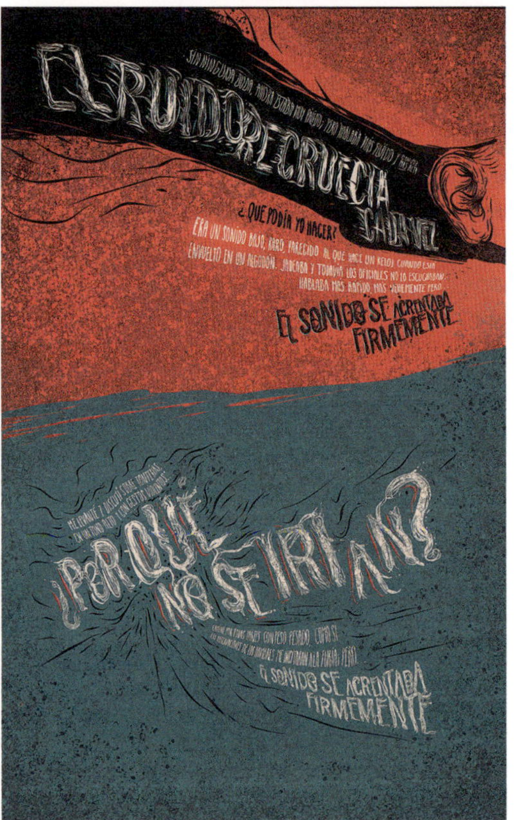
EL RUIDO RECRUECÍA CADA VEZ
¿QUE PODÍA YO HACER?
ERA UN SONIDO BAJO, RARO, PARECIDO AL QUE HACE UN RELOJ CUANDO ESTÁ ENVUELTO EN UN ALGODÓN. JADEABA Y TODAVÍA LOS OFICIALES NO LO ESCUCHABAN. HABLABA MÁS RÁPIDO, MÁS VEHEMENTE PERO
EL SONIDO SE ACRENTABA FIRMEMENTE
¿POR QUÉ NO SE IRÍAN?
EL SONIDO SE ACRENTABA FIRMEMENTE

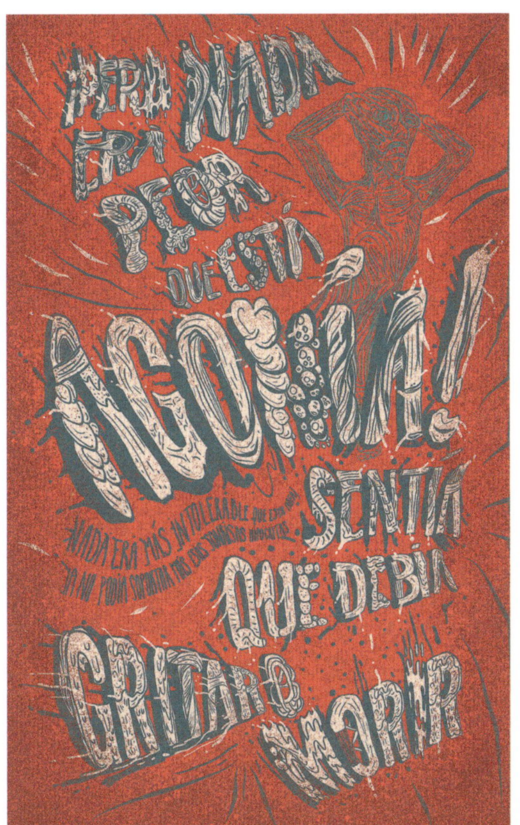
PERO NADA
ERA
PEOR
QUE ESTA
¡AGONÍA!
NADA ERA MÁS INTOLERABLE
YA NO PODÍA SOPORTAR
SENTÍA
QUE DEBÍA
GRITAR O MORIR

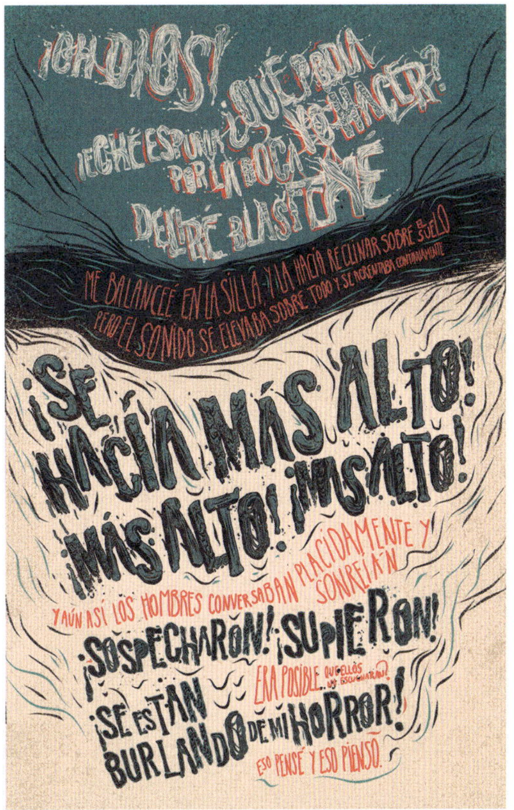
¡OH DIOS!
¿QUÉ PODÍA YO HACER?
¡ECHÉ ESPUMA POR LA BOCA
DELIRÉ BLASFEMÉ
ME BALANCEÉ EN LA SILLA Y LA HACÍA RECLINAR SOBRE EL SUELO
PERO EL SONIDO SE ELEVABA SOBRE TODO Y SE ACRECENTABA CONTINUAMENTE
¡SE HACÍA MÁS ALTO!
¡MÁS ALTO! ¡MÁS ALTO!
Y AÚN ASÍ LOS HOMBRES CONVERSABAN PLACIDAMENTE Y SONREÍAN
¡SOSPECHARON! ¡SUPIERON!
ERA POSIBLE
¡SE ESTÁN BURLANDO DE MI HORROR!
ESO PENSÉ Y ESO PIENSO.

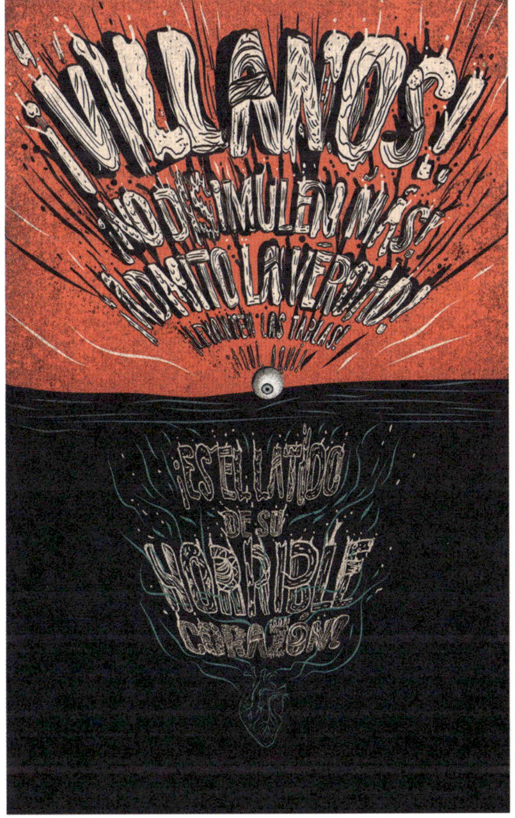
¡VILLANOS!
¡NO DISIMULEN MÁS!
¡ADMITO LA VERDAD!
¡LEVANTEN LAS TABLAS!
¡AQUÍ, AQUÍ!
¡ES EL LATIDO DE SU HORRIBLE CORAZÓN!

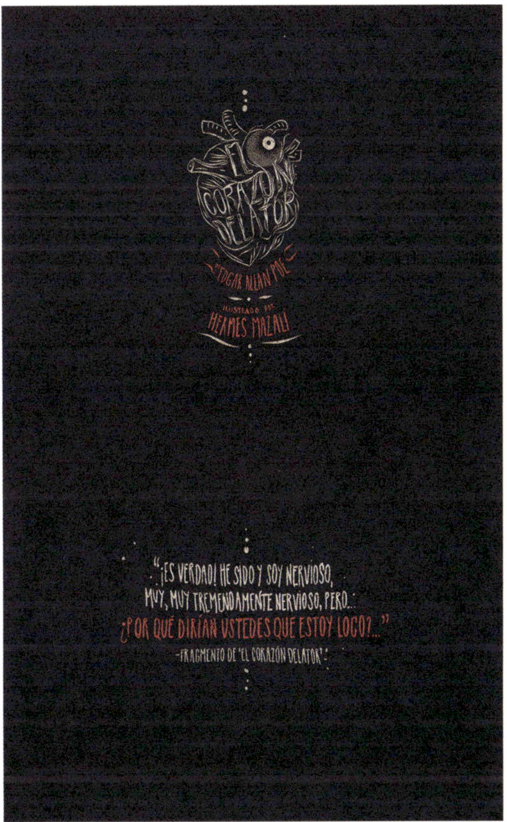
EL CORAZÓN DELATOR
EDGAR ALLAN POE
ILUSTRADO POR
HERMES MAZALI
"¡ES VERDAD! HE SIDO Y SOY NERVIOSO,
MUY, MUY TREMENDAMENTE NERVIOSO, PERO...
¿POR QUÉ DIRÍAN USTEDES QUE ESTOY LOCO?..."
-FRAGMENTO DE 'EL CORAZÓN DELATOR'.

THIS MISERY GARDEN

Designer: Aleksandar Živanov / Hardworkz

This a CD artwork for metal band This Misery Garden.

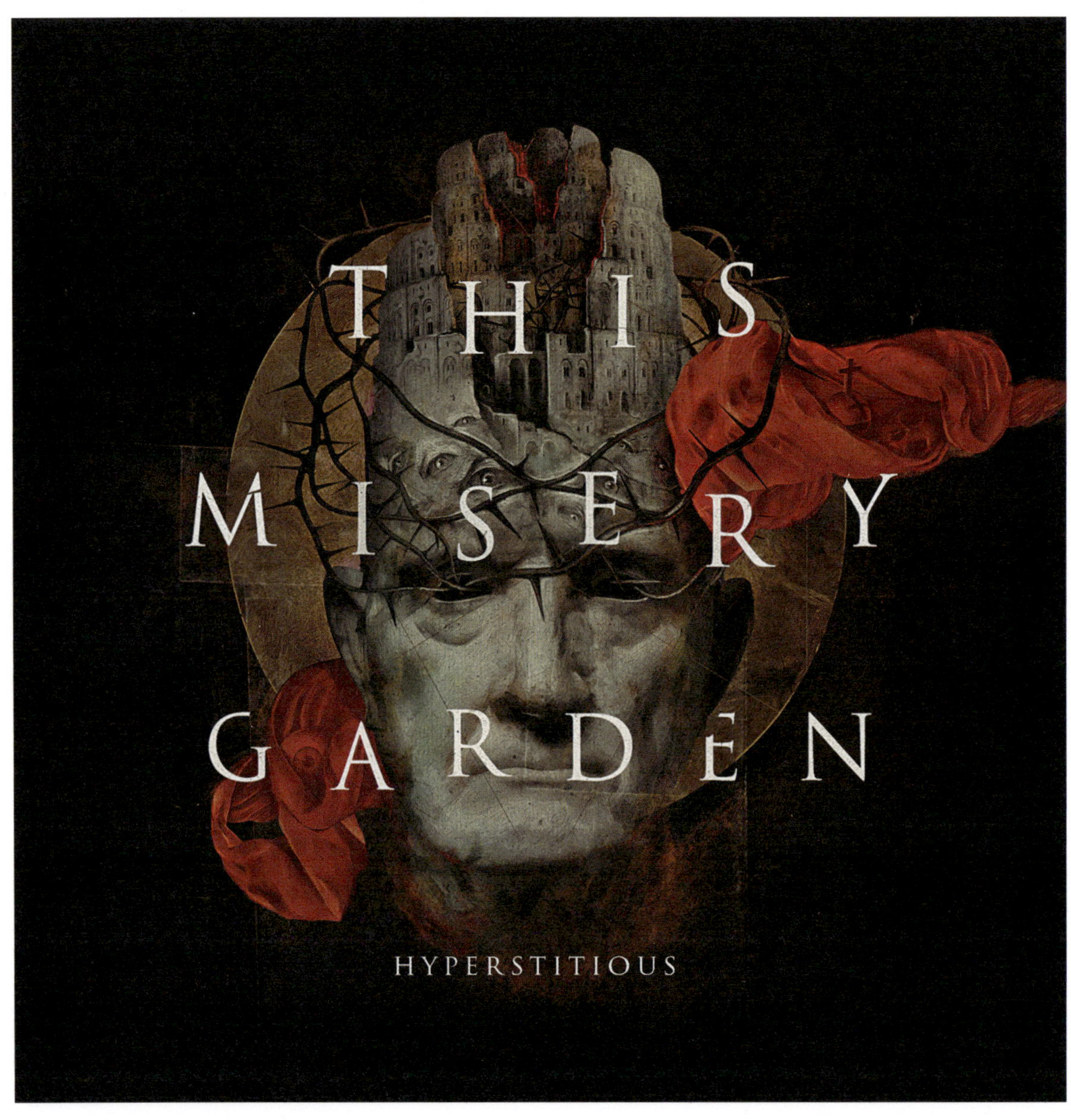

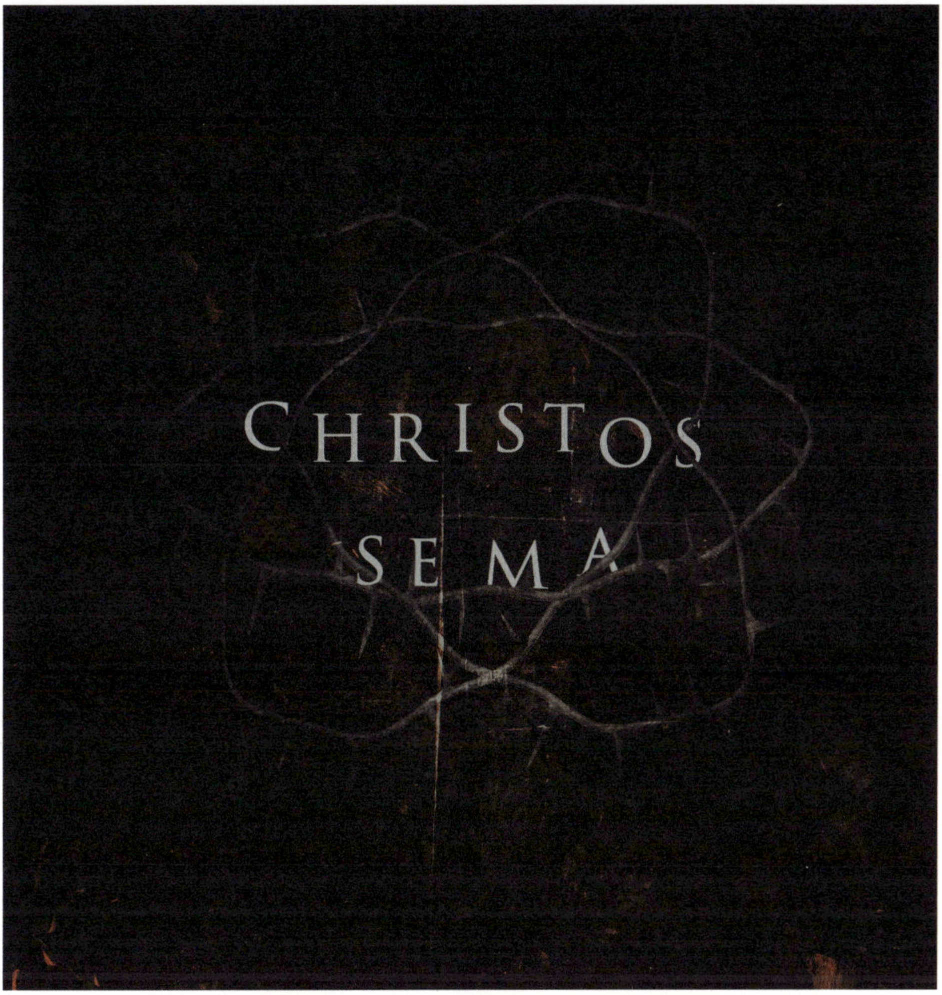

CHRISTOS
SEMA

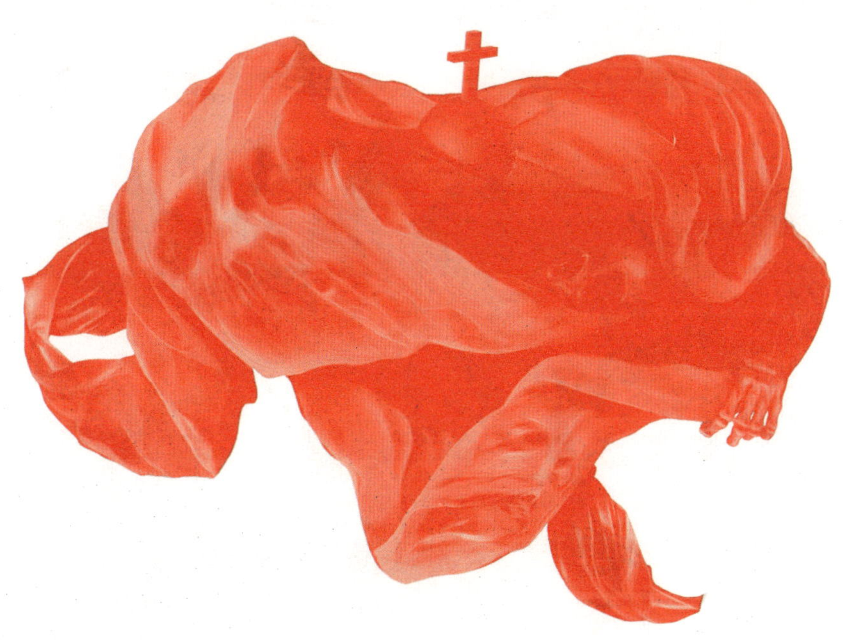

MANGE TES PETITES MORTS

Artist: Gabriel Machéta

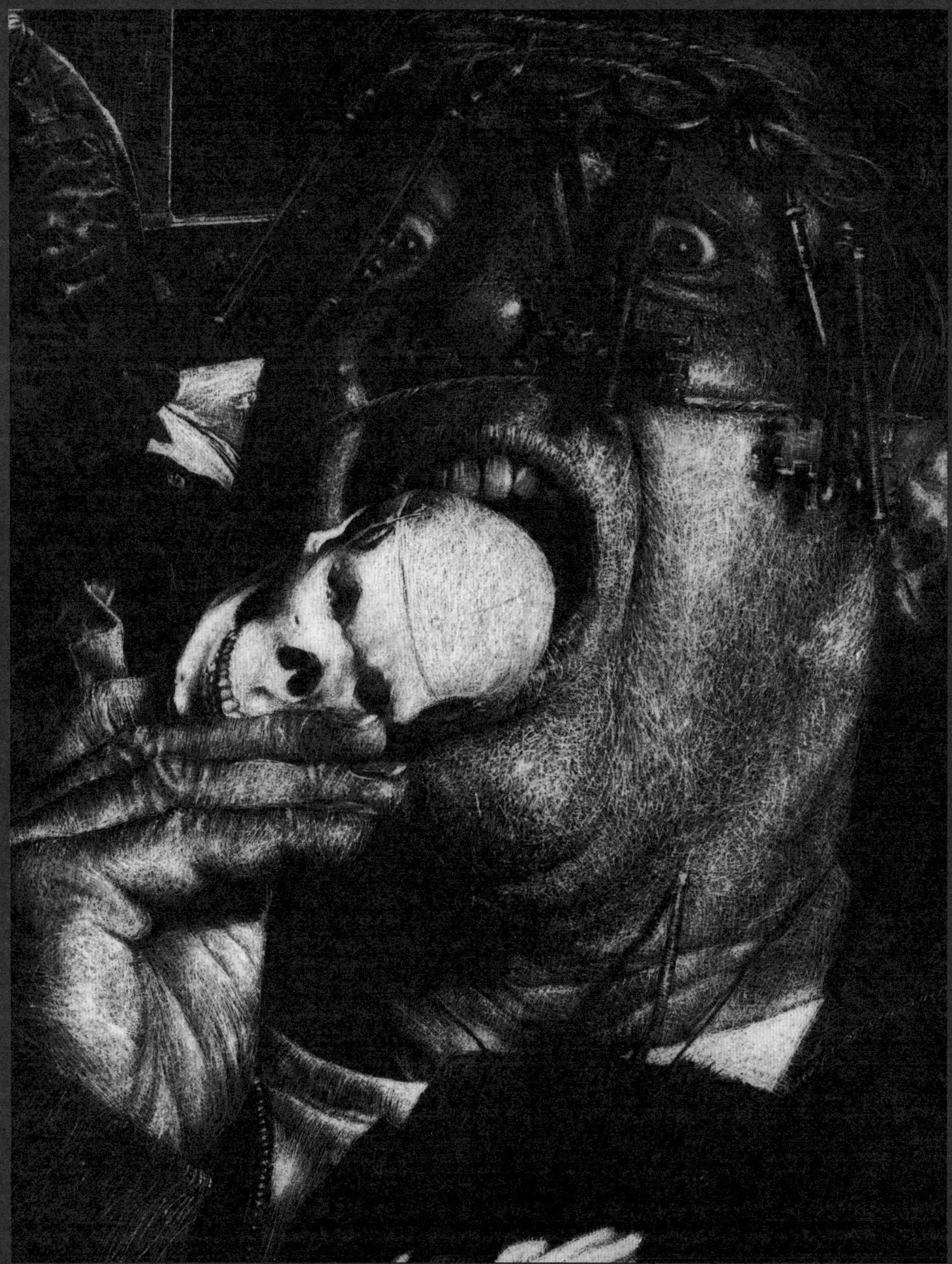

TETE DE NOEUD

Artist: Gabriel Machéta

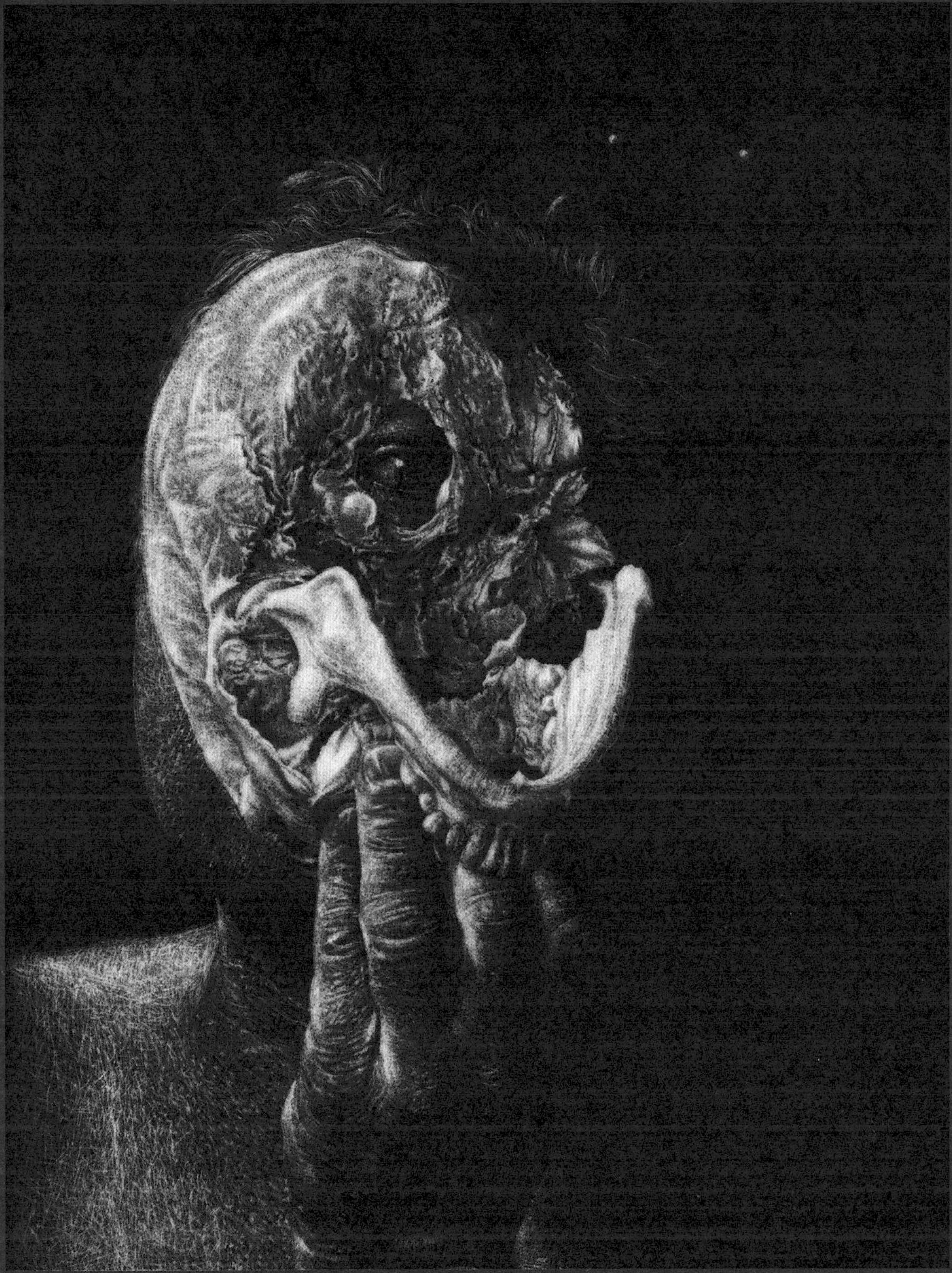

INDEX

ACKNOWLEDGEMENTS

We would like to thank all the designers and contributors who have been involved in the production of this book. Their contributions have been indispensable in its compilation. We would also like to express our gratitude to all the producers for their invaluable opinions and assistance throughout this project. And to the many others whose names are not credited but have made specific input in this book, we thank you for your continuous support.

FUTURE COOPERATIONS:

If you wish to participate in SendPoints' future projects and publications, please send your website or portfolio to

editor01@sendpoints.cn